LOCAL STUDIES COLLECTIONS
A MANUAL
VOLUME 1

*Frontispiece.   John Leslie Hobbs (1916-1964). Borough Librarian and Curator of Shrewsbury from 1946. His publications were influential in promoting public library local collections in the post-war years.*

# Local Studies Collections: A Manual Volume 1

Edited by
Michael Dewe

Gower

Reprinted 1991. Originally published as A Manual of Local Studies Librarianship.
Published by
Gower Publishing Company Limited
Gower House
Croft Road
Aldershot
Hants GU11 3HR
England

Gower Publishing Company
Old Post Road
Brookfield
Vermont 05036
USA

Library of Congress Cataloguing-in-Publication Data
Local Studies Collection, A Manual Volume 1.
    Bibliography: p
    Includes index.
    1. Libraries—Special collections—Local history—Handbooks, manuals, etc.
    2. Local history—Bibliography—Methodology—Handbooks, manuals, etc.
    I. Dewe, Michael.
Z688.L8M35 1987        026'.9        86-31999

British Library Cataloguing in Publication Data
Local Studies Collection, A Manual Volume 1        .
1. Libraries—Great Britain—Special collections—History, Local
I. Dewe, Michael
026'.941        Z688.L8

ISBN 0 5660 3522 7

Printed in Great Britain by Billing and Sons Ltd, Worcester

# Contents

# Illustrations

Frontispiece, John Leslie Hobbs (1916-1964). Borough Librarian and Curator of Shrewsbury from 1946. His publications were influential in promoting public library local collections in the post-war years. [Dorothy Hobbs]

# Plans

# Contributors

*Robin Ansell,* ALA, Reference Librarian, Yeovil, Somerset County Library since 1982. Whilst working previously for the London Borough of Merton, where one of his responsibilities was for local studies, he was invited onto the committee of the Local Studies Group of the Library Association and since June 1982 has been its Assistant Honorary Secretary.

*Chris Baggs,* BA, MA, Dip.Lib., ALA, Senior Lecturer, College of Librarianship Wales, was formerly Assistant Librarian (Media Services) at the Open University; has been teaching audio-visual studies and sources of information since 1979. Past chair of the ASLIB Audio-Visual Group.

*Andrew Blizzard,* BA, ALA, Schools Liaison Librarian, Local Studies Department, Birmingham Central Library, has worked in the Department since he was eighteen and has occupied his present post, with its responsibility for providing local studies materials for all levels of education, since August 1981. He is a native Brummie.

*Valerie Bott,* MA, FMA, Museum Development Officer for the London Borough of Wandsworth, took the Museums Studies Diploma at Leicester University in 1971, with local history as her special subject, which she converted to an MA in 1980. Formerly worked at the Vestry Museum (London Borough of Waltham Forest), and was first curator of the Grange Museum of Local History (London Borough of Brent), both of which combine artefacts with local archive and library collections.

*John H. Chandler,* BA, PhD, Dip.Lib., ALA, Local Studies Officer, Wiltshire Library and Museum Service, has worked for Wiltshire since 1974, occupying his present post since 1979. After research into the later Roman empire, his published work has all been concerned with local history, including a history of Salisbury and an edition of Wiltshire dissenters' meeting-house certificates for the Wiltshire Record Society, of which he is secretary.

*Jane V. Dansie,* ALA, Senior Librarian, Local Studies, Essex Libraries, based at Colchester Central Library, was Reference Librarian at Chelmsford from 1965 until 1978. Published articles in the professional press and author of church guide; joint author of Essex local studies publications. Committee member of the London and Home Counties Branch of the Local Studies Group of the Library Association.

*Michael Dewe,* MA, FLA, Senior Lecturer, College of Librarianship Wales, worked in a number of London public libraries until 1975. Since then he has taught library management as well as offering optional courses on local studies librarianship and the planning of library buildings and has written widely on the latter topics. Committee member of the Local Studies Group of the Library Association.

*Geraint Evans,* BSc(Econ), Dip.Lib., ALA, Senior Lecturer, College of Librarianship Wales, previously worked at the National Library of Wales. He has considerable experience as a broadcaster having worked for over seven years for the Welsh Language Service of BBC Wales. This included interviewing work which awakened his interest in oral history and he has taught courses on interviewing techniques and other areas of concern to oral historians.

*Roy Field,* FLA, MBIM, Deputy County Librarian, Shropshire County Library, having previously worked in public libraries in Leeds, Scarborough, Derby and Derbyshire. In Scarborough as Reference and Local History Librarian in the 1960s he was involved in one of the earliest public library produced publications. Since then he has been responsible for a series of successful publication programmes and is a regular lecturer and writer on this topic.

*Rheinallt Llwyd,* MA, Dip.Ed., Dip.Lib., ALA, Senior Lecturer, College of Librarianship Wales, was a mobile librarian in South Cardiganshire before becoming Cultural Services Organiser for Cardiganshire and later Dyfed County Library, 1970-1974, where he established an oral history collection. Continues to record oral evidence privately on family history, rural lore and agricultural techniques. Editor of *Book news from Wales,* 1982-1985.

*Chris E. Makepeace,* BA, ALA, Senior Planning Officer/Local Historian, Planning Department, Greater Manchester Council, was formerly with Manchester City Libraries Local History Department from 1967 to 1973. Has written on Manchester's history, ephemera, and local history bibliography. Chairman of the Local Studies Group of the Library Association.

*Bernard Nurse,* MA, Dip.Lib., ALA, Librarian, Society of Antiquaries of London, was previously Local Studies Librarian for the London Boroughs of Southwark and of Tower Hamlets after training in the Guildhall Library. Treasurer of the Local Studies Group of the Library Association, 1982-1985. Contributor to the *London encyclopedia* and author of several articles and booklets on aspects of London's local history.

*Derryan Paul,* BA, MA, DAA, Senior Lecturer, College of Librarianship Wales, trained as an archivist and took an MA in English Local History at Leicester. Has worked in local government, in the National Army Museum and at Royal Holloway College. For the past twelve years has taught palaeography, archive administration and local history.

*Paul Sturges,* MA, PhD, ALA, MIInfSc, Lecturer, Department of Library and Information Studies, Loughborough University, is the compiler of several reference works and author of numerous articles, including a number on eighteenth century Derbyshire history. In 1979 directed a BLRD sponsored investigation of local publications, and has since spoken at various meetings and conferences on local studies bibliography. Secretary of the Local Studies Group of the Library Association since 1982.

# Acknowledgements

Many contributors would wish to acknowledge the information provided by the librarians of local collections throughout the United Kingdom which has made possible the currency of detail and exemplification throughout this book. Except for Chapter 4, which is based on the results of a survey of a large number of academic libraries, much information was gained by individual authors through informal, limited surveys and in answer to requests for information. All contributors are grateful, therefore, for the speedy and helpful responses that have been given to their enquiries.

The editor would like to thank his two colleagues, Derryan Paul and Malcolm Tunley, for their support and advice and those individuals and libraries which supplied the photographs and plans used in this book: their names are acknowledged in the lists of illustrations and plans.

# 1

# Introduction

Michael Dewe

While there are other books on local collections in libraries, the standard text on the subject has long been J.L. Hobbs's *Local history and the library*, completely revised and partly rewritten by George A. Carter in the second edition published in 1973. Since that date the changes and developments that have taken place in the field of local history generally, and in library provision to support it, have been considerable. Not least of the changes in librarianship has been that of terminology; in many libraries the local history collection has been renamed the local studies collection. This reflects the fact that such collections have long been involved in collecting material other than the purely historical in subject and have been as much concerned with the present (and the future) as well as the past. Belated recognition of these factors has brought out the great potential of the local collection to support a wider range of research, educational and informational activity than had been perhaps visualised earlier. This change in image has led to a better understanding of a local collection's worth and the need for it to be provided with improved resources.

The description and analysis of the substantial changes and developments of the last dozen or so years are, perhaps, more than one individual author could handle successfully, and so this present publication is a team effort. In this way it brings together the interest, knowledge and experience of a number of contributors - practising local studies librarians, library school lecturers and others - each of whom looks at their own topic in considerable depth. The aims of the *Manual,* which have guided contributors, are to provide a 'state of the art' account of local studies librarianship, to provide practical advice on aspects of local studies work, and to promote developing areas of local studies activity such as oral recordings, video, publications and the utilisation of computers.

Local studies or local history collections have been seen largely as a public library specialism and are largely treated as such in much of the literature. In this present work, however, an attempt has been made to describe the nature and extent of such collections in university, polytechnic and college libraries, with some interesting results. Another feature of the *Manual* is the endeavour to provide a picture of local studies librarianship in the United Kingdom as a whole. Local studies work in other countries has also been referred to in individual contributions where appropriate, and useful references and readings included to reflect this wider coverage.

For obvious reasons Hobbs included information on archives and libraries and this has been emulated here, the author being both qualified as an archivist and as local historian. In addition, Chapter 2 has been written by a museum keeper who, while considering the general theme of the chapter, introduces topics dealt with more fully by other contributors and also outlines recent developments in the museum world. In this way the reader is presented with a broader view of local studies and its institutions and reminded of the interdependence of library, record office and museum and the need for co-operation. Some contributors explore the view that a much closer, more formal association is desirable and that this could benefit the user of local studies material significantly, as well as bringing other benefits.

A fundamental cause of the changes and developments referred to above has been the local government reorganisation that has affected all parts of the United Kingdom from 1965 to 1975, beginning with London. Such a recasting of boundaries and responsibilities has had a particular impact on local studies collections. Larger local authorities have provided the opportunity for a better managerial approach to local studies librarianship, which has included rationalisation, co-operation and in-service training, and for a staffing structure in which local studies has its place. The latter may be reflected in authority-wide teams, groups or working parties responsible for local studies and its development within a library system, and the creation of specialist posts at service point and co-ordinator level that provide the stimulus for improvement. There is also evidence that in many authorities the local collection is now seen not just as a large library concern but also as a service that is worthy of provision at branch level. The abolition of the Greater London Council and the metropolitan county councils will have a considerable effect on local studies provision particularly as regards archive services.[1]

A major change, hardly considered in the last edition of Hobbs, is the use of computerisation in libraries and in local studies collections. West Sussex produced a computerised catalogue of local material in 1977 and a recent advance has been the computerised production of a local studies bibliographical data base at the University of York. The ubiquitous microcomputer offers considerable opportunities for information organisation and retrieval in local studies librarianship, for example in the indexing of local newspapers and photographs.

Another development that has characterised recent years has been the increased exploitation of the unique materials of the local collection through the publication and sale of maps, prints and photographs. Such publication activity has been further extended by the publication of works by local residents.

The emergence of oral history as a significant resource for research and enlightenment about the past has been reflected in the local studies collection. Librarians have sought to augment and develop their collections through the creation and acquisition of oral history recordings. They have also made extensive efforts to increase the visual contents of their collections, particularly through copying and acquisition programmes for photographs. Ephemera too - a substantial part of any local collection - has also attracted more attention than in the past and a number of books and reports on the subject have appeared.

The most recent development is perhaps the greater awareness in the profession generally, and among local studies librarians in particular, of the almost universal need to improve the conservation of library materials. In many instances librarians have been hampered by the lack of the proper environmental facilities for storage, but the large number of new library buildings of the last few decades have seen this deficiency remedied in many instances. In the 1980s the situation as regards library buildings continues to improve, if at a somewhat slower rate. To overcome problems of conservation and heavy use of some materials, the provision of surrogates for some materials, e.g. microfilm and photocopies, is becoming a common feature of local studies libraries. The British Library (another development since Hobbs) has been a leading force in stimulating this new awareness of conservation, particularly through its sponsorship of the report by F.W. Ratcliffe in 1984 entitled *Preservation policies and conservation in British libraries.*[2] An outcome of the report was the establishment in 1984 of the National Preservation Office at the British Library, which will use its resources to promote the better conservation of library collections throughout the United Kingdom. The British Library's Newspaper Library at Colindale should also be mentioned for the excellent work it has done to improve the preservation of and access to local newspapers, for example an index to local newspaper indexes, most of them unpublished, has been compiled.[3]

The changes and developments briefly chronicled here have on the whole been of great benefit to users. However, the cumulative effects of better provision, often in new buildings, the greater interest in local studies both formally from within education and more informally from local groups and individuals, has led to a greatly increased use of the local collection. While such increased use is welcomed, it has created, and continues to create, particular problems in times of financial stringency for those responsible for the running of such collections, especially as regards the demands made on staff resources. Behind the scenes, however, hard-pressed staff have been helped by the employment of government-sponsored employees to do work which would not otherwise have been carried out. Often this has taken the form of the retrospective indexing of local newspapers, resulting in the accomplishment of much useful work and sometimes the publication of the experience and practice of a particular project.

Perhaps no greater indication of the current standing of local history or local studies work in libraries is needed than that demonstrated by the establishment of the Local Studies Group of the Library Association in 1977, which now has a membership of about 1800. The formation of such a specialist group reflects developments in historical studies generally. The group advises its parent body (as well as others) on matters related to local studies, provides a focus for those working in the field and furthers professional activity through meetings and publications, in particular the periodical *Local studies librarian.* Local branches of the group have been formed in London and the Home Counties, the eastern counties, the north-west of England and Scotland; the latter's journal *Locscot* is lively, informative and well produced. In the early 1980s the group embarked upon the formulation of guidelines for local studies libraries but as yet these have not been finalised. The American Library Association, on the other hand, published in 1979 a brief set of guidelines to assist in the establishment of local history collections.[4] While formulated for a particular purpose, these provide a framework upon which libraries, including those with existing collections, could develop fuller statements to suit their own circumstances. A year earlier the American Association

4

for State and Local History had published a manual for librarians entitled *Local history collections,*[5] which was based on processes and procedures used in Englewood Public Library Local History Collection in Englewood, Colorado. Also in the late 1970s the New South Wales Branch of the Library Association of Australia began to publish a very useful series of occasional papers on aspects of local history librarianship.[6] This professional activity in the United States and Australia mirrors the greater attention afforded to local history/studies librarianship in the United Kingdom.

Local studies work, like much else in librarianship, is in a period of transition. For a long time the local collection was often a deprived and neglected feature of a library service but this situation has vastly altered for the better in the last 30 years or so. Change has generally meant improvement and development has generally encompassed growth; the future for local studies librarianship looks exciting but also demanding.

## NOTES

1. Berry, E. Metro records refuse to die without a fight. *Local history* no. 2 September 1984, 4-7.
2. Ratcliffe, F.W. *Preservation policies and conservation in British libraries.* London, British Library, 1984.
3. *British Library news* (1976-   ) often carries information of interest to the local studies librarian; the *Newspaper Library newsletter* (British Library Reference Division), which was published from 1980 to 1982, records the considerable activity of that period, and recently resumed publication.
4. American Library Association. Reference and Adult Services. History Section. Local History Committee. Guidelines for establishing local history collections. *RQ* 19 (1) Fall 1979, 29-30.
5. Thompson, E.T. *Local history collections: a manual for librarians.* Nashville, Tennessee, American Association for State and Local History, 1978.
6. For example: Library Association of Australia, NSW Branch. *Local history resources.* Sydney, LAA, 1978. (Occasional paper no. 2.)

## FURTHER READING

Garden, E. Local history: a community resource. In: Scottish Library Association. *Aberdeen '84: conference proceedings.* Glasgow, SLA, 1984, pp. 49-54.

Jamieson, I. Local studies. In: *British librarianship and information work 1976-1980,* edited by L.J. Taylor. London, Library Association, 1982. Vol. 1, pp. 124-130.

Petty, M. The albatross inheritance: local studies libraries. *Library management* 6 (1) 1985, 1-51.

# 2

# The world of local history

Valerie Bott

No one would deny that the recent growth of interest in local history has been dramatic. It is important to remember, however, that it had already begun before the Second World War. What has happened since then has been much more than a simple continuation of that growth; the subject has not only gained academic respectability but it has also been popularised to an extraordinary degree. Today there are over a thousand local history societies in Britain, with many more devoted to related subjects such as industrial archaeology and family history. Current annual visitor figures for museums alone stand at over 50 million and although all museums do not devote themselves entirely to local history this figure serves to underline the great enthusiasm for historical pastimes of every sort. Hundreds of local history books, pamphlets and articles now appear every year, many of them made available at a modest price by local history societies and individual historians anxious to share their enthusiasm. And the media (especially television and the colour supplements), always on the lookout for a good story with human interest, find such material in abundance in local histories.

## LOCAL HISTORY COMES OF AGE

Two events which mark the beginning of the coming of age of local history took place in 1948. In that year a number of teachers of local history in the Workers' Educational Association and university extra-mural classes, members of local history societies and individual historians met under the auspices of the National Council of Social Service and established the Standing Conference for Local History. The intrinsically parochial nature of local history made it all too easy for amateur historians to work in isolation and there were intellectual as well as social benefits to be had from shared experience. By 1952 the Standing Conference was ready to launch a magazine, the *Amateur historian*, to provide a forum and a point of contact; this magazine, published quarterly, continues today as the *Local historian*. The change of title is significant; during the thirty odd years of the magazine's existence local history has become a part of historical research at every level.

Where previously the subject might have been dismissed as parochial antiquarianism, the value of studying local history, not only for its purely local interest but also for the light it sheds on other aspects of historical research, has now been recognised. In this the Department of English Local History at Leicester University has played a major part. This was the first ever university department in the subject; it was created, in the charge of W.G. Hoskins, in 1948[1]. Its emphasis has always been on postgraduate training and its interests extremely wide-ranging. It has never restricted itself to the history of a specific region, nor to a specific historical period, preferring instead to encompass all of English local history from Roman times to the twentieth century. It has included fieldwork and the study of vernacular architecture as well as the study of documentary and illustrative material and has sought to establish the basic principles and methods of local history. The existence of the department is both a result of and a part of the academic world's changing attitude towards local history. Its work has encouraged an approach to local history as the history of communities which is now widespread.

## AMATEURS AND PROFESSIONALS

The subject, which R.B. Pugh described as 'history studied through the microscope',[2] is still largely the preserve of amateurs working on a locality they already know well. The majority of the numerous histories published today remains popular in character and is researched and written by them; while the standard of such work is often very high it generally takes a different approach from that of the professional historian. Where the amateurs working for love of the place and their subject may allow themselves a little parochialism, the professional is often more detached, seeking to identify both the typical and the exceptional through a comparison of different communities. The amateur's research thus often provides the basic groundwork which the professional has neither the time to trace nor the local knowledge to relate to the place in the same way. Much has been learnt from detailed local studies which has begun to change our historical perceptions of some periods and issues of the past. Thus our picture of the complex social and political relationships of the English Civil War has been fleshed out with tremendous detail from local studies of that period and our knowledge of the processes of change which make up the Industrial Revolution has been enhanced by studies of the history of individual crafts in specific localities.

In addition a number of local studies which are entirely the work of professional historians have been published. These have been of great significance in both their content and their approach. The legacy of the antiquarians of an earlier generation was a powerful bias towards genteel history centred on the manor, the church and the lives of the rich and famous. The process of historical questioning has expanded to encompass the lives of those whose anonymity is broken only by marriage, apprenticeship or taxation; to consider the recent as well as the more distant past; and to include the town and the suburb as well as rural society. Hoskins' study of Wigston Magna, *The Midland peasant*,[3] was one of the first of these re-evaluations of the lives of ordinary people in a specific community. Professor Dyos' splendid account of the development of Camberwell in the nineteenth century paved the way for a completely new approach to urban and suburban history.[4] Historians examining the minutiae of change in the landscape have unearthed detailed evidence for the history of local communities, from M.W. Beresford's *History on the ground* to Jack Ravensdale's *Liable to floods*.[5] Another important development has been one in which people are predominant; Margaret Spufford has described it as 'the total history of village communities'.[6] Examining three Cambridgeshire villages and their villagers in her *Contrasting communities,* she was anxious not to treat the people of the past as little more than abstract statistics in the economic and social history of these places. She has acknowledged the influence of the French historian, Emmanuel Le Roy Ladurie and his circle, whose pioneering work on the lives of mediaeval peasants in the Languedoc has not only influenced other European historians but also produced a paperback bestseller, *Montaillou,* in 1980.[7]

## A WEALTH OF RESOURCES

The sheer availability of source material has had an influence on the development of local history during this period as well. The growth has been both in the quantity of material available and in its ease of accessibility. By the early 1950s almost every county in England and Wales had established a record office, whereas there had been only a handful before the war. Scotland was slower to provide archive services and the opportunity offered by local government reorganisation in the 1970s was missed. It has, however, begun the process of 'catching up'. Now in the 1980s virtually everyone is within reasonable reach of a collection of local materials in a record office, a local studies library or a museum; where communities have felt deprived of such a resource they have established their own local collections. The existence of such institutions has attracted material which might otherwise have remained in private hands and the custodians of such collections are becoming increasingly conscious that their role demands active collecting rather than simply accepting the occasional gift or loan of original material. At a national level local historians are obtaining a wide range of material for information and insights into their communities; some sources previously untapped by the local historian, such as the large quantity of parliamentary papers, are proving particularly useful. The availability of the original census enumerators' returns, especially those from 1851 onwards, after a century of official secrecy, has provided an exceptionally detailed source of information about every class of society. Although increased car ownership and more leisure time mean that a trip to the Public Record Office is no longer too daunting for the amateur historian, the willingness of local studies librarians to purchase copies of such records from national sources to supplement their own holdings has made them widely available virtually on the doorstep.

The original census returns have provided the raw materials for a considerable amount of local history research and in 1963 M.W. Beresford drew attention to their potential as a historical resource.[8] At about the same date the Cambridge Group for the Study of Population and Social Structure was coming into being, at first as an ad hoc group of individuals working part time on limited resources, but expanding over the next decade to become a research unit of the Social Science Research Council. The group's work has not been confined to the study of census material; indeed, it has made use of any source which might reveal patterns of marriage, mortality or migration. The group's work has been a remarkable partnership between amateurs and professionals; numerous classes, societies and individuals have assembled data relating to the population in their localities to contribute to the experts for analysis. The magazine *Local population studies* contains a considerable amount of information about techniques to be used in this rather specialist study, the fruits of various local and regional studies and opportunities for comparing notes, revealing that the subject is far more than a technical statistical one. Without the contribution of the amateurs it would not have been possible for the group to cover so much ground, while the professionals have been able to develop analytical techniques which can be used throughout the study of population history. As a result many amateur histories now include tables and diagrams of population growth or social structure in a community in the past.

## NEW APPROACHES TO HISTORY

This period of development in historical research has seen the creation of two new branches of the subject. Both have had a contribution to make in the move towards studying the lives of ordinary people in the past and both have had an especial appeal to ordinary people interested in history today. Industrial archaeology was the new subject of the 1950s. The study of the physical remains of industrial sites and transport systems offered an opportunity of getting close to the experience of those who worked them in previous generations. The practical approach, often involving surveying, recording, excavating and sometimes restoring industrial monuments, appealed to many who might never otherwise have embarked on historical research if only dusty old documents had been available for the purpose. The enthusiasm for the practical restricted many of those involved to a purely technological vision of the past, although few people would deny the immense dignity and power of a gleaming, restored beam engine in steam once again! If many amateur industrial archaeologists failed to interpret their evidence in terms of the effect of industrial change on society and, above all, on the lives of those who worked the machines, they did at least achieve the preservation of many sites and structures which would by now have completely crumbled away. What is more, from their pioneering efforts has emerged a new interpretative approach, site museums, of which one of the most impressive is that at Styal in Cheshire, where cotton spinning and weaving machines are at their deafening work again and twentieth-century visitors can almost step back into the world that Styal's workers knew.

Oral history was the new subject of the 1960s. It marked the recognition of personal reminiscence, for all its limitations, as a valuable historical source and the beginning of the active collecting of such material. A few people of an earlier generation had already published autobiographical works written in the conscious knowledge that society was changing and that a record of their personal experience was worthy of preservation. George Sturt's *The wheelwright's shop* and Flora Thompson's *Lark Rise to Candleford* are the classics of this type.[9] The former was first published in 1923 and the latter as a trilogy from 1939 to 1943 but both are still available, and indeed the latter is currently suffering the indignity of being marketed as the inspiration for a range of toiletries and bed linen with a rural and nostalgic flavour. This history from the horse's mouth has a powerful appeal; it is very immediate and very real. A considerable amount can be learnt from memories which cannot be discovered from any other source; used in conjunction with other sources oral history can provide new insights, confirm half-suspected ideas about past lives and pose new questions for the historian. Raphael Samuel has pointed to oral history as 'an invisible corrective and check' upon the historian and a 'forcible reminder that the historian's categories must in the end correspond to the grain of human experience'.[10]

Radio and television have made impressive use of oral history as the best source available for some aspects of recent history and some recordings made of both the unknown and the famous will be invaluable as sources for future historians. A number of impressive programmes have been made in recent years where broadcasting has provided an immediacy in communicating human experiences which the printed word could not easily match. Many local study groups have taken up oral history as a particularly accessible means of exploring their own past and Age Concern and other groups working with elderly people have discovered that reminiscence work can have a therapeutic effect for some of them. This new subject has achieved the status of university involvement and since 1972 there has been an Oral History Society with an important journal. Oral history has developed various applications of its own, such as the recording of forms of dialect or the recording on sound tape or demonstration on videotape of information about a piece of equipment or a craft tool newly-acquired for a museum collection. The historical record preserved either intentionally in this way or unintentionally for entertainment or short-life news film is beginning to be recognised as a major source for twentieth-century history.

12

# THE TEACHING OF HISTORY

Changing attitudes towards historical research have shown themselves in the teaching of history during the last 40 years. For many adults the special appeal of local history today is the fact that it is very different from the history they were taught at school. The old emphasis on politicians, monarchs and military conflicts has been replaced by something much closer to their own experience. This local history provides both an intellectual and an emotional satisfaction for them as they begin to people the streets of their own town with those they discover were there before them. The delight of this kind of historical discovery is something which needs to be shared, a fact which helps to explain the huge popularity of adult education classes and group projects within local history societies. The desire to give students a more active involvement has led to a growth of project work in adult education during this period. This has led naturally towards a greater emphasis on local history than on national history because of the availability of resources for this kind of group work. In addition the fact that some kinds of local history research are best done by groups has reinforced this approach. Population history, involving the handling of large quantities of statistics, oral history, where interviewing, transcribing and editing reminiscences can prove enormously time-consuming, and industrial archaeology, needing armies of workers to provide detailed surveys, measured drawings, muscle-power and elbow-grease for restoration work, have all proved ideal subjects for group projects.

Every aspect of the teaching of history, from university to primary school, has been influenced by the flourishing interest in and re-evaluation of local history. Undergraduate courses in history had long included the use of some original source material, usually in the form of photographs or photocopies, as a means of introducing primary evidence into their syllabuses. Real research, using a quantity of original material, used to be something only postgraduates did. Today it is common to find undergraduates preparing a dissertation from primary sources as part of their course of study. This is not an experience confined to history students alone; geographers, sociologists, planners, surveyors, architects, photographers and anthropologists are also to be found engaged on similar studies. This use of original evidence as a basis for teaching history has filtered down to the level of the primary school. It has been stimulated by the promotion of the concept of environmental education, a concept adopted and developed by town planners and natural historians alike as a means of teaching people about their surroundings and encouraging them to take an active role in planning and conservation issues. At the level of the primary school class environmental education usually means the investigation of the school's immediate surroundings; it involves fieldwork as well as the study of documentary sources, maps and illustrations. A visit to another town, to a museum or a local history library may be involved if the teachers are particularly ambitious for their pupils.

Commercial publishers were quick to see the potential market in this new approach to the teaching of history through evidence. Folders of reproduction documents on a variety of historical themes began to be published in the 1960s, the most famous name among these being the *Jackdaw* packs. Enterprising record offices began to compile packs for loan or sale from their own collections and many teachers, already aware of the value of making up their own sets of teaching material for specific purposes, began to build up their own files of source material, an activity which became increasingly practicable with the advent of good quality and inexpensive photocopying machines. History teaching in schools has become much more lively over the last 20 years. Not only has the use of primary source material provided a new approach but elements of industrial archaeology, oral history and archaeology have also found their way into the curriculum. The Schools Council's 'Curriculum Development Project, History 13-16', begun in 1972, made the use of evidence central to the teaching of history in that age group, while another of its projects, 'Art and the Built Environment', later applied similar principles to another area of education.

These developments in teaching have increased the demands placed upon the custodians of the necessary raw materials in libraries, record offices and museums and some of these institutions have added education officers to their staff to promote the use of the collections, to advise on their use and to prepare teaching material. In *Archives and local history* F.G. Emmison, one of the pioneers of this kind of educational work at the Essex County Record Office, bemoaned the education authorities' ignorance of both the facilities provided by record offices and the increasing demands being placed upon them by schools and especially universities and colleges of education.[11] In 1973 the Wright Report entitled *Provincial museums and galleries* published by the Department of Education and Science devoted a chapter to the educational role of museums, emphasising their great educational potential which could so easily be realised if the necesary resources - trained staff, suitable accommodation and funding - were

14

available and teachers and education authorities were aware of the role it could play in their work.[12]

Emmison considered that the knowledge and expertise of archivists made them 'especially well qualified to give advice parallel with that which the student receives from his academic supervisor'.[13] The same should apply to the curator and the local history librarian. The creation of an education officer post does not absolve the other professionals from carrying a responsibility for the educational use of the collections in their care; such work should draw upon the combined skills of all the staff. In the current climate of widespread enthusiasm for local history and local studies there are tremendous opportunities for the professionals to remain in very close contact with the actual and potential users of their collections, not only to welcome and advise them but especially to foster the kind of relationship with them which ensures that the institutions benefit from this work as well. The numerous research projects carried out over the last few decades have not simply extracted information from local collections; they are often the product of studying a variety of sources and whether they have been produced by children or adults are likely to have added something to the sum of human knowledge. They are worth preserving in local collections for this intrinsic value and as examples of methods of study, of success and failure in different approaches and techniques. In addition such research work sometimes leads to the discovery of hitherto unknown material in private hands which eventually finds a new home in a museum, library or record office. The fact that someone has proved the value of such a source by making use of it is often enough to convince its owner of the value of making it more widely available. Once contacts have been made those members of the community who are involved in the study of its history can provide a network of monitors, keeping an eye open for other potential acquisitions and tipping off the professionals about any impending threat of loss or destruction.

## ARTEFACTS AS EVIDENCE AND ENTERTAINMENT

Most of these developments in the study of local history have been dependant on the study of documentary sources with fieldwork, archaeological excavations, the study of buildings and building styles and industrial archaeology providing a strong link with a specific locality. Few of them, however, have made much use of artefacts as a historical resource.

Even at Leicester University, where students of the Museum Studies Department shared some of the classes of the Department of English Local History for more than a decade from 1967, material culture was virtually ignored in the study of local history. Few degree courses, except archaeology and art history, make use of artefacts as a form of evidence. The fact that museums of social history have long been regarded more as repositories of curiosities, of 'bygones', than as a source of hard evidence about past lives and have often been relegated to a lowly position within a larger local government department, has reinforced the neglect of artefacts in this context. A kind of snobbery has been involved as well as ignorance; rare, beautiful and financially valuable objects have been accorded a reverence out of all proportion to their value as historical evidence, while the commonplace and comparatively recent artefacts which can so vividly illuminate some aspect of everyday life have simply been dismissed as insignificant. Museums themselves have been guilty of a similar neglect and there are still many large towns and cities such as Manchester which have spectacular art collections but which have hitherto paid little attention to the history of their own communities. This is changing, however, as a result of growing interest in the subject and some of the best museums of the last decade have been those devoted to the history of an aspect of the history of a single town or city. The Museum of London, Watford Museum, the Museum of Oxford and the People's Palace at Glasgow are excellent examples of this type.

Even well-run, dynamic local history museums, some of them established in recent years, still find themselves rather low down in the local government hierarchy, struggling to survive on very modest resources. Many museums which were already in existence at the time of local government reorganisation in the 1970s were liberated from the neglect of a libraries department only to find themselves competing for attention in a recreation or leisure department against sport instead of books! Nevertheless, the changeover in the 1970s provided a unique opportunity for reassessment and the expansion of many museum services. At the same time, and partly resulting from the desire to get involved in local history in a practical way, a new breed of museum, dubbed 'independent' by its supporters, has been created. These still depend on public money to a very large degree, in the form of grant-aid from local authorities, tourist boards, the Manpower Services Commission and the Area Museums Services. Other income is drawn from sponsorship, either in cash or in kind and often from local businesses, from admission charges and from sales of souvenirs, publications and refreshments. The curators of such museums argue in favour of the degree of freedom they feel outside the network of local authority services. However, it can be argued that many fall under quite a different tyranny, that of having to generate an income from their users which pushes them closer and closer to nostalgia instead of history in their efforts to get the required numbers through the turnstiles. Some of these museums have succeeded, however, in finding a balance between the demands of fund-raising for survival and the need for the development and preservation of their collections if they are to have a reason for existence; Ironbridge Gorge Museum and the Weald & Downland Open Air Museum seem to have this balance about right. Others have been forced to concentrate on fund-raising to such a degree that their priorities for action are defined according to their income-generating power. The world of record offices and local studies libraries have not developed in this way, although attempts have been made to make a charge for the use of record offices in the last few years.

While new approaches and techniques have been developing in the study and teaching of local history, museums in general have been moving towards a more clearly defined philosophy. Better training has resulted in an increasing professionalism which is reflected in higher standards of documentation, conservation and interpretation in Britain's museums. Two postgraduate courses in Museum and Gallery Studies are now established at Leicester and Manchester Universities and the Museums Association's part-time diploma course has also been improved, not least because of the efforts of the junior curators themselves. From the early 1960s a kind of safety net has been provided for museum collections in the establishment of the Area Museums Services which now cover the whole of Britain. These are co-operative groupings of museums within a given area, created to provide practical help, professional advice and grant-aid. They draw funds from members' subscriptions and from fees and charges for their services and they receive half their income from government funds. They offer grant-aided feasibility studies for new projects, grants for approved display, conservation and documentation projects and training for member museums' staff, whether professional or amateur. For the most poverty-stricken little museums even the funds required to match an Area Museums Services grant may not be available but in general these organisations have been a powerful force for good, helping museums achieve higher standards and keep pace with the demands of increasingly knowledgeable and discerning visitors.

As far as most visitors are concerned museums are fun. They may be treasure houses of rare and spectacular objects from all over the world, may offer an eye-opening view of the natural world or may deal with the history of a local community. All can be equally exciting and in many ways it is the last which has the greatest potential for public involvement and a new kind of excitement. The local museum, actively seeking out comparatively modern, everyday artefacts, made or used in the locality it serves, can depend on the enthusiasm of local people for an energetic response to appeals for help in tracing particular artefacts to fill gaps in existing collections or help begin new ones. Many elderly people welcome the opportunity of finding a good home for objects they have treasured all their lives but which they fear might be destroyed after their death, while a whole range of local residents who understand the museum's purpose will offer chance finds from their gardens, architectural details and fittings removed from their homes during modernisation, the obsolete records of their family businesses, their old toys and games, in fact all those everyday things that usually end their days in the dustbin. Even the mass-produced goods of the twentieth-century are worth preserving; their presence in different parts of the country reveals trading patterns as important as finds of Roman amphorae. The products of local industries reveal clearly the predominance of heavy or light manufacturing industry or processing industries like food packaging, laundries and printing and will be as highly valued by future historians as artefacts from the more distant past are today. What is more, these artefacts offer a very immediate contact with the past as those who see them make comparisons with similar objects from their own experience. Museums house a rich and untapped source of historical information, of far greater significance than mere nostalgia, which new techniques of display and interpretation are making accessible to a wider market.

Today's most attractive museums have a theatrical element, a degree of showmanship which brings in the visitors. They maintain high standards of historical accuracy, use a variety of related material, including printed and manuscript items, maps and illustrations, to give a context to their artefacts and often inspire visitors with the wish to find out more about their subject. Potentially the most fruitful combination of local historical resources is that of artefacts and archives. There is a limit to how much can be offered in an exhibition; visitors must not be overwhelmed by the equivalent of the pages of a book on the wall. But providing direct access to a local history (or local studies) library or archive collection as a part of a museum visit offers great potential. This arrangement is to be found in a number of the London boroughs, although on a rather modest scale, and in large and small provincial authorities such as Oldham, Merseyside and Leicestershire. This is not merely a question of convenience for the researcher. The possibility of offering an almost immediate answer to an inquiry, especially to a child, which this arrangement makes possible is a very rewarding one. It is the all-embracing approach to the history of a community which emerges most successfully from such an arrangement, where artefacts, documents, pictures and maps have equal status as primary sources although the methods of using them may vary. In the London Borough of Brent, where the local history collections form an entity as the core of a local history service, many visitors to the museum galleries or to a temporary exhibition discover that there is something there about which they want to know more. By making sure that the professionals are always available to help and encouraging browsers when the library is not particularly busy, the staff ensure that no one is daunted by the prospect of embarking on their own bit of research. Conversely, small children working on a local history project can find plenty to help them in the permanent displays on the history of the borough, where material has been selected in order to help them and the language used in captions and descriptive text is simple, instead of having to struggle with fragile material in the library.[14]

## CO-OPERATING WITH OTHER PROFESSIONALS

Various officers in other local authority departments work in similar fields - planners, conservation officers, community workers, surveyors and educational advisers make use of local studies collections. Co-operation between these officers and those who care for local collections can be extremely fruitful for all involved. Where the cumbersome departmental structure of a local authority provides no formal or official relationship between officers employed in different departments one must be created. This is not always easy, particularly where more senior officers stand on ceremony and discourage direct contact between their juniors. Opportunities for co-operation are frequent but often demand more time and effort on the part of an individual if others are to be involved. Mechanisms have already been established for records management within local authorities and it should not be difficult in the the first instance to extend these to include the preservation of obsolete equipment as well. The problems, however, arise when something outside the local authority's control needs to be 'rescued' as the example outlined below illustrates.

A planning officer with responsibility for historic buildings discovers that the new owner of a seventeenth-century forge with living accommodation attached wishes to modernise the building; the last blacksmith has died but his tools still remain in the workshop. The planner recognises that the building will no longer serve as a forge and photographs it for his own files; he then calls in a local history group to make some measured drawings and record the layout of the interior. He knows from previous contacts with the local museum curator that the completeness of a survival like this has particular historical value and puts the new owner in touch with the curator who is able to arrange a visit and is very enthusiastic about preserving the entire contents of the forge. The owner had not realised that anyone would be so interested in the tools, etc. and is delighted to make a gift of everything to the museum. In the course of conversation he mentions that some old account books are in the attic and that the smith had kept his father's scrapbooks of local postcards, photographs and ephemera. The chain of contact continues as the curator calls in the local archivist and the local studies librarian to provide a new home for these. Only if the new owner himself had been a local historian would he have realised where to start in preserving so much material; the network of contacts was essential for everything to be saved.

This rescue operation would have been closer to the ideal if all local historical material for the area had been held within one department. Then the business records, the personal scrapbooks and the artefacts would not have had to be separated. In the long term our aim should perhaps be a local authority department, with some political clout, which incorporates all those whose skills contribute to the preservation of the history and study of local communities. This would be comparable to the field archaeology units which already exist but concerned with surviving material, whether artefacts or archives, above the ground. In the meantime the development of the network of contacts which is essential to achieve even a part of this ideal remains the responsibility of curators, archivists, librarians and planners.

## THE ROLE OF THE LOCAL STUDIES LIBRARIAN

While museums have developed considerably in both philosophical approach and practical skills and are enormously popular with the public, they are not a statutory local authority service. In an ideal world every community would have access to its past through a lively museum service as well as library collections and archives and, as some communities have proved, if the local council is not prepared to fund a local museum, it is not impossible to set up your own.[15] In the forseeable future there is little chance of an adequate network of museums being established for every local community in Britain so the local studies collection within the statutory library service takes on an additional significance. For many would-be local historians this will be their first and only source and the specialist librarian-in-charge will be their first contact with a professional in the field. Since local history has such a profound emotional significance for many of those who wish to study it, the local studies librarian must act sensitively towards them, especially towards newcomers to the subject. It is, after all, *their* local history and it is essential that they should be welcomed and advised in such a way as to put them at their ease, and that nothing is done to dampen their enthusiasm or extinguish their interest. Local studies librarians may find themselves working with very limited resources in a service for which demand continues to increase; such circumstances demand considerable energy and commitment on their part but must never be used to justify a patronising or possessive attitude towards the history of a place and its people. Public support is essential if our local collections are to be given the resources they deserve and can ultimately be guaranteed by creating a stream of satisfied customers!

The local studies librarian carries not only the responsibility of providing a public service of some quality but must also take on the task of developing and ensuring the preservation of the collections on which that service is based. Active collecting is important; a local studies collection can never be complete and additional material to fill gaps and supplement what is already there should be sought rather than simply accepting whatever happens to be offered. The local history librarian, the archivist and the curator have to promote interest in their collections, to educate not only those individuals and organisations who might wish to offer material to them but also to ensure that the senior managers and, above all, the local politicians appreciate the significance of the collections and their special requirements. Vital material will be lost through decay and through missed opportunities and the public will lose both the sense of community identity that local history can promote and the enjoyment and enlightenment its study can provide. Microfilming and copying can ensure that fragile originals are preserved for future generations - but they cost money. Stores need environmental control - which requires specialist equipment - to prevent deterioration or decay through extremes of humidity or temperature. Ratepayers who have used the local collections will come to understand why their rate payments should go towards such expenditure; given the current enthusiasm for local history it should not be impossible to convince the politicians that there may be votes in it for them!

Taking such responsibilities seriously results not only in a high quality of service but also ensures a high degree of job satisfaction. It is not only the shared enthusiasm which is enjoyable. Solving a complex historical problem, acquiring new material which fills a yawning gap in the existing collection, or simply strengthening an inquirer's personal sense of the past, are clearly measurable successes. Furthermore, the legacy of an active and committed local librarian will be a well-managed, comprehensive and much used collection, not only for his or her contemporaries but for future generations as well.

## WHY LOCAL HISTORY?

The present financial climate makes it very unlikely that public money will be invested in large quantities to develop local studies libraries, record offices and museums in the near future. But the growth of interest in the subject shows no sign of slowing down; indeed, it seems to be accelerating. When Hoskins considered the reasons for the growth of interest in local history in 1959 he saw it as a reaction against the insecurities of the modern world. 'We belong to a particular place and the bigger and more incomprehensible the modern world grows the more will people turn to study something of which they can grasp the scale and in which they can find a personal and individual meaning.'[16] People do object to some aspects of modern life but those who are interested in local history are as likely as anyone else to be able to cope with them and even to take advantage of some of them. Widespread car ownership has enabled local historians to travel the length and breadth of the country, following up a local connection, investigating a town with a similar economic foundation or visiting an archaeological site. Family historians arrange their holidays in the parish where a generation of their ancestors were brought up in order to follow in their footsteps and to study the parish registers there. Cheap air travel has provided the opportunity for millions of ordinary people to travel abroad; they are equally hungry for information about life in other countries as life in the past! And in a world where we are increasingly prepared to take advantage of the microchip the home computers are taking their place alongside the camera and the tape recorder as a tool for the local historian.

Increased interest in local history does not have to be explained in this rather negative fashion. The fact remains that the subject has its own intrinsic fascination. A combination of factors have made it easier than ever before for ordinary people to become involved in a pastime which was formerly the preserve of the educated and leisured classes. The 1970s saw a generation of schoolchildren who had benefited from the teaching of local history in schools emerging to follow related subjects at university or as a hobby. Working in museums and as archaeologists became fashionable and for a time there were many jobs available for those who were interested. As the demand grew, at a time when resources for the creation of more jobs in these fields were becoming scarce, more and more enthusiasts found opportunities to get involved instead as voluntary workers, helping out on museum projects or as willing workers on archaeological excavations at weekends and in their holidays. Leisure time has increased since the Second World War through reduced working hours and longer paid holidays; in addition there is now a large number of people with the enforced leisure time of unemployment. Such time can be invested in pursuing active interests such as research and fieldwork. It is no accident that the membership of the National Trust has exceeded a million during the last few years; family outings by car to historic houses or beautiful countryside have become very popular and many local societies enjoy a coach outing to such places or to a historic town in the summer.

In 1977, almost 30 years after the creation of the Standing Conference for Local History, a Committee to Review Local History in England and Wales was formed under the chairmanship of Lord Blake. This should have been an important opportunity for taking stock, for assessing the vitality and potential for growth in the subject, but the Blake Report published in 1979 was a disappointment to many involved in local history. [17] Given the fact that the review seems to have been prompted by the need to find a new identity for the Standing Conference, separate from the parent body, the National Council of Social Service, the report's primary recommendation was perhaps predictable. The report recommended the creation of a national body to promote local history and to offer advice, training and information to local historians but it offered no concrete proposals about the constitution of the new body nor did it examine its future financial viability except in terms of grant-aid.

The British Association for Local History (BALH) which emerged to fulfill this role has so far provided only a pale reflection of the vitality of the subject in spite of the efforts of its field officer whose salary was provided by a grant. The new association seems to have failed to define its function clearly and has not solved the problems inherent in offering both personal and 'institutional' membership; as a forum for local societies, classes and other groups it might have had a clearer sense of purpose. Funding is now a serious problem and it is to be hoped that the *Local historian* (the association's journal) survives as a much valued publication whatever becomes of the BALH.

That local history remains a vigorous and popular subject is not in doubt, however. There are now more books about the history of communities and more books about how to do local history than ever before and in 1984 a lively new magazine, *Local history,* began publication, the brain child of two enthusiasts from Nottingham which takes a popular approach with plenty of illustrations and does not fear controversy. All these publications give the amateur confidence in knowing where to start and what to ask when seeking a new source of information. A BBC Radio series in 1972 and its accompanying book, *This was their world,* defined the areas the local historian should consider and offered not only detail about the material available but also advice on how to interpret it.[18] Subsequent television programmes on local history and allied subjects have spread the message further. *Discovering your family history,* broadcast on BBC TV in 1979, attracted a response from 33 000 for its initial information sheet alone and boosted the popular family history movement that was already gathering supporters. Again this was the popularisation of a subject which had existed in an older form; genealogy had had a very aristocratic image, but here were ordinary people embarking on an ambitious quest for their own ancestors, a project which could evoke the same combination of intellectual and emotional satisfaction as local history. There is no reason why the passion for the subject should die down; the material and archival evidence is freely and increasingly available for those who are interested and the subject costs almost nothing to pursue. The professionals know more now about the special requirements of the evidence in their care and its preservation should be assured. Our leisure time is likely to continue to increase as technological developments change the demands on our workforce. The tourist industry and some publishers are already making

24

money out of history. We may well be on the way to being identified as a nation of local historians.

## NOTES

1. A bibliography of the writings of the members of the Department was published to mark its 30th anniversary in 1978; the introduction by Professor Alan Everitt is the best summary of the Department's work. University of Leicester. Department of English Local History. *English local history at Leicester 1948-1978: a bibliography of writings by members of the Department*...Leicester, University of Leicester, c. 1981.
2. Pugh, R.B. *How to write a parish history.* 6th edition. London, Allen and Unwin, 1954.
3. Hoskins, W.G. *The Midland peasant.* London, Macmillan, 1957.
4. Dyos, H.J. *Victorian suburb: a study of the growth of Camberwell.* Leicester, Leicester University Press, 1961.
5. Beresford, M.W. *History on the ground.* London, Lutterworth Press, 1957. Ravensdale, J. *Liable to floods.* London, Cambridge University Press, 1974.
6. Spufford, M. The total history of village communities. *Local historian* 10 (8) November 1973, 390-401. *Contrasting communities: English villagers in the sixteenth and seventeenth centuries.* London, Cambridge University Press, 1974.
7. Le Roy Ladurie, E. *Montaillou: Cathars and Catholics in a French village, 1294-1324.* Harmondsworth, Penguin, 1980.
8. Beresford, M.W. The unprinted Census returns of 1841, 1851, 1861 for England and Wales. *Amateur historian* 5 (8) Summer 1963, 260-269.
9. Sturt, G. *The wheelwright's shop.* Cambridge, Cambridge University Press, 1923. Thompson, F. *Lark Rise to Candleford.* London, Oxford University Press, 1945.
10. Samuel, R. Local history and oral history. *History workshop* no. 1 Spring 1976, p. 204.
11. Emmison, F.G. *Archives and local history.* London, Methuen, 1966.
12. Department of Education and Science. *Provincial museums and galleries.* London, HMSO, 1973. (Wright Report.)
13. Emmison, p. xvi.

14. Bott, V. Into darkest suburbia... *Museums journal* 84 (3) December 1984, 109-116.
15. Amateur museums of this kind have become so common that the Area Museums Service for South-East England has published *The local museum: notes for amateur curators,* by Crispin Paine. Second edition, Milton Keynes, 1986.
16. Hoskins, W.G. *Local history in England.* Second edition, London, Longmans, 1972.
17. Committee to Review Local History. *Report.* London, Committee to Review Local History, 1979 (Blake Report.)
18. Rogers, A. *This was their world: approaches to local history.* London, BBC, 1972.

# 3

# The historical development and present structure of public library local studies provision in the United Kingdom

Robin Ansell

## HISTORICAL DEVELOPMENT

### Early nineteenth-century

The public library movement, as we know it today, had its origins in mid-nineteenth-century Britain and consequently the consideration of any individual aspect of its development must of necessity begin there.

The year 1830 marks an appropriate starting point, as it was then that William IV appointed a Records Commission to examine the state of the national archives. Some seven years later it reported unfavourably on many of the buildings then in use as repositories - including the Tower of London, Westminster Abbey and Somerset House - recommending that the most important national records be removed to a new central building. Here they could be properly arranged and made accessible to searchers. As a direct result of the commission's findings the Public Record Office Act of 1838 was passed, which established a central repository for the national records. Under the comprehensive range of powers vested in him as Master of the Rolls, Lord Langdale devoted himself energetically to his new duties and in the course of time the nation's records found their rightful place in the Public Record Office in London.

The situation, however, was completely different with regard to local records. Apart from the legal and official records, their conditon was very largely ignored by the government at this time. A few archaeological and antiquarian societies were interested, along with a handful of libraries, but otherwise they were regarded with total apathy. Of the interested libraries, two are worthy of special mention: the Guildhall Library, London and Warrington Public Library.

The Guildhall Library had been collecting and preserving local records on all matters relating to the City since 1824, although its history extended over many centuries to the days of Dick Whittington. At this time it was not a public library as such, being maintained from the corporation's privy purse.

Warrington, like two other towns, Canterbury and Salford, ingeniously established a public library under the provisions of the Museums Act of 1845. The origin of its local collection may be traced from its first accessions register. It opens in November 1848, with the donation of a collection of books by William Beamont, the first mayor of Warrington.

## Select Committee on Public Libraries 1849

Following the passage of the Museums Act agitation had gradually been on the increase for the introduction of rate-supported public libraries. Consequently a Select Committee was duly appointed in 1849 to look into 'the best means of extending the establishment of Libraries freely open to the Public, especially in large towns, in Great Britain and Ireland'.[1] The report issued by the committee, largely 'engineered' by William Ewart and Edward Edwards, did briefly touch upon the importance of including local history - or as they were then known 'topographical' - collections within public libraries. The minutes of evidence reveal Chairman Ewart questioning a preacher named George Dawson on the desirability of such collections:

Chairman   As you have travelled much in the provinces, do you not think it might be of great advantage to have collections in the different provincial towns on topographical subjects connected with the nature of the country, its geology for instance, and its past history, and everything that concerns the local character of the neighbourhood?

Witness   Yes; they should be complete, I think.

Chairman   And would not that give an interest in the eyes of the people in the district, to the literature connected with their own country?

Witness   It would, and sometimes it would be really to their material advantage.[2]

Furthermore, the report recommended that: 'In all our chief provincial towns it is requisite that there should be Topographical Libraries...where history may find a faithful portraiture of local events, local literature, and local manners; and art and science a collection of all objects illustrative of the climate, soil, and resources of the surrounding country.' It also made a strong case for establishing 'Special Libraries' in appropriate localities, 'illustrative of the peculiar trade, manufactures, and agriculture of the place, and greatly favourable to the practical development of the science of political economy'.[3]

At this early stage there is thus an indication of the way in which local material was regarded and how it would later develop into two distinct, although related, branches: local history ('topographical') and commercial/technical ('trade, manufactures, and agriculture...').

## Public Libraries Act 1850

The Select Committee's report had shown in general terms that the existing public library provision was totally inadequate and on 14 February 1850 William Ewart was given leave in the House of Commons to introduce his Public Libraries Bill. In so doing, he referred once again to the claims of local history as an indispensable feature of the public library:

> One great advantage which might be hereafter derived from such institutions [i.e. public libraries] he [William Ewart] should mention. It was that their contents would be illustrative of the local and natural history of the places in which they were established. They would be most valuable to the future historian, as furnishing not only works illustrative of the locality in the libraries, but as preserving in the museums samples of the natural curiosities of the neighbourhood.[4]

After six months of intense opposition, led by the redoubtable Colonel Charles de Laet Waldo Sibthorp, the bill received the royal assent on 14 August. The successful triumvirate of Ewart, Edwards and Joseph Brotherton had finally convinced Parliament of the necessity of establishing rate-supported public libraries.

## Collections in early public libraries

So from the very outset local history collections were regarded, at least by some enlightened individuals, as worthwhile ventures which might rightfully find their place in the newly established public libraries.

One of the earliest libraries to open under the act was Manchester, in September 1852. This library possessed a local collection from the beginning of more than 500 works, accommodated within its reference department. Its first librarian, coincidentally, was none other than Edward Edwards himself.

A month later saw the opening of Liverpool's public library - the second major civic library. Here too the local history collection commenced in the library's inaugural year, with the purchase of the Binns Collection, belonging to a lately deceased antiquary. It was an impressive assortment of material in 26 large folio volumes, consisting of maps, drawings and engravings illustrative of the history of Lancashire in general and of Liverpool in particular. In the acquisition of this collection the library committee and the librarian, John Stuart Dalton, showed great wisdom and foresight.

Numerous library local collections originated in a similar manner to that at Liverpool. That is, through the acquisition, by purchase or bequest, of the private library of some well-known local collector or antiquary. The deposited material would then act as a nucleus around which further deposits would gradually be accumulated. Depending upon the relative importance attached to these deposits, they were either broken up or maintained as separate physical entities.

Typically the local collection at this time, and for a considerable time to come, was just one of a number of special collections housed within the general reference department. Indeed, much time was to elapse before the autonomous local history department, with specialist staff, was to become a common feature of the public library. Even today its autonomy is by no means universal.

So far the specific local collections cited have been geographically restricted to the north of England, in particular Lancashire. This has not occurred by design - but by mere coincidence. However, it does serve to illustrate what one noted library historian has previously indicated, that 'the predominance of Lancashire is a pointer to the fact that the great strength of the library movement in the nineteenth century was to be in the industrial areas.'[5] With the hope of dispelling thoughts of regional bias, however, a brief account will be given of two of the earliest collections to be found in the south - in Cambridge and in Bristol.

Cambridge's local collection commenced with the opening of the library in June 1855 - thanks to its indefatigable librarian, John Pink. Among the first donations to be received were four volumes of Cooper's *Annals of Cambridge*. Less than 20 years later Pink's published catalogue of the reference department included a local collection comprising 'some 688 items ranging from Domesday Book to a contemporary report on a proposed new cattle market...'.[6]

The ancient commercial centre of Bristol had engaged itself in the collection of local material since 1856, largely due to the vigorous exertions of its first city librarian, George Pryce. It is all the more remarkable when one considers that Bristol did not formally adopt the Libraries Acts until 1874 - an arrangement whose legality was apparently never questioned!

Thus by the tenth anniversary of the Public Libraries Act several libraries had been successful in establishing special collections relating to their localities which were steadily growing in stature.

## Historical Manuscripts Commission 1869

National interest was aroused in unpublished manuscripts and local records, with the appointment of the Historical Manuscripts Commission in 1869. Its remit was to enquire into the existence of such documents in the possession of private individuals and in institutions, and to make inquiry as to the places in which local records and manuscripts were deposited. Since their appointment 'the Commissioners have inspected and issued reports upon many hundred collections, embracing not only records belonging to private families, but to those of public authorities also'.[7] In essence the commission acted, and still continues to act, as the public watch-dog on the conservation of manuscript and record material.

Thus by the late nineteenth-century the imbalance, so clearly evident in 1830, was being redressed. The fate of at least some record material, of interest to the local librarian and historian, was being determined at a national level. Obviously the commission was not able instantly to examine all the extant material and inevitably much has been lost over the intervening period through lack of adequate protection.

## Penny rate

Local collections at this time, although steadily growing in number, were severely restricted in what could be purchased for them. Under the provisions laid down by the Public Libraries and Museums Act of 1855, town councils were allowed to levy a maximum rate of one penny in the pound for libraries. This limited greatly what a library and its constituent collections could afford to purchase. This niggardly financial situation effectively prevented any competition with private collectors, and consequently donations continued to remain the principal source of local books and documents.

Despite this lack of adequate funding, libraries were still being urged to collect local material. Edward Edwards, writing in 1869, continued to stress the need for 'a thorough collection of all printed information about the history, the antiquities, the trade, the statistics, the special products, the special pursuits, and the special social interests, of the Town and of the County in which it stands'.[8]

## Birmingham and Derby

Two interesting case studies of this period are Birmingham and Derby. Birmingham, which adopted the Libraries Acts in 1860, had as its first chief librarian, John Davies Mullins, and it was he who acquired for the library the Staunton Collection on the history and antiquities of Warwickshire in 1875. This collection had been purchased from its owner, John Staunton, with funds raised largely by public subscription. Unfortunately, however, it was almost totally destroyed - along with the famous Shakespeare Memorial Library - in the disastrous fire of January 1879. Regrettably, due to the very nature of the material involved, much that was lost was irreplaceable. Despite this tremendous set-back, a new library was constructed and eventually opened three years later by the reform politician, John Bright. From that date onwards the rebuilding of the special collections has been earnestly pursued.

Derby's local collection commenced in 1878, when the library had been open but seven years, with the donation by the seventh Duke of Devonshire of his Derbyshire books, supplemented by many local books from the magnificent library at Chatsworth House. In expressing their thanks to the donor, the library committee announced their intention of making the topography and literature of the county a cardinal feature of the library service. This was no empty gesture, as the collection was later greatly augmented by the Bemrose Library, built up over many years by Sir Henry Howe Bemrose and his two librarians. Again, it had been purchased by public subscription in 1914, following the personal intervention of Lord Curzon of Kedleston.

## 'Father of public library local history collections'

The year 1877 witnessed the foundation, in London, of the Library Association of the United Kingdom - largely through the efforts of the London Institution's librarian, Edward Williams Byron Nicholson. Its first annual meeting (later to be called conferences) was held in Oxford the following year, and interestingly one of the papers read there further advanced the cause of the local history collection. The paper was given by the librarian of Plymouth, William Henry Kearley Wright, and if any man deserves to be regarded as the 'father of public library local history collections', it is undoubtedly he. His paper stressed the necessity of local collections to be well catalogued and the desirability of such catalogues to be published, if at all possible. Wright spoke also of the role of the local history librarian, who 'should endeavour to identify himself with his work, so as to become in course of time an authority upon matters relating to his particular locality'. On the purpose behind establishing local collections, Wright was most convincing:

My plea is that every provincial library which is designed to be the central or public one of its district, should, in addition to its recognized reference department, be the repository for works connected with the city, town, county, or district of which it is the centre, and that efforts should be made to collect therein all useful books, pamphlets, or manuscripts having any connexion with the district, whether descriptive of, relating to, published in, or written by natives of, or sometime residents within the limits of such district. By this means, in course of time, a large and valuable collection of books would be made, and an interest awakened in local as well as general literature. In this way, too, local authors and publishers would be encouraged, a new impulse given to literary workers, and an additional inducement offered to the general public to frequent and use our public libraries for purposes of study and research.[9]

*1. William Henry Kearley Wright (1844-1915). The "Father of Public Library Local History Collections."*

It is quite surprising that Wright possessed such an accurate and remarkably clear view of the objectives of a local history collection, especially when one considers that he had only entered public library service some two years earlier. Devonian by birth, he had been born in the historic seaport of Plymouth on 14 September 1844.[10] After 'leaving the Plymouth Public School young Wright entered the Plymouth Bank of Deposit. His next post was at Millbay Station under the old South Devon Railway Company...'. When some of the railway workers decided to form a library, 'Wright, on account of his studious habits, was made honorary librarian. The knowledge of books gained in this position next secured for him the post of librarian of the Plymouth Working Men's Association...'.[11] In 1876 he was appointed librarian of the newly established public library - a post he was to hold until his death, almost 40 years later.

Wright was a man of boundless energy, having been a founder member of the Library Association, and a Vice-President on several occasions. The Ex-Libris Society owed its origin to Wright, who was also keenly interested in historical research, particularly in connection with his native town. In 1888 he took a prominent part in the Armada Tercentenary celebrations. Shortly before his death, he introduced 'open access' into his library - then quite a revolutionary innovation. The obituary which appeared in the *Library Association record,* written by the Nottingham librarian and historian, John Potter Briscoe, concluded: 'His commanding and picturesque figure and a marked personality will be greatly missed in Plymouth; and the name of W.H.K. Wright of Plymouth will long be remembered by those who knew him in public library and literary circles.'[12]

## Collections come of age

In 1878 Wright had been able specifically to name extensive, well-organised local collections at Manchester, Liverpool, Rochdale, Bristol, Leicester, Birmingham and, of course, his own Devon and Cornwall Collection at Plymouth. The following collections, already referred to, supplement Wright's list: Guildhall, London (1824), Warrington (1848), Cambridge (1855) and Derby (1878). Others, however, were quick to follow: South Shields (1879), Norwich (1880), Gateshead (1884), Newcastle-upon-Tyne (1884), Swansea (1887), Oxford (1890), Carlisle (1890), Cardiff (1891), and Gloucester (1891).

Devious means were sometimes employed to help finance the establishment of a local collection. A good example is that of Norwich, where its ingenious librarian, George Easter, put forward the suggestion to his library committee that a local collection be established - financed totally from the lending library fines. The obvious advantage of this scheme was that no extra expenditure was involved, and not surprisingly the committee approved the idea.

Similar local collections, of varying extent, were being established north of the border: Dundee (1869), Paisley (1870), Glasgow (1877), Perth (1879) and Dumbarton (1881), for example. As with their southern counterparts, they too frequently originated with the acquisition, by donation or bequest, of an important private collection. Indeed, at Perth for example, a collection of local literature was being formed almost 20 years before the library actually opened. Often the existence of such collections - awaiting a suitable home - would help stimulate the city elders into adopting the Libraries Acts.

By the 1880s collections of local material in public libraries had become generally accepted and fairly commonplace. By this time too, the larger libraries had finally grasped the distinction - alluded to in the 1849 report - between local history and commercial/technical collections. Thus true local history collections, in the modern sense, may be said to date from this period.

## Controversy over local records

Public libraries, particularly their local collections, had been keen to acquire and preserve local records and other manuscript material from the very outset. Two notable examples were the libraries of Manchester and Liverpool. At the Library Association's ninth annual meeting in 1886, the librarian of the British Museum, Edward Augustus Bond, reasserted the role of the public librarian in the field of local records:

> He [the public librarian] will not be long in extending the first conception of the scope of its [the public library's] action and usefulness by taking opportunities for gathering into it not only local publications and local journals, but topographical records of every character. He will seek eagerly for all documents connected with the town and neighbouring landed estates - for charters and manorial rolls and accounts - for family correspondence and papers. A cry has already been raised for the need of public action in rescuing what remains of these invaluable records from destruction. The fittest agency for the purpose is the Public Library of the district.[13]

Bond's sentiments, regarding the acquisition of local records, expressed the thoughts of many a librarian at the time: 'If no one else is willing to collect them, then I suppose we must.' Of course, this was well before the advent of the county record office, which did not arrive on the scene until the early twentieth-century. The role of the public library as conservator of local records was repeatedly raised by librarians in the latter years of the nineteenth-century. An official of the British Museum, Henry Robert Plomer, spoke at the 1891 Library Association annual meeting of how local records 'have suffered in times past from the neglect and carelessness of their custodians...'. He pointed out 'that whereas the national records are now safely housed...the local records are very little better off than they were a hundred years ago'. Plomer continued by asking: 'Why should not every library in the kingdom take in hand the records of its own district?'[14]

There was, indeed, no valid reason why libraries should not involve themselves in what was only a natural extension of their activities. Several librarians, most notably William Henry Overall, Ernest Axon, William Elliott Doubleday and the ubiquitous Wright, championed the suitability of public libraries as repositories for local records and manuscripts. It was stressed that local records had no authoritative place of deposit, and could by no means be said to be easily accessible to searchers.

However, some people, particularly William Phillimore Watts Phillimore, who had founded the British Record Society in 1888, argued the converse - that libraries were unsuitable, and that local records and manuscripts ought to be held in separate custody in record offices. He had written to the *Times,* as early as 1889, advocating that: 'In every county town there should be provided a suitable building under the direction of the county council to be styled "The County Record Office".'[15] Needless to say, he was somewhat ahead of his time.

## Local Records Committee 1899-1901

This rather confused state of affairs, with the air rife with argument and counter-argument, led to considerable public agitation as the nineteenth-century drew to a close. To quell this the First Lord of the Treasury, Arthur James Balfour, appointed a Local Records Committee in 1899, with instructions 'to enquire and report as to any arrangements in operation for the collection, custody, indexing and calendaring of local records, and as to any further measures which it might be advisable to take for this purpose'.[16] Two schedules of questions were duly drawn up and circulated to more than 850 local and ecclesiastical authorities, of which 483 replied. The first schedule alluded to the existing repositories and the second invited suggestions for improvement and for making the records more accessible. Specific mention of public libraries in these schedules fostered the hope that their claims would receive official consideration, and several librarians commented on their institutions as suitable centres for the reception of records. A resolution proposed by the librarian of Chelsea, John Henry Quinn, 'that the municipal public library authorities are the natural and best custodians of local records, and that the Local Records Committee of the Treasury be asked to receive a deputation of the Library Association to support this view'[17] was unanimously adopted. Consequently, the Library Association, along with other interested bodies, put forward the claims of local libraries and made representations urging the advantages of library custody to the Local Records Committee.

The Local Records Committee itself was composed of six members: Bishop Mandell Creighton, Sir Henry Churchill Maxwell Lyte, Sir Francis Mowatt, Sir Courtenay Peregrine Ilbert, James Bryce and Stephen Edward Spring-Rice - not a single public librarian among them! Lyte, however, was the deputy keeper of the Public Record Office.

Sitting from 1899 to 1901, the committee issued its report the following year. It had chosen to dissent from the view put forward by the Library Association, stating quite definitely that 'we do not recommend that local libraries should, as a rule, be used as depositories of records'.[18] Their objections, all remediable, were that libraries were not always fire-proof, that accommodation was often limited and that the scope of a public library differed from that of a record office.

The key question in the schedules had been Question 8, Schedule 2: 'To what extent, if any, could local libraries, under public control or managed by trustworthy local bodies, be made useful for purposes of custody?' For the committee to reach the decision it did, for the reasons stated, this following reply from the London County Council must have been very typical:

> Public libraries, which rarely have fireproof accommodation, are not always suitable for the custody of records. The regulations governing the use of records must necessarily be very different from those for the use of books, and the most competent of librarians may not necessarily possess the qualifications of a custodian of records.[19]

In fact, detailed study of the answers given in the second schedule reveal that only 74 were in favour of public libraries acting as custodians of local records; while 22 respondents gave a qualified approval of the idea. Several librarians, including John Minto, Charles William Sutton, John Ballinger, and Frank Pacy gave, as one might expect, favourable replies. Phillimore, characteristically, had contributed to the discussion from the opposing viewpoint, stating that librarians 'have rarely received the training suitable for record keepers'.[20]

As a result of the committee's findings it was recommended that local record offices be established to act as centralised repositories for record material. However, no legislative action was forthcoming, and in the absence of compulsion few local authorities took any active steps in the matter. The appointment of yet another Records Commission, sitting from 1910 to 1919, still failed to resolve the situation.

## County record offices

One person who sought to break the deadlock was Dr George Herbert Fowler, who saw the necessity for record offices, as others did, but translated his thoughts into positive action. In 1913 Fowler established the Bedfordshire County Record Office - the first of its kind in Britain. This same year marked the death of one who for so long had advocated the merits of the local record office - Phillimore. The chief function of the county record office was deemed to be the taking of full and proper steps for the better preservation of local records and to act as a centre for historical research. Following the publication of Fowler's *The care of county muniments,* in 1923, several county councils interested themselves in the custody and preservation of records and from that date the movement expanded rapidly.

## Law of Property (Amendment) Act 1924

The 1920s, however, witnessed the beginning of the final battle over custodial rights, between libraries and record offices. In 1922 the Law of Property Act abolished copyhold tenure, which effectively deprived one class of local record - the manorial document - of its legal value. It was realised at the time that in so doing there was a grave danger that many of these documents would literally vanish overnight or be wantonly destroyed, now that they no longer possessed any practical significance.

Such a situation would thereby have deprived future historians of a great wealth of historic source material. To prevent this from occuring the Law of Property (Amendment) Act was passed two years later, which prescribed legal enforcement for the custody of manorial records. Lord Hanworth, as Master of the Rolls, used his powers under the act to draw up the Manorial Documents Rules in 1926. These laid down conditions which had to be met by any institution seeking to preserve manorial records. Furthermore, Lord Hanworth encouraged the establishment of a central repository in each county for the preservation, not only of manorial documents, but of records of every description relating to that area. Surprisingly, it proved no simple matter to find a suitable repository in each county and many libraries were thus approved since other bodies were not inclined to fulfill the obligations imposed by the acceptance of manorial documents.

The first list of approved repositories, issued in 1926, included 18 libraries; while that of 1934 included 10 county record offices, 26 municipal libraries, 1 county and 13 special libraries. A 'one area - one repository' rule was introduced, so as to achieve some degree of centralisation. This, however, was in some cases rather unfair - as at Manchester, for example. Here the public library, in spite of its vast collections relating to the city and the county of Lancashire, was refused 'official' repository status because the John Rylands Library had been accepted for Lancashire and Cheshire. Liverpool, Plymouth, Leeds and Newcastle-upon-Tyne were similarly not approved although they possessed large collections of manuscript and manorial records, and qualified staff to deal with them.

Librarians were no doubt well pleased, and not a little surprised, to be so actively engaged in the local records field - especially after the 1902 report had so severely criticised their competence in this respect. Many of them, in fact, were now eminently better qualified to do this work than they had been 20 years earlier - for in 1919 the first full-time School of Librarianship was created at University College, London, which offered a course of training in palaeography and archives.

By this time, too, county libraries had come into existence, established by the act of 1919, and were also collecting local material. This was partly to meet the demands of their readers and partly because, once established, they tended to attract such material. They did not, of course, attempt to rival the major collections already held in urban libraries; Norwich's long-established Norwich and Norfolk Collection and Gloucester's Gloucestershire Collection, to name but two, were far beyond anything their respective counties could hope to achieve.

40

## McColvin report 1942

In 1941 the Library Association commissioned its Honorary Secretary, Lionel Roy McColvin, to make a war-time tour of public libraries, and in the following year his report was published. Regarding the stage of development that local history collections had reached by this time, the report stated that 'the great majority of urban libraries have excellent local collections dealing with their local history and topography, and including photographs, prints, maps and manuscripts, in addition to books and printed materials'.[21] Such a commendable situation had arisen largely due to the enthusiasm and dedication of the new century's librarians, building upon the solid foundations laid by their Victorian predecessors: David Rhys Phillips of Swansea, Harry Tapley Tapley-Soper of Exeter, George Edward Johnson Roebuck of Walthamstow, William Benson Thorne of Poplar, George Arthur Stephen of Norwich, William Charles Berwick Sayers of Croydon, Alfred Cecil Piper of Richmond-upon-Thames, Miss Ethel Gerard of Worthing, Arthur John Hawkes of Wigan and more recently John Leslie Hobbs of Shrewsbury.

Hobbs perhaps deserves special mention here. From 1946 to 1964 he was Shrewsbury's borough librarian and energetic local historian, and also author in 1962 of *Local history and the library,* which became the standard work in the field. He had been personally involved in the formation of the Standing Conference for Local History (now the British Association for Local History), being the Library Association's representative. Until his untimely death he was generally regarded as the 'apostle' of modern local history librarianship.

## Present position

During and since the Second World War, with the movement for better preservation of records and the establishment of county record offices growing apace, there has been an unannounced, yet significant, change of policy on the part of the Master of the Rolls. The 'one area - one repository' rule was no longer applied, and the policy became instead to recognise each new county record office, as it was created, as the appropriate repository for each county. Where an existing library or other body had previously been an approved repository, it continued to function as an additional repository but was no longer regarded as the primary repository for the area, however well it had fulfilled its obligations in this respect in the past. It has now become generally recognised that 'although libraries were decades earlier in the field it must now be conceded that the normal means of collecting archives is the county record office...'.[22]

This decision, of course, was only relevant in so far as documents deposited under the direction of the Master of the Rolls were concerned and public libraries were still at liberty to collect manorial records, providing they complied with the Manorial Documents Rules. For those libraries who wished to retain, or even commence, a local records and archives collection, the Library Association issued a policy statement in 1968.[23]

After reading a historical survey such as the above, one might be tempted to pose the question: 'Why local history libraries/librarians?' Perhaps Hobbs offered the best testimony in their defence, when he stated:

> But the real reason why the librarian should participate in this work of collecting local historical materials is simple. He really has no alternative: it is a duty - one thrust upon him by the logic of circumstance and by virtue of his position as custodian of the literature which is of potential interest to the community he serves and which gives him his livelihood. Local history material constitutes a vital part of this literature and the librarian who neglects it is not fulfilling his whole duty to his community.[24]

## PRESENT STRUCTURE

The present structure of local studies provision dates essentially from the last reorganisation of local government: London (1965), Northern Ireland (1973), England and Wales (1974) and Scotland (1975). Library authorities in London became the boroughs; in Northern Ireland the education and library boards; in England and Wales the metropolitan districts and non-metropolitan counties (plus a handful of Welsh non-metropolitan districts); and in Scotland the districts, regions and islands.

Many of the structures now in existence bear a marked resemblance to those recommended in the 1973 Department of Education and Science report *Public Library service: reorganisation and after*. This is particularly true with regard to the creation of 'a strong central collection relating to the area as a whole...' and the report further stipulated that:

'Outside this central collection, each identifiable community within the new authorities will have a need for material relating to its own history to stimulate and to satisfy the interest of local residents, who may subsequently turn to the central collection to pursue their further studies.' The report emphasised 'that these two considerations - the need of local historians for comprehensive collections, and the need of residents for conveniently accessible local collections - should determine the deployment of local history material within each new authority'.[25] These then were the guidelines.

## London

London boroughs are amalgamations of previously independent local authorities and 'most areas had independent collections of differing quality prior to reorganization'.[26] This can be said to be true of practically all the reorganised authorities. A good example is the Local Studies Section at Bexley which 'was set up in 1972 to integrate the local history material inherited from the former Boroughs of Bexley and Erith, the Urban District of Crayford and the Sidcup part of the Urban District of Chiselhurst and Sidcup with the museum collections of Bexley and Erith'.[27] Not surprisingly, perhaps, the statement continues: 'Naturally with such a variety of former local authorities the local history coverage is rather erratic.'(!) London boroughs are relatively small in both population and area, consequently the centralisation of local studies provision - covering the needs of the whole borough - is a common feature. Travelling distances tend not to be too great and public transport generally of the first order. However, this centralisation is frequently supported:

> by strong local collections in area libraries serving well-defined areas, often areas previously independent, the emphasis being on the history of that local area. The central collection usually has copies of all the local material in the Borough, and if unique publications are in an area library these are moved to the central collection and photocopied.[28]

One distinct advantage of centralisation is that it often facilitates the employment of specialist staff, that would otherwise prove totally uneconomic. The boroughs of Bexley, Lewisham and Waltham Forest all maintain centralised collections. However, strong local interests (often of a 'political' nature) may militate against such centralisation, as at Croydon (Croydon, Purley); Islington (Islington, Finsbury); Merton (Wimbledon, Mitcham, Morden). The Guildhall Library, although part of the City of London, acts in a sense as an 'unofficial' centralised collection for older London material in general.

## Northern Ireland

The public library service in Northern Ireland has been administered since 1973 by five education and library boards: Belfast; North Eastern; South Eastern; Southern; and Western. Irish and local studies collections (as they tend to be known in the Province) are generally centralised at a divisional or library headquarters. For example in Western the Local History Department is housed at library headquarters at Omagh, Co. Tyrone, with lesser collections at two divisional headquarters (Londonderry, Co. Londonderry and Enniskillen, Co. Fermanagh); in South Eastern the Irish Section is based at library headquarters at Ballynahinch, Co. Down; in Southern the Local History Service is at the divisional headquarters at Portadown, Co. Armagh. The largest single collection of Irish material is that held at Belfast. Its Irish and Local Studies Department, within the central library, has more than 40 000 books and pamphlets, and in addition has extensive holdings of newspapers, periodicals, government publications and other special collections (including archives).

Inter-library co-operation is given a high priority in Northern Ireland, examples being the publication of *Northern Ireland local studies* (a Province-wide current bibliography of material added to the stock of the five public library services) and the compilation of union lists of newspaper holdings, both in hard copy and microfilm. The former is a product of the boards themselves, edited by North Eastern; the latter being the work of the Library Association Northern Ireland Branch and the Public Record Office of Northern Ireland.

## England and Wales

### Metropolitan districts

Like the London boroughs, metropolitan districts tend to favour centralisation of resources on account of their relatively small geographical area. Usually such centralisation is based on the main centre of population and almost certainly a former library authority in its own right. Those local collections based on the major cities such as Manchester traditionally undertook to cover their 'hinterland', but now the districts 'are widening the area for which all material is collected, if only up to the new boundaries'.[29] Again like London boroughs, in most districts 'the maintenance of a central local studies research collection is accompanied by a decision to build or develop strong branch local collections, sometimes with the aid of duplicates and commonly with microforms from the central collection'.[30] The resultant structure of the local studies provision within a local authority is very largely determined by two factors: the availability of suitable accommodation and geographical size. Hence, in 1972 Salford created a central local history collection at Salford Central Library because there was sufficient space there and it was 'the nearest to Salford University where a Department of Local Studies has just been established...'.[31] However, it still 'continues to provide district local studies library services in Eccles, Irlam, Swinton and Walkden' as a response to 'local traditions and local interests'. Indeed, such is the strength of local feeling that 'the people of Broughton, whose town became part of Salford over a hundred years ago, have recently established their own local history society'.[32] Such consideration of local loyalties and prejudices within the community can be crucial in the effective provision of local studies services. Geographical considerations dictated that Sandwell should retain its 'four separate local history collections in West Bromwich, Wednesbury, Tipton and Smethwick...and not build a large central collection, because of shortage of space...and because the District is comprised of several distinct medium-sized townships'.[33] A similar situation exists at Rochdale, where three area local collections are maintained at Rochdale, Middleton and Heywood.

## Non-metropolitan counties

There is probably more variety in the administrative structure of local studies in the non-metropolitan counties than for any other category of local authority. Some have remained virtually unaffected by the reorganisation of a decade ago, retaining their 'existing pattern of local studies provision';[34] some have established central research collections; and yet others have adopted a decentralised approach. Typically the latter library structure - not solely restricted to local studies - is divided administratively into groups, areas or divisions. West Sussex has three divisions, with local collections at Crawley, Chichester and Worthing; Somerset also has three divisions, with collections at Taunton (main collection), Bridgwater and Yeovil; Dorset three areas, collections at Dorchester (main collection), Bournemouth, Poole and Weymouth; Devon five areas, collections at Exeter (main collection), Plymouth, Torquay, Exmouth, Barnstaple, Bideford, Newton Abbot, Tiverton and Sidmouth; Wiltshire three divisions, collections at Trowbridge (main collection), Devizes, Salisbury and Swindon; Cumbria five groups, collections at Carlisle (main collection), Barrow-in-Furness, Kendal, Whitehaven and Workington; Derbyshire fifteen groups, collections at Derby (main collection), Buxton, Chesterfield, Glossop, Heanor, Ilkeston, Long Eaton, Matlock and Swadlincote. Frequently the policy of county libraries is to 'have a Local Studies Librarian, with county-wide responsibility, based at the library with the major research collection'.[35] The smaller collections within the county library service are usually administered by the appropriate group, area or divisional reference staff, rather than designated local studies librarians.

To summarise: London boroughs and metropolitan districts tend to neglect the provision of 'local' (i.e. branch) local collections and over-centralise. On the other hand non-metropolitan counties have a tendency to be unconvinced 'of the desirability of building comprehensive research collections...'.[36]

## Scotland

Scotland underwent reorganisation last of all and it resulted in a dramatic reduction in the number of library authorities, from 80 to 40. Of these, three are regions, three islands and the remainder districts.

### Regions

The number of local collections administered by a regional library service can vary from as few as two, to as many as seven. They are invariably based at the main libraries of former authorities. For example Borders maintains local collections at Duns, Galashiels, Hawick, Kelso, Peebles, St Boswells and Selkirk.[37]

46

## Islands

They tend to administer their collections from a central repository, as befits a highly scattered population in a small geographical area. For example Orkney has a centralised collection at Kirkwall, founded in 1683 and boasting '1,000 linear feet of local authority, business and private records from 16th. century onwards'.[38]

## Districts

Typically they have a central local collection, often long established, based on the main centre of population. Examples are Dundee: central collection at Dundee (founded 1869); Motherwell: Motherwell (1904). Occasionally a secondary collection may exist elsewhere in the district, usually to be found at the principal library of a former independent authority. Examples are Angus: Arbroath and Montrose; Dumbarton: Dumbarton and Templeton (Helensburgh); Monklands: Airdrie and Coatbridge.[39]

To summarise: in general Scottish library authorities show 'an even stronger interest in centralisation than English counties, with of course a parallel development of local interest collections in branch libraries'.[40] This is hardly surprising when one realises that most library authorities in Scotland are considerably smaller than their English counterparts. However, the major collections, as in England, are largely to be found in the great conurbations. Two particularly fine collections being those at Glasgow ( founded 1877) and Edinburgh (1932).[41]

## Local studies centres

The initial concept of the local history resource centre, as they were first known, is credited to Michael F. Messenger, borough librarian of Shrewsbury, back in 1972. However, it only became widely known among practising librarians some three years later, with the appearance of an article on the subject in the professional press. Its author, Philip C. Cruttenden, senior assistant curator of Kirklees, referred to such centres as 'unlimited media bureaux containing the total contents of the record office repository and local history sections of the reference library and museum'.[42] It aroused much interest at the time, with librarians responding from Oldham,

Wiltshire and elsewhere. At Oldham there had been what was called a Local Interest Centre since 1972, where library and museum had successfully been combined - although the record office was still awaiting approval. Its librarian, Richard Peroni, considered that his centre operated 'on a wider basis...for it deals with local studies as opposed to purely local history: local studies in the sense that both current and historical information is treated equally. The Centre provides an information point dealing with all aspects of the town today, as well as most aspects of the town yesterday.'[43] Likewise Wiltshire's then director, Frederick Hallworth, described their local studies service as intending to 'contribute to a better understanding and appreciation of the geological, archaeological, climatic, historic, demographic, geographic, economic, domestic and other factors that moulded the scenery, culture and society of the county'.[44]

Over the decade since then many authorities have made attempts, with varying degrees of success, to implement the local studies centre concept. The London Borough of Bexley has its Local Studies Section at Hall Place, which combines library, museum and archives; the London Borough of Waltham Forest has similarly established the Vestry House Museum at Walthamstow, integrating library, museum and archives collection; the London Borough of Lewisham's Manor House at Lee has an Archives and Local History Department; at Manchester the Local History Library and Archives are two special departments of the central library; likewise at Birmingham where Local Studies and Archives are housed under the same roof. In the non-metropolitan counties, Norfolk shares accommodation with the local record office at the central library in Norwich, and in Devon a similar arrangement exists at Exeter central library. Suffolk operates the reverse of this structure, where 'the County Library and the County Record Office have set up local study centres in the County Record Offices at Bury St Edmunds and Ipswich, where both printed and archival materials are available'.[45] In Scotland plans are presently afoot in the Borders Region to establish a library and archive resource at regional library headquarters, Selkirk. Belfast provides in its central library probably the best example in Northern Ireland - archives being housed alongside printed material.

'These Centres, occupied by local studies libraries with museums and archives, all appear to show a common theme - the grasping of an opportunity which presents itself when a building, seemingly appropriate for housing local studies materials, comes into the ownership of the local authority'.[46] They also demonstrate a common desire on the part of

48

librarians, archivists and curators to provide an improved and more integrated service to the public they serve.

With the impending abolition (at the time of writing) of the Greater London Council and the metropolitan counties, there is a possibility that archival powers may be devolved upon the London boroughs and the metropolitan districts or alternatively that special arrangements will be made for London and archival powers in the metropolitan counties will go to Commissions or committees set up to handle various public services.[47] If this does indeed take place, then the creation of many new local studies centres - combining library and former record office functions - may well be one of the more positive results.

## NOTES

1.  Hansard. *Parliamentary debates.* 3rd series. Vol. 103, 1849, col. 755.
2.  Select Committee on Public Libraries. *Report.* 1849, p. 84.
3.  Ibid., pp. x-xi.
4.  Hansard. *Parliamentary debates.* 3rd series. Vol. 108, 1850, col. 762.
5.  Kelly, T. *A history of public libraries in Great Britain, 1845-1975.* 2nd edition. London, Library Association, 1977, p. 24.
6.  Petty, M.J. Cambridgeshire Collection, 1855-1982, p. 2. (Unpublished typescript.)
7.  Hobbs, J.L. *Libraries and the materials of local history.* London, Grafton, 1948, p. 13.
8.  Edwards, E. *Free town libraries.* London, Trubner, 1869, p. 37.
9.  Wright, W.H.K. Special collections of local books in provincial libraries. In: *Transactions and proceedings of the first annual meeting of the Library Association of the United Kingdom... 1878.* London, Whittingham, 1879, pp. 44, 45.
10. Sources vary as to Wright's exact date of birth; 15 September 1844 is also cited.
11. Tapley-Soper, H.T. William Henry Kearley Wright. *Devon and Cornwall notes and queries.* 8(7) 1915, p. 193.
12. Briscoe, J.P. ('J.P.B.'). Obituary: Wright (W.H.K., Plymouth). *Library Association record* 17 15 July, 1915, p. 30A. The attribution

of the initials 'J.P.B.', which appeared at the foot of the obituary, to Briscoe is entirely the author's.

13. Bond, E.A. Address to the Library Association. *Library chronicle* 4 (35/36) January/February 1887, p. 3.
14. Plomer, H.R. Local records and free public libraries. *Library* 4 1893, pp. 138-139.
15. Spufford, P. The British Record Society - eighty years of an index. *Indexer* 6 (1) Spring 1968, p. 20.
16. Hobbs, p. 14.
17. Hobbs, p. 15.
18. Local Records Committee. *Report.* 1902, p. 46.
19. London County Council. London County Council's views as to the custody and arrangement of local records. *Library Association record* 2 (part 2) August 1900, p. 427.
20. Local Records Committee. *Appendices.* 1902, p. 246.
21. McColvin, L.R. *The public library system of Great Britain.* London, Library Association, 1942, p. 67.
22. Hepworth, P. Archives and the local collection. *Librarian and book world* 44 (8) September/October 1955, p. 157.
23. Library Association Council. The place of archives and manuscripts in the field of librarianship. *Library Association record* 71 (1) January 1969, 15.
24. Hobbs, J.L. *Local history and the library.* London, Deutsch, 1962, p. 17.
25. Department of Education and Science. *The public library service: reorganisation and after.* London, HMSO, 1973, p.11.
26. Nichols, H. The administration of local studies collections in Great Britain and Northern Ireland. *Journal of librarianship* 8 (4) October 1976, p. 245.
27. Bexley, London Borough of. A guide to local history resources. London Borough of Bexley Libraries and Museums Department, Local Studies Section, April 1983, p. 1. (Typescript).
28. Nichols, p. 246.
29. Nichols, p. 247.
30. Nichols, p. 247.
31. Nichols, p. 247.
32. Howard, S. and Howard, R. Local history in Salford. *Local history* no. 1 July 1984, p. 8.
33. Nichols, p. 247.

34. Nichols, p. 250.
35. Nichols, p. 251.
36. Nichols, p. 262.
37. Armstrong, N.E.S. *Local collections in Scotland.* Glasgow, Scottish Library Association, 1977, pp. 82-86.
38. Armstrong, p. 116.
39. Armstrong, pp. 79-80, 89-90, 93-94, 111-112, 114.
40. Nichols, p. 251.
41. Armstrong, pp. 97-98, 101-102.
42. Cruttenden, P.C. Local history resource centres. *Library Association record* 77 (8) August 1975, p. 179.
43. Peroni, R. Local history resource centres. (Correspondence.) *Library Association record* 77 (10) October 1975, p. 246.
44. Hallworth, F. quoted in Nichols, p. 249.
45. Robertson, A.K. Local studies and the new authorities. In: Library Association. *Proceedings of the study school and national conference, Brighton 1978.* London, LA, 1979, p. 154.
46. Nichols, p. 250.
47. Seaman, A. Archives services in danger. *Local historian* 16 (5) February 1985, 278-281.

# 4

# Local studies collections in academic libraries

Derryan Paul and Michael Dewe

Local studies collections in Great Britain have traditionally been the responsibility of public libraries. It is these libraries which provide a basic and systematic coverage of the country, county by county, city by city and town by town, and it is on these collections that the professional literature of the subject has been based. Alongside them, however, there are now a considerable number of local collections in academic libraries, built up in the main as working collections for the support of teaching, project work and research in the academic institutions which they serve. It is not their function, however, to duplicate the collections and services provided in public libraries and record offices or to supplant them, but to supplement them. Hitherto these academic collections have received no separate attention as a group, so that this chapter constitutes a preliminary attempt to remedy this omission by reporting on the results of a survey carried out in the summer of 1984.

A questionnaire and a letter were sent out to 218 libraries in universities, polytechnics and colleges in England, Wales and Scotland. The questionnaire is printed as an appendix to this chapter. In the university sector questionnaires went to university libraries, to the constituent colleges of the Universities of London and Wales and to a number of university departments and institutes, principally schools of education and librarianship. The colleges chosen outside the university sector were, in the main, those which offer courses leading to degrees in the arts and social sciences and to professional qualifications in education and librarianship. These are fields in which local studies have figured most prominently in recent years, but it is quite probable that there may be small, highly specialised collections in institutions which concentrate on more technical subjects or on individual fields such as agriculture and horticulture. Overall

56 per cent of the libraries replied - 64 per cent of universities, 62.5 per cent of polytechnics and 46 per cent of colleges. Of those who replied, 55 per cent have local collections - 54 per cent of universities, 64 per cent of the polytechnics and 54 per cent of the colleges. What is said below, therefore, is based on information provided by 66 libraries - 26 in universities, 16 in polytechnics and 24 in colleges. The collections in the Bodleian Library at Oxford and in Cambridge University Library lie outside the scope of the survey, but they are discussed briefly at the end of the chapter.

## HISTORICAL DEVELOPMENT

The chronological development of the local collections appears to be at least as closely linked with the expansion of higher and further education as it is with the growth of local studies as an element in academic and professional training courses. It is perhaps worth recalling that before 1798 there were precisely six universities in England, Wales and Scotland - four in Scotland and two in England. Between 1798 and 1960 there was a steady, if modest, growth in higher and further education, followed by more intensive development in the 1960s and early 1970s. This is reflected in the development of local collections to the extent that half of those covered here have been formed since 1960. In universities there has been a fairly gradual acceleration. Ten libraries now hold collections set up in the nineteenth century, a further nine introduced local collections between 1900 and 1960 and six have been established since then.[1] At the opposite extreme is the Library of the Dean and Chapter of Durham. This has substantial holdings of local material and is run in conjunction with the university's theological library. The collection was begun in the tenth century and pre-dates the university by some nine hundred years.

In the polytechnics and colleges a different pattern emerges. Only two polytechnics have collections which were certainly started before 1960. Most of the rest have come into being in the last 25 years, including two set up since 1980.[2] Three colleges have collections established before the Second World War, while two more began to collect in the 1940s and 1950s. The majority started between 1960 and 1980, with three others joining them since then.[3] In five cases polytechnic and college libraries cannot say with any certainty when their collections of local material began.[4]

## SCOPE OF COLLECTIONS

In geographical terms the coverage of the individual collections varies since they are not tied, like local collections in public libraries, to specific administrative units. A substantial number of libraries favour regional collections in the sense that they collect material relating to the three or four counties that are closest physically to the institutions that they serve. Half of the universities and polytechnics and over a third of the colleges work on this basis.[5] The scope of each collection is fairly clearly defined by each library in terms of the area it covers, although collections are not necessarily pinned to county boundaries, whether old or new. Teeside Polytechnic has a deliberate variation on this pattern. Their main collection covers the county of Cleveland, with a selection of items for Durham, Northumberland and North Yorkshire. In addition they acquire a further selection for Essex, Cornwall and Lincolnshire as a basis for comparative study between one area and another.

Most of the libraries that do not collect on a regional basis confine their collections to one or two counties or to one county and its immediate borderland, including four that cover London or Greater London specifically.[6] A small number of libraries for various reasons do not conform to either a regional or a county pattern. The University of St Andrews has a collection which covers the town itself and places within a ten-mile radius. In Wales the university collections in Swansea and Bangor extend over the whole of Wales, with special emphasis at Swansea on West Glamorgan. The Welsh collection at Bangor has a strong literary emphasis but aims to cover all aspects of Welsh life. In strictly local terms it is especially strong on Anglesey and Caernarfon, but it is worth noting that, in addition to Wales itself, it aims for limited coverage of the border counties of England, the other Celtic countries and Welsh communities outside Wales, including those in London, Liverpool, the United States and Patagonia. The University of Leicester has a collection which covers all the counties of England and Wales and the Library at the Institute of Historical Research in the University of London has printed materials for all the English counties and for London, as well as substantial amounts of local material for Scotland, Ireland and Wales.

Manchester Polytechnic, like the University of St Andrews, has drawn a circle and collects material on all subjects for the area within a 20-mile radius of Manchester. Two other polytechnics possess collections whose scope is limited for special reasons. Huddersfield has the library of G.H.

54

Wood, a reformer and free thinker, who was appointed secretary of the Huddersfield Woollen Manufacturers Association in 1907. The collection reflects his interest in the labour movement, in welfare and in reform, and includes local material on wages and trade union affairs. It co-exists with a small collection of local monographs and three collections of local archives. The School of Librarianship at Newcastle Polytechnic has a small teaching collection containing good and bad examples of the source materials used by local historians. This serves to supplement the limited local collection in the Polytechnic Library and the principal collection for the area at the Central Library in Newcastle.

Two colleges maintain small collections relating to the towns where they are situated and to the surrounding area,[7] while Liverpool Institute of Higher Education confines itself specifically to Liverpool. In Wales there are two colleges which have developed national collections which reflect the scope of their work. Coleg Harlech, which offers one-year and two-year courses in a range of subjects to students over 21, collects materials to support its courses in Welsh studies which, in local terms, are particularly good for the county of Gwynedd. The College of Librarianship Wales has a Welsh collection, which aims to cover all aspects of Welsh life with a particular emphasis on language and literature. In addition it has selected materials for the rest of the British Isles which are integrated into its main stock.

## USE OF COLLECTIONS

The use of the collections varies between one institution and another, and between the different sectors. It is difficult, however, to proffer any very cut-and-dried comment in this connection for a number of different reasons: the structure of the courses appears to be different in the different sectors; the level of use as between research, undergraduate work and general study varies according to the declared aims of different institutions; and the data relates to the pattern of use as perceived by librarians, although there is no reason to think that the latter would differ very significantly from that perceived by academic staff and students.

Nonetheless, three things emerge very clearly. The first is that the collections are most heavily used for historical study. The returns indicate support for a total of 57 historical courses, including 38 specifically devoted to economic and social history, regional history or local history.[8] To these one might reasonably add the six places in which the study of history and literature is evenly balanced, sometimes across a range of courses. All other subjects trail. The polytechnic and college collections support 19 courses in the humanities and a variety of combined studies, many of which would have some historical content.[9] Between them the three sectors offer support for 15 courses in education (8 of them in colleges) and 12 in geography, including one in historical geography as such.[10] In other subject fields they support anything from one course to five. The institution which uses its local collection most intensively over a wide range of subjects is the University of Nottingham. The material is used in the pursuit of archaeology, architecture, economics, education, geology, planning and social administration, apart from its use for the study of geography and three forms of history. Among the colleges, six have reported that their collections exist for general use within the college and are not related to any specific courses. The most innovative collection is at Bridgend College of Technology. This was started in 1984 to provide current information about the area. The emphasis is on bus and rail services and material from business firms.

The second thing to emerge is that in some universities the local collections exist primarily for the benefit of specialist departments and regional centres. At the University of Leicester, with its Department of English Local History, the local collection is seen primarily as a resource for that department, although it is used as well by undergraduates taking options in other academic disciplines. Similarly in the Universities of Lancaster and East Anglia the main function of the local collections is to support the activities of the Centre for North-West Regional Studies and the Centre for East Anglian Studies.

Thirdly it is very clear that universities, with their separate departments of adult education, use local collections much more heavily in this field, than polytechnics and colleges.

## RELATIONSHIP TO MAIN COLLECTIONS

Just over half the libraries house their local collections separately from the rest of their stock, in the main as distinct and independent units,[11] although in a few instances the local collections form part of a larger special collections unit, within which they have a distinctive identity.[12] Otherwise local material is generally integrated with the main stock; but there are six libraries, in addition to that in the College of Librarianship Wales, where some local material is separately housed and some integrated. This is the case in the University of Glasgow where several named collections are housed with other special collections, and in the Universities of East Anglia and Leicester which have named collections, originally formed by private individuals, which are stored on their own. In three polytechnics, North Staffordshire, Preston and Wolverhampton, most of the local material is kept apart from the rest of the stock, but a little is integrated where appropriate.

Where local material is treated in whole or in part as an element in the main stock, it is shelved in a relatively small number of subject categories, and it seems that some stock is classified in subject areas for which no specific course is provided. History still predominates, but its dominance is much less marked. The principal subject areas in which local items are included are: history (33 libraries), geography and geology (23), architecture (21), archaeology (19), natural history (15) and environmental studies (14). Since the libraries in question support only five courses in archaeology and four in architecture, it is immediately apparent that material in these subject fields is more widely acquired than the distribution of courses might suggest. The same is true of natural history. Nearly a quarter of the libraries have local items in this field in their stock, although it is apparently not used in the study of the natural sciences. Thirteen libraries also have stock in other areas.[13]

This state of affairs is probably due to a number of factors. Much of the material on archaeology and architecture may well be acquired at the request of lecturers in history and education for use in supporting different facets of their own courses. In addition a library attempting to maintain a balanced stock in any particular field will be influenced by the pattern of publishing, and it is noteworthy that local items tend, in these academic libraries, to cluster together in those subjects in which there has been a significant growth of interest in regional and local studies over the past ten or fifteen years. There is, therefore, a wider range of potential acquisitions in these fields. It is clear, too, that in quite a number of cases collections have started simply in order to provide material on the locality of the parent institution for the use of anyone who is interested in knowing more about it. Several colleges have stressed that this is the main function of their collections to-day,[14] and in the past it seems to have been the primary function of a number of university collections in places where the collections appear to be older than the courses which they now support.

## FINANCE

The local collection does not normally feature as a separate item in the budget of an academic library. Of the 66 libraries discussed in this chapter only nine allocate separate funds for the acquisition of local material at all. Elsewhere, even in places where the local collection is separately housed, there is no separate purchase fund. In those libraries where money is earmarked, the size of the funds and the basis on which they are available varies considerably. The University of Exeter, which staffs the Library of the Devon and Exeter Institution, has a small allocation derived mainly from private funds, while at Glasgow there is an endowment, also small, associated with one of the special collections. At the University College of Wales in Cardiff local material is bought out of the budget for the Salisbury Library of which it forms a part. In Southampton University Library, which houses the Cope Collection with its other special collections, money is allocated every year from the library's acquisition fund. At the University of Leicester and at the University College of North Wales in Bangor there is a different pattern with a certain similarity in the basis of funding. At Leicester there are two allocations, one for departmental selection and one for new and second-hand material selected by the library. In Bangor much material for the Welsh Library is purchased from the funds allocated to the Department of Welsh and the Department of Welsh History. These acquisitions are complemented by purchases from the money available to the Welsh librarian.

Separate budgets are virtually unknown in polytechnics and colleges. The Polytechnic of Wolverhampton is alone in having a specific annual allocation for its West Midlands Studies Collection. Elsewhere, Huddersfield Polytechnic has had temporary access to funds through the Manpower Services Commission in order to catalogue the G.H. Wood collection and the archives of the Huddersfield Mechanics Institute. The College of Librarianship Wales has a separate allocation for its Welsh collection, which includes local material for Wales. Otherwise it follows the normal practice in most institutions, which is to buy such material out of allocations for the main stock of the library.

## STAFFING

The pattern of staffing corresponds with the pattern of budgeting, that is to say that it is unusual in academic libraries for staff to be specifically allocated to local collections in any sense of the term. Eight university libraries have provided information from which it emerges that in six cases the staff concerned have responsibility for special collections or some other larger unit, within which local material is included. These include Aberdeen, Keele, Nottingham, Southampton and the University College of North Wales in Bangor. Only Manchester Polytechnic has a separate staff allocation and the College of Librarianship Wales has an allocation for its Welsh Collection. The normal practice is for the local collection to be serviced by the staff on the same basis as the rest of the stock.

## TYPES OF MATERIAL

The questionnaire distinguished nine categories of material that might be found in a local collection. All of them are acquired to a greater or lesser extent in academic libraries and for the most part there do not seem to be any very significant differences in collecting practice between the different sectors. Books and pamphlets, newspapers and periodicals, and maps are the categories of material most widely acquired. Apart from the Clwyd Centre for Educational Technology, which specialises in modern audio-visual media, all the libraries hold books and pamphlets. Newspapers and periodicals feature in the collections of 80 per cent of academic libraries and maps in 67 per cent. A substantial number also hold theses and photographs among their local material, the figures being 44 per cent for theses and 43 per cent for photographs. Here it is perhaps appropriate to recall that in some institutions maps are the responsibility of one or more academic departments and their absence from library collections is not an indication that an institution has no map collection at all. Theses are very commonly held by academic libraries, but they are not necessarily housed or administered with local collections even if they deal with a relevant locality.

Other categories of material are less widely acquired. Ephemera forms an element in 32 per cent of collections and so do archives other than those of the library's parent institution and its predecessors.[15] Prints, drawings and paintings feature in 26 per cent of the libraries and oral recordings in 19 per cent.[16] The relative absence of prints, drawings and paintings from collections may be attributed to a combination of factors. They are expensive to buy and special measures have to be taken if they are to be properly cared for. In addition they are also widely collected by other institutions, not least museums and art galleries, which have been collecting for more than a century and already have the right facilities for storing the material and for carrying out restoration work where necessary.

The small number of libraries with oral recordings is, perhaps, on the face of it more surprising, given the recent surge of interest in oral testimony and in its value as a supplement and a counterbalance to written evidence. Its absence may in part be due to the growth of sound archives and oral history projects outside academic libraries, but again cost is almost certainly a significant consideration. A library may not have to bear the cost of making the tapes, with all that this implies in terms of time spent on recording and on background research, but it will need to provide and pay for the right storage facilities and will also have to share or bear as a whole the cost of transcribing and indexing.

A further 18 per cent of libraries have reported that they have materials which do not fit conveniently into any of the listed categories. Except in one case, it is clear from the information provided that the materials in question stand apart from specific categories not because they are different in kind, but because they fall into special categories of their own on account of their origins. In some cases the items all derive from a similar source, like the collection of school log books and administration books held by the library in the School of Education at the University of Newcastle, and the collection of semi-published 'grey literature' developed at Oxford Polytechnic. This consists of items issued to the public by a variety of local organisations including local authorities. Some collections stand apart because they were originally formed by private individuals or by groups engaged on specific projects. Apart from the G.H. Wood collection at Huddersfield Polytechnic, there is the Warwick Collection at Derbyshire College of Higher Education which came from the library of Professor Warwick of Birmingham University; and at Wolverhampton Polytechnic there is a collection deposited by the Wolverhampton Film Archive group. But the only collection which seems to be genuinely exceptional in terms of format is at Durham University Library which holds coins from the Durham mint.

## CLASSIFICATION SCHEMES

Classification practice varies, with a majority of university libraries having a scheme of their own and a majority of polytechnics and colleges using Dewey. In the universities, 15 libraries use their own scheme, 4 use Library of Congress, 3 use Dewey, 3 use Bliss and 1 London college uses the Guildhall Library scheme.[17] Among the polytechnics 12 have Dewey, 2 have their own scheme and 1 in London uses the Guildhall scheme.[18] The collection in the School of Librarianship at Newcastle Polytechnic is too small to merit classification. Of the colleges, 21 use Dewey[19] and 2 use Bliss, while Bridgend does not yet classify its local information resource. Occasionally, where libraries make use of one of the standard schemes, they may modify it themselves or introduce elements from other schemes, but there is no indication that any scheme poses major problems when applied to local collections. Where a library has its own scheme this also appears to be generally satisfactory, although two librarians have expressed strong dissatisfaction with schemes inherited from their predecessors.

## CATALOGUING AND INDEXING

Most libraries include their local collections in their main catalogues, with a small number making duplicate catalogues for local items only. A third provide additional catalogues or special indexes to give improved access to this material. More emphasis is placed on this practice in universities, where half the libraries have some kind of extra aid for those using their local collections, as against a third in polytechnics and a tiny number of college libraries. What is done in practice seems to depend entirely on local priorities. Seven university libraries, five polytechnics and one college compile either classified catalogues or subject indexes. Three universities index topographically, including the University of Lancaster, which maintains a regional studies index based on map references. Three universities and one college provide selective indexes to local periodicals. University College London has a separate map catalogue and the University of Southampton compiles indexes to local imprints and illustrations. The University of Durham has an index of material printed or published in the North-East before 1865 which is held in its library. In overall terms the most thorough catalogues and indexes are those provided in the Universities of Nottingham and Southampton. Apart from special catalogues and indexes for material relating to the university itself, Nottingham has name and subject catalogues, its own subject index to *East Midland geographer* and a visible index of periodical holdings. Southampton has a catalogue of books comprising author and classified sequences, a subject index and the index of local imprints. In addition it maintains sheaf indexes to illustrations and to the text of miscellaneous volumes and periodicals.

## PUBLICATIONS

A library may also promote the use of its local collections by producing a variety of leaflets, lists and bibliographies. This practice does not appear to be as widespread in academic libraries as it is in public libraries, in part because in some academic institutions publications of this kind are the responsibility of a research unit or a teaching department. Only 12 of the 66 libraries surveyed here prepare special guides or bibliographies, eight in universities, three in polytechnics and one in a college. Four other university libraries draw special attention to local material in their general library guides and in leaflets and bibliographies for special subject areas. The University of Lancaster, for example, issues leaflets on the census and on Ordnance Survey maps in its series of guides to library services and these include specific detail on material relating to Lancashire. Where individual guides for local collections are prepared in university libraries they usually take the form of leaflets. Durham University Library has a leaflet entitled *Local studies resources* which explains the scope of the collections and draws attention to a number of special indexes and bibliographies which are only available in the library. Its occasional publications have included a list of some of its manuscript material. The University Library at Keele issues factsheets for its readers, among them one for its special collections which includes the local collection. In addition its Education Library has produced a list of its holdings on the history of education in the area around Keele, which covers parts of the counties of Staffordshire, Cheshire, Shropshire and Derbyshire. The University of Nottingham has a guide to its East Midlands Collection in its series of reader's information leaflets. This covers the scope and contents of the collection, classification, catalogues, arrangement on the shelves, borrowing and hours of opening. It also alerts readers to the presence of local material in government documents found in its Documents Division and to the existence of the local studies collections in public libraries throughout the East Midlands. From time to time the library has produced regional bibliographies and the special collections librarian contributes to the annual bibliography in *Bulletin of local history: East Midlands region,* as well as supplying book notes for *Nottinghamshire historian.*

The most impressive publications have come from two polytechnics - Manchester and Teeside. Manchester has issued a list of its local studies periodicals which runs to 34 pages. This is regularly supplemented by an index to periodical articles drawn from a range of national, regional and local newspapers and journals in which items are listed under broad subject headings. It also produces a quarterly accessions list. Teeside Polytechnic Library compiles and publishes a *Cleveland County bibliography.* The first part, for the years from 1974 to 1980, appeared in 1981 and this has been followed by annual supplements for 1981 and 1982. There is only one college among those surveyed which produces any kind of guide for its local collections and that is Derbyshire College of Higher Education which has an introductory leaflet.

## CO-OPERATION AND FUTURE PLANS

Competition between academic libraries and others is exceedingly rare. Only 3 of the 66 libraries surveyed have experienced any problems of competition at all and these appear to be slight. Five libraries operate formal schemes of co-operation and in two more schemes have lapsed, in one instance as a direct result of local government cuts. A further 19 libraries co-operate with others on an informal basis and in the remaining 40 a pattern of peaceful co-existence appears to be the norm.

Plans for the future are inevitably modest and tempered both by lack of resources and by the libraries' declared aim of meeting the particular needs of their own institutions. Twenty specifically intend to continue as they do at present, thirteen hope to produce additional guides, catalogues or indexes and eight express an interest in widening the range of materials which they hold. Two university libraries would wish to develop a more systematic policy of acquisition and Bridgend College of Technology hopes to expand its new local information resource, which consists mainly of publicity material that is available free of charge.

## OXFORD AND CAMBRIDGE

In trying to assess the findings of the survey it is essential to consider the extent to which the 66 libraries concerned constitute only part of a very wide and varied network of provision for local studies. The University Libraries at Oxford and Cambridge stand apart from all others in this field because of their role as copyright libraries. Like the British Library they hold a wide range of materials for the whole of the British Isles, including much for specific localities. In addition both have, until recently, served as diocesan record offices. Cambridge University Library continues to fulfill this function for the diocese of Ely, but the Bodleian has now transferred the diocesan, archdeaconry, parish, tithe and probate records for the diocese of Oxford and its archdeaconries to the county record offices in Oxfordshire, Berkshire and Buckinghamshire.

## CONCLUSIONS

A significant number of the libraries which returned questionnaires have no local collection at all. They constitute a total of 45 per cent overall - 46 per cent of universities, 36 per cent of polytechnics and 46 per cent of colleges. Their response serves to underline the fact that provision of a local collection is not seen as an essential function in an academic library. Such a collection will only exist if it serves interests and needs in the parent institution which cannot be met in other ways. Sometimes these needs can be met by other units within the parent institution. Geography departments, for example, will hold substantial working collections of maps and may cover the area in which they are located in considerable depth. At Leicester the Department of English Local History has a working collection of maps for the whole of England and also a small reference library for the use of its members. Other departments with different specialised interests develop collections of their own. An excellent example is provided here by the Regional Buildings Record at the University of Bath where there is no local collection in the university library. The Record, which covers primarily Bristol and Bath with the surrounding counties, was established in 1962. It has a collection of prints, drawings, measured drawings and documents relating to buildings of all ages, and lays especial emphasis on making photographs and drawings of buildings that are threatened by demolition and of groups of buildings and areas at risk on account of development schemes. At present it is a source of reference for architects, students and others, but its ultimate object is to provide a record for future historians.

Externally members of any academic institution will have access to the collections maintained by local authorities and to a wide variety of local societies devoted to the study of both humanities and the sciences. It is taken for granted in academic libraries that readers working on local and regional topics will use public libraries and, where necessary, record offices and museums. Hence the location of these institutions, together with their individual strengths and weaknesses, will be a factor in determining the development of academic collections. The inter-relationship between libraries and local societies is more difficult to determine and is usually confined to purchase of the societies' publications. In three places, however, local societies have placed their libraries under the care of a university library. The City University holds the Library of the London Society, the Library of the Devon and Exeter Institution is staffed by Exeter University Library and the Library of the Thoroton Society is on deposit with the East Midlands collection at Nottingham.

Academic libraries may fulfill one or more of three different roles in providing a local collection. In a small number the sole purpose of the collection is to provide material for the use of anyone who wishes to know more about the area, while Bridgend College of Technology is alone, at present, in developing a local collection in the form of a current information service for its area. Most libraries, however, have local collections designed to support teaching and research. Within the collections there is a heavy bias towards an admittedly wide range of historical and topographical studies. Only three institutions, one in Scotland and two in Wales, apparently look to their local collections to support the study of national or regional language and literature to any significant extent. These are the University of Aberdeen, the University College of North Wales in Bangor and the College of Librarianship Wales in Aberystwyth. Two places also depart, for different reasons, from the usual practice of collecting material from within clearly defined geographical or administrative boundaries. Teeside Polytechnic supplements its collections for Cleveland and the neighbouring counties with a selection for Essex, Cornwall and Lincolnshire to be used for comparative study in its courses; while the Welsh Library at Bangor extends its coverage to take in at least some material relating to Welsh communities outside Wales and to other Celtic countries.

This report amounts to no more than a preliminary inquiry into the scope and administration of collections which have not been examined before as a whole, but there is much more that could usefully be done. At present it would be particularly helpful to know more about the practice of individual libraries and to have some discussion of the total range of local and regional collections held in specific institutions both in libraries and in academic departments.

## NOTES

1. Examples are: nineteenth century: Dundee, Southampton; 1900-1959: Leicester, St Andrews; 1960 to date: East Anglia, Kent.
2. Examples are: before 1960: N.E. London, Huddersfield; 1960-1979: Brighton, Sheffield; since 1980: N. London, Oxford.
3. Examples are: before 1939: Coleg Harlech, Derbyshire College of Higher Education; 1940-1959: Loughborough Technical College, St Andrew's College, Glasgow; since 1981: Liverpool Institute of Higher Education, Neath College.
4. Examples are: Preston Polytechnic, N.E. Wales Institute of Higher Education.
5. For example, Aberdeen University, Lancaster University, Manchester Polytechnic, Sunderland Polytechnic, N. Cheshire College, College of St Mark and St John.
6. Examples are: University of Kent, University College London, N. London Polytechnic.
7. Bridgend, Rumney.
8. Examples are: University of Kent - history, social and economic history, local history; University of Essex - history, local history; University of Lancaster - local history, regional history; Sheffield Polytechnic - history, local history; Wolverhampton Polytechnic - regional history; Aberdeen College of Education - history; Gwent College of Higher Education - local history.
9. For example, Brighton Polytechnic, N. Staffordshire Polytechnic, Humberside College of Higher Education, Liverpool Institute of Higher Education.
10. Examples are: Education - Newcastle University, Portsmouth Polytechnic, Aberdeen College of Education, Hertfordshire College of Further Educaton; Geography - Nottingham University, Newcastle Polytechnic, Homerton College; Historical Geography - Dundee University.
11. Examples are: Exeter University, University College of North Wales, Oxford Polytechnic, Nene College, Hertfordshire College of Further Education.

12. Examples are: Nottingham University, University College of Wales Cardiff.
13. Universities: Glasgow, Kent (religion), Lancaster (social sciences), Newcastle School of Education (education), Reading (local printing and imprints), Swansea (Celtic Studies); Polytechnics: Newcastle, Sunderland (urban and regional studies), Teeside. Colleges: Coleg Harlech (sociology), N. Cheshire College (drama, children's literature), College of St Mark and St John (economics), College of Librarianship Wales (sociology).
14. For example, Bridgend College of Technology, King Alfred's College, Winchester, Loughborough Technical College, Nene College.
15. Examples are: ephemera: City University, Glasgow University, Huddersfield Polytechnic, Newman College, Hertfordshire College of Further Education; archives: Dundee University, University College of Wales Swansea, Newcastle Polytechnic, Humberside College of Higher Education, St Andrews College, Glasgow.
16. Examples are: prints: Exeter University, Nottingham University, City of London Polytechnic, Rumney College; oral recordings: Essex University, Oxford Polytechnic, Coleg Harlech.
17. Examples are: own scheme - East Anglia; Library of Congress - St. Andrews; Dewey - Durham; Bliss - Lancaster; Guildhall - University College London.
18. Examples are: Dewey - Manchester, Preston, Teeside; own scheme - N.E. London; Guildhall - City of London.
19. Examples are: Dewey - Aberdeen College of Education, Cambridge College of Technology, Neath College.

## APPENDIX: LOCAL HISTORY/STUDIES COLLECTIONS IN ACADEMIC LIBRARIES: QUESTIONNAIRE

1. Does your library have a local history/studies collection? YES/NO
2. When was the collection begun? (Indication of decade will suffice)
3. What is its 'local' coverage? Town/County/Regional? Please describe appropriate category/ies briefly.

4. What courses or other activity does the collection support?

5. Is the collection separately housed? (i.e. as a special collection or subject department) YES/NO. (If answer is NO, please see question 7.)

6. Is the collection known by a distinctive name?

7. What subject sections are local material integrated with?
   History
   Geography and Geology
   Archaeology
   Architecture
   Natural History
   Environmental Studies
   Other

8. Does the collection have a separate budget allocation? YES/NO. If yes, please give details.

9. Is the collection separately staffed? YES/NO. If yes, please indicate numbers and professional status.

10. Please indicate whether the following categories of material are contained in the collection. Please delete those not in the collection
    (a) books/pamphlets
    (b) newspapers/periodicals
    (c) theses
    (d) prints, drawings, paintings
    (e) oral recordings

(f) photographic, e.g. slides/film/photographs

(g) maps

(h) archives

(i) ephemera - please indicate range of ephemera, e.g. posters, handbills

(l) other - please specify

11. What scheme is the local collection classified by?
    L of C/Dewey/Own scheme/Another scheme. Please give brief details if either of the last categories apply.

12. Are a special catalogue and indexes provided to the collection? If yes, provide details please.

13. Are publicity and publications produced?

14. Relationships with other local collections in the area.
    Are their problems of competition?
    Is there a scheme of co-operation?

15. Future plans and development for the collection.

# 5

# Archives in libraries

Derryan Paul

The development of archive departments in public libraries, like that of local record offices has been an exceedingly uneven one. Some are now very highly developed indeed, while others are still in a relatively embryonic state. The aim of this chapter is to examine the basis on which such departments should be run and to provide guidelines for the librarians who are responsible for them, whether or not they have a staff of professional archivists and conservation officers. It has been written with public libraries in mind, but what is said on conservation, and at least parts of the sections on acquisitions and services, apply equally to academic libraries.

Local archive services in England and Wales are provided under the terms of the Local Government (Records) Act 1962, the London Government Act 1962 and the Local Government Act 1972. These acts require all authorities to make proper provision for their own records and they permit the metropolitan counties (whose continued existence is threatened at the time of writing), the counties and the London boroughs to provide an archive service as of right. Other local authorities must obtain a ministerial order before they can do so. In practice the acts allow the authorities a certain measure of choice and this has produced a network of services that does not yet conform to any very coherent pattern. By 1985 there were county archive services in all the counties and metropolitan counties, except for the West Midlands and Avon, and eleven of the thirty-two London boroughs had exercised their right to provide one. A number of other authorities have applied for ministerial orders but only a few have been granted, all of them to councils governing sizeable conurbations. The rest of the local authorities discharge their responsibility for their own records either by using the appropriate county or district service or by making their own arrangements locally.

Public libraries with archive departments have responded to the situation in a number of ways. Some, like Nottingham, closed their archive departments in 1974 and transferred their collections to county record offices. Others have become a base for archive services in metropolitan areas. This is the case, for example, in Huddersfield, which provides the service for Kirklees Metropolitan District. This is one of the five districts which, together with the West Yorkshire Metropolitan Council, have formed the West Yorkshire Archive Service. Some libraries have developed links of various kinds with county record offices. In a few places, as at Darlington and Folkestone, there are branches of the county archive service in the library building. Where this happens the relationship between the two is worked out on a local basis. Elsewhere, as at Burton-on-Trent, a library receives administrative assistance from the county record office. In addition a number of libraries, such as Rochdale and Chesterfield, run their archive departments without having any formal links with other archive services.

In Scotland the present network of local archive services dates from the reorganisation of Scottish local government in 1975 and is governed in the main by the Local Government (Scotland) Act 1973. This allows for the same sort of flexibility that obtains in England and Wales. By 1985 eight of the ten regional councils possessed an archive service and these are supplemented by a number of district, city and burgh services. As in England and Wales some services take the form of a record office, while others are based on libraries. In Northern Ireland there are no local archive services and their place is supplied by the Public Record Office of Northern Ireland.

The present legislation is not entirely helpful. It aims to ensure that local authorities running an archive service have the resources to sustain a heavy and unremitting financial burden, but it does to some extent militate against the preservation of archives in the areas and in the communities where they belong. As the most distinguished of French archivists, Michel Duchein, has put it: 'Archives, like paintings, sculptures and books, are part of a living culture. Their place is among the people who create and use them.'[1] A possible framework, which would fill the gaps and help to establish a more integrated pattern for local archive services, is provided by the Association of County Archivists in the set of recommendations entitled *Yesterday's future.*[2]

They have recommended in the first place that there should be a national archive service in Great Britain comprising both national and local record offices. This would be supplemented, in the second place, by a network of licensed repositories holding archives other than their own which they make available for public use. This licensing system would cover libraries, including the British Library, and a number of museums and other specialist institutions. Thirdly, the association has proposed registration for archive collections of obvious importance which are still in the custody of their owners; and it has also suggested a more clearly defined role for organisations such as the Historical Manuscripts Commission and the British Records Association which exist to foster the preservation and use of archives. To establish such a framework would certainly take time. Detailed discussion would be necessary and legislation would be required. But if it were to happen, it would clearly provide a much better basis for the professional administration of archives and for closer co-operation between local record offices and public libraries.

*Yesterday's future* was issued as a contribution to the debate on the need for a national archives policy which has been taking place recently within the archive profession as a whole. The Society of Archivists devoted a session at its annual conference in 1983 to discussing the need for such a policy and two papers presented then were published in the *Journal of the Society of Archivists* in 1983. In one Mr A.A.H. Knightbridge of the Public Record Office discusses the slender legislative and administrative framework within which archive services operate in Great Britain, and in the other Dr Felix Hull, formerly county archivist of Kent, discusses the development of local archive services and the various factors that have shaped and that now inhibit their development.[3] Dr Hull's article deserves to be read and carefully pondered by anyone who is responsible in any way for local archives. More recently the Society of Archivists has formulated a discussion document entitled 'Towards a national archives policy' which is intended as a basis for discussion with other bodies.[4] This examines the deficiencies of the present situation, in particular the lack of finance and the haphazard and uneven nature of both legislation and government concern and involvement in the preservation of archives. It draws very explicit attention to the fact that archives are very poorly protected compared with other parts of our national heritage in the shape of buildings, museum objects and archaeological sites. Archive services are poorly funded and there is a lack of proper advisory bodies both at a national level and at a regional level. We are undoubtedly living in times of financial constraint but, as the society points out, if we can afford to spend on artefacts we can also afford to spend on archives. It is in part a question of attitude, a problem well summed up by Dr Hull: 'There is at present a significant gap in the heritage concept which concentrates on artefacts, but which largely ignores documentary material.'[5]

## INTRODUCTORY LITERATURE

Librarians working with archives are familiar with at least two basic texts: the statement of policy issued by the Library Association in 1969 and Philip Hepworth's pamphlet *Archives and manuscripts in libraries.*[6] The Library Association's statement sets out guidelines for the management of archive departments in libraries, but is necessarily brief. *Archives and manuscripts in libraries* is in the main a bibliography of published catalogues and guides and it relates to the situation as it was 20 years ago. Since then the library and archive professions have changed and their literature has changed with them. The books, articles and journals discussed below are a small selection of the most essential. All the books have bibliographies, and further references can be found in the two international bibliographies 'Basic international bibliography of archive administration' by Michel Duchein and *The history of archive administration* by F.B. Evans,[7] as well as in the articles and journals mentioned below.

The most useful general introduction to archives in the UK is *Enjoying archives* by David Iredale, which is intended for amateur local historians and genealogists.[8] It includes national as well as local archives and the main emphasis is on the content of documents and their relevance to particular topics of research. The most recent manual of archive administration published in Britain is *Archives administration* by Michael Cook.[9] This was written specifically with small and medium-sized organisations in mind and five of its thirteen chapters deal with records management as a normal part of the activities of an archive service. There are also some very valuable chapters in an American book entitled *Norton on archives.*[10] This is a collection of papers published between 1930 and 1956 by Margaret Cross Norton who was state archivist of Illinois from 1922 to 1957. Some of the papers on more technical aspects of archive administration are now out of date and some relate to American state archives only. It should also be recognised that there are variations in the practice of archive administration between America and Great Britain and that in some respects the divergences between archive and library practice have increased since Margaret Cross Norton wrote, particularly in the area of cataloguing. In addition to these two books there is now a new series of information sheets issued by the Society of Archivists, which is designed to provide concise guidance on specific and problematical aspects of archive administration.

Cook's manual does not deal with buildings apart from the layout and equipment of searchrooms and there is a brief chapter only on the essentials of conservation. The standard international manual on archive buildings and their equipment is that by Michel Duchein and this should be consulted before any building is planned or accepted for use as an archive department.[11] More is also said in Chapter 8 of this *Manual* on accommodation for a local studies collection including archives. Some aspects of both building and conservation are covered in BS5454:1977, *Recommendations for the storage and exhibition of archival documents.*[12] This too is essential reading and should be consulted not least before any institution commits itself to an exhibition of documents. Exhibitions, unfortunately, remain a source of damage and Section 13 of BS5454 sets out succinctly the precautions that need to be taken with written or printed materials including bound volumes.

There has been a whole spate of books in recent years on the conservation of 'library materials'. *Conservation in the library* is one of the best, together with a vital article by D.G. Vaisey on the 'Archivist as conservator' and an excellent, brief and authoritative source of plain advice on good conservation practice, *Caring for books and documents* by A.D. Baynes-Cope.[13] Anyone who has to preserve photographs within the limits of a local authority budget will almost certainly be grateful for Madeleine Gray's article 'Photograph storage in Gwynedd', while the problems associated with modern technical media are clearly summed up in an article by Michael Roper, 'Advanced technical media'.[14]

There is a vast range of journals - academic, professional and technical - which are of relevance or potential relevance in archive administration. There are three, however, of paramount importance for anyone responsible for archive collections. These are *Archives,* published by the British Records Association twice a year; the *Journal of the Society of Archivists,* also published twice a year; and *American archivist,* issued four times a year by the Society of American Archivists. All contain the usual range of articles, book reviews, notes and news and advertisements. Both *Archives* and the *Journal of the Society of Archivists* include lists of publications received and *American archivist* at the time of writing has short bibliographies entitled 'Professional reading'. Until 1980 it included, once a year, a select bibliography of new publications in several different languages.

## DEFINITION OF ARCHIVES

Before discussing the administration of an archives department, it seems as well to define the term 'archives', not least because it now has two quite distinct meanings. In the original and primary sense of the word, 'archives' are groups of documents made or used in the course of everyday transactions, whether public or private. They may be created by official administrative units such as local authorities, private enterprises such as business firms, voluntary organisations such as clubs and charities, and also by families and individuals. Their salient characteristic is that they are groups of documents assembled for specific practical purposes - legal, administrative, financial or purely private. The people who create these groups of documents are not normally concerned with the future needs of research and they would probably be very surprised indeed if they could return in a few hundred years' time to see some of the uses to which their archives were then being put. The word 'archives' is also used in another, much looser sense, to describe any collection of written or audio-visual materials which might be used in the study of the past. And so we have data archives, film archives and sound archives. Of the latter, only the BBC Sound Archives are archives in the primary sense of the term, since they consist of materials prepared by the BBC for its own working purposes. The salient characteristic of most other collections in this category is that the items in them have been acquired individually and from many different sources. Most of them also have been assembled deliberately for reference and research: so that, whatever their historical value and significance, they are different in origin and purpose, and therefore in kind, from archive collections in the primary sense. And it is with archives in the primary sense that archive services are concerned. They may or may not, according to circumstances, collect other items.

## AIMS OF AN ARCHIVE SERVICE

Any archives service has two aims - to preserve the documents in its care and to make them available for use. Unhappily these two aims conflict, since use involves handling and wear and tear, which militate against preservation. Generally it is possible to resolve the conflict satisfactorily in one way or another, but if this cannot be done, then conservation must take priority. If a document is so fragile that it cannot safely be handled, then it must be withdrawn from use until it can be repaired and strengthened. Archive services have a duty to ensure the survival of their collections for future generations of enquirers as well as for those of the present generation, some of whom may return in five or ten or fifteen years' time to check on information or to pursue a new line of research using archives which they or others have used before for very different purposes.

Any record office or archive department may, according to circumstances, fulfill a number of different functions. One of these, seen as fundamental, is to provide a service for the administrative unit to which the archive department belongs. This entails responsibility for an organisation's older archives, and also the provision of a records management programme with all that this implies in terms of close co-operation with other departments within the organisation. The archivist in charge of the programme needs to be closely concerned with the management of current as well as semi-current records and must be able to meet the requirements of administrative departments and services, while maintaining a programme based on sound principles of records management. A second function in a local authority is the custody of archives deposited or given to the archives department. In addition to taking responsibility for the physical care and protection of the records, the department has to negotiate terms of acquisition with a wide variety of organisations and individuals. These may include restrictions on access which have to be scrupulously observed thereafter.

A third function is to make records available for use. This rests primarily on facilities for individuals to come and carry out research. But it is also useful to consider a programme of talks and exhibitions both for the general public and for specific organisations. These are unfortunately time-consuming but they are an excellent way of bringing the archive service to the notice of people who have no yearning to do research. They are encouraged to take a sympathetic interest in the service and may support it with gifts and deposits. Finally it is appropriate for a local archives department to provide an education service, which should comprise an adult education programme, as well as activities and facilities designed to meet the special needs of colleges and schools. Outline standards for local government archive services were issued by the Society of Archivists in 1971 and are printed as Appendix A in *Archives administration* by Michael Cook.[15] These deal with functions and organisation and specify the duties that can appropriately be assigned to professional and non-professional staff.

## ACQUISITIONS

Any local archives department will collect within a specific geographical area, which will probably be determined by administrative boundaries. Where existing provision consists of a county archives service together with district services and archive departments in libraries, it is helpful to agree as to which set of boundaries will be used since in any area there will have been boundary changes within the last century and a half if not before. It is also useful to have a framework of agreement as to which institutions will collect specific categories of material for a given area, in cases where the materials are not an integral part of an archive collection. Many archives include very substantial quantities of published maps, photographs and printed items of a kind that librarians usually see as printed ephemera; so that any archive service will acquire such items as a normal part of its work. Beyond that the systematic collection of published maps and photographs has been a function of the library service in some areas and of the archive service in others. Agreement as to who collects what should help to avoid expensive duplication and will be determined by a number of factors, including the existing pattern of provision and the extent to which individual institutions can provide facilities to preserve and exploit materials. A number of local agreements now exist but their details are not available in writing.

The archive collections which come the way of a local archives department divide into official archives and deposited archives. The official archives divide again into those that are public records under the terms of the Public Records Act of 1958 and those that are not. The public records comprise the records of courts of law, including courts of quarter sessions and coroners' courts, records of the local and regional offices of central government departments, and records of institutions run by government departments, most notably hospitals. The Public Records Act allows the Lord Chancellor, who is the minister responsible for public records, to appoint places of deposit for public records outside the Public Record Office. The resulting arrangements are made by the Public Record Office through a liaison officer and there are three points that should be noted. In the first place the Lord Chancellor's freedom of action under the act is limited. He must pay attention to the wishes of the courts and officials who have created the records and if they say that an archives service 40 miles away is inconveniently remote, then somewhere nearer must be found. This may mean that the Public Record Office will approach an institution that has only minimal facilities. The basic requirements are adequate storage and a place where records may be consulted under proper supervision. Secondly before an institution can take public records its buildings must be approved. The liaison officer from the Public Record Office will visit and inspect the buildings and may ask for improvements and modifications to be made. If, later on, an institution holding public records wishes to move them to a building that has not been approved already, it must obtain approval before doing so. Thirdly an institution must be specifically appointed as the place of deposit for each separate group of public records. This means, for example, that a library which is the designated place of deposit for the records of one coroner's district may not automatically take those of another coroner's district. Approval must be obtained first from the Public Record Office. Official archives created by local authorities and by the boards and commissions whose work they inherited are not under the control of the Lord Chancellor. Many had already reached local archive services before 1974 and they continue to accrue within the limits set by the Local Government Act of 1972.

Apart from the official records, archives come into local repositories under the terms of the Local Government (Records) Act of 1962 from a wide variety of sources. These include churches, business firms, solicitors, clubs and societies, landed estates, families and individuals. The records of the Anglican church are deposited in a number of different record offices and libraries within each diocese. One will usually hold the archives of the diocese itself, together with those of one archdeaconry and some or all of its parishes. The others will hold the archives of the remaining archdeaconries and their parishes. In urban areas an archive service may hold parish records only for the parishes in and near a particular town. Under the Parochial Registers and Records Measure of 1978 parishes must either deposit their records with the appropriate archives service or, if they wish to keep the records in the parish, they must comply with the standards of care laid down in the Measure. For other denominations arrangements vary. In some, individual meetings and congregations are given guidance from the governing body of the denomination as to where they should deposit their archives if they wish to do so. In others it is up to the meeting or congregation to approach an archive service themselves. Many archives will come in either as a result of an approach from their owners or as a result of a survey, conducted by the archive service itself or as part of an academic research project by some other body. It should be noted that some collections will contain manorial or tithe records. These records are by law the ultimate responsibility of the Master of the Rolls. Registers of manorial and tithe documents are maintained on his behalf by the Historical Manuscripts Commission, which should be consulted about the requirements of the relevant legislation.

The terms on which collections are taken into public care may vary, but the most usual practice in Britain is to accept archives on deposit. The records are placed with an archives service on the understanding that they will remain there permanently, but the ownership of the collection is not transferred. Because this form of arrangement generally works well, gifts and bequests are rare. Where they are made they are normally subject to the conditions that apply to deposits, in particular where access is concerned. It is not very desirable for access to be limited to one individual or to a specific group of individuals. This practice has been more widespread in America than in Britain and libraries and archives there have found that it can pose considerable problems for institutions which hold collections on such terms. In addition it inhibits research on topics which have nothing to do with the lines of inquiry being pursued by those who do have access and which are most unlikely to have any unfortunate repercussions for the donors of a collection. Deposits, gifts and bequests remain with an archive service in the long term, but archives may also on occasion come into a record office or library on loan for a limited period for some specific purpose - so that a researcher may consult them, for listing, for exhibition or for repair.

It is helpful for all concerned if an archive service has a schedule of the conditions that normally apply to collections in its care. It should be made clear that a depositor has the right to withdraw documents either temporarily or permanently, giving reasonable notice. Permanent withdrawal is unusual, but in recent years archives placed on deposit with record offices or libraries have occasionally been withdrawn and sold at auction. Clearly documents in good condition, cleaned and repaired, will fetch a higher price than those that are dog-eared and dirty; and a collection which has been put in order and listed has a higher value than one that consists of unsorted bundles and individual items. In these circumstances an archive service may reserve the right to charge for the cost of work done on a deposit which is later taken away. Temporary withdrawal of documents is another matter, as are temporary restrictions on access. There are no statutory periods of closure for private records, but if documents are very recent or highly personal in content it is perfectly reasonable for an owner to ask that no one should be given access to them for the time being. The standard period of closure in such instances is 100 years, but it may be varied a little in either direction. Sometimes an archive service may have to close records on its own initiative, if their owner places no restrictions on access and papers are found to contain information about named individuals which might cause distress or embarrassment to the people concerned or their near relations.

Conditions of deposit should specify in outline the procedures that will be followed in administering a collection and the terms on which it will be made available for use. In Britain records will not normally be produced for any legal query without their owner's permission, since it is part of the responsibility of an archive service to protect depositors as well as their documents. It is also normal practice for researchers wishing to publish documents to obtain the owner's consent. This gives the owner an opportunity to ask that particular documents or pieces of information should not be published and is a useful alternative to total restriction on access. This is something distinct from copyright which is discussed below, and also from the question of making facsimile reproductions for which fees may be payable. Conditions of deposit should specify, too, the circumstances under which documents may be taken off the premises of the archive service which holds them. A schedule of such conditions, based on those used by Liverpool University Archives, is printed as Appendix C in Cook, and can be used as a guide to the various points that need to be raised.[16]


## CONSERVATION

It has been said, very rightly, that conservation is an attitude of mind. It is also something that continues round the clock throughout the year. It is not confined to what is done by conservation officers in their workshops, usually at the eleventh hour, when things have patently gone wrong. It is the responsibility of all members of staff, including the archivist or librarian at the head of the service as well as the remaining professional and technical staff, assistants, porters and cleaners. Good security is essential. The buildings occupied by an archive service should be secure against break-in from outside and there should be no question of anyone gaining access from the public areas of the building to strong rooms and workrooms without the knowledge of the staff. Buildings should also be proof against flood, fire and explosion and it is as well to bear in mind that on many occasions these come from within. If an archive service has to share a building, it is vital to know what happens on all the floors above and below the service not simply in the areas which are immediately adjacent to its accommodation. If burglar and fire alarms are fitted there should be a swift and effective means of contacting the police and fire services to ensure a prompt response.

Documents may be damaged in different ways for different reasons and, unfortunately, many of the factors involved are insidious ones, so that damage is not always immediately obvious. Common and ordinary causes of damage are fluctuations in temperature and relative humidity which place a stress on the physical fabric of the documents; bad ventilation creating pockets of damp and stagnant air; excessive humidity which encourages the growth of mould; and dirt. The dirt stains and may attract moisture, mould and insects. Other potential sources of serious damage are heat, light, atmospheric pollution, insects and rodents. Cold in itself is not a source of damage and, while archive departments must be heated for the benefit of their human occupants, it is important to grasp that the heat has nothing to do with the welfare of the collections. Ultra-violet light, it seems, is everywhere. Windows, showcases and fluorescent lights should be treated to filter out the ultra-violet rays and the filters regularly renewed. Atmospheric pollution is now associated primarily with industrial areas, but in the past it was widely present wherever houses and offices were heated by gas or coal; hence the fact that effects of atmospheric pollution are to be found in documents from non-industrial areas. Insects and rodents will tear, eat and stain a wide variety of materials and may deposit eggs and droppings. It is sadly true that much damage is done to documents by the people who come into contact with them every day. Ignorance and indifference have contributed to bad storage, mishandling and, last but not least, inexpert repair. The latter has been a frequent and serious source of damage, since the use of poor materials and unsuitable techniques has in the long run aggravated the damage that the repair was designed to remedy. Deterioration is inevitable. We have to accept this and to recognise that we cannot entirely prevent it. But there is no need for us to make an active contribution to the process and the least we can do is to provide the best protection we can for the documents in our care. Much of the solution lies in awareness of the problems, in good housekeeping practice and in careful attention to the environment in which the documents are kept and used.

*2. One of the strongrooms, Calderdale District Archives, Calderdale Central Library.*

Environment is of paramount importance. It should above all else be stable, with constant levels of temperature and relative humidity. Differences in temperature and relative humidity between strongrooms and working areas should be minimised as far as possible, which generally speaking implies that strongrooms will be kept near the upper end of the permissible range of temperature and working areas near the lower end. Ideally different materials - parchment, paper, photographs, films, sound recordings - should be kept in different environments. The correct levels of temperature and relative humidity for different media are specified in BS5454 and for modern audio-visual media in an article by Michael Roper, 'Advanced technical media'.[17] For small repositories where a variety of different materials have to be kept in the same storage areas, the British Standard suggests a compromise environment which is suitable for most media. For many archive services it is not a practical proposition to keep colour film. If it is to survive indefinitely it has to be stored near freezing point and must be raised gradually to ordinary room temperature before it can be used. Film on nitrate base (that is film made before 1950) is a dangerous substance and its storage and disposal are governed by Home Office regulations. It is highly flammable and can explode. It should be taken out of its container and isolated in a cool, well-ventilated place where damage will be minimal if it does catch fire. Advice about copying the film on to safety base and dealing with the original may be obtained from a regional film archive, if there is one, or from the National Film Archive. Further advice on the conservation and storage of film and photographs will be found in Chapter 16 of this *Manual*.

Ventilation and circulation of air should be good throughout the archive department. It needs to be particularly good in strongrooms where there is less natural circulation of air and extra measures may be necessary in workshops and photographic studios where the work involves processes that generate heat, moisture and fumes. Air-conditioning and ventilation systems should be designed to filter out dust as well as atmospheric pollution, as a contribution to keeping the building clean. All areas of an archive department must be regularly and thoroughly cleaned including the strongrooms, and the cleaning programme should be supplemented by frequent inspection. Responsibility for formal inspection should be assigned to one member of staff, either an archivist or a conservation officer, who should go round the strongrooms looking for signs of damp, insects, rodents, damage to documents and packing materials, and items that have not been properly put away. To supplement inspections all members of staff should be trained to watch for these things as a normal part of their work.

Storage is not just a matter of environment. In order to provide maximum protection it is essential that suitable storage units and the right packing materials are used. Archives are heavy and some media are particularly vulnerable to chemical damage. It is therefore important to ensure that storage units are strong, suitably constructed and made of materials that will not cause adverse chemical reaction. Shelving should be open-backed and should not be placed against walls. Ordinary cupboards and filing cabinets are not suitable unless they can be fitted with louvres or vents to improve circulation of air. On the continent archive services frequently place files and bundles of documents on the shelves as they are, without any form of covering. In Britain files and bundles are generally placed in boxes. This may inhibit circulation of air to some extent, but it has the advantage of providing extra protection against dirt, light and fluctuations in the environment. Boxes should be made of acid-free board with loose fitting lids and may also have ventilation holes. Any staples used must be non-corrosive. Special care should be taken to ensure that packing materials and labels used for modern audio-visual media are chemically inert to avoid the risk of adverse reaction. Once a photographic image is gone it is gone for ever.

Mishandling is a major and continuous source of damage to documents. All staff should be given specific instruction in how to handle documents in their everyday work, in how to pack them and in how to bring them in and out of storage. Regulations for readers normally include guidance on the precautions that they should take while carrying out research on original documents. Few readers probably realise how much they can help in preserving archives by handling the documents they use with the greatest possible care. Over-handling of books, newspapers and documents that are in frequent use is another problem and one that has become widespread in recent years in both libraries and record offices. It is now common practice to ask readers to use copies in the shape of microforms, photocopies or transcripts if possible in order to reduce wear and tear on the originals. Many documents are damaged while on exhibition on account of a widespread belief that anything is safe as long as it is kept under lock and key. This is not necessarily so. Documents on display still need a stable and well-ventilated environment and they still need protection against dirt, damp, heat, light and atmospheric pollution. The documents should also be given suitable and adequate physical support and the materials and fabrics used for showcases and display stands should be chosen with as much care as those for storage units. One does not expect to see live insects or mice in a show case, but it is not for nothing that the major museums place thermometers and hygrometers in their showcases alongside rare and fragile exhibits.

Even with first-class standards of care, materials will deteriorate to a point where they need attention and much will reach an archives service in poor condition in the first place. Such a service therefore needs workshops and photographic studios in which documents can be copied, repaired and strengthened and, if necessary, bound or re-bound. It is also essential to have staff with the appropriate training in binding, repair work and photographic techniques. It cannot be too strongly stressed that repair should never be undertaken by anyone who has not been trained, since it is highly probable that they will do more harm than good, for instance by mending damaged items with sellotape. The work requires a sound scientific knowledge of materials, techniques and processes and a high degree of manual skill which has to be maintained by constant practice. At one time record offices and libraries with trained conservation officers and their own workshops could occasionally do a little work for those who lacked the staff and facilities. This is no longer possible, not least because of financial constraints, but they can still offer informed advice. There are commercial services available, but anyone using them will need to provide detailed written instructions as to what is to be done to each item. A commercial service will not be able to provide a precise estimate of costs until it has seen the documents and had an opportunity to assess what is required in terms of materials and time. However, any library approaching a commercial service should ask for an approximate scale of charges and a list of institutions which use the firm's services. A cross-section of these should be consulted as to whether the standards of work and service are satisfactory.

## SERVICES

The object of preserving archives is to make them available for use. The needs of users take a variety of forms, but whatever the limitations imposed by shortage of money and lack of staff any archive service will provide facilities for individuals to consult records for research. These facilities are intended in the main for enquirers engaged in historical research, and service to those carrying out legal enquiries is normally confined to depositors inspecting their own records and to others who wish to see official documents available for public inspection. The latter may include documents up to 200 years old such as enclosure awards. In general terms the greatest bar to effective use of archives is short and inflexible opening hours. At present there is little that most archive services can do to extend their opening hours, but many are experimenting with a fairly flexible pattern and may close on a weekday in favour of opening on a Saturday or on one or two evenings during the week. In libraries it is sometimes possible to extend opening hours by making items from the archives department available in the reference library by appointment at times when the archives department is closed. This should only be done in places where the reference library staff are able to provide constant supervision and it is essential to be realistic about the limitations of this practice. It is only useful for the more experienced researchers who can specify in advance what they need and who can work without guidance or assistance from the professional staff of the archive department. An

*3. Search room, Calderdale District Archives, Calderdale Central Library.*

increasing number of local record offices and archive departments in libraries now ask researchers to make an appointment before coming. Even where it is not compulsory it is highly desirable that readers should do this, since opening hours change, search rooms are becoming more and more crowded and queues develop for microfilm readers.

Reading rooms are discussed in Chapter 8, so the following paragraph contains only a summary of what is required in an archive department. The search room must be arranged so that the archivist on duty has an uninterrupted view of the desks. This is in part a security measure, but the main aim of supervision is to ensure that readers do not inadvertently overlook the rules and mishandle documents. The small tables provided in modern libraries are not adequate for researchers using documents. The tables should measure 1 metre by 70 centimetres and, if the department holds large maps or other outsize documents, there should be at least one big table where these can be consulted without risk of damage to the documents or disturbance to users working on other documents. As a basic rule of thumb each reader will require 5 square metres of space and it is absolutely essential that the lighting is good and that chairs and tables are comfortable, since some people will be working in the search room for several hours at a stretch. Other facilities will vary according to the size and resources of the service. If it is at all possible soundproof carrels should be provided for researchers who wish to use typewriters or tape-recorders, with glass in the upper part of the partitions to allow for supervision. The search room should have its own microfilm readers where necessary and a good service should be able to supply photographs and microfilm of documents as well as photocopies, all at a reasonable cost. In order to reduce the risk of damage to a minimum, copying should always be done by staff, and an institution may reserve the right not to copy very fragile documents and to decide on what form of copying should be used.

Unpublished written material may not be freely copied or published without permission; once publication has occurred normal copyright practice applies. In the case of photographs the duration of copyright depends upon when they were taken. An increasing number of archive services now ask researchers who order copies to sign a copyright declaration stating that they have not received a copy of the same item from any other source and that they require the copy for private research and will not use it for any other purpose. These declarations should be kept as evidence that the service has drawn the attention of its readers to the provisions of the Copyright Act. It is not always appreciated that the copyright in a letter belongs to the writer and not to the recipient. It is therefore not sufficient to ask the owner of the letter alone for permission to publish. In some cases it may be difficult if not impossible to find the owner of the copyright, but there are circumstances under which the Copyright Act allows publication, provided that suitable efforts have been made to trace the person concerned. There is an excellent basic guide to the main requirements of the Act in an information sheet prepared for the Museums Association by Charles Gibbs-Smith, which should be available in the library of every archives service for the use of both staff and readers.[18] Even this is not entirely straightforward and it has been suggested that researchers should be asked not to publish without reference to the head of the archive service, so that any potential difficulties can be discussed at an early stage.

It is essential to have a clear-cut policy defining the limits of the enquiry service, since an archive department can expect a lot of postal and telephone enquiries in addition to those made on the spot. In the ordinary way a department will provide by post or telephone information about opening hours and facilities, about the scope of its collections, the range of material relevant for specific topics and the extent of its lists and indexes. In the search room professional guidance is given on using lists and indexes, on finding additional information from sources which may not seem obviously relevant and on the existence of possible source materials in other institutions. Archivists also expect to help in translating or transcribing short sentences or phrases in records which are obscurely worded or difficult to read. But the staff will not expect to transcribe or translate entire documents or to carry out time-consuming research on behalf of individuals. Here again policy should be defined and in the case of enquiries which are likely to take more than a specified time, the enquirer should be asked to come in person or to employ a records agent. In recent years a few local authorities have authorised arrangements under which their professional archivists do research for individuals during working hours at a fee which is paid to the authority. Such arrangements bring in a little income, but they take professional staff away from the preparation of lists and indexes without which many records remain inaccessible to large numbers of people who might usefully consult them; so they inevitably mean that an enhanced service for individuals undermines the standard of service to the general public. An alternative, tried by one county record office, is to appoint a graduate research assistant to carry out research for family historians and to charge fees which cover the cost of the appointment. This allows the record office to provide a research service without taking professional staff away from the preparation of finding aids. A few archive services have been compelled by their employers to charge for access to search rooms. It is difficult to see the justification for such a practice when the authorities concerned continue to provide free access to museums and libraries and such schemes are invariably cumbersome to operate. Exemptions have to be made for large categories of users - senior citizens, the unemployed, teachers, full-time students - and at least one authority has abandoned charges because the exemptions reduced income to a level at which it was uneconomic to collect the money. A few local authorities have considered making a charge for researchers who are not local, but no one has yet succeeded in producing a fair and satisfactory definition of a 'local person'.

An archive service compiles a separate list or set of lists for each collection and analyses the content of these by producing a cumulative index in three sequences to draw together scattered references to places, people and subjects. These lists and indexes, available in the search room, are frequently supplemented by leaflets describing the department and its services and by leaflets and pamphlet guides to sources for broad fields of inquiry, such as family history, topography or education. Since 1976, and in particular since 1980, substantial strides have been made in developing computer systems for use in archive administration. For purposes of information retrieval there are two different types of system. The first type is designed to list documents (in some cases at two or three different levels) and to generate indexes from the lists. The data can be used in some instances for administrative purposes to produce location lists; and one application of this type, based on a system devised by the Museum Documentation Association, provides fields for describing the physical condition of documents and recording details of conservation work. The second type of system is designed to generate detailed indexes to the content of documents and is typified by schemes for producing detailed analysis of specific types of record such as parish registers, wills and maps. A variant of this type of scheme has been used by the National Maritime Museum, initially as a security measure, to index all documents signed, annotated or written by Lord Nelson. Details of schemes under development and in use can be found in a report prepared for the British Library by Rachel Bartle and Michael Cook.[19]

Service to the general public can be extended by talks and exhibitions, which may or may not be integrated into the framework of a formal education programme catering for students and teachers in both schools and colleges and for adult education classes. An archive service can run such a programme on its own, it can work in partnership with other institutions or it can contribute on a regular basis to programmes organised by local education authorities, universities, colleges or the Workers' Educational Association (WEA). An article by R.A. Lewis, published in the *Local historian* in 1979, describes the local history service provided for Staffordshire schools through the education office and the county record office; and it discusses the materials and projects that have been found useful and some of the constraints.[20] The University of Nottingham and the WEA run a very wide-ranging programme of adult education classes which comprises research groups for those wishing to join a research team, training classes for beginners and local history classes for those who do not wish to do research. Some details of these are available in a leaflet on local history in Nottinghamshire issued by the county library which also covers sources and gives some information about the scope of collections in the county and university libraries and the county record office.

Provision of an official archives service to a local authority entails running a records management programme which will involve commitment of staff, accommodation and resources. Most records pass through two or three stages in their existence. They are current, then semi-current and finally, if they survive, they become part of an organisation's permanent archives. Records management is primarily concerned with the second stage, but effective records management entails active participation in the first stage. With semi-current records the programme will have three principal aims. One is to keep the records for as long as they are needed, the second is to make them readily available and the third is to dispose of them efficiently when their useful life is over. It is an important subsidiary aim to maintain the records as efficiently and economically as possible, but financial savings should not be given absolute precedence over effective preservation and retrieval. Participation in the management of current records needs to focus on three things - the fabric and format of the records, the way in which they are handled and stored and the organisation of filing systems. Considerable problems arise in records management on account of the condition in which documents reach archive services. They are made of poor materials, assembled in unsuitable formats and have often been badly stored and carelessly handled. Records may arrive in such a dilapidated state that it is difficult to ensure their survival for even a short period;

and while it may be technically possible to strengthen and repair them or to put them on microfilm, these are expensive procedures and very much more costly than taking positive steps to minimise the problems in the first place. The archives service should be allowed to specify the materials and format used for any records needed for any length of time and should be able to offer guidance and training on the storage and handling of current records. It is also helpful if the service is consulted on the organisation of filing systems as this can ease both the transfer of records and their appraisal.

Appraisal is fundamental in records management. It is in essence the process of deciding how long records should be kept. It involves two levels of decision: decisions about which records to keep indefinitely and decisions about when to destroy the rest. In some cases it is not possible to take an immediate decision about when to destroy records and they are then ear-marked for review at a specified date. In deciding which records to keep permanently staff will apply a range of both administrative and academic criteria; whereas decisions about when to review or destroy records will be taken on administrative grounds. The mechanics of the process vary from one system to another, but there are broadly speaking two approaches. One approach, used by the Public Record Office, involves reviewing the records at specified intervals in their life cycle. Those that survive a first review are reviewed again at a later date and some are retained indefinitely. In the other approach each new series of records is appraised when it first reaches the archive service and is marked for either indefinite retention or review or destruction at a specified date. It cannot be too strongly stressed that all decisions on the administrative life of the records must be taken by the people who create them. The closest co-operation is necessary between the archives service and the administrators, lawyers, accountants and filing staff in its parent organisation. The object of administrative appraisal is to ensure that records survive for as long as they are needed for practical purposes and that the periods of retention specified by law are observed.

Running a records management programme involves continuous intake of records and a continuous process of appraisal, review and destruction. Before records are destroyed they must be scheduled and the schedules signed and counter-signed by the head of the department from which the documents come and by the archivist or librarian in charge of the archives service. The schedules constitute a precise record of which documents were destroyed and when, and they provide clear evidence that the material has been destroyed on proper authority in the ordinary course of an official records management programme. The regular destruction of documents generally ensures that the need for storage space is relatively limited and the strongrooms need not be expensively equipped. They should be secure and have an environment that is stable, well ventilated and clean. Some institutions store at least part of their semi-current records in outstores from which documents are fetched at specified intervals. If outstorage has to be used for all semi-current records then consideration must be given to the need to retrieve documents on occasion as a matter of urgency at short notice. This can now be achieved if the level of demand warrants it by installing a facsimile transmission system.

The enquiry service will in the main be concerned with the issue of documents, since most enquirers will need access to the precise text of the documents they wish to consult and will need to take semi-current records back to their own offices for several months at a time. The circulation system must therefore include provision for making regular checks on items on issue to ensure that they are either returned promptly to the archive service or re-issued at intervals. In essence the service is comparable with the lending systems in a library rather than with its reference services, although much stricter controls will apply. It is the usual practice to issue documents only to the department from which they came and it is essential to ensure that documents are transmitted direct from the archives service to the department of origin. The ordinary internal mail should not be used, as it does not allow for full control of access to documents and has no mechanism for retrieving material quickly if it goes astray. On occasion administrative staff may need to consult bulky records or it may be necessary for a group of people to examine records together. In these circumstances it is useful to have several small search rooms or enlarged carrels equipped with big tables, so that one user or group of users does not disturb others. Requests for information as such are relatively rare and this has implications for computer use. The computer is not used fundamentally for information retrieval but to establish administrative control, so that it generates the various schedules that are required for acquisition, review, destruction and management of storage and can also control the circulation system. Successful computer applications have been in operation for some years now in Dyfed and in Tyne and Wear. Brief descriptions of these systems and references to more detailed accounts can be found in the report *Computer applications in archives* by Bartle and Cook.[21]

## STAFFING

An archive service will require professional archivists and conservation officers together with records clerks and typists. It may or may not have, in addition, its own ancillary staff of porters, drivers and cleaners. Staffing levels vary enormously from one institution to another, most being seriously understaffed. There should, however, be enough archivists to ensure that professional advice is available to readers during the hours when the search room is open. This means that due allowance must be made not only for leave, but for the fact that the archivists will need to be out of the department at times, consulting with council staff on the operation of the records management programme and visiting potential depositors and donors to inspect collections. Whatever the level of staffing the ratio between professional and non-professional staff is in practice a fairly constant one. Most institutions work to a ratio by which professional staff outnumber non-professional by two to one or by three to two, depending on the size of the ancillary staff. It is probably true to say that most archive services could use more ancillary staff, but it is always essential to maintain a fully professional standard of service and to achieve the appropriate distribution of duties.

The Library Association in its statement of policy has taken the view that no repository for archives can be considered satisfactory unless the collections are large enough to justify the employment of a full-time archivist. For a variety of reasons not all libraries have been able to meet this ideal and there are still librarians who have to administer archives without a professional archivist on their staff. Where this happens it should be clearly recognised that the librarians concerned are being asked to undertake a range of duties and responsibilities for which they have not been trained. In these circumstances they should at least be given the opportunity of taking professional qualifications in archive administration. It is also essential to recognise that a training in bookbinding is not an adequate preparation for the range of work that is required in the conservation workshop of an archive service, although it provides an excellent foundation. The pattern of training for both archivists and conservation officers has varied over the years, but up-to-date information on recognised qualifications and on the range of courses available can be obtained from the Society of Archivists. All professional staff will need the opportunity to attend the meetings and courses run by their professional associations in order to keep in touch with current thinking and current developments. Membership of the Society of Archivists is open to practising archivists, conservators and to anyone who is directly engaged in the administration of archive collections. Most archivists also belong to the British Records Association and many conservation officers join the Institute of Paper Conservation. The British Records Association holds an annual general meeting and conference in London each year and is the only organisation which provides a meeting point for owners of documents, curators and researchers regardless of their subject fields and qualifications. Membership is open to any organisation or individual who cares to join.

The Society of Archivists holds its annual general meeting in London in the winter and an annual conference outside London in the spring. It has, like the Library Association, a substructure of committees, regional meetings and subject groups. Its training committee maintains close contact with the five universities in the British Isles which offer full-time professional qualifications and the society has recently set up its own diploma in archive administration. This is a two-year correspondence course open to suitably qualified candidates who are already employed in an archive service. There is a separate training scheme for conservators, which includes periods of placement in different record offices, culminating in an assessment based on both practical and written work; while for those already qualified in either archive administration or conservation the society organises a number of short, annual courses. The society has its own publications programme and its groups issue occasional papers, often based on the proceedings of their own meetings. Those of the records management group, which has strong links with the Records Management Society of Great Britain, are a particularly useful source of advice and information on current thinking and on recent developments in this field.

## CONCLUSION

In the first section of its statement of policy the Library Association has set down a very thorough list of the facilities that should be provided by a good archive service. Its first requirement is that any good repository should have permanence and a secure income. Beyond that it is also important that the organisation that runs the repository should accept that it has a permanent obligation to devote a due part of its income to maintaining good standards of care and service. There is no possible justification for taking archives into public custody if the resulting standards of care are poor and if the archives cannot be made fully available because there is a shortage of professional staff to list, index and interpret them. Any institution, including a library, which accepts archives as a gift or on deposit accepts a responsibility to donors and depositors, as well as to the research public. This responsibility should be properly discharged in accordance with the accepted norms of professional archive administration.

## NOTES

1. Duchein, M. *Archive buildings and equipment*. Munich, Verlag Dokumentation, 1977, p. 24.
2. *Yesterday's future: a national policy for our archive heritage*. Association of County Archivists, 1983.
3. Hull, F. Towards a national archives policy - the local scene. *Journal of the Society of Archivists* 7 (4) October 1983, 224-229. Knightsbridge, A.A.H. National archives policy. *Journal of the Society of Archivists* 7 (4) October 1983, 213-223.
4. Towards a national archives policy: a discussion document. Society of Archivists, 1984. (Unpublished.)
5. Hull, p. 228.
6. Library Association. The place of archives and manuscripts in the field of librarianship: a statement of policy.... *Library Association record* 71 (1) January 1969, 582. Hepworth, P. *Archives and manuscripts in libraries*. 2nd edition. London, Library Association, 1964.
7. Duchein, M. Basic international bibliography of archive administration. *Archivum* 25, 1978. (Complete issue.) Evans, F.B. *The history of archive administration: a select bibliography*. Paris, Unesco, 1979.
8. Iredale, D. *Enjoying archives*. Newton Abbot, David and Charles, 1973. 2nd edition, Phillimore, 1985.
9. Cook, M. *Archives administration: a manual for intermediate and smaller organisations and for local government*. Folkestone, Dawson, 1977.
10. Norton, M.C. *Norton on archives: the writings of Margaret Cross Norton on archival and records management*. Edited by T.W. Mitchell. London, Feffer and Simons, 1975. Chapters 1-5 and 13.

11.  Duchein (1977).
12.  British Standards Institution. *Recommendations for the storage and exhibition of archival documents*. London, BSI, 1977. (BS5454: 1977.)
13.  Swartzburg, S.G. (ed.). *Conservation in the library: a handbook of use and care of traditional and nontraditional materials*. London, Aldwych Press, 1983. Vaisey, D.G. The archivist as conservator. *Journal of the Society of Archivists* 6 (2) October 1978, 67-75. Baynes-Cope, A.D. *Caring for books and documents*. London, British Museum, 1981.
14.  Gray, M. Photographic storage in Gwynedd: an ad hoc solution. *Journal of the Society of Archivists* 5 (7) April 1977, 437-440. Roper, M. Advanced technical media: the conservation and storage of audio-visual and machine readable records. *Journal of the Society of Archivists* 7 (2) October 1982, 106-112.
15.  Cook, pp. 202-205.
16.  Cook, pp. 210-211.
17.  Roper (1982).
18.  Gibbs-Smith, C.H. *Copyright law concerning works of arts, photographs and the written and spoken word*. 3rd edition. London, Museums Association, 1978.
19.  Bartle, R. and Cook, M. *Computer applications in archives: a survey*. Liverpool, University of Liverpool, Archives Unit, 1983. (British Library research and development reports, no. 5749.)
20.  Lewis, R.A. A local history service for Staffordshire schools. *Local historian* 13 (5) February 1979, 291-296.
21.  Bartle and Cook, pp. 31, 50.

## FURTHER READING

Brodie, C. The local historian and the local archivist. *SLA News* no. 186 March-April 1985, 28-31.
Foster, J. and Sheppard, J. *British archives: a guide to archive resources in the United Kingdom*. London, Macmillan, 1984.
Ratcliffe, F.W. *Preservation policies and conservation in British libraries*. London, British Library, 1984.

# 6

# Management: Objectives, Policies and Finance

Michael Dewe

This chapter is not concerned with library management per se, there is a large professional literature on that topic,[1] but is a plea for the utilisation of a management approach to the administration of the local studies collection, particularly through the formulation of objectives and policies, and to the resources it needs to attract - staff, stock, accommodation and finance. The first three resources are the subject of separate chapters and will not be given detailed consideration here other than within the general theme of this chapter.

Some librarians may see their professional work in local studies as an escape from management - the librarian as an historian, or broader subject specialist, but not as a manager. Indeed they may be encouraged in this attitude by senior management, who also may not see local studies work as demanding a managerial as well as a subject expertise. However, given the increasing demand for local collections and services, which has often been reflected in an increase in resource allocation, it is vital that good management practice is followed if resources are to be made the best use of in the interest of users and staff. In the large public library authorities of today, with a number of service points offering local studies provision, a number of staff involved county-wide and other organisations and institutions, such as local history societies, museums and archive repositories, working in the same subject field, good management is vitally important. What the management literature and the experience of successful library managers stress is the importance of a planned systematic approach.[2] Among the important benefits such an approach brings about is the focusing of attention on objectives. Library systems, departments, units and individuals are obliged to answer the question 'What business are we in?' And it is this question that has to be asked of local studies.

## OBJECTIVES

There does not appear to be a published general statement of objectives for the public library local studies collection. Although the responsibility for local studies provision is clearly stated in the Library Association's *Guidelines for reference and information services to public libraries in England and Wales,*[3] no statement of objectives appears in the Public Library Research Group's *Public library aims and objectives* published in 1982, where local history appears as a special support service under adult reference services: an understandable but possibly restricting location, although the 'provision of specialist staff and resources according to the particular need' are seen as necessary implications.[4] The following general statement of objectives is therefore offered: the local studies collection exists to promote the study, knowledge and awareness of all aspects of a locality, past and present, through the acquisition, preservation, organisation and exploitation of printed and non-printed material related to it. The implementation of such objectives within a single public library authority is likely to be achieved at various levels by the constituent libraries (e.g. headquarters, district and branch libraries) and this will relate to such factors as their age, the organisational structure of the library service, and the need for a continuity of provision. Objectives must, however, be firmly based on a study of user needs and therefore this general statement would be likely to be different if the collection was serving an academic institution, such as a university or college, with its likely emphasis on the need for the collection to support academic courses and research. Objectives will also be affected if the local collection is seen in terms of local history rather than local studies. The framing of objectives should also take into account the work of other local agencies such as record offices and museums. In a specific situation the general statement of objectives given above would benefit from further elaboration as to the individuals and groups that the collection existed to serve - there is need for them to be identified if relevant services and facilities are to be offered - and a geographical description of the locality in question. The general statement isolates four functions - acquisition, preservation, organisation and exploitation - and, while these functions are not peculiar to a library's local studies work, their precise significance to that field of library activity poses many questions and problems that need to be answered and solved by decisions as to policy and practice.

With a planned approach, objectives are also likely to be given a time-scale as well as being spelled out in greater detail. For example, there will be long-term overall goals or objectives (growing out of needs) which are for the general guidance of the service. Then there will be mid-term (say, five-year) objectives for collection building, cataloguing and service development, for example; plus short-term (one-year or less) objectives which it might be possible to implement reasonably quickly and with the minimum of additional resources. What this illustrates is that planning is a continuous, cyclical and flexible process; objectives, policies and plans have to be adapted to changing needs and circumstances.

## POLICIES

A basic feature of good management, therefore, especially in the complex and demanding world of local studies, is the production of one or more documents which set out objectives and policies and provide a firm foundation for planning, that most fundamental of managerial activities. Documents that set out agreed courses of action in such areas as acquisitions, classification, and staff training in the context of local studies provision can also be helpful in other ways. They ensure a common approach to agreed aims (to collect or avoid the collection of certain forms or types of material); they encourage certain standards of service or provision; they assist the standardisation of library practices and procedures (such as conservation and acquisition), and provide the basis for continuity where staff succeed one another. Policy documents may also be used to point out areas for improvement and development; long-term goals such as improved accommodation or the use of computerisation in local studies work. Also as libraries and record offices are usually part of the same local authority (and sometimes responsible to the same committee), the creation of a policy statement provides an opportunity to formulate the results of agreement on matters of policy between the two services (or with other agencies) on such questions as readers' services, publicity and even cataloguing. The following paragraphs indicate the public library's obligations in the field of local studies and the kind of policy decisions that need to be taken in respect of the four functions noted earlier.

## Acquisition

The public library is part of the community it serves and so it is in a unique position to learn of and acquire material of a local nature. It can be seen as the librarian's duty to collect material of interest to the community he/she serves, but of course this must not be done haphazardly, as the result may be an uneven, unrepresentative collection, but through a properly organised acquisition programme described in a policy document. Such a document could range from a consideration of the acquisition responsibilities of constituent collections, through the variety of materials to be collected, to questions of comprehensiveness and selectivity. It would also need to take into account the legitimate acquisition concerns of other libraries and institutions and the need for co-operation.

## Preservation

A policy statement on preservation would reflect the local collection's dual responsibility to preserve (that is, store material for posterity) and to conserve (to keep that material in good condition). Much would be lost, especially ephemeral material such as programmes and posters, if it was not acquired with a view to its preservation for future use rather than to serve the immediate needs of researchers and enquirers. In many instances the local public library is the only institution concerned to preserve fully the print and non-print material about its immediate locality. For some libraries it may be their only attempt at specialisation. In this role the library has the advantage over organisations, such as local history or civic societies, which may wish to acquire and preserve material from time to time, in that its continuity is guaranteed, while that of local societies, and their ability therefore to preserve material, is not. Preservation is virtually synonymous with conservation: but the latter requires librarians to ensure that the materials in their charge are not only stored for posterity but are kept in a sound state, free from damage, deterioration and possible destruction. Preservation is nullified without a proper policy for the conservation of materials, at their receipt (if necessary) and while they are in the library's care. The financial implications of such a policy will probably be considerable in terms of accommodation and equipment for local studies provision and these may well become the subject of long-term goals.

## Organisation

The organisation for use of local studies materials may also be considered from two points of view: the physical housing of materials for access and use, and their organisation for the retrieval of individual items and the provision of information. The first is very much a matter of policy as to what degree of direct and immediate access to local materials will be permitted to users. The second relates to policies on cataloguing, classification and indexing. The indexing of local newspapers, for example, is a local studies activity that benefits enormously from a considered policy as to how it should be approached (e.g. what is to be indexed) and details of practice as to how it should be carried out (e.g. the form of entry).

## Exploitation

Exploitation and use of the local collection and its services is not something that can be left to chance. How such activity can be maximised must be a matter of policy which should indicate how the librarian can inform, publicise and encourage the use of the local collection. Nowadays library managers are paying increased attention to public relations aspects of their work. Despite dwindling financial resources many librarians see it as essential to communicate with their communities. Publicity in various forms is a major feature of this work and local studies is a particularly interesting service area to publicise via local radio and television, talks, exhibitions and publications of one kind or another. Exploitation is also concerned with the range of services to be offered to users and it is suggested that these could be legitimately widened in many instances to include a local information service. A lot of the enquiries received by librarians are of a local nature, concerned with such matters as planning schemes, local activities and community facilities. Many such questions might be answered from material acquired by the local studies collection as a matter of course and these would form the basis for such a service. Such a contribution to local information provision could be reflected in a fuller departmental title such as the Local Studies and Information Department, which could indicate its link with, or responsibility for, community information.

## Lancashire's report and policy statement

One example of the management approach to local studies provision, which is well worth consideration here, is to be found in the document produced by Lancashire in 1981 entitled *Standards of provision for local studies: report and policy statement.*[3] The report was the outcome of a working party set up in the previous year which had in mind the discussion of four key issues: standards for provision; objectives and in some cases guidance as to practice; definitions as to the functions of the many Lancashire collections; the relationship with other organisations concerned with local studies. These concerns reflect the points made earlier about the need for policy statements and the following description and discussion of the report is perhaps helpful in indicating the wide range of local studies issues that require consideration in such a document.

The introduction to the document states that an effective local studies service must be one of the priorities of any public library, but gives no indication as to its place in the priorities of Lancashire. Also there is not a full statement as to the purpose of providing such local collections, nor for whom they are intended, although some of these questions are answered to some extent in the body of the document.

The 'Topographical scope of collections' is concerned with the pattern of provision in Lancashire (district and headquarters collections) and the need to define boundaries, recognising that other factors than administrative ones, e.g. historical links, and shopping centres, play their part in such a definition. The section called 'Content and function of collections' comes nearest to defining the objectives of the various collections, differentiating between those of the districts and headquarters (which includes an extensive loan collection), and recognising that while some archive and three-dimensional material is held in libraries, the collection and exploitation of such material is the province of the county record office and museums. The section on acquisition is rather short but recognises that sources and procedure depend very much on local knowledge and the alertness of staff; current, retrospective and secondhand sources for acquisition are briefly described. An appendix lists forms of material to be acquired for permanent retention, indicating minimum requirements for district collections, which for good local reasons exclude certain types of printed ephemera and oral recordings. 'Organisation of collections' is concerned with classification (there is a Lancashire local studies scheme), the computerised cataloguing programme and with the storage and care of local studies material. Much useful advice on this latter topic in terms of equipment and conditions is given in a lengthy appendix, emphasising the elementary steps that can be taken even in less than ideal circumstances. In addition to the two appendices already mentioned, there is also a third on copyright, which covers books, periodicals, photographs, maps and oral history, with a note of the sources used in its compilation. 'Special services' is concerned with developing links with local radio and with the promotion and encouragement of the recording of oral and visual history: reel-to-reel and cassette recorders are available from headquarters, where there is also a photographic unit.

The staffing section of the report has important recommendations to make about the provision and training of staff. It recognises that since local studies is a priority of the library service, each district must have a post on its establishment with responsibility for such work. The need for staff training is seen to be required at three levels - for qualified local studies staff, for junior staff and for all new professional staff as part of their induction training.

The next section deals with the promotion of co-operation with outside groups and organisations. This is seen as part of the work of the librarian responsible for local studies, who is to be encouraged to join such bodies; co-operation with the county record office, with its microfilming and conservation facilities, has proved fruitful. The report recommends that the bi-annual meetings of local studies staff continue, as these not only provide a forum for the exchange of ideas and information, but also have a unifying effect, which is important as there is not a large number of full-time specialist staff. Here, and elsewhere, the report thus endorses indirectly the need for a good communications system among the staff involved in local studies. Such a system is vitally important; how it is to be provided for must be spelled out for all the staff concerned.

The section headed 'Exploitation' emphasises the importance of this work with the collection 'subject to the limitations imposed by its physical care... we are not in business only to ''preserve'' ' It goes on to identify not only specific activities, such as exhibitions, local studies packs for schools, holiday activities and competitions, but also some of the various groups and individuals in the community which could be served by the collection. The report would have benefited perhaps from a fuller discussion of present and potential users of the collections and from the placement of such a discussion in the early sections of the document.

The report concludes that an official policy is necessary if progress is to be made towards an acceptable minimum standard of provision throughout the county (which is an expressed long-term aim) and that the report provides clear guidelines by which a district could judge its collection. It is noted that many of the most important recommendations are concerned merely with changing procedures and attitudes and will cost very little. The report's final sentence reads: 'Only when it is possible to fully implement the aims of this policy statement will Local Studies achieve the position it merits within the full range of library activities.' The report does not, however, indicate any time-scale or mechanism by which improvement can be implemented, nor a date by which progress should be reviewed. An essential part of such a document should be the provision for a review and evaluation of performance. This provides an opportunity for checking on progress and to determine the effectiveness of objectives, policies, practices and plans. Such an assessment would involve the keeping of statistical and other records and a requirement of local studies librarians to report regularly on problems and achievements.

## Wiltshire's policy statement

Another such document is the unpublished local studies policy statement produced by Wiltshire Library and Museum Service in 1981. Less ambitious and therefore shorter than the Lancashire report and policy statement, it covers, among other things, three of the four functions noted earlier, under the headings of 'Collection', 'Arrangement', 'Bibliographical control' and 'Publications'. These sections are concerned with the scope of collections, acquisitions, classification (including reclassification using a new scheme), bibliographical control (both retrospective and current, which features a monthly current awareness service), and details of a publications programme which is to include a directory of information of use to local historians and parish history competitions.

Some interesting and important features of the statement occur under the headings 'Provision', 'Special user groups' and 'Future developments'. Following a short note on general policy (or objectives), the first of these sections says that: 'Wiltshire Library & Museum Service makes available local studies materials in three ways: in reference collections designated 'Local Studies Libraries'; as part of the lending and reference stock of public libraries throughout the county; and in connection with services to specialised user groups ...'. The 'Provision' section then goes on to outline briefly the relationship, availability and administration of the four local studies libraries, which includes that at headquarters administered by the county's local studies officer. 'Special user groups' draws attention to the needs of educational establishments, further education tutors, library and museum staff and archaeologists in Wiltshire, of local organisations such as the Wiltshire Buildings Record and the Wiltshire Folk Life Society, and the need to support the current information work of the reference libraries. 'Future developments' notes the requirement to be aware of changing demands, the 'dangers inherent in rejecting material on the basis of present-day values', to keep abreast of new techniques and developments, and of taking an active role in co-operative projects both locally and nationally.

The document ends by asking for the endorsement of an earlier decision to make an annual report on local studies a standing item on the relevant county council committee's agenda. Such a report would act clearly as a valuable record of achievement and of proposed future plans and developments. This intention to report regularly, the document's short statement of objectives and the listing of target user groups, makes good some of the suggested deficiencies of the Lancashire policy statement and report.

Whatever criticisms there might be of the contents and arrangement of Lancashire's published policy document and that of Wiltshire, they are clearly significant steps towards better local studies provision throughout their respective counties. Information about the contents of such statements provides guidance for others to follow in compiling their own policy documents or a means of comparison where they exist already.

## FINANCE

Agreed objectives and policies that aim at better practice and higher standards of service and provision, give not only a sounder basis for planning generally but also for financial planning. It is important therefore that the financial requirements of local studies provision within a library system should receive due recognition in its estimates. As a separate and distinctive service, even where provided in association with or as part of reference library facilities, it needs to be specifically budgeted for. Such a situation is more likely to obtain where local studies provision is physically separate from the reference library with its own staff, for its librarian is more likely to be given the opportunity to ask for local studies items to be included in the library's estimates and therefore to be provided with an annual departmental allocation for books, binding, stationery, furniture and equipment, etc.

If there is no separate detailed financial estimate made for local studies provision then a number of disadvantages accrue. First, the financial implications of providing such a service are not appreciated and it is impossible therefore to evaluate it in terms of money which must have been spent on its provision. This is clearly undesirable for what has become a fundamental part of public library provision - some authorities, such as Lancashire, seeing it as a priority service. Secondly, it is likely that little or no money will be spent in a regular fashion in building up the collection, perhaps in the mistaken belief that it can be built up almost without cost through gifts, donations and photocopied extracts. While it is true that much will be gathered in this way (the nature of the material dictates it), regular funding would enable a more balanced stock building programme through purchase, and could provide the financial resources for photographic work or oral history recording to be carried out to provide visual and sound material for addition to the collection. Thirdly, the servicing of the collection may be neglected if funds are not regularly earmarked for such matters as binding and proper storage equipment.

Because it is difficult to forecast expenditure on local studies provision, particularly in respect of acquisitions, this may be used as an excuse for not attempting it at all, it being understood that money will be made available, either through another department or centrally, as it is required. The preceding paragraphs suggest that this is an unsatisfactory state of affairs. However, there may be one situation where an appeal for access to a reserved sum may be appropriate and that is where unexpected and/or expensive items come up for sale. For example, the expenditure of £2800 could not have been anticipated presumably by Northampton Public Library when it acquired a series of autographed letters from the Northamptonshire poet John Clare to his publishers at Sotheby's in June 1972.[6] Libraries buying census enumerators' returns for a large area on microfilm, or occasional sets of the Victoria County History which become available, will also require sums which are probably in excess of the regular expenditure. It is important, therefore, that such a fund exists, if manuscript material, first editions and rare maps, for example, are not to be lost to other institutions or collectors because of the delay in organising the availability of the purchase sum.

## NOTES

1. See for example: Rizzo, J.R. *Management for librarians: fundamentals and issues.* London, Aldwych, 1980. Stueart, R.D. and

Eastlick, J.T. *Library management*. 2nd edition. Littleton, Colorado, Libraries Unlimited, 1981.

2. See for example: Wilson, A. *The planning approach to library management*. London, Library Association, 1979. Palmour, V.E. et al. *A planning process for public libraries*. American Library Association, 1980.

3. Library Association. *Guidelines for reference and information services to public libraries in England and Wales*. London, LA, 1981, pp. 5, 9.

4. Public Library Research Group. *Public library aims and objectives: policy statements*. PLRG, 1981, p. 5.

5. Lancashire Library. *Standards of provision for local studies: report and policy statement*. Preston, Lancashire Library, 1981.

6. *Daily Telegraph* 28 June 1972.

## FURTHER READING

Lynes, A. *How to organise a local collection*. London, Deutsch, 1974. Chapter 1.

Nichols, H. *Local studies librarianship*. London, Bingley, 1979. Chapter 1.

# 7

# Staffing

Jane Dansie and Michael Dewe

## STRUCTURES

The term 'local studies' is of comparatively recent origin but local history collections have been part of public libraries since their inception. Yet the concept of specialist staff has developed mainly during the last 20 years. In the early days the collection was in many cases the jealously guarded province of the chief librarian and often housed in his office. As numbers of library staff increased, the local collection was usually placed in the care of the reference librarian. Only with the reorganisation of London government in 1965 and local government generally in the mid-1970s, however, did library authorities attain a scale of activity sufficient for the creation of designated local studies posts to become more than exceptional, as was the case earlier. The creation of specialist posts was also perhaps encouraged by the need to staff the accommodation provided for the local collection in the many large new buildings of the post-war period, the opportunities afforded by professional education to study local studies librarianship and the increasing demands of library users. The period since reorganisation has, however, unfortunately coincided with the onset of recession. This has meant that many authorities have been unable to keep pace with the increase in demand which they have helped to promote. Many local studies librarians find themselves in the one-man-band category and totally dependent on non-professional staff for support, meal and holiday relief.

There is no consistent pattern of staffing in public libraries in the United Kingdom and the place of local studies posts in relation to the overall library establishment varies considerably. In some instances the local studies librarian is for the most purposes outside the normal chain of command of the library service and works with the record office or museum service. For example, in Suffolk the local studies librarian, although appointed by the county librarian, works at the county record office, which is separate from the library, and in practice comes under the jurisdiction of the county archivist. The Wiltshire local studies officer's post is part of the Archaeological and Museums Section of the Wiltshire Library and Museum Service. The holder is responsible to the museums officer, who is in turn answerable to the assistant director, public services. In the hierarchy the post is on a par with the county field archaeologist and museum conservation officer.

In many practical ways these staffing arrangements may be seen as user-orientated. Users of local studies collections and record offices are seldom acquainted with the niceties of the distinctions between librarians and archivists, and, where a joint search room is provided, will probably be unaware that any such distinctions exist. Local studies librarianship clearly has much in common with record office and museum work so that a formal recognition of the three aspects of the service has many advantages in terms of avoidance of duplication of effort or competition for the same materials. The librarian may be somewhat isolated from professional colleagues, however, and will need to ensure some form of regular contact with the mainstream of the library authority. A post of this nature, paid on a basic salary grade, may pose particular problems for younger librarians and those needing supervision for the purposes of the Library Association's charter requirements may find themselves unable to accept employment in which suitable oversight is so difficult to arrange. Even for the more experienced, qualified librarian, a post in local studies is not without problems, as the break with mainstream librarianship may prove a barrier to subsequent career development. On a day-to-day level, arrangements will have to be made for clerical and administrative support if the location of the local studies library is remote from the main library.

In authorities where the local studies librarian is more directly covered by the library management structure the post is usually of a 'one-off' nature. The chain of command may be complex and the local studies postholder may be responsible to different senior staff on various policy matters and to the librarian of a service point for the day-to-day running of the department. In this respect the location of the main local studies collection is a determining factor. In Kent, the county local studies librarian is based at county library headquarters and is responsible to the assistant county librarian (bookstock and public services). In Oxfordshire, where the local collection is situated at Oxford Central Library and not county library headquarters, the local studies librarian reports to the assistant county librarian (central public services) on a daily basis and to the county librarian on policy matters. Essex's local studies post is one of seven for senior subject librarians (arts, music, technical, etc.) who are based at principal area libraries within the county. These senior subject librarians operate within the area teams in which they are based and run a public department in their subject specialism (the local studies specialist and major collection are at Colchester Central Library) but have additional county-wide responsibilities for stock control which are co-ordinated by the assistant county librarian (resource management).

In a field in which much of the material handled and the nature of activity differs significantly from that of the rest of the public library service, the flexibility afforded by one-off arrangements allows the local studies specialist to establish suitable procedures for stock control and exploitation which are appropriate to the subject. The danger of becoming a separate unit is that it may be difficult to provide adequate access to support services such as typing and general clerical work. The more structured approach of a team of senior subject posts within the authority has the advantage of a more clearly defined framework in which there is likely to be a more defined relationship between the specialists and other staff. This may involve the inclusion of a subject element in posts at area level. It should be realised, however, that local studies may not slot conveniently into a framework devised for a wider group of subject fields. Some authorities (e.g. Derbyshire) may also employ local studies specialists at the local level as well as at the headquarters or main collection.

Counties, London boroughs and other metropolitan authorities face similar problems in co-ordinating collections inherited from two or more previously independent libraries. It will probably be found desirable, as well as politically prudent, to maintain these collections in parallel to the main one, with attendant implications for staffing. Local studies may only form part of the duties of those responsible for subsidiary collections. Nevertheless, the inclusion of a designated local studies element in a post in each major area is desirable to ensure a continuing commitment to the collection. The Lancashire Library policy document particularly emphasises this point: 'The designation of a post, not simply a person, is essential to ensure continuity when staff leave, and to establish Local Studies as a permanent function of the District activity.'[1] The Lancashire Library has implemented this within its own districts and the county local studies librarian is responsible for co-ordinating the work of these staff. In contrast, the three regions of Cambridgeshire have theoretically autonomous collections. In metropolitan authorities, all but the largest collections are usually administered by reference library staff, as was common practice before amalgamation. The Metropolitan Borough of Wigan, for example, has a separate post of local history librarian at Wigan itself while at the constituent library at Leigh the post is combined with that of reference librarian.

The Welsh counties, Scottish regional authorities and Northern Ireland education and library boards have in many instances the additional difficulties of wide geographical areas and scattered populations. These are dealt with in various ways. The Welsh county of Clwyd has its main local history collection at county library headquarters at Mold but there are four other substantial collections at Colwyn Bay, Wrexham, Rhyl and Ruthin. The local history librarian is based at the county library headquarters; there are no other designated local studies posts elsewhere within the library system. Three of the main local history collections, together with the accompanying general reference collections are staffed by qualified senior assistant librarians and one collection is staffed by a library assistant. In the Highland Regional Council library service in Scotland, local studies is the responsibility of the senior librarian (reference), who is a member of the headquarters staff responsible to the regional librarian. However, he is based at Inverness Library where most of the local material is housed. There are small local collections in a number of other libraries, and these are run by the local branch staff under the supervision of the senior librarian. An interesting experiment, reported in the Library Initiatives column of the *Library Association record* for August 1985, is the temporary appointment of a 'genealogist-in-residence' based at Inverness library to answer queries in more depth than had been possible previously. In Northern Ireland, the local history department of the Southern Education and Library Board is located at present in a divisional library headquarters at Portadown but will eventually be moved to share a building with a branch library in the town in which the library headquarters and board offices are situated.

Harold Nichols has written about the way in which the new post-organisational structures have affected local studies collections in England and Wales.[2] Although largely concerned with county library structures, Nichols provides a useful source of further information to the above paragraphs and assists in the formulation of the following summary.

Broadly speaking it may be said that whether local collections are centralised or decentralised there is usually a senior member of staff, the local studies librarian, who is responsible for this subject area and who also has an advisory and co-ordinating role throughout the service. Elsewhere this responsibility may be exercised by an assistant county librarian or county reference librarian at senior management level. In decentralised structures for local studies, divisional/area librarians or reference librarians may carry out this responsibility, or there may be a specialist local studies librarian appointed for each district or area. Whether work with local studies is a full-time specialist job or part-time 'team' responsibility under divisional or area leadership, a common feature of the library organisational structure is the existence of an authority-wide local studies team, panel or working party. This meets regularly and consists of representatives from headquarters and the divisions or areas to:

> produce active development of local studies and to stimulate co-operative growth in the interests of local studies users... but most particularly to stimulate and maintain local studies development at local branch levels and to encourage the Local Studies Librarian, so much involved with the central research collection, to assist the branches in providing 'local' local collections.[3]

Such meetings help overcome the possible isolation of local studies librarians, whether occupied full time or part time with this area, enables planning, ensures better communication and provides local studies with a voice in the library system.

## DUTIES AND NUMBERS

Although the aims and objectives of local studies posts are usually similar, the daily work may vary considerably. The position of the local studies post within the library structure and the location of the department have a considerable bearing on this. A local studies librarian whose main base is a department in a public library service point will obviously spend a higher proportion of time in dealing directly with the public than one based at library headquarters. The level of enquiries will also vary, as a local studies department within a central library will be expected to deal with basic enquiries such as street directions and current local papers, which would otherwise be regarded as part of the general information service. In a department which is run in conjunction with a record office, it will be impossible to segregate local studies library enquiries from archival ones, and it may also be thought undesirable to do so. In this arrangement, and that where the local studies library is located in an independent building, personal callers will be more likely to be more purposive, although not necessarily more knowledgeable. The library staff may find themselves offering a slightly more academic level of service. However, they may also be required to undertake duties relating to the security of buildings and the supervision of cleaning staff which are not required of staff whose departments are sited within larger service points. A post based at the headquarters of the library system will probably have a higher element of co-ordination of field services, and will have more of a back-up role in relation to its own collection.

## Staffing standards

The most thorough attempt to formulate staffing standards has been *The staffing of public libraries,* issued by the Department of Education and Science in 1976,[4] which was concerned with providing the bases for calculating the number of staff required for different library services. Based on research undertaken by the Local Authorities Management Services and Computer Committee (LAMSAC), this report pointed out that the only staffing guide previously available for public libraries was in terms of staff ratio to population. The staffing formula produced by LAMSAC for reference and information services included a consideration of the requirements for local studies provision.[5] The formula was based on a capability of each staff member to handle 3000 enquiries a year; the average time to handle an enquiry in different subject areas; the inclusion of an additional element to cover extra functions; and the ratio of enquiries to other support duties in a 50/50 ratio. It is expressed as:

$$\frac{(E)}{(3000 \times F)} + A = \text{number of full-time staff required}$$

where

$E$ = annual total of recorded enquiries
$F$ = a factor representing the average time to handle an enquiry in a given subject area

$3000$ = average number of enquiries per staff member per year
$A$ = additional element

The single most interesting fact to emerge from the LAMSAC survey, from the viewpoint of local studies, was the confirmation that the average time spent on a local history enquiry was longer than in any of the other broad subject areas identified: 10.52 minutes compared with 7.64 for science and technology and 4.88 for quick reference and information. With the mean of all enquiry, work stated as 1, local studies is considered to have a factor of 1.6 in the formula for staffing requirements. The report also points out factors that militate against its simple application, including one such observation about local studies - the need for staff, over and above the basic formula, 'to liaise with the museum service, archivists, local educational resource centres, schools, colleges and academic institutions, local societies and organisations concerned with historical research, with a view to achieving the fullest possible exploitation of local studies material'.[6]

The LAMSAC report provides an example of how its formula could be applied to a local studies library;[7] it recommends that about 50 per cent of such staff should be professionally qualified.

One of the difficulties in implementing the formula is that it is related to the total number of recorded enquiries in a year. This statistic will not be available if a new local studies department is to be established and the grossing up of sample figures (as recommended in the report) for shorter periods, in assessing present staffing levels, may not necessarily reflect the overall pattern of use. Nevertheless, the formula provides for a set of criteria in creating an establishment based on the *use* made of the department and indicates those conditions which attract a possible additional staff allowance. The report does not, however, consider the necessity for non-library staff, which the size, nature and use of the local collection might dictate, e.g. archivists, conservationists and reprographic specialists.

The Local Studies Group of the Library Assocation, which at the time of writing is formulating guidelines for local studies librarianship, is expected to state that every public library authority should have at least one designated local studies post, even when the local studies service is provided in conjunction with the record office under the direction of an archivist. It is also expected to recommend that the local studies officer should be a chartered librarian whose education has included a course directly concerned with local studies. It is anticipated that a career grade salary will be recommended to provide an alternative to the administrative path to seniority.

## Job descriptions

Some, but by no means all, authorities issue job descriptions. These are usually couched in general terms, allowing scope for the post to develop with the service and as suggested by changing circumstances. The job description will almost certainly include an indication of the place of the local studies post within the hierarchy of the library establishment, usually in terms of the officer to whom the local studies librarian is responsible, and the numbers of staff to be supervised. Other details likely to be included are responsibility for maintaining links with other relevant departments of the authority and outside organisations, providing training for other members of staff and the promotion of local studies in the library and the community. The detail included in relation to stock work will vary. The emphasis may be on the maintenance of a central collection, but in most instances there will also be an element of co-ordination of the work of other collections elsewhere in the system. The librarian of the central local studies collection may be directly responsible for the selection of material for these supporting collections or the function may be exercised by field staff with the principal local studies librarian offering advice and assistance as required. Some job descriptions give only general guidance on duties and responsibilities, while others are more specific in describing the methods to be adopted, in, for example, acquisition work, where the principal local studies librarian may be required to inform staff responsible for field services of newly published fugitive material on the area, perhaps by the issue of a weekly or periodic list.

The senior local studies librarian in a library system has a management role which will include responsibility for other staff working within the department. Few local studies departments, with the notable exceptions of those in large libraries such as Birmingham, are large enough for this to be a major function. In most cases a small staff of one or two is the extent of the workforce to be supervised, and some local studies librarians operate as one-man bands without any regular staff at all. All, however, will have responsibilities concerning the training of staff throughout the system and assisting in arranging cover for the local studies service during their own absence.

The local studies librarian may attend the meeting of a management team at which developments and problems in the service are discussed. The post holder will thus have the opportunity of influencing policy on local studies matters and once a policy has been formulated will be responsible for its implementation. In most authorities a budget will be allocated for the purposes of the local studies service and spending within these limits will be a responsibility of the local studies librarian who should also be involved in the preparation of the estimates for such an allocation. If specific needs for additional resources arise, as indicated in the previous chapter, then where possible they should be planned in advance and included in the department's estimates or a case made for additional funds. In some instances oversight of the spending of field staff in charge of supplementary collections may be required or implied in a stock control responsibility.

## Non-professional staff

The proposed Local Studies Group guidelines are likely to state that non-professional library assistants working full time in a local studies department should be certificated library assistants who have a recognised interest in the history of the locality. This presupposes that the placement of non-professional staff is on a long-term basis, which is not universally the case at present. The range of duties undertaken by such staff could include such matters as the ordering, receipt and processing of materials, binding routines, the mounting of illustrations, cutting and processing newspaper articles, simple repairs, photocopying, typing catalogue entries, simple indexing and filing. Other work might consist of assisting in the preparation of displays, exhibitions and publications and answering simple enquiries. It has been pointed out that: 'Local studies asks far more of junior staff than any other department.' And that they may have to answer enquiries without professional supervision which would not be allowed in the lending library.[8]

## EDUCATION AND TRAINING

### Formal education

Until the late 1960s the idea of subject specialists in local history and its librarianship was not provided for nor encouraged by professional education. On the whole librarians learnt about this area by doing it, usually as part of wider reference and information duties. As the profession was

116

largely a non-graduate one, few librarians would have had a degree in a subject of relevance to local studies work, such as history or geography. With the emergence of postgraduate qualifications in librarianship, the Library Association introduced an elective paper in 1967 on local studies librarianship and a similar one was introduced by the association in 1971 for its now defunct two-year non-graduate course. On the establishment of degree courses in librarianship and the adoption of internal examining by the library schools, various courses in local studies are now being offered in their postgraduate and degree programmes. Some schools have apparently made no provision for specific education in local studies, while the option papers offered in the other schools are taken up by a small number of students.

While it is not to be expected that all students will wish to take a specialist local studies paper, the inclusion of a local studies element in the core syllabus of professional education is to be commended. All service points of a public library and many academic libraries may be in receipt of local enquiries, not just those where an appropriate member of staff is based. The basic course at the Polytechnic of North London covers, albeit briefly, national public records and those most often found in county record offices and libraries, and also considers landscape sources, organisations in local history, oral history and the exploitation of local collections.

Optional local studies courses offered may be sub-divided into two separate papers: the management of local studies collections, and the sources for local history, as in the undergraduate course at the College of Librarianship Wales. The topics covered by the former include the context of local history libraries in the community in both the public library service and academic libraries, the building and organisation of a collection, including classification and cataloguing, management and services. The sources course covers cartographical, field, pictorial and written evidence. The casework approach is also employed based on the use of directories, newspapers, guide books, reminiscences, Ordnance Survey maps and aerial photographs. Undergraduate students have the opportunity to take one or both courses. Although now a little dated, Michael Reed has described the course content at Loughborough in an article published in 1975.[9]

The need for continuing education once the librarian has started work is particularly acute in local studies. The post-college, pre-charter period in a librarian's career is one in which time must be allowed for attendance at courses and this can be particularly difficult to manage in a field of service consisting mainly of small units. A sense of isolation can often occur where the local studies librarian is working without much contact with professional colleagues. There is a need to retain links with the profession and to forge them with others active in the local history field. Since 1977 the Local Studies Group of the Library Association has provided a much needed forum. Courses and one-day schools, on such topics as library local publications, and newspapers and local studies, have been well received. The group is aware of the need for interaction between its members, archivists, museum curators and educationalists. Joint meetings with these professionals, or attendance at their events where possible, are clearly of relevance to the local studies librarian's desire to keep abreast of current problems - problems often not understood by non-specialist librarians! Short courses are also organised, notably by the College of Librarianship Wales and the Polytechnic of North London. Some librarians will clearly benefit from the opportunity to participate in more prolonged, formal further education, such as a diploma course in local history.

## In-service training

No matter how many external courses are provided and supported, there remains a need for in-service training in local studies. The need may be felt at various levels of staff: the local studies librarian of a main collection, who will probably be employed full time in this capacity; staff whose job descriptions include responsibility for a local collection, usually of a subsidiary collection within the library service, among other functions; professional staff not specialising in local studies but likely to be in receipt of local enquiries; and non-professional staff.

## Professional staff who are to work full time with a main local studies collection

Staff in this position are likely to have had some relevant experience before appointment and may already be acquainted with some of the material in question. They will need to familiarise themselves with the collection at a basic level as soon as possible after appointment. It should be more widely appreciated, however, that this is a process which can continue for many years. It will also be necessary for the new post-holder to become acquainted with other related collections within the library's own organisation, within the local authority and under the control of other bodies. These could include other major collections within the library

118

service, possibly inherited from previous authorities. The appropriate county or metropolitan record office must be included in the introductory tour where it does not form an integrated department with the local studies library. Other candidates for introduction within the first few months of taking up appointment are the local museums and major societies (especially if they maintain libraries), the Victoria County History if still active and the local branch of the Historical Association. One advantage of regarding visits to these organisations as induction training is that most local authorities are prepared to make both time and travelling expenses available under this head which may be less easily obtained at a later stage. Early introduction to the staff of these organisations will also be advantageous to good working relationships in the future.

## Staff working with other local studies collections within the library service

On taking up a post involving responsibility for local studies, other than at a main collection, the recruits should spend a minimum period of a week at the principal collection and should be afforded the opportunity of working with the collection as much as possible. They can gain an insight into the work of the principal local studies librarian and be encouraged to explore ways in which the resources of the local studies centre can be best used to supplement their own collections. Their co-operation may also be enlisted in prospecting for publications of local interest which appear within their own areas with minimal publicity which could otherwise be missed. It may be advantageous for this visit to take place after the new members of staff have been in post for a period of approximately a month and are in a position to view the central collection in relation to the ones with which they are concerned. They should also be encouraged to contact local organisations operating within their own area. This may involve further visits for which reasonable time should be allowed.

Continuing training for all involved in local studies should be provided as part of a regular staff development programme. This should ideally be planned to widen the horizons of participants. Possible themes could include the work of related local government departments such as the planning officer or a national source such as the Public Record Office. Training may also take the form of case studies or a joint exercise by those concerned such as the preparation of a guide to resources. Such an exercise has the added benefit of increasing awareness of the total resources of the local authority and enabling newer or less experienced staff to benefit from working with established experts.

## Professional staff not specialising in local studies

As local studies enquiries may be received at any service point at any time, it is important for non-specialist staff to be given training in referral techniques. This may be best achieved by organised visits to the main collection where sample cases can be examined and attempts made to enable staff to share the viewpoint of the local studies department in relation to possible areas of difficulty. Role playing is one means of making such points, as is the need for the observance of any booking scheme in operation for reserving facilities and equipment, or the desirability of giving prior notice when specialist advice is required. Enormous problems and loss of confidence in the service can result from failure in this aspect of referral, as for instance when staff omit to mention to potential users such basic facts as the reference nature of a collection.

## Non-professional staff

Non-professional staff, particularly in smaller libraries, may be in the position of advising potential users of the local studies collection and, in this respect, have similar needs to those of non-specialist professional staff. The most important single piece of advice to them could be to recommend the enquirer to contact the local studies library by telephone or letter before making a visit.

For non-professional staff employed as support staff in the same library as the local collection, the need is for training in the mechanics and care of equipment and materials. Those with some experience of library work may have a general background of routine processing and repair work, which will need to be developed further, but are likely to require technical training in the use of equipment such as tape recorders, microfilm and microfiche readers, and any special requirements in photocopying. They may also be expected to deal with clerical operations connected with the smooth running of the department. In many local authorities a brief course on office practice will be available to assist with this aspect.

## VOLUNTEERS AND GOVERNMENT-FUNDED SCHEMES

The acceptance of voluntary workers within the public library service has become more widespread and more structured during the last decade. Voluntary work has had a long history, for example in housebound reader and hospital provision, and local collections too have often benefited from the assistance provided by individuals and groups in undertaking such tasks as indexing materials in the collection. This activity has probably taken place throughout the existence of most local collections without being formally labelled as such. Partly because of the effects of recession on the public service, trade unions have become particularly sensitive on the issue of work being carried out by unpaid labour. This cautious approach has been extended more recently to the Manpower Services Commission Community Programme. There may be some justification for the view that the work undertaken by volunteers or those participating in government-funded schemes should properly be performed by members of the library's own paid staff. However, realism suggests to the local studies librarian that the alternatives to these schemes are that the projects in question are not attempted at all, or that they are performed by staff members in their own time, which in effect constitutes voluntary labour in itself. The criterion for approval of a scheme must be that there is no likelihood of the work being carried out by paid library staff within the foreseeable future.

Where the library service is co-operating with other organisations in the establishment of a scheme, it is important that clear objectives should be agreed and understood by all parties from the start. Partners are likely to be local societies, whose expectations from the scheme may differ from those of the library, or the Manpower Services Commission, whose primary concern is that the skills and experience acquired by the participants should improve their chances of obtaining permanent employment at or before the conclusion of the project. Variations of emphasis must be discussed and decisions reached on procedures to be followed in the event of unforeseen difficulties or developments. These discussions should take place before the volunteers or trainees begin work to avoid confusion and waste of time. The outcome of these consultations will affect financial budgeting, as the responsibility for equipment may devolve partially on the library authority, although provision for staffing is not required. Items which may be required include additional microfilm readers or reader/printers, including consumables, stationery and access to a computer.

A member of the local studies library staff should be involved in the selection of participants and in their subsequent training. Even though no salary payment is involved, some degree of selection and assessment of those concerned is essential. A measure of supervision is likely to be required from library staff and inept workers can be a charge on the library in terms of the time involved in providing constant repetition of instructions and the reinstatement of material left out of order. Other workers may also be demotivated if a volunteer or trainee negates the value of their own efforts by incompetent work. A method of sample checking the work must be incorporated in the arrangements. Some Community Programme schemes provide for the appointment of a supervisor. Liaison between the scheme supervisor and the local studies library staff will be vital. Mutual agreement must be reached on the times to be worked by those involved in the scheme. The projects most frequently involved in work by volunteers or participants in government schemes are indexes to census returns and newspaper files and oral history projects.

## Census indexing

The nineteenth-century census returns and the extensive information they contain have long been underused because of the difficulty of extracting information from the schedules. The mushrooming growth of interest in family history over recent years has provided both an exacerbation of the problem and indirectly the possibility of solving it. The obvious interest of genealogists in the production of indexes to census returns has led to many family history societies becoming involved in indexing projects. In many instances there will be projects undertaken jointly by the family history society and the library or record office. Alternatively the Family History Society may act as sponsor for a Manpower Services Commission scheme.

The scope of any index to census returns needs to be considered in advance in relation to the quantity of data available, the methods to be used and the projected end product. The availability of a microcomputer will obviously permit greater sophistication than a card index. However, it should be remembered that the capacity of the equipment likely to be employed is not unlimited. Careful consideration should be paid to whether the intention of the project is to produce a transcription of the original (microfilm) returns or an index to them; the latter concept is the more readily achievable. It should be remembered, however, that many users of the index will not have access to the films of the returns and when the index is released the library will be inundated with requests for information to be extracted for telephone and postal enquiries!

As well as the equipment required for the consultation of the film and input for computer, participants will require access to gazeteers of place names, dictionaries of Christian or first names and checklists of occupations if these are to be included. Some training in reading nineteenth-century handwriting will be needed, and in the early stages of the project some checks on accuracy should be made to ensure that the work is of a sufficient high level.

## Newspaper indexes

The value of newspaper indexes is beyond question but faced with a file of perhaps 200 years in some cases for which no index exists, the librarian will be unlikely to be able to find the staff time to tackle the problem. The possibility of involving voluntary or government-funded labour in an indexing scheme may often present the only opportunity for the work to be attempted. This opportunity has been grasped in recent years by various authorities, including the Cambridgeshire Collection.

The need for predetermined guidelines to be formulated by the local studies librarian for the guidance of volunteers and others is, perhaps, given the complexity of the work, even greater in the case of newspapers than census returns. The index may be to selected features of the newspaper: an index to the village news pages, the personal columns or the sports pages, for example. If a general index is envisaged, these columns may be excluded. Guidance will also be necessary on the choice of headings for the index, and it may be desirable to establish an authority file. Mike Petty has indicated what can be done, under supervision, by the 'growing army of unemployed or early-retired who need something interesting to do'.[10]

A factor in gaining approval for an indexing scheme and of motivating its participants may be the possibility of a resulting publication, such as a village history, or the publication of the index itself, although the latter may be more difficult to sustain financially. More often the index will remain either in card form or entered into a computer so that entries may be retrieved on demand or printed out for use within the library.

## Oral history projects

A considerable amount of work has been undertaken in the field of oral history during the past decade but there is little effective co-ordination of effort between the various bodies involved. Before undertaking a major project the librarian should investigate therefore any work already in progress in the area. This may involve contacts with public library authorities, universities or colleges, talking newspapers and organisations for the blind and local societies.

When the above possibilities have been taken into account, it may still be decided that a gap exists which could usefully be filled by a Community Programme scheme or voluntary work. The objectives of the scheme should be clearly stated and may involve the acquisition of information not previously available, such as details of a craft or occupation which is becoming extinct. In a submission for a Community Programme approval, benefit to the community must be established. In oral history work this justification usually takes the form of the value of the information to be collected and also the psychological benefit to the subjects of the interviews. Usually senior citizens, they are enabled to feel that they are still able to contribute to the community. The need for the work to be undertaken as soon as possible once approval has been granted is obvious considering the age of the main resources of any oral history project, the interviewees.

The training required for participants is both technical and social. Most may have some acquaintance with tape recorders, but will need to become confident in handling the equipment in a variety of locations, to checking recording levels and dealing with some of the more common problems which are likely to arise. Equally important will be the ability to reassure those interviewed who may be unjustifiably and irrationally troubled by the presence of the equipment. Although a difficult quality to impart in a brief period of training, sensitivity is an essential requirement and this should be borne in mind if selection of the participants is possible. In the event of unsuitable personnel being assigned to the project, it may be possible to direct them into clerical aspects of the programme. These are also essential to the success of the project, as ideally all tapes should be copied and transcribed before any further recording work is undertaken, and this can be a large part of the exercise in terms of work-hours. Much useful guidance which would assist the formulation of oral history training programmes is offered in Chapter 15.

For the project to achieve maximum results, a co-ordinator should be appointed. The functions of this post could include assisting in the allocation of interviewers to interviewees, co-ordinating travel arrangements and the processing of completed tapes. If sufficiently competent, the co-ordinator could assist in the indexing of transcripts to facilitate the exploitation of the information which they make available.

It has been pointed out that long-term projects under the Manpower Services Commission Community Programme involving unemployed young people can achieve great results, 'but need time to set up and administer and considerable participation by specialist staff which may overwhelm both the individual librarian and the department to which they are attached'.[11] The same writer has commented that there may also be problems with individual volunteers 'who come to see the department as a second home and the staff as their confidants' but feels that these are acceptable because of the resultant benefits.[12]

## CONCLUSION

Local studies librarianship has now become more firmly recognised as a professional specialism that warrants a place in a library system's organisational structure. Library education provides the basis for those who wish to adopt this specialism as their long-term career and job prospects have opened up in this field with the potential to rise to senior management in some public library services. However, as a unique public library specialism, the local studies service must attract more staff resources if it is to respond to increasing demands from users, and if dedicated staff are to get job satisfaction and rewards for their dedication to a field of professional activity of accepted importance to the community. While the contribution to be made by volunteers will always have a place, and the major projects accomplished by government-sponsored workers will make lasting contributions to local studies resources, there is a need to ensure that there are the staff resources to build on these endeavours.

## NOTES

1. Lancashire Library. *Standards of provision for local studies: report and policy statement.* Preston, Lancashire Library, 1981, p. 8.

2.  Nichols, H. The administration of local studies collections in Great Britain and Northern Ireland. *Journal of librarianship* 8 (4) October 1976, pp. 252-254.
3.  Nichols, p. 253.
4.  Department of Education and Science. *The staffing of public libraries.* London, HMSO, 1976. 3 vols.
5.  *The staffing of public libraries,* Vol. 3, pp. 215-224. A summary of the formula is given in: Library Association, *Guidelines for reference and information service to public libraries.* London, LA, 1981, pp. 4-6.
6.  *The staffing of public libraries,* Vol. 3, p.217.
7.  *The staffing of public libraries,* Vol. 3, pp. 221-223.
8.  Petty, M. The albatross inheritance: local studies libraries. *Library management* 6 (1) 1985, p. 41.
9.  Reed, M. Local history at Loughborough. *Journal of education for librarianship* 16 (2) Fall 1975, pp. 100-101.
10. Petty, M. The exploitation of newspapers in the Cambridgeshire Collection - a few notes. *Newsletter* (Library Association Local Studies Group) 4 (1) Spring 1981, p. 5.
11. Petty (1985), p. 42.
12. Petty (1985), p.42.

## FURTHER READING

Hobbs, J.L. *Local history and the library.* 2nd edition revised by G.A. Carter. London, Deutsch, 1973, pp. 238-245.
Library Association. Research and Development Committee. *Professional and non-professional duties in libraries.* 2nd edition. London, LA, 1974.
Lynes, A. *How to organise a local collection.* London, Deutsch, 1974, pp. 92-98.
Tunley, M. *Library structures and staffing systems.* London, Library Association, 1979.

# 8

# Accommodation

Michael Dewe

While there was a strong commitment to collecting local materials by the early public librarians, this did not appear to be evidenced in the provision of special accommodation to house such material in the numerous municipal public library buildings erected before the First World War. Public library buildings of that pre-war period were to be found with strongrooms (which may have housed local materials) and separate rooms for rare books and patents, for example, but the local collection was usually a part of the reference department and not separately accommodated.

Three examples - Birmingham, Plymouth and Glasgow - indicate the more exceptional arrangements made for the accommodation of the local collection during this early period and of subsequent development. In the 1860s Birmingham had an assistant in charge of its local collection, which was housed separately in its first building of 1866. In the replacement Birmingham building of 1882, necessitated by the disastrous fire of 1879 which destroyed local history materials among much else, a fireproof room, the 'iron room', was provided to accommodate the local collection. Today the Local Studies Department occupies substantial accommodation in the large central library opened in 1973. A fairly large local room (190 square metres) was provided on the first floor of Plymouth's Carnegie Central Library erected in 1910, perhaps explained by the fact that the librarian, W.H.K. Wright, was an early advocate of local collections. During rebuilding (1954-1956) following wartime damage the Local History Room was reduced in size to 95 square metres and basement strongrooms were provided to house city muniments and archives of the Local History Department. The archives were handed over at local government reorganisation in 1974 to the West Devon Record Office, which is housed in an industrial unit in Plymouth. The Glasgow Room in the Mitchell

Library (1911) provided separate accommodation for local materials but items were not separately catalogued and were issued on application at the main reading hall counter. A proper subject department with its own accommodation, catalogues and specialist staff was not introduced until 1959 following an internal rearrangement of the Mitchell Library. The extension of that library in 1981 made possible even better facilities for the Glasgow Collection.

Edinburgh under Savage is credited with being the first public library to make the local collection a subject department in its own right in 1932. Better provision for such collections was a feature of the major library buildings of the 1930s. Birkenhead, Manchester and Sheffield, all opened in 1934, provided separate (although not necessarily separately staffed) accommodation, as did Huddersfield (1939) and St Marylebone (1940).

In 1948 Hobbs noted that a number of smaller libraries had made special provision for their local collections and instanced Hove, Worthing, Gloucester, Northampton, Lancaster and Newark.[1] However, for many, only the provision of a new building would make possible separate and suitable accommodation for the local collection, which by this date was often of some size and in a number of places inadequately and inaccessibly housed. In many instances this requirement became a reality in the library building boom that began in the late 1950s and continued until the mid-1970s, when recession saw the slowing down, but not the halting, of new library construction. Holborn, Kensington, Exeter and Norwich were all major new libraries of the 1960s that provided local collection accommodation, as was the case with Bradford, Dundee, Portsmouth and Birmingham in the 1970s, and Aberdeen (extension and modernisation of existing building), Calderdale, Colchester, Ealing and Shrewsbury in the 1980s. While the accommodation arrangements for the local collection may have changed in some of the less recent of these libraries since they were built (Exeter and Holborn, for example), their plans are well worth looking at for a conspectus of possible approaches and they provide some of the exemplification given below. While small local museums were often a feature of early public library buildings (e.g. Shoreditch, Worcester), this is very much less the case today. One recent example, however, is the central library (with its local history collection) and local history museum at Thurrock, opened in two phases in 1969 and 1972.

Provision of improved accommodation for the local collection has not been confined to new, large library buildings. Guildford, Crawley, Nuneaton, Swinton and Pendlebury, Tamworth, and Waterlooville are examples of a range of provision in other libraries of varied sizes. New county library headquarters buildings, such as Flintshire (now Clwyd) and West Sussex, also provided special accommodation, as will the new central library and headquarters for South Glamorgan in Cardiff.

In many instances libraries are also responsible for the custody and use of archives, and in a number of cases this has meant the provision of an archives department within the library building, for example in Calderdale Central Library. Elsewhere the library may house the county record office (Bedfordshire county headquarters; Norwich) or its branch (Southend). The requirement to accommodate archival material (and in some cases museum items) adds to the complexity of planning suitable accommodation.

As far as is known, there is no local collection that is housed in a separate, purpose-built building, independently sited, although such an arrangement would have benefits, as more attention could be given to the special requirements of such a local studies library, particularly as regards fire

*4. Reading Room, Guildhall Library*

hazards, security and noise prevention. The Guildhall Library's 1974 building whose collections centre round material relating to London and the City, perhaps comes nearest to such a preferred situation. It is understood that the idea of a purpose-built local history library combined with record office has been mooted in Plymouth. However, there are a number of examples of collections which have been separated from their parent libraries. They are usually housed with the museum and/or archives collections, often in converted buildings. There are three London examples of such an arrangement: Haringey's Bruce Castle; Brent's Grange Museum of Local History; Walthamstow's Vestry House Museum of Local History. Others are to be found at Salford, where the local history library is housed in what was originally the central library together with the museum and art gallery, and in Somerset, where it is accommodated in Taunton Castle along with the county museum.

The local studies collection as a section of the reference library still survives in library buildings of today, for example, at Worthing, Maidenhead, Oxford and Caernarfon, and may be appropriate in certain circumstances. Elsewhere it may exist as a feature of an integrated open-plan library (Barnsley, Hoddesdon, Sutton), as a separate room (Holborn, Calderdale, Cardiff), or a subject department in its own right (Birmingham, Bradford, Dundee, Norwich, Nottingham, Shrewsbury) occupying a substantial amount of space and with a wide variety of accommodation. In certain cases, as examples in London, Salford and Somerset have demonstrated, something close to the resource centre approach - local studies, museum and/or archival material in one building - has been possible, although not (with the exception of the Guildhall Library, London) in purpose-built facilities. For historical and administrative reasons libraries are perhaps more often required to house archival than museum material, and this has been given due consideration in the following sections dealing with the planning of local studies accommodation.

## PRE-PLANNING CONSIDERATIONS

Because accommodation for the local collection is provided within a building offering a range of library and library-related activities, it may be tempting to describe its requirements in a very basic manner in the architect's brief, without relating them to the objectives of the collection or indicating its uniqueness within the total library building. The opportunity to plan the accommodation for a local collection provides an occasion to formulate or reformulate the collection's objectives, taking into account local needs and circumstances, as these will dictate the range of services and facilities to be provided. The amount of space, the range of spaces and their location within the building, as well as environmental standards, will all be affected by, for example, objectives relating to educational activities and the provision of local information, in addition to the traditional preservation and study provision objectives.

Policy decisions, as well as objectives, will also affect the planning of the accommodation. The location of the collection in the building and features of the layout will be influenced by a decision as to whether the local collection is to operate as an independent department or as part of another department, the reference library for example, or in association with another department such as a museum or archive repository. This decision will in turn be influenced by such factors as the overall size of the library, the size of the collection, staff structure and whether the library is to be organised by function or subject. Policies about the content of the collection, particularly those which relate to the geographical area to be covered and the forms of material to be collected, will affect the growth of the collection and thus future space requirements, while the forms of material to be collected will influence environmental conditions and the range of storage and other equipment that will be needed. Consideration should also be given to the question of whether loan facilities of duplicate material will be provided from the local studies department, or whether such material will be available through another department, such as the lending library.

Another important policy decision is concerned with whether the local studies collection is to be on closed access, as at Birmingham, or open access, as at York. An in-between approach utilises locked glass-fronted cases, as in an integrated open-plan library such as Mansfield, or the local history collection housed in the Reference Library at Chester. Only closed access, however, provides for the optimum conditions for the secure preservation and conservation of the collection. Some people have, perhaps, been rightly critical of the public librarian's emphasis on the use of local history materials, almost to the exclusion of other considerations, and recognition is growing of the need to balance the desire for readers to see, handle and use material with the duty to conserve and preserve it for posterity. Much of the material of the local collection, while not unique in the archival sense, is irreplaceable. Those items for which there is a financial worth, rare books, for example, are often given protection, at least in terms of security, but this may not be applied to the bulk of the collection, which may be unsuitably housed from a conservation as well as a security point of view. An Australian publication makes the point 'that unique materials cannot be made available to the public as freely as ordinary holdings; if necessary, access must be restricted and photocopying and microfilming utilised to save wear and tear of originals'.[2] Such surrogates have considerable implications for space and equipment provision.

It would appear, therefore, that in many cases serious consideration should be given to adopting the archivist's approach to the local collection (excluding reference works, duplicates, etc.), with the consequent separation of the user from the materials of the collection (or most of it), with all the implications this will have, not only for the planning and design of the accommodation, but also for staff, users and the provision of catalogues and indexes. Separation of user and materials will also make possible more appropriate conditions for the latter - the environment that public libraries have created for users is perhaps the opposite of what is required for the proper preservation of the collection.[3]

At this pre-planning stage the librarian is handicapped by the lack of standards for local studies accommodation, e.g. at what size service point should collections be provided, and what space and environmental standards should be utilised. A Department of Education and Science publication of 1981 on medium-sized public library buildings (those for populations of between 15 000 and 30 000) recognised that collections of local material were a feature in central and district libraries and in many large branches. Given certain conditions it is suggested for medium-sized public libraries that 'local studies seldom justify a separate room, though a clearly separate space may make it easier to accommodate school classes and study groups'.[4] This provides guidance of a kind. Proposals for standards of provision by Cumbria County Library in 1976, stated that local history collections should be provided in full-time libraries serving populations of beween 10 000 and 20 000 and in those serving higher population bands. The Australian view in respect of conservation is that 'guidelines are needed to ensure that appropriate physical facilities exist for the preservation of the local collection within the public library complex'.[5]

## LOCATION AND SPATIAL RELATIONSHIPS

Where should the local collection be located in a library building? In very large libraries, such as Bradford and Birmingham, where the local collection is a subject department, it is on the uppermost floor; the sixth in the case of Bradford, where together with the Archives Department it occupies virtually the whole floor, while at Birmingham it shares the top floor with the Language and Literature Department which includes the Shakespeare Library. A smaller library, such as Runcorn, places the collection along with the reference library in the more 'formal' part of the building on level four. Except for essentially single-storey libraries, the local collection appears never to be housed at ground floor or basement level in modern public library buildings. Two new buildings, Cardiff and Reading, place the local collection on the third and first floors respectively, while older buildings, Barnsley, Colchester and Solihull, have first-floor locations. It is interesting to note that Nottingham University Library does have its collection below main floor level, while like many public libraries (e.g. Sutton and Portsmouth), Manchester Polytechnic houses its collection in its Special Collections Room on the second floor.

When the local collection essentially forms part of the reference library (although perhaps occupying a 'separate' room), then clearly its position in the building is dictated by the location of the latter department, although its placing within, and relationship to, the reference library requires special consideration. If the local room is serviced and supervised from the reference library, or at those times when specialist staff are off duty, particular attention must be paid to the relationship between the local studies room, reference library and its enquiry desk. Holborn, opened in 1960 (Figure 8.1), shows one approach: the Local Collection is separate from but adjoins the first-floor Reference Library with a common service desk; lower-ground-floor strongrooms house archive and manuscript material.

Practice then would seem to confirm the requirement for the local collection to be housed on an upper floor, in a quiet zone away from main traffic routes, and near or adjacent to the reference library. Such a location provides a wider range of reference sources, saves on the duplication of material and provides overflow seating if that in the local room is minimal or fully utilised at peak periods. At Dundee (Figure 8.2), readers requiring materials from the local collection outside its opening hours may request any item to be made available in the adjacent Reference Library. Wherever the local collection is located, however, there is a need for it to be clearly signposted.

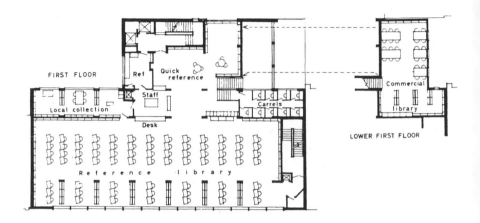

*Figure 8.1    Holborn Central Library (first floor): Commercial Library, Reference Library and Local Collection*

Where an additional factor is the existence of a separate archives department, then consideration needs to be given to locating it in close proximity to the local studies department and possibly to the reference library. At Norwich, however, all three are on separate floors, while Calderdale places all three on the second floor. At Stoke Central Library opened in 1970, where archives form a substantial collection, the Local Studies suite (276 square metres) is located on a third-floor mezzanine above the second-floor Reference Library (Figure 8.3). At the time of its opening the Local Studies suite provided stack accommodation for 12 000 books, 35 000 documents and 1500 maps in compact storage and a workroom. Seating for 35 people (including 4 carrels) was provided in the study room.

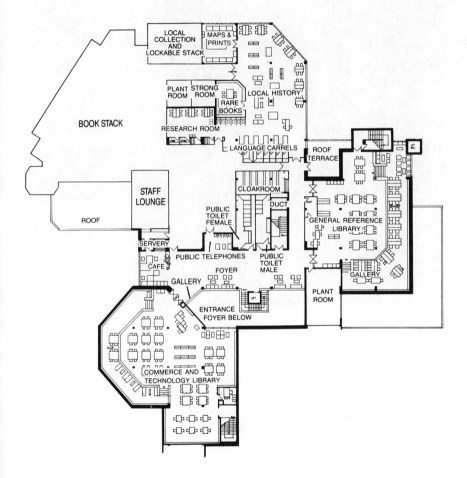

*Figure 8.2   Dundee Central Library (first floor): Local History Suite, General Reference Library, etc.*

Other relationships that will be important are those with group, lecture and exhibition rooms and those with the stack and other storage rooms, which should be adjacent and easily accessible to staff rather than at a

5.  *Local History Study Room, Dundee Central Library.*

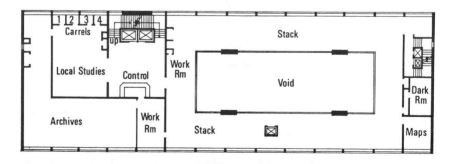

*Figure 8.3   Stoke Central Library (third floor): Local Studies Suite (the area shown as 'stack' is largely the store for the Reference Library below).*

136

lower (often basement) level. If the latter is to be the case, then the need to provide a convenient lift for staff and materials must be taken into account. Where the collection is completely housed on an upper floor and organised on the closed access principle, then storage requirements will be considerable and will have implications for floor loading, especially if compact shelving is to be used.

## RANGE OF ACCOMMODATION: FURNITURE AND EQUIPMENT

The range of local studies accommodation will not only be decided by decisions taken at an earlier stage as to objectives and policies but also by what other facilities are to be provided in the building. The inclusion of an exhibition room, for example, will probably obviate the need for large-scale display and exhibition facilities. Provision of photographic darkrooms, bindery and archive repair rooms within the building will influence what needs to be provided for the work of the local collection. The following range of accommodation might be considered.

A central feature of local studies accommodation will be the study room or area (which would also house the service desk or counter, if provided) giving a variety of seating for short-stay and long-stay use of the collection. This could include browser seating (Dundee has easy chairs and low tables), seating at tables of varied sizes (large tables offer the potential for extra seating and facilitate the consultation of material such as maps) with sloping stands for the use of bound newspapers and folio volumes. A suggested general space allowance for readers is 2.3 square metres; for the consultation of maps 3.25 to 4.6 square metres; for the use of microforms 3.7 square metres. Facilities for microform use in local studies libraries are often mean in their allocation of space, makeshift in the desk provided and poorly located in terms of lighting. It is important therefore that microform readers and computer terminals are housed on purpose-built furniture under suitable lighting conditions if they are to be comfortably and successfully used by readers. Varieties of carrel may be provided, both enclosed and open ('dry' or 'wet'), to cater for the use of audio-visual materials, typewriters, word processors, etc. and for prolonged research. The enclosed carrel, lockable if required, should be about 3.5 square metres. The use of a wide variety of equipment means that adequate sources of power must be given careful consideration. Task lighting should be provided where appropriate, but particularly in enclosed carrels, to raise the general level of illumination for the detailed study of maps and other documents: a range of 500 to 1000 lux has been suggested,[7] but the upper figure seems rather high.

The study room or area may also accommodate all or part of the collection, depending upon the size of the latter and taking into account questions of supervision, conservation and security. A variety of shelving and storage equipment to house and display materials as varied as slides, microform, prints and maps will therefore need to be accommodated in the study room itself. In small collections some secure storage would make possible the loan of archive material from the county record office or elsewhere.[8]

Special rooms and departments are unnecessary for the use of microforms or particular types of material, unless in the latter case they form an especially large collection, e.g. the Print, Manuscript and Newspaper Rooms at the Guildhall Library, London; the Maps and Prints Room at Dundee; or a separate identity is required for a notable part of the collection, e.g. the Dickens Room, Portsmouth, the Cecil Roberts Room, Nottingham; or secure accommodation for rare books (Dundee). The latter may be housed in a strongroom, along with archive material, where this forms part of the collection. Strongrooms are often the only part of the local studies accommodation where an appropriate environment for local material is provided, for example at Shrewsbury, where a specially air-conditioned and humidified strongroom in the basement accommodates archives and older local studies material.

Workroom accommodation for local studies staff should be generous. Plenty of desk and work table space should be provided because of the varied work that goes on with local materials, such as cutting and indexing newspapers, mounting photographs and simple repairs. An office for the departmental head may be provided in large libraries.

The variety of shelving required in the local studies library will reflect its size, the formats to be housed and the policy on access to local materials. A stack area, particularly for large, closed access collections, will be required. Dundee has a locked stack, entirely separate from the library's other stacks, and adjacent to the study room which holds a collection of 3500 books on open display in glass-fronted cases. Bradford too has an adjacent stack, while in Kensington material is housed on the lower ground floor. Calderdale has a mixture of adjustable open and glass-fronted, lockable shelving. Wood is usually preferred for study room shelving, while metal shelving may be used in the stack. Choice of shelving should take

138

into account possible damage from the finish and construction of the shelving and the book support. Shelving should provide a range of storage sizes if materials are not to be uneconomically shelved or housed in a manner likely to lead to damage. Folio, elephant volumes, or bound newspapers, which should be shelved flat, often suffer through lack of suitable shelving and aisle space to manoeuvre them. It has been recommended that each such volume should have a separate shelf, or as a more economic alternative, three or four volumes to a shelf, 'but with adequate and clearly designated "transfer stages" where the top volumes of a stack may be placed while a lower one is being extracted'.[9]

Consideration should be given to the method of moving books to be shelved. In large libraries this may suggest a mechanical system but this must ensure that books and other materials will not suffer damage in transit. At the Guildhall, London, the counter is connected to the main stacks in the basement by a Lamson tube vacuum system and a book hoist.

One or more rooms of differing sizes will be needed for lectures, exhibitions, talks to school classes, group work, and committee and other meetings of the local history society and similar bodies. If a lecture room is provided this should be equipped for audio-visual presentations. Other furniture and equipment requirements will range from catalogue furniture, photocopier, photographic equipment to display and exhibition boards and cases.

As mentioned earlier, a variety of storage equipment - boxes, folders, envelopes, cabinets, chests, vertical and lateral filing - will be required to house microfilm, maps, prints, sound tapes, films, etc., and methods, and the capacity and effectiveness of particular makes of equipment should be carefully examined, including perhaps, in the case of items such as cabinets and chests, the protection they might give against fire and water. Storage facilities for hardware, such as cassette recorders, slide viewers, etc., should not be overlooked.

Separate accommodation from the local collection is often made for archives in a library building, either because they form a substantial collection with specialist staff or because they are not the responsibility of the library service. Such a separation seems wasteful from an accommodation point of view, as archives basically require the same range of accommodation: search (study) room, offices, repair and workrooms, muniment rooms (strongrooms) and lecture and exhibition space. However, some specialist facilities would be required for conservation work, as well as fumigation and sorting rooms. Such facilities would also be useful for handling other types of material.

## HOW MUCH SPACE?

While deciding upon the range of areas or spaces to be provided may be relatively easy, given clear statements of objectives and policies, the calculation of how many square metres are required for each is less so, because, as was mentioned earlier, there are no standards or guidelines for local collections. There are, therefore, considerable problems in calculating how much space to allow for readers as a whole (i.e. the number of seats), for housing the contents of the collection, and for special areas and rooms such as a viewing area or photographer's darkroom. Little advice is given in the literature about the number of seats to provide or the size of the reading or study room to accommodate them.[10] However, Table 8.1 gives study room size and seating provision for a number of local collections. While the figures in Table 8.1 provide some guidance for the planners of local studies accommodation, there are considerable variations dictated by local circumstances. For example, Tamworth Area Library (Staffordshire) allows 24 square metres out of a total of 1668 square metres for local history, while Ambleside (Cumbria) provides a room of 79 square metres to house the Armitt Library in a branch library of 371 square metres.

Works on physical planning such as Godfrey Thompson's *Planning and design of library buildings* and Keyes Metcalf's *Planning academic and research libraries*[11] provide general guidance on space calculations for library materials and their storage, particularly as regards books and periodicals, but are less helpful in respect of the varied range of non-book materials to be found in the local collection. The librarian will need, therefore, to turn to more specialised publications for detailed help in calculating the space requirements for the storage and use of microforms, maps, slides, films and cassettes, for example, where these materials form a substantial part of the collection.[12]

Space allowances for the local collection, particularly as regards stock, require a commitment to the future and thus allowance must be made for growth. The local collection is the one collection where there will always be material to add yet probably nothing will be discarded. While the

140

projected life of a public building may be seen in planning terms of 25, 40 or 60 years, major library buildings may have longer lives in excess of the last figure and this needs to guide long-range planning. Consideration should be given, therefore, as to how the design and layout of the library will cater for the future expansion of the local studies collection.

*Table 8.1   Study room size and seating provision*

| Library | Total size (square metres) | Study room (square metres) | Seats |
| --- | --- | --- | --- |
| Aberdeen | 4 000 | 115 | 12 |
| Birmingham | 21 368 | 309 | 48 |
| Calderdale | 4 000 | 75 | 6 |
| Cardiff | 8 500 | 572 | 54 + 24 shared |
| Colchester | 2 708 | 201 | 9 + 32 shared |
| Coventry | 3 067 | 200 | 26 |
| Dundee | 9 135 | 500 | 61 |
| Glasgow | 49 776 | 494 | 30 |
| Plymouth | 1 810 | 95 | 20+ |
| Reading | 2 500 | 200 | 30 |
| Shrewsbury | 1 179 | 160 | 25 |

A number of other factors affect the space required. First, whether the users have access to the local collection materials. If the collection is a closed access one, as at Birmingham, then this permits stock to be stored more economically (taller stacks, narrower gangways) than an open access collection. In other instances a major part of the stock - books, pamphlets, minutes, directories, etc. - are readily available on open shelves, as at Exeter, Portsmouth and York. Elsewhere a working collection is placed on open shelves, the remainder being available on application. Secondly, the choice of storage method will also affect space requirements. The most obvious example is the use of mobile shelving in preference to static shelving, where there may be a space gain of 50 per cent or more depending upon the particular system chosen. Lateral shelving is generally considered to be less space-consuming than vertical files, although it has its disadvantages. Choice of product therefore may be just as important as method - the claims for the storage capacities of microform cabinets vary considerably. Lastly, the effects of modern technology - the use of

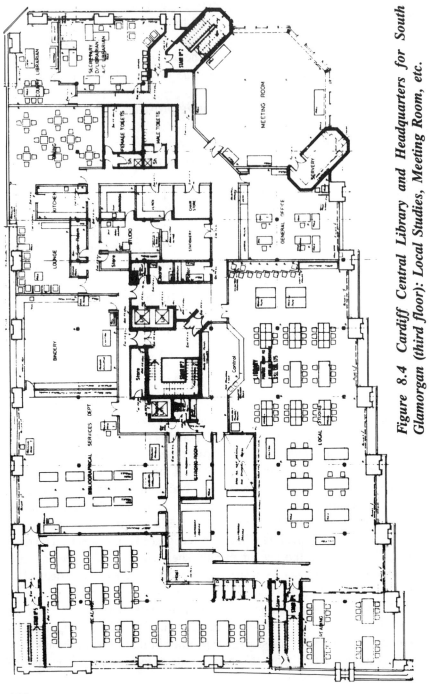

Figure 8.4 Cardiff Central Library and Headquarters for South Glamorgan (third floor): Local Studies, Meeting Room, etc.

microforms and computerisation - may mean less space is required for some stock, catalogues and indexes but more (and better-designed) space for readers. The availability of important source material on microfilm, and the demands of genealogists in particular, mean that new local studies libraries must be planned for considerable microform use, as for example in the major new libraries at Cardiff and Reading (Figures 8.4 and 8.5).

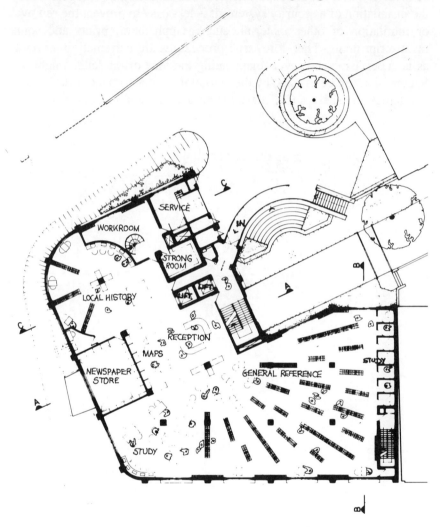

*Figure 8.5   Reading Central Library (first floor): Local History and General Reference*

## SECURITY

The security of local studies material is not only a matter of library design and layout but also a question of library procedures related to the issue and return of items made available for consultation. While the removal of local books from the department or building may be safeguarded by the installation of a security system, it is less easy to prevent the removal or mutilation of other material, such as ephemera, prints and some manuscript items. Therefore issue procedures are extremely important, as is supervision, however unappealing the idea of the latter might be. Supervision can be assisted by the layout of the department in such a way that tables and shelves (if material is on open access) can be easily seen.

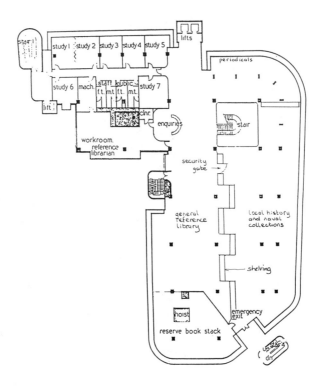

*Figure 8.6  Portsmouth Central Library (second floor): Local History and Naval Collection and General Reference Collection*

A design solution for the local studies collection that makes it part of an open-plan layout poses particular security problems, however skilfully that solution might be implemented. Portsmouth (Figure 8.6) was opened

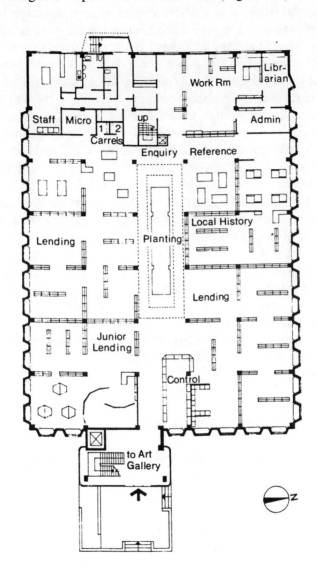

*Figure 8.7 Leigh Central Library (ground floor)*

in 1976 with its Local History and Naval Collection on the open-plan second floor and the point was made at the time that special collections of books, some of them rare and previously kept in reserve stores, were now to be found on the public shelves. The shelves were arranged in such a way that there was only one way in and out of the local collection area and that was close to the librarian's desk. While the whole library's stock was protected at the main library exit, there were still security problems for the Local History and Naval Collection and further steps were taken recently to safeguard them by placing a security turnstile at the exit to the area itself. A somewhat similar, but smaller-scale approach to the open-plan arrangement, is to be found in the 2392 square metres Leigh Central Library (Figure 8.7) designed to serve a population of 46 000 and opened in 1971. The building has an open-plan, modular interior whose ground floor has an elevated central area of flowers among fountains and pools. This very flexible space has its constituent areas defined by the furniture and shelving; the enclosed Local History collection (approximately 149 square metres) adjoins the Reference section.

Locked glass-fronted bookcases, for all or part of the local studies collection, which places it on view to users in the study area, may be seen to overcome some security problems. But this arrangement should not be used as an excuse for not making staff available in the area: lack of supervision after books have been unlocked for readers may nullify the whole arrangement. The choice of showcases for the display of local studies items should take into account the adequacy of their locks and security fastenings.

## ENVIRONMENTAL CONDITIONS

Paul Banks, conservator at the Newberry Library, Chicago, points out in an article on environmental standards for the storage of books and manuscripts that:

> One very important general principle is the separation of books and people insofar as this can be achieved without violating the basic *raison d'être* of a library. The conditions which make a favourable environment for people are not the same as those which are conducive to the preservation of library materials, the oft-repeated myth to this effect not withstanding.[13]

He adds that the employment of such standards are affected by 'difficulties in balancing differing scientific opinions, reasonable cost and desirable goals, or conflicting goals'.[14] He thus points up the professional dilemma which faces those responsible for planning local studies accommodation and the factors that will affect the decision that is made. His principle would seem to support the view that, where it is appropriate and possible, the local collection should be a closed access one. For only in this way can the potential enemies of the local collection - extremes of temperature, humidity and light, and polluted air - be controlled or excluded.

## Temperature

Banks recognises that it has been widely stated that temperatures in the range of 68 °F (20 °C) are optimum for the preservation of library materials, but recommends that the temperature level be set at 60 °F (16 °C) +/- 5 °F for book storage areas.[15] He is arguing for an ideal temperature in storage areas that hitherto has perhaps only been provided in rare book strongrooms from which material is only occasionally taken for consultation. Such ideal conditions are endorsed by Baynes-Cope, who also states that it is easy to demonstrate that books are safe at temperatures very much below 55 °F (13 °C). Heat rather than cold would appear to be the enemy.[16] Morrow suggests a wider range of possibilities that might reflect what can be achieved in many local studies libraries: 'Optimum temperatures are 70 °F [21 °C] in the stacks, 72 °F [22 °C] in the departmental libraries, and 60 °F [16 °C] in limited access storage areas.'[17]

## Humidity

Deterioration of library materials due to changes in humidity are more readily noticed than those caused by fluctuations of temperature. Banks's recommendation, supported by other writers, is for a 'design figure' of 50 per cent relative humidity +/- 3 per cent daily and +/- 6 per cent seasonal tolerances. If parchment or vellum is present a steady relative humidity of between 55 and 65 per cent is required.[18] The need to control temperature and relative humidity in the bookstacks argues for air-conditioning to be provided. At Dundee the whole library building is air-conditioned.

## Air cleanliness

Polluted and dust-laden air is harmful to books and should be extracted from the air entering the library. Particulate matter can be removed from the air by filtration and gases by washing/absorption. Morrow recommends that equipment should be 90 per cent efficient: other authorities say 95 per cent.[19]

## Ventilation

Banks states that: 'The circulation of cleaned and tempered air must be adequate to prevent pockets of stagnant air and ''micro-climates'' which are at variance with the stated standards.'[20]

## Light

Light, whether natural or artificial, damages library materials through ultra-violet radiation, its intensity, and according to the length of exposure. In many ways it is, perhaps, the easiest environmental problem to combat in the planning of new local studies accommodation through the choice of appropriate building design and light fittings. Banks recommends that: 'For storage and exhibition areas, all ultra-violet radiation should be eliminated ... [by the use of ultra-violet filters]; intensity levels should be kept as low as possible, and periods of exposure should be kept as short as possible [using time switches].'[21] Clearly the shelving of local studies materials in heavily fenestrated rooms, with a high intensity of overall fluorescent light, is undesirable. A poor situation such as this is exacerbated by a shelving layout that exposes shelved material to direct sunlight. While such a situation can be improved by blinds, filter glazing, UV filters on fluorescent lighting or a change to incandescent bulbs (which are less damaging) and a new shelving arrangement, it can only be completely remedied by the removal of the material to a more suitable environment.

## Exhibition of materials

It is pointed out by Banks that exhibited materials are also vulnerable in respect of changes in temperature, humidity and light and he makes a number of recommendations, in particular that all light sources should be outside the exhibition cases themselves.[22]

148

## Other library materials

Much audio-visual and non-book material has a plastic base and therefore requires similar storage conditions for conservation: controlled storage environment, regular inspection, use of inert storage containers and assurance that no residual chemicals are present after processing. Where collections of such materials, e.g. photographs, microfilm and gramophone records, are not large and special conditions are not justifiable, 'the following range is broadly acceptable for the principal media: temperature: 13 °C to 16 °C, relative humidity: 50% to 60%'.[23]

Baynes-Cope summarises the main considerations for the proper storage of books and documents as: a sound building and storeroom in all respects; a room that is easy to clean and inspect thoroughly; the free circulation of air; an even climate, and recommends that a room is better cold than warm.[24] In the interests of security and conservation, Banks recommends that all buildings should have the best possible monitoring system 'which should probably have centralised read-out and be continuous, and some of them might perhaps usefully be automatically recorded'. He also believes that a research library of any size - a large local studies collection can readily be seen as such - needs a full-time conservator of sufficient seniority to influence those library policies that affect the preservation of library materials.[25]

## DISASTER PLANNING

The benefits gained from the storage of library materials in carefully controlled environmental conditions may all be rendered worthless if the design of the building does not take into account the need for above-average protection of local studies material from the potential dangers of fire and water. Fire detection, alarm and extinguishing systems will need careful consideration, particularly the nature of the lastnamed. Water sprinkler systems, however sophisticated, are now less preferred than extinguishing systems using Halon gas for example. Banks states that 'the air-conditioning must be designed with automatic dampers to prevent the spread of smoke and flame in the event of fire, and means should be provided for exhausting smoke from the building following a fire'.[26]

Book storage areas should be kept free from water and steam piping and it is recommended from a conservation point of view that heating and air-conditioning systems are well isolated from such areas.[27]

149

# DESCRIPTIONS OF LOCAL STUDIES ACCOMMODATION

## Shrewsbury

Castle Gates Library, Shrewsbury, Shropshire opened in September 1983 in the extensively (and expensively) remodelled and renovated group of historic buildings formerly occupied by the town library of Shrewsbury from 1882 to 1974 but originally erected for Shrewsbury School. 'The building now houses the main Shrewsbury lending services and Local Studies department together with Area administration. The Reference and Information Unit for the town (and the county) are in premises not far from the complex.'[28]

*6. Local Studies Department, Shrewsbury Library.*

*Figure 8.8 Shrewsbury Library (upper floors): Local Studies Department and Adult Lending Library*

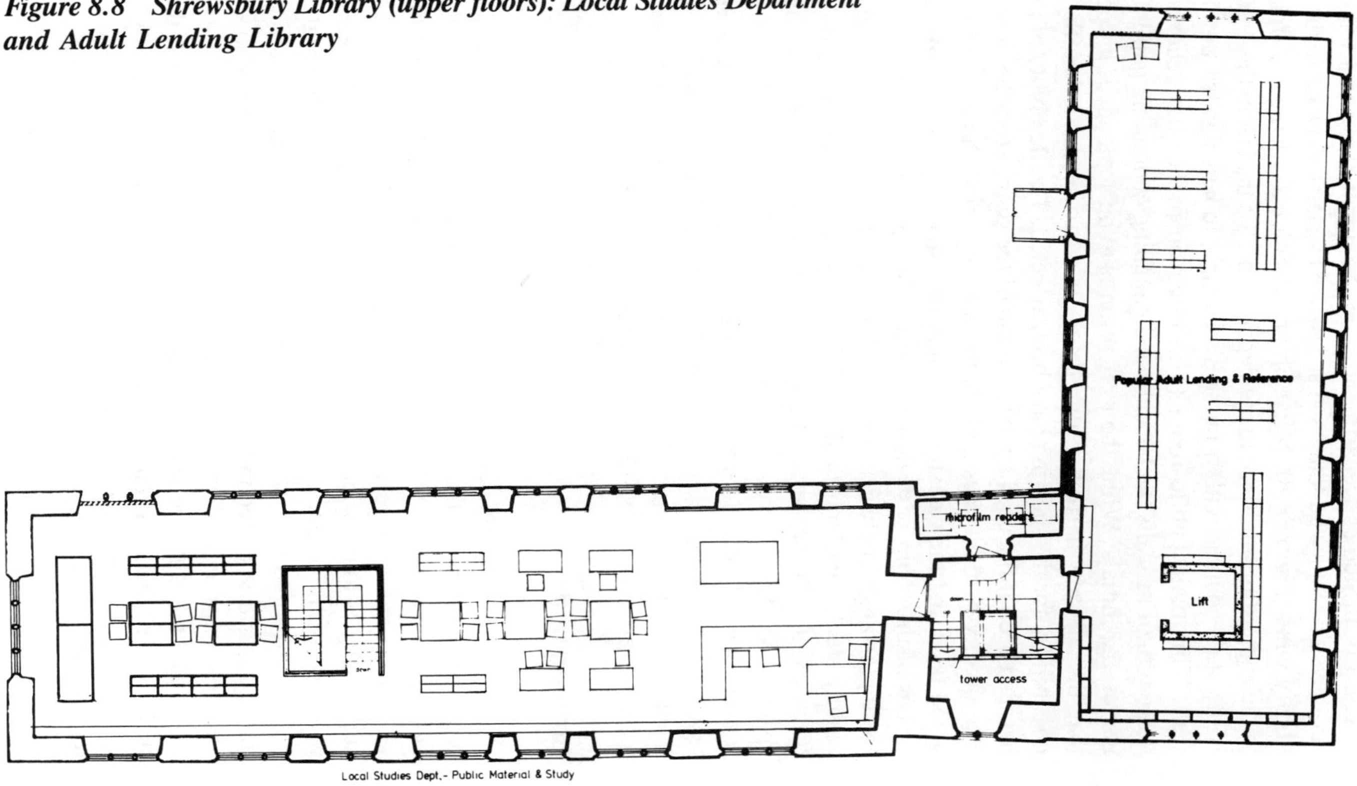

Popular Adult Lending & Reference

Lift

microfilm reader

tower access

Local Studies Dept.- Public Material & Study

The Local Studies Department is on the upper floor of a wing of the seventeenth-century building and accessible by stairs and a lift in the lending library wing (Figure 8.8). Microfilm readers are available in a small room to the right of the entrance to the department. To the left in the department is the staff counter with a number of map cabinets against the opposite wall. This main public room (illustrated on p.150) has retained along the length of its walls the benches and panelling containing pupils' carved names and initials. While their retention is to be applauded, it does mean that the already narrow room is made narrower and that the layout possibilities for the shelving have been affected. The flexibility of the room has also been influenced by the location of the staircase to the floor below. The quality of the tables and chairs is exceptional, both in terms of the wood used and their design, but only one size of table is provided. The layout of the room is straightforward - shelves parallel to the walls with seating arranged between them. Below the study room is the substantial mobile stack area, and facilities for newspaper storage and group study (Figure 8.9). The basement strongroom has already been commented upon (page 138). Elsewhere in the complex is a meeting room, the 'Hobbs Room', named after a former borough librarian and author of a standard text on local history librarianship. This beautifully restored building is a marvellous achievement but it does illustrate some of the difficulties of adapting an historic building for library purposes.

## Birmingham

In the Birmingham Central Library, the Local Studies Department occupies quarters on the sixth floor ranged round two sides of the large central void (Figure 8.10). The local studies reading area (illustrated on p.155) has a large number of four- and two-person desks (placed at right angles to the windowed void), about a third of which are equipped with microfilm readers. A service counter runs along the length of the reading area and here staff deal with enquiries and issue materials from the closed access collection. The space behind the counter is also a storage area for maps and other local collection items.

At one end of the counter, the local collection stack begins; the static shelving originally installed has now been largely replaced by mobile shelving. Other stack areas, with special deep shelving and cabinets, house bound volumes of newspapers, oversize books and maps. The department contains some 108 000 books, pamphlets and periodicals, together with

19 000 maps and plans and 252 000 photographs relating to Birmingham, its suburbs and surrounding counties.

7.  *Newspaper Stack, Birmingham Central Library*

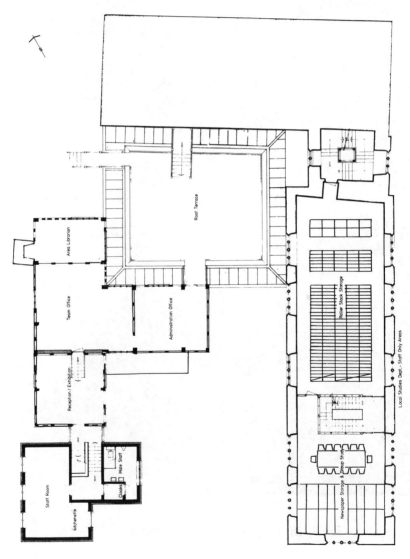

*Figure 8.9  Shrewsbury Library (first floors): Local Studies Department Storage Areas and Group Study*

Staff facilities consist of a workroom and an office for the department head. Those for users include a large general purpose room and four enclosed carrels, one of which is a double carrel. The department is served by staff stairs and lift and a Lamson hoist in addition to the public escalators.

*8. Local Studies Department, Birmingham Central Library.*

## Glasgow

The Mitchell Library, with its thirteen-storeyed extension opened to the public in 1981, claims to be the biggest public reference library in Europe. The Glasgow Collection, located on the third floor at the very heart of the new extension (Figure 8.11), has been in existence as long as the original library itself. It contains over 20 000 books and pamphlets, many bound volumes of newspapers from 1740 to the present, and over 5000 engravings, photographs, watercolours and other illustrations.

The Glasgow Collection room (illustrated on p.158) is panelled in teak and is separated by a glass partition from the mezzanine gallery of the Social Sciences Department. Seating is spaciously arranged on a patterned, carpeted floor: some tables have microfilm or microfiche readers; others have sloped surfaces for reading large volumes. There are also a number of study carrels, as well as a seminar room (now found to be too small because of the demands made on it) for group project work. Little material is displayed in the study room itself, which is serviced by a counter in one corner fronting onto a staff area. There is an adjacent stack of 218 square metres and a large exhibition area of 226 square metres outside the department. The building now also houses the Strathclyde Regional Archives.

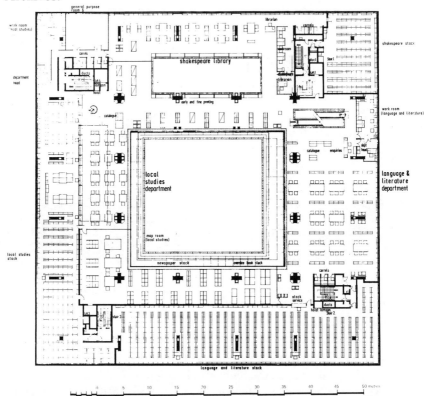

*Figure 8.10 Birmingham Central Library (sixth floor): Local Studies Department, Language and Literature Department, Shakespeare Library*

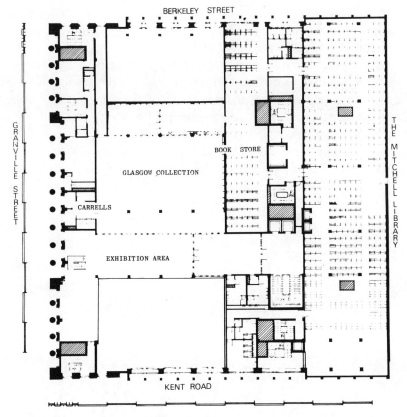

*Figure 8.11 Mitchell Library extension, Glasgow (third floor): the Glasgow Collection*

## ARCHIVE DEPARTMENTS IN LIBRARIES

While archive repositories, like local studies departments, are often housed in other buildings, there are examples of repositories, both in the United Kingdom and abroad, which are independently sited. Recent examples in this country include the Public Record Office at Kew (1977) and the Lancashire Record Office, Preston (1974). Consequently, unlike local studies accommodation, there is a body of published information about their physical planning which will be useful to those concerned with archival facilities in libraries.

157

It was suggested earlier that much may be gained from an integration of local studies and archive accommodation where such a solution is feasible. However, where for one reason or another separate accommodation within a library building is necessary then it will require special consideration. As with local studies accommodation, attention must be given in the brief to objectives (perhaps a records management responsibility needs to be acknowledged); to the department's location (unprotected basement locations are not desirable); to spatial relationships within the department (e.g. search room with stack) and with other departments (particularly the local studies department); to the range of accommodation (is an exhibition area required?); to space requirements; to environmental conditions; to disaster planning; to layout, furniture and

*9. The Glasgow Room, Mitchell Library, Glasgow.*

equipment. Much of what has been said about planning physical facilities for local studies - the need to allow for a continually growing stock and to take into account what other facilities are to be provided in the complete building, for example - will also be true in the planning of archive accommodation within the library building.

## RANGE OF SPACES FOR ARCHIVE DEPARTMENTS

The basic requirements were described earlier in this chapter; three examples are provided here.

The Norfolk Record Office (Figure 8.12) is housed in the basement of Norwich Central Library, which was opened in 1963. The accommodation

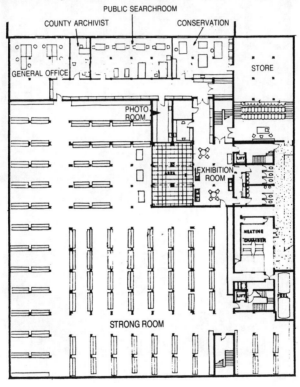

*Figure 8.12   Norfolk Record Office (in basement of Norwich Central Library)*

consists of a public search room and small reference library; a conservation room equipped for manuscript repairs, fumigation and bookbinding; the county archivist's office; general office; stationery store; and two photographic rooms (one shared with the library). The strongroom of nearly 13 000 square feet (1208 square metres), in which most of the record office's holdings are stored, extends under most of the central library building and contains over two million documents. The strongroom is fitted with fire detectors connected through brigade headquarters with the adjacent fire station.

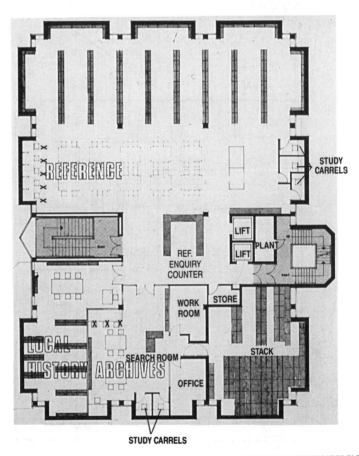

X INDICATES MICROFILM READER FACILITY

*Figure 8.13   Calderdale Central Library (second floor): Local History, Archives and Reference*

160

Archive accommodation at Calderdale Central Library (Figure 8.13), opened 20 years later in 1983, consists of a search room with study seating, carrels and shelving for reference books; an adjacent strongroom with a shelf capacity of half a million documents; offices; and a conservation room; occupying in all 240 square metres of the second floor. The basement includes an archives stack of 340 square metres with a shelf capacity of two and a half million documents. Archive strongrooms are fire and flood proof, have controlled humidity (55 to 60 per cent) and temperature (between 13°C (55.4°F) and 18°C (64.4°F)) and a $CO_2$ fire extinguishing system. Public areas of the library are fully air-conditioned.

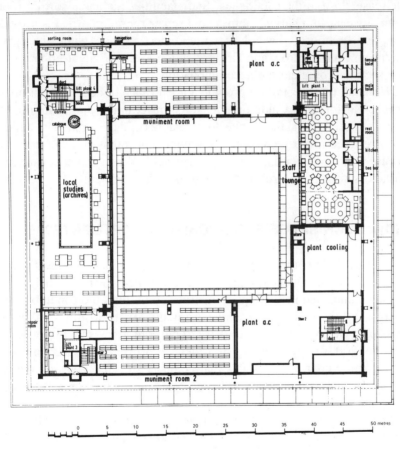

*Figure 8.14  Birmingham Central Library (seventh floor): Archives Section*

The Reference Library Archives Section in Birmingham Central Library (Figure 8.14) is the official repository for archives and records in the Birmingham Metropolitan District and an Anglican Diocesan Record Office. It is located on the seventh floor and reached by a spiral staircase from the Local Studies Department below. A lift or ordinary staircase can be made available for readers unable to use the spiral staircase. The Archives Section occupies a long rectangular space planned round a central void. Some archive material is (surprisingly) shelved on open access round the walls of the section and seating for 20 readers, including two study carrels, is provided. An enquiry desk is situated near the top of the spiral staircase close to the catalogues. Staff facilities include a sorting room, with adjacent fumigation room, and a repair room; an office is provided for the archivist. Two large muniment rooms, with appropriate environmental controls and fire protection system, one at either end of the section, complete the accommodation.

While all three examples provide a good range of accommodation and that at Norfolk and Calderdale make compact units, the location of the Archives Section and the architectural features of the Birmingham building have resulted in a search room with muniment rooms at either end. This would seem to mean that staff and materials have to travel considerable distances with the search room used as a thoroughfare.

## HOW MUCH SPACE FOR ARCHIVE DEPARTMENTS?

In calculating the storage requirements to house quantities of archives, Michel Duchein suggests that 1000 linear metres of shelving can be accommodated in 170 square metres and outlines the conditions as to gangways and shelving measurements that would make this possible. He further suggests that strongroom areas should not exceed 150 to 200 square metres, in order to prevent fire and to ensure atmospheric control. He states that compact shelving gives an increase in linear shelving of 30 to 100 per cent, depending upon the system adopted.[29]

Space requirements for administrative and all other areas might be guided by Victor Gondos's rule of thumb, based on European and American archive plans, which indicate a 60:40 relationship - 60 per cent for storage areas and 40 per cent for the rest. This is in contrast to most libraries, he adds, where it is a 20:80 ratio - 20 per cent for stack space and 80

162

per cent for other activities. Both sets of figures offer rough guidelines in allocating space within the archives department and within the library building as a whole.[30]

As with local studies libraries, there are difficulties in calculating how many reader seats to provide. Attendance records for the old facility may be helpful in this respect. It is instructive to note that the Norfolk Record Office is having considerable problems with seating adequacy 20 years after its present premises were opened.[31] It was suggested in the late 1970s that the public demand for access to archives will continue and possibly intensify and that much of the demand will be for group access.[32] If such trends have been monitored locally this will help both with decisions as to seating and the provision and planning of group facilities.

## FURNITURE AND EQUIPMENT FOR ARCHIVE DEPARTMENTS

There are many similarities with regards to the furniture and equipment requirements of archive departments and local studies libraries. Generally speaking, archive material is housed in acid-free boxes on shelves. The question of archive shelving is discussed very thoroughly by Duchein, who points out that library shelving is not necessarily suitable for archive strongrooms if only on the ground of its lack of depth. However, library shelving is available with a depth of 300 millimetres or above (which depths are wanted, and in what quantities, is dictated by the range of document formats and the manner in which archive boxes are stored) and might be suitable if they meet Duchein's requirements for strength (a 1 metre shelf must be capable of supporting 100 kilograms); safety (it will not damage documents or injure staff); and convenience (it must be adjustable). The maximum length of a range of shelving should not exceed 10 metres. Metal shelving is preferred for archive strongrooms, although wood may be used in offices and search rooms.[33] The storage equipment for maps, plans, microfilm, etc. is similar to that required in the local studies library. Information on storage equipment, including static and mobile shelving, is given in British Standard 5454.[34] Furniture and equipment requirements for staff areas, public areas and offices are given by Duchein.[35]

## CONCLUSION

The examples given in this chapter demonstrate the great improvement that has been made in the last 25 years in the accommodation of local studies and archive collections in libraries. An evaluation and consolidation of the present position, as well as further progress, would be helped considerably through the formulation of professionally sponsored standards and guidelines for local studies collections. These could cover such matters as when separate facilities should be provided, guidance on space requirements, the range of accommodation, furniture and equipment and the appropriate environmental standards for good conservation practice.

## NOTES

1.  Hobbs, J.L. *Libraries and the materials of local history*. London, Grafton, 1948, pp. 66-67.
2.  Library Association of Australia NSW Branch. *Local history: conservation and restoration procedures for public libraries*. Sydney, LA of Australia NSW Branch, 1981, p. viii.
3.  Library Association of Australia, NSW Branch, p. 3.
4.  Department of Education and Science. *Designing a medium-sized public library*. London, HMSO, 1981, p. 31.
5.  Library Association of Australia NSW Branch, p. viii.
6.  Metcalf, K. *Planning academic and research libraries*. New York, McGraw-Hill, 1965, pp. 111, 112, 129. Metcalf's figures have been converted to metric.
7.  Department of Education and Science, p. 31.
8.  Department of Education and Science, p. 67.
9.  Banks, P.N. Environmental standards for storage of books and manuscripts. *Library journal* 99 (3) 1 February 1974, p. 342.
10. Hobbs (1948) suggested that the size of the local room could be calculated by allowing 75 to 80 square feet per reader and that the number of readers to be accommodated could be roughly estimated at one in ten thousand of the population, slightly increased for small towns and reduced for large cities (p. 67).
11. Thompson, G. *Planning and design of library buildings*. 2nd edition. London, Architectural Press, 1977. Metcalf (1965).

12. For example, Irvine, B.J. *Slide libraries: a guide for academic institutions, museums, and special collections.* 2nd edition. Littleton, Colorado, Libraries Unlimited, 1979.
13. Banks, p. 339.
14. Banks, p. 339.
15. Banks, p. 340.
16. Baynes-Cope, A.D. *Caring for books and documents.* London, British Museum, 1981, p. 5.
17. Morrow, C.C. *A conservation policy for research libraries.* University of Illinois, Graduate School of Library Science. 1979, p. 5.
18. Banks, p. 340.
19. Morrow, p. 5.
20. Banks, p. 341.
21. Banks, p. 341.
22. Banks, p. 341.
23. British Standards Institution. *Recommendations for the storage and exhibition of archive documents.* London, BSI, 1977, p. 5. (British Standard 5454).
24. Baynes-Cope, p. 28.
25. Banks, p. 343.
26. Banks, p. 342.
27. Banks, pp. 342, 343.
28. Field, R. Two Shropshire libraries. *Service point* no. 29 September 1984, 4-9.
29. Duchein, M. *Archive buildings and equipment.* Munich, Verlag Dokumentation, 1977.
30. Gondos, V. (ed.). *Reader for archives and records center buildings.* Society of American Archivists, 1970, p. 15.
31. Norfolk Record Office. *Information for intending searchers.*
32. Cook, Michael. *Archives administration.* Folkestone, Dawson, 1977, p. 165.
33. Duchein, pp. 38-45.
34. British Standards Institution, pp. 4-5, Appendix A.
35. Duchein, pp. 63-94.

## FURTHER READING

Other than the chapters in the three editions of Hobbs (see above) and in Lynes's book *How to organise a local collection* (London, Deutsch, 1974), little has been published on the planning and design of local studies accommodation. There is a short section in *The American public library building* by J.L. Wheeler and A.M. Githens (New York, Scribner, 1941), which includes a model plan of a local history department - about which there must be certain reservations, e.g. bookcases facing windows, exhibits in the study room - and a list of furniture requirements. The Department of Education and Science publication *Designing a medium-sized public library* provides some basic advice and illustrations and includes the design details of the Penrith Library project, which is planned to incorporate the disused Queen Elizabeth Grammar School as a local studies area in the new library building. The following publications may also prove useful.

Bell, L. Archival accommodation in the United Kingdom. *Journal of the Society of Archivists* 6 (6) October 1980, 345-364.

Byrd, C.K. Quarters for special collections in university libraries. *Library trends* 18 (2) October 1969, 223-234.

Brawne, M. *Libraries: architecture and equipment.* London, Pall Mall Press, 1970.

*Care of books and documents.* London, Library Association, 1972.

College of Librarianship Wales. *Library Equipment Centre: a list of exhibitors and exhibits.* 3rd edition. Aberystwyth, CLW, 1984.

*Conservation in the library,* edited by S. Swartzburg. London, Aldwych Press, 1983.

*Disasters: prevention and coping.* Stanford, California, Stanford University Libraries, 1981.

Evans, Frank B. *Modern archives and manuscripts: a select bibliography.* Society of American Archivists, 1975. Preservation: buildings and storage facilities, pp. 29-34.

Faulkner-Brown, H. Protecting the library against fire. In: Fuhlrott, R. and Dewe, M. *Library interior layout and design.* Munich, Saur, 1982, pp. 57-69.

Faye, B. The design of archives buildings. *Unesco journal of information science, librarianship and archives administration* 4 (2) 1982, pp. 88-93.

Fennelly, L.J. *Museum, archive and library security.* Butterworths, 1983.

O'Connell, M. Disaster planning: writing and implementing plans for collection-holding institutions. *Technology and conservation* 8 (2) Summer 1983, pp. 18-24.

Perotin, Y. *A manual of tropical archivology.* Paris, Mouton, 1965. Chapter V: The construction of archive buildings in tropical countries.

*Preservation: your responsibility.* New Haven, Connecticut, Yale University Library, 1982.

Thompson. A.H. *Storage, handling and preservation of audiovisual materials.* The Hague, Nederlands Bibliotheek en Lektuur Centrum, 1983.

Thompson, G. Library security. In: Fuhlrott, R. and Dewe, M. pp. 51-56.

A great deal is to be gained from the study of the plans of individual library buildings, a number of which appear in the library and architectural press from time to time. Retrospective collections of plans are to be found in *British public library buildings* by S.G. Berriman and K.C. Harrison (London, Deutsch, 1966) and in the volumes published by the Library Association since 1965, of which the most recent is *New library buildings, 1976 issue: years 1973-1974* (London, LA, 1976). A new volume in this series is in the course of preparation.

The library of the College of Librarianship Wales maintains a Library Planning Collection and tries to acquire plans of all new major library buildings and representative examples of smaller libraries. A Library Equipment Centre and an indexed collection of trade literature on library furniture, equipment and supplies is also maintained by the college library. Enquiries about plans of libraries with local studies accommodation and for information about manufacturers and suppliers are welcomed; a descriptive leaflet is available on request.

# 9

# Bibliographic control

Paul Sturges

> Amid thick forests and deep swamps, on the slopes of a hill, level
> at the summit, lay the village of Frampol. Nobody knew who had
> founded it, or why just there. Goats grazed among the tombstones
> which were already sunk in the ground of the cemetery. In the
> community house there was a parchment with a chronicle on it, but
> the first page was missing and the writing had faded. Legends were
> current among the people, tales of wicked intrigue concerning a mad
> nobleman, a lascivious lady, a Jewish scholar, and a wild dog. But
> their true origin was lost in the past.
>
> *Isaac Bashevis Singer*[1]

The mentality of the stetl, that physically inaccessible and spiritually
isolated Jewish village community of Eastern Europe, so hauntingly evoked
by the Yiddish writers such as Shalom Aleichem and Isaac Bashevis Singer,
still frequently provides the dominant tone of British local history writing.
The authors of histories of single villages or hamlets still struggle
inconclusively with legends, sunken tombstones and old manuscripts. They
produce pamphlets or articles that have little reference to any world outside
their own boundaries. What is more, unless both professional and amateurs
are encouraged to compare their own community with others, both similar
and dissimilar, from both nearby and afar (even from other countries if
possible), local history will remain an inward-looking discipline scarcely
capable of producing significant contributions to knowledge.

New courses in universities, such as the part-time MA in local and
regional history at Nottingham University which started in 1983, and the
certificates and diplomas of other institutions, such as the three-year
certificate in local history at Leicester University which began in 1984,

are a major contribution to opening the horizons of the discipline. The work of the editors of the *Local historian,* the *Journal of regional and local studies* and now *Local history* (founded in 1984) also facilitate the exchange of ideas and experience beyond the narrow confines of the parish or the suburb.

Local studies librarianship too can make its contributions to a more mature discipline of local studies. Bibliographical work is one of the most significant of the areas in which it can achieve something of this kind. There is a tendency, however, for local studies librarians to look on the creation of a local or regional bibliography as something of a luxury. This is partially a product of the sense of defeat which the financial problems of the 1980s seem to produce, but it also reflects a scepticism about the day-to-day usefulness of a local studies bibliography. Unlike many topics covered by this book, there seems to be a need to argue through the case for local studies bibliography before discussing practicalities.

The existence of a catalogue of the local studies collection may seem an adequate aid to the reader who needs to trace a publication on the area. Either the reader can make a personal visit to the library or the librarian can answer an enquiry by 'phone or post. There are at least two weaknesses in this. In the first place there may not be just one catalogue which is going to have the answers the reader requires. Consultation of the catalogues of one or two service points in a public library system, plus a nearby university library, the collections of a local history society, or perhaps even of a cathedral library, might all be necessary. Secondly, for the reader who does not live near the local studies library, to require him to use the catalogue for bibliographic information presupposes he is either able to travel, or can effectively get the information he requires via 'phone or post. A journey may just simply be impossible for someone at the other end of the country, and the enquiry may be just too complex or lengthy, or hard to formulate, to make it possible for the librarian to supply an answer to a distant enquirer.

For certain kinds of researcher there may not be a really good substitute for a bibliography which draws on the holdings of various collections and which he can either buy or consult in some library close to his home. A bibliography is also usually easier to browse in than a card catalogue. Its compilers can indeed iron out some of the eccentricities to be found in old-established catalogues, and actually create a more effective tool. The argument for bibliographies for use in the locality itself is a strong one, but one might question whether the numbers of people interested in the history and geography of a locality from a distance are sufficiently significant to merit the existence of bibliographies for their benefit. In fact it is on this group that the particular strength of the case for bibliographies can be built. In the first place, enquiries from other parts of the country are already an important feature of the local studies librarian's work load. Secondly, if the much-needed comparative element in local studies is to be effectively fostered, such enquiries should become an even more important part of local studies librarianship.

Any illusion that the problem can be dealt with by existing national bibliographic listings is soon dispelled. Gaping holes in their coverage of local material are apparent. The British Museum's *General catalogue of printed books* does not list a significant percentage of local items from previous centuries and it is unreasonable to hope that the British Library will ever acquire copies of most of the items at present unrepresented. For present-day material, the spread of items that is likely to be acquired as a result of an effective local studies collection policy is such that the Copyright Receipt Office of the British Library Bibliographic Services Division could not cope with its volume, even if the producers sent it all in as the law requires them to do. Even less likely is it that the *British national bibliography* could include it all in its pages - particularly since a policy of exclusion of certain categories of material is already necessary to keep the bibliography at a publishable size. Research in 1980 confirmed that for two selected areas the *British national bibliography* only appeared to include about 10 or 20 per cent of material that it would be worth the while of local studies librarians to acquire.[2] Although the particular method used in this research may conceivably somewhat under-represent the *British national bibliography*'s coverage of local studies material, there is still clearly a major proportion of the relevant literature which can only be discovered via the catalogues of local studies libraries or via local studies bibliographies.

The state of the art of local studies bibliography is fortunately a fairly healthy one, despite the slight scepticism among librarians, mentioned earlier. A survey carried out by Linda Julian in the first half of 1984 brought information from public libraries all over England on both retrospective and current bibliographies, in progress now or compiled in the past.[3] Most of the account of county bibliographies in England which follows is based on her findings.

In virtually every county there has been some form of bibliographic activity at one time or another. The first real wave of county bibliography was in the years immediately preceding and following the beginning of this century. This seems entirely natural, for this was a time when major local studies projects were in the air. Most notably, the Victoria County Histories were being started in many parts of the country, but they were not the only monumental histories being written. There was a certain sense that definitive work could be done in local studies. Looking back on the pedestrian and limited content of many county histories of the late nineteenth century this no longer appears justifiable, but it certainly seems to have been the way people felt. They were encouraged by the existence of county archaeological and historical societies which in most areas had been thriving for up to 50 years, producing volumes of transactions, editing texts and calendars of documents and frequently accumulating libraries of local material. It was also, significantly, a time when the cities, Manchester, Birmingham and others, had had public libraries for a number of years. The creation of local collections had been one of the explicit aims of the promoters of the 1850 Public Libraries Act, and their hopes had not been disappointed. The new public library local collections were undoubtedly a foundation of local bibliographic activity.

The titles of some of these early bibliographies betray a common inspiration: *Bibliotheca Cornubiensis* (3 vols, 1874-1882); *Bibliotheca Dorsetiensis* (1885); *Bibliotheca Staffordiensis* (1894); *Bibliotheca Lincolniensis* (1904). They contrive to sound like parts of one series. Other titles such as *The bibliographer's manual of Gloucester literature* (3 vols, 1895-1897), or *A catalogue of books printed at or relating to the university, town and county of Cambridge from 1521 to 1893* (1894), have titles which demonstrate a different approach. As might be expected, the content of the bibliographies differs sharply from one example to another. There had been less work done on the standardisation of bibliographic references but the chief differences arise over the expected content of a bibliography. Books and pamphlets everyone agrees on, but what to do about maps, prints, manuscripts, broadsheets, periodical articles, government publications, town guides and the other less obvious categories brought, then as now, no unity. Subject content varied too, with various permutations of history, topography, biography and natural history. A.L. Humphreys's *Handbook to county bibliography* is a full record of the output of these important years and gives a picture of the level of activity.[4]

The second generation of bibliographies mainly dates from the early 1950s onwards. That momentous period for British bibliographic activity (the *British national bibliography* was founded in 1950) also saw the publication of a guide to the compilation of county bibliographies[5] and the beginnings of the *Lancashire bibliography*. The work done in Lancashire, which still continues although carried on by the North West Regional Library System, has been the most substantial of all the bibliographic efforts.[6] From its earliest days the consortium of local authorities which supported the work funded full-time staff based at Manchester Central Reference Library. With the great volume of literature emerging from the Merseyside and Greater Manchester conurbations and the large number of sizeable towns scattered through the county, it is clear that voluntary labour could never have coped. Since 1968, when the first volume appeared, nine volumes have been published, the first five dealing with specific categories of material and those subsequent treating particular historical periods. Even with the remarkably persistent support of its backers, the expense of publishing the various sections of the bibliography which have appeared over the years has proved a constant problem. The issues involved in planning, funding, compiling and publishing a major local bibliography are undoubtedly all shown up in sharp relief by the experience in Lancashire.

The modern period of local bibliographic work has been one in which the public library has been the main force. This is hardly surprising, for after as much as 100 years of collecting, and with professionally trained staff available, public libraries are much better equipped than the individual scholars or the historical and record societies which had earlier dominated the field. Interestingly though, it has been libraries grouped together, or acting via branches of the Library Association, which have had most success. The individual scholar does, however, still feature as a compiler: Mr R. Coutts Smith in Hertfordshire has done an enormous amount of work towards a county bibliography. Societies can also be found doing successful work, as for instance in Devon where the current *Devon bibliography* is the product of the Devon History Society. New additions to the group of interested parties are institutions of higher education. Teeside Polytechnic is responsible for the current *Cleveland bibliography,* while the Centre for East Anglian Studies at the University of East Anglia published E. Darroch and B. Taylor's *Norfolk bibliography* (1975), and the University of Keele's Centre for Local and Community History is compiling a Staffordshire bibliography. The fine bibliography of Essex, *A history of the county of Essex: a bibliography,* published in 1959 by the editors of the Victoria County History, so far remains the only example of major VCH involvement in county bibliography. Between them, libraries, societies and higher education institutions provide a wide basis of expertise and access to potential funding.

So far most of the bibliographies referred to (only Devon and Cleveland are exceptions) have had retrospective coverage. The present output does also include a number of current local bibliographies. This is the area where libraries, individually or grouped together, have most to offer. Their permanent salaried staff are best able to cope with the constant, year in, year out demands of a current bibliography. Surrey County Library's *Current bibliography of Surrey* and the *Sussex bibliography* produced by East Sussex County Library are among the best examples of current county bibliography, although the latter has suffered in recent years from the difficulties created in the library service by shortage of staff and money.

The main progress in work on current bibliography has come in the form of regional bibliographies, but before discussing them it is important to mention those retrospective bibliographies which have successfully been brought up to date by supplements. The excellent *Kent bibliography* (1977), published by the London and Home Counties Branch of the Library Association, has already had one supplement. The *Bibliography of printed works relating to Oxfordshire* (1955) has been updated by a supplement published in 1981 by the Oxfordshire Historical Society. But the best example is set by the Bedfordshire Historical Records Society, which has updated its *Bedfordshire bibliography* (1962), with supplements published in 1967, 1971 and 1978. Work is in progress on a further supplement and, even better, serious thought is being given to cumulating the series into a single edition. Possibly a retrospective bibliography with fairly frequent supplements is the most manageable way of providing good coverage.

In some areas, however, the heavy burden of a current bibliography is shouldered on a regional basis. In Scotland it is done at a national level, for a considerable volume of material which could be regarded as regional or local is gathered together in the annual *Bibliography of Scotland.* The National Library of Scotland assembles not only material published between separate covers in Scotland, but periodical articles and material on Scotland published elsewhere.[7] There are also the four regional bibliographies: *East Anglian bibliography* and *East Midlands bibliography,* which are published by the regional Branches of the Library Association; *Northern bibliography* which comes from the Northern Regional Library System; and *Northern Ireland local studies,* which is a co-operative enterprise of the five public library services of the province.

Each of the three English examples is attached to an organisation with a call on the loyalty of the library systems of the region. This is an essential starting point if the coverage is to be good. All three then rely on the libraries to supply information about their acquisitions to the editor on a regular basis. In East Anglia, the editor sends out a formal letter at approximately three-month intervals to remind contributors that entries are needed. The response to all three bibliographies varies greatly in quantity and quality between different contributors. Cataloguing variations are a major problem and necessitate the re-editing of much of the information. In East Anglia, contributors are being encouraged to conform to something like AACR2, but even that is not easy as several of the contributors are record offices, which are not so used to library cataloguing standards. The editor of *Northern bibliography* has a small standard form which can be sent to contributors to request an annotation when, as is often the case, the local element in a publication is not obvious in the title. Only Tony O'Neal, the editor of *East Midlands bibliography,* until 1983, had rather less problem with this, since he contributed a good proportion of the entries himself, direct from the publications.

Once the bibliographic information is collected and edited into as near a standard form as is possible, the production of the published bibliography is the next concern. All of the bibliographies adopt an informal method of production, for obvious reasons of speed and economy. *East Anglian bibliography* for instance, is duplicated and *Northern bibliography* uses photo reproduction. There is a certain amount of difference between what appears on the page in each bibliography. This does not just mean that the bibliographic entries differ (the entries in *East Anglian bibliography* being very full and informative, for instance) but that the arrangements also differ. *Northern bibliography,* which began with material in a single author sequence, now has a simple and straightforward subject system backed up by an annual index. *East Anglian bibliography* and *East Midlands bibliography* have an arrangement which is basically topographical.

The finished product, published quarterly in each case, sells for an extremely reasonable price somewhere between £5 and £10 per annum. In no case does this represent a true cost for the bibliography. The expense most consistently ignored in pricing is, of course, the time and effort of the editor. At these prices, each of the bibliographies has about 100 subscribers. They consist of the local public libraries, each of which takes a number of copies, libraries in education, and a miscellaneous scatter of other interested libraries, including some in other parts of the country and overseas. Although each of the bibliographies is viable at the current level of subscription, and indeed may provide a nominal but valued profit to its sponsors, all the editors are concerned to increase the number of subscriptions. Standard letters to potential new subscribers are occasionally tried, but the effect is only sufficient to preserve current numbers rather than producing a great increase.

Alongside their concern to have their bibliographies more widely distributed and producing more income, the editors are also interested in improving the quality of what they produce. The editor of *Northern bibliography* is very seriously examining the possibilities of producing it on a microcomputer. The editing, printing and possibly indexing would all be much more efficient if mechanised. The emphasis at *East Anglian bibliography* is on producing an index, which at present the bibliography lacks. Some recent market research suggested that an index would not only make the bibliography more useful, but might also make it easier to obtain new subscriptions. The index would almost certainly be produced by some mechanical method.

*Northern Ireland local studies,* which has been published three times a year since 1981, is particularly interesting because it is the result of a free co-operation between a group of library authorities, not acting through an umbrella organisation, as in the cases of the other regional bibliographies.[8] Indeed the organisation of the bibliography is very much a collective effort, with the North Eastern Library Board providing the impetus. Each board has agreed, for instance, to index a specified group of newspapers and journals for relevant material. The vexed problem of establishing guidelines on what to include and what to omit is tackled by the editors circulating a list of indexed items which have been omitted from each issue so as to indicate a set of indexing principles by example. Although AACR2 and Dewey 19th edition are the bases for entries and arrangement, the editors have attempted to match subject arrangement to reader expectations rather than library norms. The meetings of the editorial panel after each issue has been produced have been used to modify and improve the bibliography. The planning of cumulative indexes, annual at first, then in five-year units, has also been discussed.

In the organisation of regional bibliographies we are fortunate in not having to rely on United Kingdom experience alone. In France there is a long tradition of work in regional and local history which has also produced a number of good bibliographic enterprises. The *Bibliographie annuelle de l'histoire du Dauphiné, Bibliographie Bourguignonne* or the

*Bibliographie annuelle de l'histoire du Finistère* all cover a group of departments and towns with their own library and archive services. The *Bibliographie Alsatique,* produced by the Bibliothèque Nationale et Universitaire in Strasbourg, likewise covers a region and is produced with the aid of computerised methods. The completeness of its coverage is much aided by the regional legal deposit privilege for Alsace enjoyed by the library.

Regional legal deposit privileges are also the source of the extremely comprehensive geographical coverage of the Federal Republic of Germany by its system of regional bibliographies. The states of the Federal Republic each have provision for the deposit of a copy of each new publication at a library, or libraries (as many as half a dozen in some states). In North Rhine Westphalia, for instance, the bibliographic information derived from deposit is being collected at the University Libraries in Münster (for Westphalia) and Düsseldorf (for the Rhineland), then processed and stored in a computer at Köln for a new *Nordrhein-Westfälische bibliographie.*[9] The computer program is one already used for the *Hessische bibliographie* which results in a very attractive and readable printed product.

A different, but equally effective computerised system, is used for the *Niedersächsische bibliographie* which is produced at the Niedersachsische Landesbibliothek in Hannover. Dr Reinherd Oberschelp has for some years been the chief promoter of the concept of regional bibliography in West Germany and is responsible for a 'photo-cumulative' retrospective bibliography of Niedersachsen, *Niedersächsen-bibliographie 1908-1970.* This latter work has been achieved by collating entries from eight previous printed bibliographies of the state. Photocopies of the entries from the earlier bibliographies have been edited and reorganised into one new sequence, pasted together into page sizes, and the bibliography has been printed from photolitho plates produced from the newly-made-up pages.

The imaginative use of the potential of computers in recent German regional bibliography could only be matched or topped by a system which creates a national database for local and regional material. The feasibility of such a scheme has more than amply been demonstrated at the University of York Library. Using work she originally did for the library's own computer systems, Margaret Evans has designed a system to accommodate bibliographic data from different geographical areas in one database. This involves original recording of the data on microcomputer discs. When ready these could be fed into the mainframe computer which was to hold the central database. The advantage of this arrangement was that bibliographic recording could take place at any number of different points where suitable microcomputers were available. In March 1983 a full-scale pilot project on the literature of the City of York began and publication of a bibliography arising from the project was expected in 1984. At the same time a sizeable body of entries from Warwickshire was also fed into the computer.

The more than 10 000 entries from these two sources were easily numerous enough to test the feasibility of the system. On-line searches of any section of the subject arrangement of the database, on any subject term used in the index, or any word used in the author, title or other fields of each entry, either throughout the whole of the database or in any specified topographical area, proved perfectly effective. Not only are full bibliographic details provided, but up to 99 locations for each document can be indicated. Production of the bibliography in hard copy or microfiche, area by area from the whole of a county to individual towns, has also been successfully tested. With the printing techniques now available, up-to-date bibliographies can be produced virtually on demand, thus removing the need to estimate the length of print runs required.

Given the availability of sufficient financial resources, the necessary number of different geographical areas to cover the whole country could be included on the database. A number of library systems have expressed their firm interest in this. The financial arrangements necessary to make this possible have two elements. First, each library system or other organisation involved needs to have the staff to put bibliographical entries on to a microcomputer with the appropriate disc storage. Secondly, there has to be an office with sufficient computer and editorial resources to maintain the database itself. In the full plan for the York Local Studies Database there exists the potential for a new generation of bibliographic development in local studies. The scope for researchers to strengthen the comparative element of their work would be ever-widening as bibliographic data on more and more areas were included on the database. The more mature discipline of local studies envisaged at the beginning of this chapter would be brought much closer to reality.

In the meantime, the conventional bibliographic project will be with us for some years yet. As an intermediate step towards a national database, some guidelines for local bibliographic projects would be useful. In Denmark a scheme called the *Dansk lokalbibliografi* does exist and a set of detailed guidelines has been prepared by a national committee.[10] Some very good bibliographies have been prepared to this scheme, for instance Gentofte Kommunebibliothek's *Litteratur om Gentofte Kommune* (1976),

177

and supplement (1977). As yet there is no indication of any move to develop a parallel system in the United Kingdom, but a few points can be made about the chief areas on which local bibliographers need to make decisions.

First, the organisations to be involved need to be decided. A scheme which draws in local libraries, historical societies, higher education institutions and other interested bodies would be useful in many ways. Library and scholarly expertise, the views of potential users, and the greatest potential for access to possible funds, computer time and other facilities would all be represented.

Secondly, the question of funding must be given serious examination. Manpower Services Commission schemes have proved an effective short-term source of funds for personnel, although the problem with this sort of funding can be considerable. It is likely that this type of help will be available in some form or other for some time to come. Substantial sums of money are needed in addition for the expenses of publication. It is salutory to note that in 1983 an available sum in excess of £20 000, which would have been provided by a charitable foundation, was considered insufficient for the whole range of expenses that would be involved in the compilation and publication of a new Lincolnshire bibliography.

Thirdly, questions of limitation and definition arise. The area to be covered may seem unlikely to cause problems, since Britain is neatly divided into a convenient number of manageable administrative units. However, boundary changes have done away with many entities which captured people's loyalty. How many Yorkshiremen, for instance, will accept that the reorganisation of 1974 effectively destroyed Yorkshire as a unit? What kind of loyalty can new units such as Avon or Humberside command? Specifying whether a bibliography of Leicestershire is to include Rutland, or if Hereford and Worcester are to be treated as the unit they now form, will not prove easy. The types of material to be included will also require some hard work. Printed material between separate covers may or may not bring unanimity, but if audio-visual materials are considered, how will they be defined and incorporated, to instance only one problem of this type.

Fourthly, there is endless scope for disagreement over arrangement, bibliographic citation and indexes. Wherever two or more bibliographers are gathered together, two or more schemes will be offered in opposition to each other. There is much to be gained, and no true pride to be lost, in adopting an existing and proven scheme. The Staffordshire bibliography now in preparation has adopted the published *Norfolk bibliography* as its model in both scope and arrangement. This, if done more often, would make it easy for the user to check through a number of sources using the same search strategy, with an expectation of finding the same basic description of items. While no set of rules is laid down in this chapter, it can be said that the inclusion of locations for items is absolutely essential for any worthwhile local bibliography.

Fifthly, the use of the computer has become almost essential for the convenient production of finished bibliographies, and the creation of indexes. The widespread access to microcomputers and wordprocessors is not particularly helpful here. To do useful things with large bodies of information, a sizeable storage capacity is needed and the discs used in micros at present are not capable of meeting requirements. Small parts of the total body of data, before it is finally sorted and indexes generated, can be held in micros for future input to a mainframe (as in the York database), but the mainframe is essential in the end.

Finally, a timetable for the bibliography's creation is vital. The time-scale chosen will depend on the definition of the scope of the task and the resources which can be assembled to attempt it. An open-ended commitment will, however, almost certainly condemn the bibliography to that limbo of uncompleted projects of which so many examples can be quoted. Good local studies bibliographies are needed too much for that to be anything less than a minor tragedy.

## NOTES

1. Singer, I.B. The gentleman from Cracow. In: *Penguin collected stories of Isaac Bashevis Singer*. Harmondsworth, Penguin, 1984, p. 15.
2. Sturges, R.P. and Dixon, D. *An investigation of local publications.* Loughborough, Loughborough University, Department of Library and Information Studies, 1983. (British Library research and development reports, no. 5645).
3. Julian, L. An assessment of local and regional bibliographies in England. MA dissertation, Loughborough University, Department of Library and Information Studies, 1984.
4. Humphreys, A.L. *A handbook to county bibliography.* London, Dawson, 1974. (Originally published 1917.)
5. *The compilation of county bibliographies.* London, National Council of Social Service, 1948. (Local history series no. 2).

6. Cotton, G.B. and Tupling, G.H. The Lancashire bibliography. *Library Association record* 61 (5) May 1959, 119-121.
7. Smith, D. The *Bibliography of Scotland. Locscot* 1 (7) Autumn 1984, 125-127.
8. McFettridge, L. The *Northern Ireland local studies* list. *Local studies librarian* 2 (2) Winter 1983, 7-11.
9. Haller, B. *Die nordrhein-westfalische bibliographie Mitteilungsblatt* (Verband der Bibliotheken des Landes Nordrhein-Westfalen) 32 (2) June 1982, 107-146.
10. *Dansk lokalbibliografi, DLB: en vejledning til brug ved udarbeidelse af lokalbibliografier.* 3rd revised edition. Arhus, 1982. Supplement, 1984.

## FURTHER READING

Marshall, J.D. The study of local and regional 'communities': some problems and possibilities. *Northern history* 17 1981, 203-230.
Oberschelp, R. *Die Bibliographien zur deutschen landesgeschichte und landeskunde.* 2nd edition. Frankfurt am Main, Klosterman, 1977.
Sturges, R.P. Local and regional bibliographies: a state of the art report. *Local studies librarian* 2 (2) Winter 1983, 3-6.
Sturges, R.P. and Dodds, E. *Seminar on ephemera and local publications: report on proceedings.* London, British Library, 1980. (British Library research and development reports, no. 5594.)

# 10

# Acquisition

Chris E. Makepeace

Those responsible for the care and maintenance of local studies collections not only have to make the resources of their collections available to those who wish to use them, but also have to acquire material in order to maintain the growth and development of the collections. Any acquisition policy in a local studies library or department, however, will not be directed solely towards obtaining current or contemporary material, but also to acquiring older material which has either never been acquired by the library, or is to replace that which is missing or is in such a poor condition that it is not possible to allow it to be used. The acquisition of local studies material, whether it be contemporary or older material, is not as straightforward as acquisition work can be for other departments or sections of the library for a number of reasons.

First, there is no 'set list of sources that can be recommended for systematic searching'.[1] As a result, there can be problems in trying to establish what has been published, by whom and when and where it is available from.

Secondly, local studies collections are not composed entirely of books and pamphlets with a small amount of other types of material, but include large quantities of ephemera, newspapers, illustrations, maps and local publications. All these have to be acquired in order to achieve a comprehensive range of materials covering the area represented by the collection.

Finally, there are the problems associated with the mechanics of the acquisition of local material by the library. Such material tends not to fall within a library's usual acquisition procedures, with the result that special provision may have to be made, either within the department responsible for local studies or, if material is acquired centrally, within the department which undertakes that work.

The purpose of this chapter is to look at the problems of obtaining local studies material and to make suggestions as to how it may be acquired. It will also suggest that a policy should be adopted for the acquisition of material which should be formalised as a written statement. It is essential to have such a policy statement if the collection is to grow and develop as it should and not in a haphazard, unplanned fashion, and if there are to be different levels of provision at a library system's service points.

## COLLECTION POLICY

Before any local studies material is collected, it is important to establish the acquisition aims of the collection, such as the geographical area to be covered and the type and formats of material to be collected or excluded. Defining the acquisition policy will also help to establish the credibility of the department or collection in the eyes of other parts of the library, as there may be still some librarians who tend to regard local studies work as not being as important as their own particular specialism. It is also important for reasons of inter-departmental co-operation to establish this credibility, because so much local material is to be found in items which are in the stock of other parts of the library. For example, there are a great many references to local matters in periodicals like the *Builder* or the *Engineer,* which will almost certainly be found in the arts and technical libraries, if such departments exist. It has to be agreed policy, therefore, that the local studies department has access to this material in order to provide a full service to its users.

In his book *Local studies librarianship,* Nichols summarised the aim of a local studies collection as to serve 'the locality in the same manner as a national library serves the nation'.[2] Putting this another way, the aim of a local studies collection should be to collect and make available to its users as much material on the area as possible, irrespective of its format, bias or source. It should be pointed out that the material collected will not be always 'historical' in the usual sense of the word, as it is important to collect everything that relates to the area, whether it is geological, political, educational or demographic. Such a broad frame of reference requires careful delineation because of the inherent problems it presents.

Thus it is necessary to define very carefully the area to be covered by the collection, not only in terms of material and possibly subjects, but in terms of the geographical area. Usually, this will be the same as the local authority area. Therefore, in the metropolitan counties, where districts have library responsibility, the collection should coincide with the area covered by the district council. In the non-metropolitan counties, where the county councils are the library authorities, many have central district libraries which house the local studies collections for their areas. It is important that in the non-metropolitan counties (especially where there is no comprehensive central collection) that the district libraries play a major role in the acquisition and preservation of local material, as they are in an ideal position to be aware of that material which is only available locally. Where there is a central county collection, its acquisition responsibility and that of other libraries needs to be clearly spelt out. Even within the metropolitan districts, it may be necessary to use the local branch and district libraries to ensure that as much local material as possible is collected and that nothing is overlooked.

There are occasions when collections will have to take an interest in the area outside the local authority boundaries. This usually arises where there is some historical connection between two areas. For example, the modern local government boundaries go against the historical relationship between Preston, Walton-le-Dale and Penwortham; or that larger area covered by the mediaeval parish of Manchester. The acquisition policy statement will need, therefore, to take into account such historical connections as well as the local perception of the community or area, as this may well disregard man-made boundaries, both past and present. There may also be a need for the collection to take an interest in the wider area such as the region, county, or mediaeval parish or hundred. This should ensure that the local material is placed in context and items which include local references are not excluded. Once again, the extent to which the acquisition of 'background' material is collected should be a matter of policy.

Alongside the question of what is the geographical area with which a local collection is concerned, are the problems of defining what is meant by 'local' in terms of individuals and authors, as well as what is to be the library's policy with regard to works published locally but not concerned with the locality. Clearly such policy decisions will be affected by questions of space, likely public expectation, the quantity of material involved (of locally published works, for example) and the collection policies of other libraries and institutions. A few years ago, Wiltshire drew up a list of 32 names of local authors which it was felt should be collected; a further list of 15 it was suggested should be ignored. Such a precise policy would obviously need review from time to time. Collections of material on local authors or individuals, or of local publications, may well become special collections within the local studies collection, for example, D.H. Lawrence (Nottingham), H.G. Wells (London Borough of Bromley), Charles Dickens (Portsmouth) and Chiswick Press (London Borough of Hounslow).

When it comes to deciding what should be collected, therefore, the easy answer, namely 'everything' irrespective of its subject or format (or current usefulness), has to be tempered by local circumstances. The local studies librarian, however, should be open-minded and should not act as a censor in deciding what material on the locality should be collected and what should not, if it falls within the declared policy of the collection. Interests change over the years and it is not possible to tell what might concern those engaged in research in two years' time let alone twenty years'. What might appear to have little significance today may be of great significance in the future and even the smallest item may help to answer a query at some point in the future. Nichols comments that: 'The criterion of all materials added to the local studies library is that they should concern the locality; quality is not a factor.'[3] Anything which reflects the work, leisure and domestic activities of the community for which material is available and falls within the library's acquisition policy is the province of the local studies collection of the area. However, even for material which is clearly the responsibility of the local collection, it might be possible to make the case for some form of selective collecting, as is argued for photographs in Chapter 16.

## THE SCOPE OF MATERIAL THAT SHOULD BE ACQUIRED

The stock of any local studies collection can be divided into four main sections, ignoring for the moment the wide variety of different formats of material. First, there is the material which deals with local history and local studies generally as subjects in their own right. Secondly, there are those works which provide essential background information for the department about its locality, such as county histories and histories of specific industries. The third group are items which provide background information on the sources which might be used by readers in the department, such as those publications dealing with tithe maps, or the interpretation of census returns or parliamentary papers. Finally there are those publications and other material which relate specifically to the area itself. All four groups of material feature as part of the range of stock acquired for the department.

## General publications on local history studies

It is important that a local studies collection should include those publications which relate to the theory and practice of local history in general terms. They can provide not only the theoretical background but also give an indication of the type of local history/studies work that can be done, the sources that can be used and which, by implication, should be available within any local studies collection. For example, one would expect to find books by Hoskins, Rogers and West on the shelves of a local collection and also new publications, including new editions of older works.

Among this type of material one should also include items on the librarianship of the subject, such as those by Hobbs and Nichols, which are essential for the staff and which even members of the public might find useful in indicating, for example, the type of material which is to be found in a local studies department.

General bibliographical resources are usually found in other departments of the library, but it is important that the librarian of the local studies collection ensures that they are obtained and has regular access to them, for they can be very useful in tracing material which has appeared in journals (for example, through *British humanities index*), and which might not be picked up from other sources.

## Regional and subject publications

All towns, villages and cities are part of a larger community, even the large cities fall within a county boundary. It is, therefore, important to ensure that the local studies department acquires those works which relate to the larger region within which the authority is situated, such as the county or the hundred. In most local studies libraries, for instance, one would expect to find the Victoria County History for the area, as well as other histories of the county in which the area is located.

Similarly, there are many books and publications which deal with a topic on a wider basis than just the local area under consideration. In order to place the local scene in context, it might be essential to have some of this general background material, or at least access to it. For example, in

Lancashire, especially the eastern part of the pre-1974 county, one would expect to find works dealing with the cotton industry in general as this played a major role in the area's economy. (Just as the Great Western Railway played a major role in the development of Swindon, and it is there one would expect to find a reasonable coverage of material on that railway company.)

## Publications on sources, etc.

Anyone working on a local studies project will usually need to consult a wide variety of sources, and they may not fully understand the problems and the pitfalls of the use of some of them. It is, therefore, important that within a local studies department, guides to those sources are available, such as those on tithe maps, hearth tax returns and ecclesiastical records. Many of these guides are in book or pamphlet form and can usually be traced and obtained through the usual channels. The availability of catalogues, bibliographies and guides to local collections, archive repositories, museums, etc. will assist users and staff in locating relevant material held elsewhere.

## Local material

When it comes to local material, there should be no need to explain why this is collected as it is the *raison d'être* of the department or collection. What is important to remember is that it is not purely books and pamphlets that have to be acquired, but all types and formats of material which relate to the area, such as journals, society transactions, newspapers, directories, maps, illustrations and ephemera. Although intended for the guidance of district libraries, a good list of this material is given in the Lancashire Library's *Standards of provision for local studies: report and policy statement,* which indicates the items which should be considered for any collection:

1. Books and pamphlets.
2. Church magazines. Local magazines published by church organisations of all denominations.
3. Cine film.
4. Directories and year books. Trade and street directories; alphabetical and classified telephone directories; local trade year

books, e.g. those produced by local Chambers of Commerce; local industrial handbooks.

5. District Council publications. All material published by the District Council, including printed minutes.
6. Election material. Publicity material issued by all local parties and candidates at each election.
7. Electoral rolls. Registers of voters for the District area, including the provisional lists issued prior to each revision.
8. Illustrations. Photographs, prints... slides...
9. Industrial literature. House journals of local firms; trade catalogues.
10. Maps and plans.
11. Newspapers and magazines. All local newspapers and magazines with local content, ...
12. Posters and handbills.
13. Programmes of civic events. Galas and festivals.
14. Sale catalogues. Printed catalogues of local auctions.
15. Society publications. All publications of local societies, especially journals.
16. Oral recordings. Tape or disc.
17. Events arranged by local organisations. Programmes of amateur and professional events, including theatre programmes and those of sporting events.
18. Timetables. Timetables of local transport services.
19. Books by local authors on non-local subjects.
20. Locally printed material with local content.
21. Locally published material without local content.[4]

Of the items listed above, the statement indicates that items 1, 2, 4, 5, 6, 8, 9, 10, 11, 14 and 15 form the basic collection, 3, 7, 12, 13, 16, 17 and 18 form part of a more well developed collection, and items 19, 20 and 21 are optional, their acquisition dictated by local circumstances.

Although the list includes most types and formats of material, there is no provision made for the collection of miscellaneous material which is referred to as ephemera, although some such items are included under other headings. It is, therefore, important that this category of material is added to the list.

Ephemera, such as lottery tickets, menus, timetables and trade literature, can be defined as that:

material which carries a verbal or illustrative message and is produced either by printing or illustrative processes, but not in the standard book, pamphlet or periodical format. It has the following characteristics:

(a)  it is usually flimsy or insubstantial;

(b)  it is a transient document produced for a specific purpose and not intended to survive the topicality of its message or event to which it relates. Consequently, most items have a limited useful life, although the life of an item will vary according to the purpose for which it is produced and may well be of interest to scholars and collectors after its topicality has expired;

(c)  its acquisition, storage, classification and cataloguing may not fall within the conventionally accepted methods of treatment within libraries and record offices and consequently, may require special consideration. It is, however, classifiable;

(d)  its availability will depend on where it was produced, by whom and for what purpose and where it is available from;

(e)  it can be either primary or secondary source material.[5]

It is important to understand what is meant by ephemera because this type of material may be the only reference or source of information that has survived on a subject and, therefore, may be of great importance to the researcher.

When the acquisition policy for the local studies library is formulated, there is, therefore, a need to bear in mind these four different groupings of material and not to be concerned solely with the acquisition of what is local. This other material will help with the interpretation of the stock, as well as providing the necessary background for the reader and for the staff answering enquiries.

## THE ACQUISITION OF STOCK

The acquisition of stock for a local studies library must of necessity be looked at from two different angles: that of filling the gaps that exist in the collection (retrospective stock maintenance) and the acquisition of all the different types of current or contemporary material. Although it is difficult to trace what has been published, there are bibliographical aids which can assist in establishing what has been written and published in the past. It is, therefore, possible to find out where the gaps are and what should be sought, although for many types of material, including ephemera, this facility will not exist. It is with the current or contemporary material that the greatest problems lie in trying to discover what has been published, as there are many local publications which do not reach the pages of the usual bibliographic tools and which are only traced after a great deal of hard detective work on the part of the staff of the department. This applies not only to ephemera, but also to books and pamphlets, local newspapers and serial publications.

In order to acquire 'new' stock for the department, different sources have to be checked depending on whether it is retrospective stock maintenance or whether it is current material that is being sought for acquisition. No one way is mutually exclusive of others. Therefore, it is necessary to have a systematic method of checking those sources which exist to ensure that all approaches are covered.

## RETROSPECTIVE STOCK MAINTENANCE

Retrospective stock maintenance is a very important part of the acquisition of stock in a local studies department. Although most libraries have acquired local material in the past, it has not always been done in such an intensive or comprehensive way as is now demanded in order to respond to the requests for information by users. If better collecting policies had been practised in the past, the problems of filling the gaps would not loom so large as they may do at present for some local studies librarians. Coupled with the selective nature of the material which was acquired by previous generations, there is also the fact that there were very definite views as to what constituted local history so that only material on certain subjects was collected by libraries, although private collectors might have had a wider view and collected more extensively.

In addition to filling gaps created by the failure of libraries to appreciate the scope of the subject in the past and the changing demands of the readership, there is always the need for acquiring older material for reasons indicated earlier, as well as acquiring duplicate material for loan purposes.

There are a number of ways in which the retrospective maintenance of stock can be carried out. For worn-out or missing material, it should be obvious what is required from regular checks of the stock and the catalogue, but for material which has not been acquired, it is necessary to check bibliographies of all subjects in case they refer to unacquired items. In addition to the information gathered from bibliographical sources, there are also references and reviews in past newspapers and journals. If a regular programme of retrospective indexing of these sources is carried out, provision can be made for references to publications, in the widest sense of the word, to be collected and checked against the stock of the library. It is not proposed to enumerate these potential bibliographical sources for retrospective acquisition here, as they are covered elsewhere in another publication,[6] but to concentrate on the places and methods which should be utilised in order to acquire material.

## Second-hand booksellers

Most towns have second-hand and antiquarian booksellers where local items can be found. Sometimes these shops will inform the library if they have acquired material which they consider of interest to the library, but it is always worth while spending some time looking through their stock as there may be material of local interest which the owners have not informed the library of because they did not think the library would be interested in it. This is especially true when it comes to minor publications (e.g. locally published pamphlets), illustrations and items of ephemera. It is always possible to arrange with the bookseller to let the library know if particular items are acquired by the bookshop, but there is a drawback to this, and that is that if it is known that there is a ready market for local material, the price may rise.

If it is possible, not only local second-hand and antiquarian booksellers should be checked, but also those outside the area concerned, for local material can be discovered in the most unusual of places. For example, a programme for the dinner to celebrate the centenary of the *Manchester guardian* was found in a bookshop in London, while postcards are often more readily available outside an area than inside it, the reason being that local people would send local postcards to their friends and relatives, who may have lived some way away, and these items, if they find their way onto the market, do so in an out-of-the-way place, not local to the town where they originated. It is also worth bearing in mind that prices for material are often lower outside the area. For example, the prices charged for illustrations of prominent public buildings will often be higher than for the less well-known buildings, although the illustrations of the latter may be scarcer and, therefore, for the library, more useful; lack of local knowledge means that they are marked down as being of relatively little interest.

## Second-hand booksellers' catalogues

All libraries receive copies of second-hand booksellers' lists and catalogues when they are published. In many cases they will contain little or nothing of local interest, but it is important that they are scanned as soon as possible after receipt in order that the library will have a good chance of acquiring what it wants. Not only should the topographical section be checked for material, but all other sections in the list. For example, there may be material on local industries in the sections dealing with technology or trade and commerce. Likewise, subject booklists which deal with topics which have no apparent local connection should also be checked in case local items have found their way into the list. Some second-hand booksellers do, of course, specialise in topography or local history and issue appropriate catalogues.

It is important that as soon as the library receives a list, the local studies librarian checks it immediately for required local material, as copies of the list will have been received by many other libraries, although it is likely that they will only be interested in their own local material. However, there are also private collectors who will be interested and who may often order items on receipt of the catalogue before the library has had chance to make a decision about purchase. This means, that in addition to checking as quickly as possible, the library must have a procedure for ordering the material urgently, rather than waiting for the usual ordering channels to be followed. Preferably, if the local studies department sees an item it requires, the order should be telephoned through and then confirmed later by post.

Most second-hand booksellers' lists contain books and minor publications. There are some, however, who issue specialist lists and others which include illustrations and ephemera among their books. For instance, there is one bookseller who issues a special catalogue devoted solely to maps, whereas there is another who includes all types of material in his lists, and yet another who has issued a special list of ephemera, although it must be pointed out that 'ephemera' in his terms includes pamphlet material as well as ephemera as librarians understand it.

When dealing with second-hand booksellers, either directly or through their lists, it is noticeable that over a period of time, prices rise, sometimes quite considerably. This is often due to private collectors, who indirectly force prices up. This can create difficulties for libraries when budgets are tightly stretched. However, special financial provision should be made for local studies libraries so that they can acquire material they seek to fill gaps in their collections. For if the local studies collection does not acquire material, the chances are that it will be acquired by a private collector and, if it is unique, lost to the public sector for a long time or even forever. It is possible that other public institutions would acquire a local item but rarely can such items be borrowed through the national inter-lending system, unless it is a recently published work. Thus, if the local collection fails to acquire something when it is available, when the next opportunity arises the price may have risen very considerably, and the financial situation still may not be right for its purchase.

## Junk shops

Looking round junk shops and shops engaged in house clearances can sometimes yield material of local interest which might not be obtained in other ways. In many cases, there will be a lot of material of non-local interest, but sometimes books, postcards, minor publications, illustrations, especially family photograph albums of a local interest, can be found and acquired relatively cheaply.

## Donations

Members of the public and organisations should be encouraged to donate local material that they do not want to the library. In many cases they may think that local items have a monetary value whereas usually the value is purely their local interest. Often material which is donated to libraries is discovered when people are clearing out for one reason or another. Usually, the type of material that is offered is books or minor publications rather than illustrations or ephemera. The latter tends to be thrown away, rather than given to libraries, simply because the public are not aware of its historical value. For example, in the early 1970s, Manchester's local history librarian and the librarian from one of the districts were asked to visit a house to look at some books for possible donation to the library. During the course of the conversation it transpired that only the previous day a large number of invitations to civic events had been sent to the tip because the people concerned did not realise that the local history library would be interested in them. It is, therefore, necessary to educate the public that local studies libraries are interested not only in books and minor publications, but also in all other types of material which reflect life in the local community.

If material of a local nature is donated, or offered to a library, and it is not of the area collected, local studies libraries should be encouraged to accept it and point out that they will pass it to the relevant local library. In this way, local collections can help each other to fill gaps by passing on material.

Business organisations can also assist local studies libraries in acquiring older material. Today, space means money for industry and business with the result that older, unused material is often discarded. It is a good idea to try and encourage firms throwing out material to pass it on to the local collection. Sometimes, however, it may be decided that such material should be kept together as an archive and deposited in the local record office. However, there is often a lot of material which is discarded haphazardly, which can include histories of the company, copies of house journals and advertising literature. For example, when the Reddish crane makers of Craven Bros. closed down in the early 1970s, Dr R.L. Hills, of the North Western Museum of Science and Industry[7] was invited to collect the company's official records. In addition to the company's records, he was able also to acquire a complete set of the firm's house journal, advertising literature and illustrations. Although this material was kept as an archive collection, there were sufficient copies of the house journal to enable the holdings in Manchester Central Library to be completed and to provide an almost complete set of the trade literature as well. If the North Western Museum of Science and Industry had not been able to acquire the material, or had not heard about it, all would have been destroyed. The only way the company heard of the museum's activities was through publicity and, once they were aware of the interest of the museum, they gladly allowed copies to be taken for the museum and the library.

In addition to the donation of material by those who want to create space, or have no further use for it, there are also those donations which arrive in the library because the person who has found them does not know what to do with the find and takes it to the library because they are aware that the local studies department collects material of local interest.

Another way of securing donations is to acquaint other sections of the local authority of the interests of the department and its need to acquire material. Sometimes, such sections can put people in direct contact with the library, while on other occasions the department itself may be instrumental in ensuring that material reaches the local collection. The architects' department, for example, may be involved in surveying empty property and may discover material. If those involved in the work are aware of the needs of the local studies collection, they should be encouraged to ensure that the local material is passed on. When a former railway office block was being surveyed prior to refurbishment, for example, the architects concerned were instructed that no paper should be removed until a suitably qualified person had looked at it. As a result, the Manchester Local History Library was able to acquire, free, copies of leaflets and pocket timetables issued by the railway in the early 1950s, none of which were to be found in the existing collection.

## Publicity

In order to educate both the public and the staff of the library about the need for old material not to be thrown away, but passed to the local studies department, it is necessary to use all the means of publicity that are available. Not only should local newspapers be used, but also local radio, both BBC and commercial stations, and television. Sometimes, when a particularly important acquisition has been made, an article in the paper or on radio or television can be used to explain why the library is interested in certain types of material and to appeal for other items to be donated.

Exhibitions of the more unusual types of material in the library can also be used to draw the attention of the public to the fact that it is not only books and minor publications that are of interest, but that in the local studies field items of ephemera, newspapers, illustrations, etc., are equally important and valuable for those interested in the history of an area. Where the library has lent local material for an exhibition, it is good policy to ask that the library is acknowledged not only in any catalogue, but also on the caption or title to the item. This will help to draw people's attention to the fact that local collections are not only concerned with books and minor publications.

## Microform

Sometimes, when it is not possible to acquire the original of an item, means have to be adopted to acquire a copy which will do in its stead. The most usual way is either to acquire a photocopy, if it is not too long, or a microfilm. Local studies libraries have already acquired microfilms of census enumerators' returns, newspapers and parish registers and so they should not be afraid to acquire microfilms of books, pamphlets and other material which is required to make the collection as complete as possible. In order to obtain a microform copy, it is necessary to trace which library or institution has a suitable copy of the item or items for filming, although some materials may be available commercially.

## THE ACQUISITION OF CURRENT OR CONTEMPORARY MATERIAL

It is much more difficult to identify and trace current or contemporary local material; it involves a much greater use of an individual's time because there is no accurate way of establishing fully what is being produced. It is a problem that applies not only to books and minor publications, but also to all types of material which local studies libraries collect and preserve, such as illustrations, maps, newspapers, directories and ephemera.

Within the framework of its acquisitions policy, there must be a basic principle that the local studies collection will try and acquire as much as possible of the material that is published currently in order that gaps will not exist and that all possible angles of research by future users are covered. However, the staff time that can be devoted to acquisitions work is limited, bearing in mind that most local studies departments are under very severe pressure from the number of people using the department and its resources, that many of the readers need help to find what they are looking for and guidance as to other possible sources, and that often there are insufficient staff to man the department properly.

The acquisition of current material can be divided into two main approaches: the acquisition of that material which finds its way into national and other bibliographies and the acquisition of that material which does not, and therefore requires special efforts to ensure that the library is able to acquire it for its collection.

### The bibliographical approach

The bibliographical approach to the acquisition of local material is one which can be done in the library itself, using the bibliographical tools which are found in any library, such as the *British national bibliography* (BNB),

*British books in print* and the *Bookseller*. It involves checking the entries for those which might have local relevance and ordering them in the normal way.

There are, however, drawbacks to this method of ordering material. First, the entries may be published so late that the library has already acquired copies due to local demand, and, therefore, the bibliographical tools merely become a means of checking what the library may have missed.

Secondly, the national bibliographical tools do not cover all the material in which a local studies library is interested. The BNB is not exhaustive in its coverage even of books and minor publications and does not include ephemera or illustrations, except in book form. In addition to the selection which the editors of BNB must make, there are items in book and minor publication format which will never reach its pages simply because they are privately published and the person responsible for the publication does not know of the laws of legal deposit, with the result that copies are not even found in the national libraries or anywhere else except the local library. Some of the material might also fall into the borderline category and be excluded by the editors as not fitting the criteria of what they include in the BNB entries. For example, a history and guide to Christ Church, Moss Side, Manchester is merely a duplicated sheet folded, yet it is a minor publication in the sense that it is meant to be a book or pamphlet. It never reached the BNB because it was not submitted, but even if it had been, there is every likelihood that it would have been excluded as ephemera.

Thirdly, by the time some local items appear in the BNB and the other bibliographical tools, they may be out of print because entries tend to be slow in getting into such publications. If a local item is a limited run, it is possible that all copies will be sold out before the library orders. This will be especially true if the library refuses to order except when an item appears in the BNB. Fortunately, most local studies departments are able to order their material as soon as they become aware of its existence and not wait for the BNB or other book-ordering tools to include it.

The acquisition of local studies material using the usual bibliographical tools is, therefore, not ideal for current material because of the material excluded and the lateness of entries. They are useful for ensuring that all listed contemporary material, especially in peripheral areas, is noticed and acquired.

## Publishers' catalogues

Most publishers produce catalogues of forthcoming publications, and sometimes leaflets on particular books, so that advance orders can be made. Publishers' catalogues are often produced quarterly or annually, although some come out irregularly. It can be very useful to check these catalogues so that the department is aware of what is being published and when, although the date of publication may be very vague and publication dates may not be strictly adhered to.

It is not only the major publishers which issue catalogues of forthcoming publications, many small publishers also do so. It is often these small publishers who publish local items and their catalogues often include, as well as forthcoming works, a list of their previous publications. Both Hendon Publishing Company and the Willow Press, for example, produce lists of previous publications and forthcoming books and pamphlets, together with some information about new work, its price and approximate date of publication. This type of leaflet is very helpful to local studies departments as it enables checks to be made to see if anything has been missed and also orders to be placed in advance of a new book being published.

## Recent publication lists

Another useful source of information on what has been published in the local studies field is the lists of recent publications that local history and related journals publish. For example, the *Local historian*[8] publishes reviews and lists of publications received on a regular basis, whilst the *Urban history yearbook*[9] does so for a given year and includes lengthy reviews of some items received. Although a local studies department might have picked up those items of local interest from other sources, it is possible that some might have been missed. These lists of recent publications often include pamphlet material from a wide range of small and private publishers which are not picked up by the national bibliographical tools and may be unknown until they appear in such lists.

## Reviews

A very valuable source of information on what has been published locally in the form of books and pamphlets is the local newspaper and the local periodical press. Often local authors will send copies of their publications to local newspapers and journals in the hope that they will receive a mention and review. Sometimes, in addition to the review, there may be an article on the author or the organisation featured in the publication, or even serialisation of parts of the work. For example, a recent publication on the Moston district of Manchester [10] was referred to several times in the *Manchester evening news,* the most recent being to say that it had sold out and was being reprinted. It is very important to scan local newspapers carefully to ensure that references to new publications are not missed, especially those of local organisations such as churches or schools. Articles can also give a hint that something may be being prepared. For example, an article seeking information about a subject, or asking for old pupils of a school with memories to get in contact with someone, should alert the local studies librarian to the fact that a publication may be in the offing and the need to write to the person to find further information about what is proposed.

The checking of newspapers and periodical publications can be a tedious task, but one which should be done regularly. Most local studies collections either clip or index local newspapers and, therefore, it should not be too difficult to arrange for references to new publications to be collected and passed to the person responsible for ordering the stock for the department. With periodicals and magazines, the library may not check these so regularly (if at all) so it is necessary to institute some procedure to enable this to be done. As most local periodical publications do not appear weekly, but usually monthly, there should be no difficulty in quickly looking through them for any mention of a new item, whether it be a short history of the area or a new guide to the parish church.

In addition to local newspapers and periodicals, the national press or nationally circulated journals will sometimes include reviews of local items, especially if the subject is one which might have national interest. If the library takes this type of publication, such as *Economic history review* or *Agricultural history,* then they too should be checked, although they might be held by another department.

In order to ensure that as many local publications as possible are acquired, it is, therefore, necessary to check all the bibliographical aids which the library holds, as even the most unlikely source, e.g. HMSO lists and catalogues, may yield a useful item which has not been noticed elsewhere. The use of bibliographical tools for local studies acquisitions mainly relates to books and minor publications as other types of material are rarely covered in such works.

## Special means of acquiring material

Although bibliographical tools can be of assistance in tracing published material, what is recorded there is only a small proportion of the range of material in which local studies libraries and departments are interested. Books and pamphlets are relatively easy to trace but with some types of minor publication, illustrations, newspapers, local periodicals and serials, maps and ephemera, the situation is more difficult and special means of acquisition have to be employed. There is a great deal of local material that is published that is never recorded in the way that books and pamphlets are listed and so it has to be sought out.

In additon to trying to establish what has been produced, there is the added problem of ensuring that the machinery exists within the library system for not only acquiring this material, but also processing it so that it is available to the general public to use. Given the ideal situation, there should be someone whose sole responsibility it is to try and trace this material and acquire it for the library. However, as staff are never sufficient, it has to be fitted into the routine with other responsibilities. From the cost point of view, much of this material is either free or available for a very small charge so that the drain on tight financial resources is not great.

There are several ways in which the material which is not listed in any bibliographical work can be traced and acquired for the library. They do involve time and effort but result in a reasonable coverage of material that is currently produced and reduce the gaps that future generations of local studies librarians would have to try and fill.

### Educational activities

If members of the public are made fully aware of the wide range of material that is produced and in which the local studies library is interested, they may pass on material they are involved with the production of, or, if they are given or receive local material, pass it on to the library. Therefore as mentioned earlier, every opportunity should be taken to acquaint the public with the material in which the local studies library is interested.

Often local studies librarians are asked to give talks on various subjects to local societies and groups. If a title is not suggested, it is always possible to talk about some aspect of the stock of the library and attract people's interest that way. A talk on the ephemera of a particular area can result in members of the audience realising for the first time the value to research of such material and passing it over to the library. This was the case with a talk that was given on the ephemera of the North-West, when afterwards a member of the audience said that he had a copy of the menu for the centenary luncheon for the *Manchester guardian* and that he would let the speaker have it in the near future. Similarly, talks to school children, or their involvement in projects which result in the collection of material of local interest, can be of value, and result in resources being acquired which might not otherwise have been the case. The more who know about the library and the type of material which it collects, the better the chance of ensuring that the collection is as comprehensive as is possible, especially given the fact that a lot of the non-book material is very difficult to trace.

## Library staff

One very useful way of discovering what has been published and having it drawn to the attention of the local studies library is through the staff of the library service, not merely the staff of the local studies department. Often, staff in branch libraries hear about local publications or are asked to put out leaflets for the public to pick up or to display posters which are of local interest and which are not sent to the central library or to the local studies library. Where a book and pamphlet or other minor publication is concerned, and a financial transaction is required, the staff at a branch could possibly forward details of title, author, price and where it can be obtained from. In the case of leaflets, etc., it should be easy enough to organise a system whereby when leaflets are received for distribution, a copy is forwarded for the local collection. In the case of posters, these too could be passed on in the same way when they are finished with.

In addition to local material which libraries are asked to distribute or display, the staff themselves will receive a great deal through their letter-boxes at home. They should be encouraged to pass this on to the local studies library rather than throw it away when it is finished with. The big problem is trying to get the message across to the staff in the branch libraries that the local studies department is interested in this material. This can be overcome by the use of staff training. Most libraries have in-service training courses for new staff and refresher courses for the older, more long-serving members. The local studies department should take the opportunity when explaining about the department and its stock to talk about the way in which all members of staff can help to build up the collection. This can be reinforced by the occasional memo from the local studies department at certain times of the year. A good time is just before an election, when staff can be asked to bring in copies of local election material that they have received, as this will supplement that which is obtained directly from the candidates or their agents.

The type of material that can be obtained from staff in this way is mainly ephemera, although they too may pass on other material. Such items as free local newspapers circulating in a small area, which are difficult to know about, advertising literature from local firms, unsolicited material sent through the post, local leaflets advertising jumble sales or exhibitions and so on. The list is endless, but it is this type of material which it is difficult for a centralised local studies department to collect, especially in a large area.

A further way in which the staff can assist in the collection and acquisition of material, especially ephemera, is by collecting material which is left for members of the public to pick up in public places such as information bureaux, railway and bus stations, information kiosks and shopping centres. It should be part of the duties of the staff of a local studies collection to visit these places regularly to ensure that nothing new has been put on display. This may appear to be time-consuming on the surface, but very often members of staff pass through bus or railway stations, information kiosks or shopping centres either on their way to and from work or at lunch time and could easily collect such material. The important thing to remember is that all the potential places where material is displayed are visited at some time or another. Once the initial collection of material is made, it is likely that only a relatively few items will be obtained on subsequent visits, although when railway and bus timetables change there may be a sudden rise in the number of items acquired in this manner.

The type of material that can be acquired by this method includes pocket timetables, leaflets for excursions, leaflets for local places of entertainment including both amateur and professional productions, sports events, information on local places of interest, guides to shopping centres, society programmes and so on. The more that can be acquired from such places, the greater the comprehensiveness of the collection and the more complete the picture of life at a given point of time.

Sometimes, in a large district or authority, a branch library may wish to build up a collection of local material. This is to be encouraged as in addition it will make the staff aware of the type of material local collections are interested in. However, the collection of material at a very local level should not be to the detriment of the main local collection covering the whole of the local authority area. In the case of currently available material, an extra copy should be taken for the branch library's own collection, but unique material should be forwarded and housed centrally and a photocopy placed locally, as the risk of loss or destruction at a local library is possibly greater than it is at the central local studies collection. Once again matters of collection policy are involved here and the decisions taken will obviously be affected by the structure and organisation of the library service within individual local authorities.

## Bookshops and newsagents

It is worth looking round local bookshops and newsagents from time to time to see if they have material of a local interest which has not been discovered from one of the more usual sources. For example, the local newsagent may well have programmes for the local church or school fete which may contain useful information on the church or school as well as local advertisements.

Newsagents can also be useful when it comes to special issues of newspapers. These may not be included in the library's subscription and are either advertised within the paper itself or on the newsagent's and newspaper seller's bill-boards. Such items can often be overlooked if the library does not keep abreast of what the local newspaper is doing. If it is possible that one has been missed, a newsagent may have one or two left on display and thus a gap can be filled. In many cases, the items which are found in local bookshops and newsagents, and which have not been acquired by other means, only cost a few pence and can usually be paid for out of the petty cash, provided a receipt is obtained. This cuts out the usual ordering procedure and ensures that the library obtains its copy.

## Local authority publishing

Local authorities are major publishers in their own right, but few are fully conversant with the laws of legal deposit and even less aware of the need to ensure that copies of their publications go to the local library. Major publications may be sent, but often not leaflets, pamphlets and the like and it is only as a result of a request for an item by a member of the public or an article in the paper that it is drawn to the library's attention. The major problem is to try and discover what each department has produced and then to try to obtain a copy from the publishing department. In many cases, the publishing department does not think that the library would be interested in the publication, whereas the opposite is the case. When the Manchester Ship Canal Steering Committee published a pamphlet on the canal,[11] which was intended to encourage public discussion on the future of the waterway, copies were sent to local industry and commerce, local authorities, trade unions, and other local interested parties, but none was sent to the local libraries, until it was pointed out that the aims of the committee would receive wider publicity among the public at large if it was available in public libraries. As a result, copies were sent out to libraries, including local studies departments. Very often the publishing department may not keep spare copies, or only a single copy, and if it gets lost, they turn to the local library and then express surprise that it has not got a copy.

It is with minor publications and ephemera that the main difficulties lie, as it is this material, rather than the lengthy detailed reports that are published and are acquired, which is often overlooked. Therefore, it is a question of educating the staff of the various local authority departments into thinking of the library as a place to automatically send material. Sometimes material reaches the library because there is a member of staff in the publishing department interested in local studies, but this is not entirely satisfactory as that person may leave or may not be fully conversant with what other sections of the department are producing. There are three ways in which this problem might be overcome.

The first, and probably the most satisfactory, way is to encourage the council to make it a standing order that one or two copies of everything that the local authority prints, whether it be a leaflet, report, pamphlet, or public notice, is collected centrally and passed on at regular intervals to the library for inclusion in the local studies collection. One way this can be done is to encourage a councillor to ask questions of the various departments or in council so that the whole issue is looked at in depth. This happened at Edinburgh and resulted in local material being collected and passed to the library under the terms of a council resolution.

The second approach is for the head of the libraries department to write to the heads of other departments asking for their co-operation in obtaining material and allowing the local studies department to make the necessary arrangements. Material could be accumulated in a centralised place in each department and collected at regular intervals. This could be done through the producing department's administration section. When invoices for printing are received and payment authorised, the administration department could insist that one or two copies of the printed item are included with the invoice and then put them out for collection by the library. This should, theoretically, ensure that all items are received, particularly if the administration department refuses to accept invoices that have been authorised for payment unless they are accompanied by copies of the printed matter.

A third alternative is possible where all the authority's printing is done in house. Provided that the heads of the other departments agree, copies of all items that are produced could be collected centrally and arrangements made to pick up the material at regular intervals, possibly weekly or fortnightly, so that the amount is not too great and can be dealt with in the library and does not clutter up the printing department. This method, coupled with a council resolution that the library should have a copy of everything produced, should result in an almost complete coverage of the local authority's publications, although it might be necessary to have a safeguard such as the invoice suggestion made above to cover items which might be sent to outside printers.

## The library

As mentioned earlier, the library itself often displays many leaflets and posters. The latter may require some means of internal organisation before the local collection gets those of local interest. This involves arrangement with those departments which have notice boards to take down those posters which are out of date and pass them to the local studies department, which will then decide what is relevant and what is not. For example, a procedure was established in Manchester Central Library in the early 1970s whereby the Technical Library, which had the main display area for notices in the building, passed on all the out-of-date posters and notices to the Local History Library for the local collection. Where they were not of local interest, the material was passed to the arts library or was discarded. The final decision as to what to retain and what to discard or pass on was taken by the Local History Department staff on the grounds they were in the best position to decide what was local and worth preserving and what was not. As a result, items which otherwise would have been missing from the collection were acquired without any great difficulty and at no expense, except for that of staff time.

## Handouts

Walk down any street in the centre of a town or city and there is a strong possibility that there will be someone or some organisation trying to give pedestrians leaflets or free newspapers. If this is the case, copies should be collected by the staff of the library and added to the local collection even if their local connection is tenuous. For example, in 1976 there was a group handing out material in Manchester on the Cyprus situation. This may not have appeared to be of local significance yet it did show what was being distributed in Manchester by those concerned with the issue and as such the material should be added to the local collection.

## Circular letter

A major way of acquiring material is by means of a circular letter addressed to organisations and sometimes to individuals asking them to donate or let the library know of material that they are publishing. For example, Manchester Local History Library writes to all the candidates before an election asking for copies of their election material. The response varies between different parties, but overall a fairly good coverage is achieved, as most candidates and political parties are aware of the historical importance of election literature.

To acquire material by means of a circular letter requires considerable organisation and a decision to approach various types of organisation according to a predetermined plan. For example, it might be decided to approach all the churches in an area to ask for copies of parish magazines. In many cases copies will be donated, but there are always those who will seek payment. Records have to be kept of those approached, their response and when material is received, so that if the copies fail to arrive they can be chased up. It must also be remembered that the library might already receive copies of this material and a check should be made before bodies are approached. Other types of material that might benefit from such approaches are schools for their magazines, societies for their newsletters and firms for copies of their house journals and advertising literature, including estate agents and their literature. When seeking material through a circular letter, it is often a good idea to explain why the library is interested in acquiring copies for preservation, especially if the organisation approached is what might be described as a 'fringe' one which may be suspicious of authority and local or central government organisations.

The response from organisations approached by circular letter can be very patchy, depending on the attitude of the person receiving the letter. Sometimes it will be thrown away while on other occasions large amounts of material will be forthcoming. Where there is no response, a reminder might be sent after a time in the hope that the material will be supplied.

## Donations

Another source of acquiring material that is current is through donations. Most local studies librarians know when they have readers working on a particular subject, whether with a view to publication or not, and it is often worth while suggesting that they might consider donating a copy of the book, pamphlet, thesis, project or notes to the collection as a sort of 'thank you' for the assistance of the library and its staff. Even if a copy is not forthcoming, it is helpful to know that a book or pamphlet is being prepared so that an eye can be kept out for its appearance in the shops and booklists.

## Commissions and the creation of material

Although libraries rarely commission books and pamphlets, there are areas where libraries are active in commissioning new work or even creating new material themselves. Sometimes, it might be decided that the local collection requires a photographic survey of a particular area or subject. It may be that the local studies staff have to take the photographs themselves, but it might also involve the active co-operation of a local photographic society or a professional photographer. If these latter methods are involved, it will involve a cost greater than just the cost of film and processing. Where a commercial photographer is involved, the charges will normally be those charged to the general public, although it might be possible to negotiate a special price. In the case of local photographic societies, those taking part will want their expenses covered. In all cases, it is necessary to ensure that what is required is photographed and that the resultant prints are processed to archival standards. A good example of the co-operation between a local studies library and an amateur society is afforded by that of Manchester's Local History Library and Manchester Amateur Photographic Society. This co-operation resulted in the library building up a fine record of the City of Manchester between the early 1950s and mid-1970s. To achieve coverage on such a scale, it is necesary to have

206

a specific budget to work to and an awareness of gaps in the library's holdings.

Another field where outside individuals might be commissioned to undertake work for the library is in the field of oral history, an area in which many libraries are now becoming involved. Although library staff may undertake recording of people and events, it is time-consuming and often outside individuals, or schemes using the unemployed, undertake the work. Whichever method is used, there will be a capital outlay for equipment. The result, however, should be to enhance the collection and the material which is available to researchers. As with photographic surveys, it is necessary to ensure that a specific plan is carefully drawn up so that those individuals who are the oldest in the community and who have the most vivid memories of events and places are covered first.

Sometimes, the library itself creates new material on the locality. Many local studies libraries have become involved with publishing material from their collections. Sometimes this is in the form of postcards or books of old photographs, sometimes it consists of maps of the locality or broadsheets which might have a popular appeal. It is very easy to forget to add such material to the permanent collection when it is published, but it is important to ensure that copies are treated as new items, even if a reprint of older material, so that the collection is as comprehensive as possible for all editions of local publications. The same also applies if the library asks an outside person to write something which used library material. It is surprising how much local material published by libraries, as well as more general library publications, is overlooked and fails to reach the local collection.

## Local radio

There are many local radio stations in the country producing a wide variety of news and educational programmes whose content will be of local interest. In some cases, the material is destroyed, thus losing a valuable source of information. In other cases, however, the local radio station will be prepared to let the library have copies or the original tapes of material, provided certain guarantees are given regarding copyright. If an approach is made by the local radio station to the library about taking such material, it should never be turned down. Alternatively, the library itself could approach the radio station and make suggestions about its material.

## Maps

Although tracing and purchase of maps may appear to be straightforward from the point of view of those issued by the Ordnance Survey, there are increasing problems due to the fact that they are becoming computerised and instead of new editions being issued at intervals, individual sheets are updated when there have been a certain number of units of change. Thus, it can be very difficult to keep track of the changes that take place and the resultant issue of sheets. Usually, arrangements are made with the local Ordnance Survey stockists to supply copies of all new maps they receive. It is, however, useful to keep in contact with the local engineers' department or planning office, as they may have copies of interim updates which are not available to the public or which have been prepared for their own use. Again it is a question of establishing a contact and ensuring that it is maintained.

## Newspapers

In addition to the regular newspapers that are published, there is also, as has been mentioned before, a large number of free, local newspapers issued. Wherever possible the publishers should be contacted and asked to send copies to the library. It should be stressed that it is not the one edition that is required, but copies of all editions if the content varies according to the area in which it circulates. The problem is trying to discover what is produced and by whom. As noted earlier, it is often necesary to rely on members of the staff to draw the local studies department's attention to the existence of such a publication.

## THE MECHANICS OF ACQUISITION

Although various methods can be used to acquire material, within the system itself there should be a means of ordering and checking what has been received and what has not. In many libraries, the acquisition of material is through a centralised system with orders and requests for material having to be submitted to an ordering department. This takes much of the work off the local studies department itself in having to acquire books and deal with the resultant paper work. However, there should be a mechanism within such a system whereby urgent orders for local material, especially

208

that from second-hand lists, is dealt with quickly. Wherever possible local studies departments should make full use of any centralised system of ordering or periodicals administration. For example, if an arrangement is made for a church to send its parish magazine regularly, and the library has a centralised system of periodical control, the arrangement should be reported to this section who can then keep track of material that has and has not been received and follow up items when necessary.

For non-book material, it is often the local studies department itself that is responsible for acquiring material for its collection. This might involve delegating the responsibility for acquiring certain types of material to various members of staff. This may also be the case where no centralised system exists for dealing with periodicals which are donated. In the latter case, a card containing the title, frequency of issue, contact and year should be made out with a grid system for marking off when copies are received. This should be checked at regular intervals to ensure that all items have been received and if not, followed up with a letter.

## CONCLUSION

The aim of acquiring material for a local studies library or department should be to ensure that, working within its collection policy, as much material as possible is collected and preserved for those interested in a specific area and its community. It involves the use of a wide range of methods of acquisition as no one method will ensure that all the material that is available is acquired. Each district or area within a library system should be responsible for ensuring that the material on that area is acquired, as it is no use relying on other authorities or areas to acquire material on its behalf, unless some specific arrangements have been made to that effect. It is essential for a local studies librarian to be prepared to go out and use unusual methods to ensure that all the relevant material is acquired. A librarian who expects to acquire material merely utilising bibliographical tools will build up a collection with many gaps which may not be apparent at present, but will be so in the future. The local studies librarian should not try to limit what types of material are acquired because no one knows what will be of interest or in demand in the future, and should resist attempts which may be made to prevent the acquisition of some types of material with a particular view which do not agree with that of the controlling committee. The acquisition policy of the local studies library should be clearly spelt out in order to guide the collection of that which relates to the area and the activities that go on within it, in the past, present and future.

## NOTES

1. Lancashire Library. *Standards of provision for local studies: report and policy statement.* Preston, Lancashire Library, 1981, p. 5.
2. Nichols, H. *Local studies librarianship.* London, Bingley, 1979, p. 10.
3. Nichols, p. 14.
4. Lancashire Library, pp. 11-12.
5. Makepeace, C.E. *Ephemera.* Aldershot, Gower, 1985, p. 10.
6. Higgens, G.L. *Printed reference material.* London, Library Association, 1984. Chapter 14, pp. 385-422.
7. Now the Greater Manchester Museum of Science and Industry.
8. The *Local historian* (formerly the *Amateur historian*), quarterly, British Association for Local History, 1952-.
9. *Urban history yearbook.* Leicester University Press, 1974-.
10. Seale, B. *The Moston story.* Moston, the author, 1984.
11. Manchester Ship Canal Steering Committee. *Manchester Ship Canal: the way forward.* Manchester, Greater Manchester Council for the Manchester Ship Canal Steering Committee, 1985.

## FURTHER READING

Hobbs, J.L. *Local history and the library.* 2nd edition revised by G.A. Carter, London, Deutsch, 1973, pp. 43-70.
Petty, M. The albatros inheritance: local studies libraries. *Library management* 6 (1) 1985, pp. 25-30.
Sippings, G.M., *Local history materials in public libraries: the framework for an acquisitions policy.* M. Lib dissertation, University of Wales, College of Librarianship Wales, 1986.

# 11

# Cataloguing and classification

John Chandler

Whatever else it may be - antiquarian repository or contemporary archive - the local studies library is at heart a pool of information which must earn its keep, on shelf and in cabinet, in the same way as any other department of a library system. It should be capable of responding with a prompt, accurate and comprehensive reply to any enquiry which falls within its specialisation. Its performance should not, and need not, be inferior to, for example, a medical library on which a life may depend, or the technical library of a multinational company. There is no shortage of textbooks to explain in general terms the techniques of successful information retrieval; this chapter is concerned solely with the special problems and possibilities which the local studies library presents.

## CONSTRAINTS

Any policy for local studies cataloguing and classification is likely to be compromised by two factors beyond the policy-framer's control. These may be labelled interdependence and inertia.

Interdependence affects the local studies library in various ways. Most collections form part of a larger organisation, usually a county, district or borough library authority. With the advent of computerised acquisition and cataloguing procedures administered centrally in most authorities it is becoming less frequent for the local studies librarian to be the creator of his own catalogue. To abandon this role runs contrary to the recommendations of some earlier writers on the subject,[1] and the implications are discussed below. Automated centralised cataloguing tends towards a uniform level and method of cataloguing and a single, union catalogue (other factors permitting) to the authority's entire stock. The local studies librarian must consider his cataloguing needs very carefully, therefore, since he will have to justify with cogent arguments any plea for special treatment.

Mention of a union catalogue raises another problem of interdependence: What constitutes an authority's local studies library? One effect of local government reorganisations has been to bring under a single umbrella (and potentially into a single catalogue) any number of overlapping local studies libraries, each reflecting the different acquisition, cataloguing and classification policies adopted by the defunct authority from which it was inherited. Such amalgamation involves not only reference stock on the hallowed shelves of the traditional local collections but also lending copies which may be scattered in 50 or more service points. The extent to which such disparate collections should be co-ordinated is a question which will not be decided on local studies considerations alone.

Leaving interdependence on one side, inertia is perhaps the most potent force limiting progress in local studies cataloguing and classification. By their nature local studies libraries cannot be self-renewing and so any change in processing should ultimately be applied not only to accessions but also retrospectively to the existing stock. Local studies libraries are rarely overstaffed; there is an understandable reluctance, therefore, to embark on any project which requires the recataloguing and rearrangement of the entire library, even though maintenance of old card catalogues, to use a common example, long after the authority has installed a computer, may mean that all new local studies items are catalogued twice. Likewise a post-1974 county library service, successor to a dozen independent authorities, may find itself classifying the same new book in twelve different ways. Inertia and interdependence, therefore, are likely to temper any innovation which the local studies librarian may think desirable; they must underlie most of the discussion which follows.

## THE TRADITIONAL CATALOGUE

Until very recent years the card catalogue has been the accepted medium for local studies cataloguing. Consequently very few local studies libraries (Durham's sheaf catalogue is an exception) do not rely to a greater or lesser extent on catalogue cards. Such catalogues may be used to supplement earlier printed catalogues (as at Belfast and Bristol), although they are more commonly intended to suffice by themselves. Vigorous enhancement of a card catalogue may lead to rapid growth, such as a twenty-fold increase at Cambridge between 1966 and 1981.[2] Card catalogues are reasonably well suited to the concept of a single, centralised local collection, such as those developed in municipalities before reorganisation. They are positioned alongside, and form an integral part of, the collections they describe. In the context of county or region, possessing several or many local collections scattered at various locations, the unique nature of a card catalogue is a serious drawback. This problem of dissemination may be tackled by publishing the catalogue in microform so that it acts as a comprehensive county bibliography (as in Cambridgeshire) or as an annual cumulating catalogue of local material acquired after a given date (Nottinghamshire). The maintenance of card catalogues may rest with the staff of the local studies library, whereas all other processing is undertaken by a centralised cataloguing department (as in Dorset, Essex and Norfolk). This may lead to duplication of effort.

The arrangement of a card catalogue, as inherited by the local studies librarian, will have been the result of a now long-forgotten debate about the merits of dictionary versus classified catalogue, and it would be inappropriate to rehearse the arguments here. A questionnaire in 1970 revealed that rather more than one-third of local catalogues were dictionary catalogues,[3] but an informal circular suggests that in 1984 the proportion was much smaller (only eight out of more than fifty responses mentioned dictionary catalogues). A few authorities appear to have rejected both the traditional arrangements, either under the influence of related disciplines such as archives (e.g. Borders), or by concentrating on an index (Brent). It is possible that in some libraries computerised retrieval methods will overshadow the traditional catalogue as a finding aid; the inadequacies of an inherited catalogue will be side-stepped rather than remedied.

The special qualities of a local studies library and the demands put upon it have often been appealed to as justification for more detailed cataloguing than required by other departments of the public library. In consequence many local studies catalogues contain a high proportion of analytical entries as well as providing detailed bibliographical descriptions for a wide range of materials. Detailed cataloguing of local studies material is designed to overcome problems shared with three other disciplines - special, multi-media and rare book librarianship.

In its role as a special library the local collection's comprehensive stock must be capable of being exploited to the full by, or on behalf of, a wide cross-section of the public sharing a common interest. The catalogue is, of course, one of the ways in which this goal may be achieved. Analytical cataloguing will always be necessary to draw attention, for instance, to one in a volume of essays, or for the parishes covered by Victoria County Histories. But the amount of staff time spent on refining the catalogue will depend on whether or not it is projected as the single point of access to the entire stock, and this will be a matter of personal preference and tradition. Some of the information which might be included in the catalogue could instead be assigned to discrete indexes. It is of course a trait of special libraries to compile *ad hoc* indexes on the basis of the readers' requirements, and in many cases this may be a more efficient response than analytical cataloguing *ad nauseam,* aimed at satisfying never-asked and never-likely-to-be-asked enquiries.

As a multi-media library the local collection has a long history. The need to provide catalogues to material in a variety of forms, such as maps, serials, images, microforms and sound recordings, at a time when other departments of a library service had little experience of them, created problems for the cataloguer. But as other branches of librarianship have caught up so the problems have diminished. It may well be that some media are best described by separate catalogues or indexes but it is now perfectly possible to catalogue them altogether. This was becoming apparent when Nichols wrote in 1979,[4] and since the adoption by the British Library of the revised Anglo-American Cataloguing Rules (AACR2) in 1981, which incorporates the International Standard Bibliographical Description for Non-Book Materials, virtually everything in a local studies library may, if required, be catalogued according to internationally prescribed rules. Diversity of form need no longer present problems.

There remains the rare book aspect of local studies librarianship, for which AACR2 may be less than ideal.[5] The cataloguing problems encountered when dealing with rare materials are of two kinds - those bound up with the obscurity of the material itself, and those anticipating the special uses to which the material will be put. The former category includes anonymous and pseudonymous works, works describing a deliberately unnamed or re-named locality and its inhabitants, and undated works. Whereas a centralised cataloguing department may cope with such problems when the solutions can be easily found in reference works, a rare, perhaps unique, item in a local studies library will normally call on the knowledge and ingenuity of its specialist staff. It is, of course, important for the users of such material that this information be supplied wherever possible[6] and it is therefore essential that, where the local studies librarian is not master of his own catalogue, he maintains close links with the cataloguers and assists them with problem material.

For the special uses to which rare material in local collections may be put by researchers for whom the information contained about the locality is not paramount, an empirical approach has been suggested.[7] Interest may be in the literary output of a local author, the work of a locally based private press or a genre such as broadsides or playbills. The form and arrangement of catalogues - published, card or computer database - and the level of description for such items should be appropriate to the needs of the potential users; such special catalogues, of course, should be in addition to the normal cataloguing procedures, and rare works should also appear in the library's main catalogue, described according to AACR2 or whatever code is in use, and classified so that their local studies content will not be neglected.

## THE CATALOGUING DILEMMA

The foregoing discussion has attempted to pinpoint some of the principles and problems enshrined in traditional local studies cataloguing, so that they may be applied to the current dilemma facing the local studies librarian. The dilemma centres on our response to what must be seen as the two most important developments in British public librarianship of our generation - the reorganisation of library authorities (outside London) in 1974/1975 and the introduction of computerised systems into many areas of library economy. The two developments are related because they jointly conspire to impose conformity on the local studies librarian, both in the way he carries out routines within his own library and in the way he regards collections outside. It will be the contention of the following paragraphs that, despite the loss of autonomy, these developments are to be welcomed.

Although computers have been used in libraries for more than 20 years, and 'the use of computer-based systems in libraries . . . is no longer a controversial issue'[8] little has appeared in print about their specific application to local studies cataloguing. The student text by Nichols, published in 1979, has no index entry for computers, and their possible use in cataloguing is only mentioned in passing.[9] A weekend school on 'Local studies and the new technology', held in 1983, although useful in other ways, included no speaker on cataloguing implications.[10] Apart from one published description of a system,[11] local studies librarians have been left to work out their own responses to the revolution in computer cataloguing, and it will be helpful to describe a few of their initiatives.

In West Sussex computer cataloguing was extended to the county's three main local collections in 1977, having been in regular operation in lending libraries since 1973.[12] The local studies catalogue was produced separately from the main library catalogue, so as to permit fuller descriptions, analyticals and a different, incompatible, form of headings. With these modifications the suite of cataloguing programs was the same as for the main catalogue, and copies were distributed to all libraries, although lending copies of local studies titles appeared on the main, not the local, catalogue. Retrospective conversion of the three manual card catalogues was proposed, but had not begun in 1979.

Leicestershire's centralised cataloguing department catalogues local studies material in the same way as ordinary non-fiction stock and it appears on the microfiche library catalogue; but the computerised catalogue record includes a specific field for local studies items resulting in a separate listing near the beginning of the classified catalogue. Some further indexing on cards is carried out in particular libraries to suit local requirements.

Clwyd inherited from Flintshire a computer catalogue of the local collection at Mold, copies of which were also held in each branch of the former authority.[13] Details of local studies items, including serials and oral history recordings, with locations, now appear on the county microfiche catalogue, collocated at the end of the classified sequence by prefixing 999.1 to the numerical local classification scheme.

Somerset and Wiltshire are both (in late 1984) in the process of adding catalogue records to different computer systems, permitting on-line access in larger branches to the entire holdings of the respective counties, and microfiche catalogues elsewhere. In both cases local studies items are catalogued in the same way as non-fiction lending stock, and the catalogues include details of the number of copies at individual locations. Retrospective conversion of manual files in Wiltshire is by no means complete, and some early conversion work using Manpower Services Commission labour has not been entirely satisfactory. Reclassification of all local studies material in Wiltshire is accompanying recataloguing.

Any discussion of the merits of particular brands of hardware at this point would guarantee immediate obsolescence, so swift is the pace of the new technology. Until the computer age settles down, works of this kind must content themselves with principles and desiderata. It may be helpful to analyse the uses for which a local studies catalogue might be designed, in a perfect technological world untroubled by considerations of cost and compilation time.

The librarian may serve the actual or potential local historian in three ways: by advising him, if he needs advice, on historical methodology; by retrieving for him, or enabling him to retrieve for himself, all pertinent material in the library; and by referring him to other agencies - libraries, record offices, museums - which can supply him with relevant sources of information not in the library. The first of these, reader's advice, necessary (and how!) although it may be, is not the function of the catalogue. The catalogue should not try to explain that pollbooks are useful for the study of elections, that inns are listed in trade directories, or that a certain village lay in a certain rural district. It is the job of the librarian as reader's adviser to explain to the researcher, in person or in print, how various categories of local studies materials may be used, and what sources exist to answer various types of enquiry. His introduction to such sources must include a description of any locally produced indexes, finding aids and catalogues of special categories of material which may be useful, but these should not be incorporated wholesale into the main library catalogue.

The catalogue should, however, assist the librarian to carry out his second (retrieval) and third (referral) functions. Having taken the librarian's advice the researcher now needs to know from the library catalogue what specific items exist, how useful they are likely to be to his enquiry (by virtue of age, length or medium), in which library and at what point on the shelves they are to be found, and whether he will be able to take them home. If the library's database can concisely but comprehensively give him all this information the researcher is not concerned whether it is a catalogue or a bibliography - for in a perfect world it will be both.

In a less than perfect world local studies librarians must weigh this ideal against realities of time, money and existing catalogues. A long-established card catalogue may approach this ideal, although it will probably not describe other libraries' holdings nor itself be available in other libraries. When the parent authority computerises its lending stock new titles will have to be catalogued twice if the card catalogue is to be maintained. Even so, local circumstances may dictate that what staff time is available may most usefully be employed in indexing specific categories of material rather than in converting existing catalogues. Camden, Dorset and Kent (Maidstone) are examples of authorities which retain card catalogues but are currently experimenting with microcomputer indexing applications for specific projects.

Creation and enhancement of other methods of retrieval may, as suggested earlier, lower the status of the catalogue by acting as a substitute for it.

But for those willing to computerise their catalogue the rewards are considerable for both user and librarian. To satisfy our ideal the catalogue should include the authority's entire holdings of local studies items, reference or lending, with locations; it should give sufficient description to indicate to the user an item's likely usefulness and to distinguish a specific issue of a work from all others; and it should be available in all the authority's service points, and perhaps in related agencies, such as the local record office and the libraries of neighbouring authorities. So far as is possible a union catalogue of this kind satisfies the referral function of the local studies library in addition to the retrieval function. In the context of a rural county this is particularly beneficial to the researcher because it enables the village historian to find out from his local library not only what is available locally or through the request service, but also what rarer or more specialist works about his village may be worth seeking in the local studies library 40 miles away. It is also a boon to the researcher who is studying a particular aspect of the history of a whole county or larger area, and who may therefore need to visit in turn all the relevant local studies libraries. For these reasons alone we must reject emphatically one view expressed in 1978 by a county librarian: 'To consider the harmonisation of cataloguing, classification and treatment over such a widely spread area, where all the collections, bar one, were very localised, was just a waste of time.'[14]

But the production of a computerised union catalogue of local studies material alongside, or incorporated into, the authority's main catalogue, carries advantages for the staff as well as the public. If proper liaison exists between the local studies librarian and the centralised cataloguing department, there is no reason at all why local studies cataloguing (apart from the creation of catalogues and indexes to special materials) should not be carried out centrally, thus eliminating pointless duplication (even triplication and multiplication) of effort. A union catalogue is also likely to throw out a few surprises: a lending copy of a rare Victorian pamphlet inexplicably and neglectedly lurking in the store of a small branch library; two copies of an early directory in one local studies library and none in another; a new church guide held in multiple copies at the local library on the clandestine initiative of the librarian, who has omitted to inform the local studies library of its existence. Anomalies are not only identified by these means, but can be speedily rectified and the relocation of stock amended in catalogue records at the press of a key.

218

If it be accepted that, despite the constraints, a computer catalogue along the lines described should and eventually will become normal in the local studies library, then two further developments become possible which could not only mark a dramatic improvement in the service that the local studies librarian is able to provide, but might also raise the status and practice of local history itself.

First there is the prospect of custom-made bibliographies on demand. If the database includes records of not only the entire monographic stock of a comprehensive collection, but also each component of all relevant serials, and certain categories of non-book materials, it becomes to all intents and purposes a bibliography - a bibliography, furthermore, which is continuously updated. And if, through an appropriate classification scheme or some other means of searching, all records relating to a place or subject may be retrieved and printed, then every researcher can be provided with an instantaneous place or subject bibliography tailored to his precise research needs.

Second is the even more exciting possibility that local studies libraries in co-operation may work towards a national database of local studies material. In one specialised field of great relevance to local studies - the Eighteenth Century Short Title Catalogue Project - this is already being realised.[15] The York University Local Bibliographic Project, which commenced in 1983, is seeking to secure funds which will enable it to hold on computer, 'a national data-base of printed publications in local studies . . . and eventually to provide a commercial on-line information service in the subjects and materials included'.[16] It is clearly a matter of the greatest importance to local studies that, whether or not this project proceeds, some means is found of co-ordinating at a national level access to the computerised records which all local studies libraries, record offices and museums will, eventually, find themselves using.

## WHY CLASSIFY?

After the rigours of cataloguing, the librarian's fancy lightly turns to thoughts of classification. The tradition is maintained in this account, but before comparing and evaluating different classification schemes it is important to be clear about the role of classification in the local studies library, and aware of the arguments against its perpetuation.

The most telling argument against classification is perhaps that it is a librarian's obsession not shared by other local studies professionals - archivists and, to a lesser extent, curators. The sanctity of the archive group imposes on a record office an arrangement by origin rather than by subject; successful retrieval is achieved by a combination of reader's advice (not only on the part of the archivist, but also in the form of textbooks on the use of primary source materials) and indexing, both of record office catalogues and of specific categories of records themselves. Recent developments in museum cataloguing propounded by the Museum Documentation Association are similarly shying away from classification (other than a basic form distinction) towards automated post-co-ordinate indexing. Indeed much of the information contained in the local studies library - in the form of periodical articles, for instance - does not rely on classification for its shelf arrangement, and is normally retrieved through an index, a subject bibliography or analytical cataloguing.

Classification as a means of subject retrieval can only dwindle in importance as automated searching and indexing techniques become more sophisticated. A degree of classification is needed, of course, to underpin any thesaurus of indexing terms, but the various conventional enumerated schemes in use throughout local studies librarianship were not in general conceived as adjuncts to keyword searching and so do not necessarily perform this role satisfactorily. Especially in the case of an authority which has inherited several idiosyncratic local classification schemes from its predecessors, exigencies of time and cost may decide against reclassification, preferring to see obsolete schemes die, so that resources can be channelled into other retrieval methods.

But before condemning classification to its fate a number of arguments should be put in its favour. Classification schemes are generally used also for shelf arrangement. Clearly some consistent shelf arrangement - whether alphabetically by author, by date of accession or classified by subject - is essential if anything is to be retrieved; inertia dictates, therefore, that it is easiest to continue the existing arrangement, which in most cases is according to a subject classification. The fact that classmarks are probably in use for shelf arrangement in other departments of the library (albeit constructed according to a more or less different scheme) further militates against their abandonment in the local studies library.

Inertia is hardly sufficient justification, however, for continuing to employ a classification scheme, and it would certainly not justify reclassification of material nor the practice of training potential local studies librarians to devise new classification schemes.[17] Retrieval considerations aside, the classmark shelf arrangement's great merit is that it allows staff and, where possible public, to browse. It may be hard to quantify, but the value of browsing to the contemplative historian is immense. In local history, where the predominant interest of researcher and classification scheme is more often than not the locality (of which more presently), the provision of all works about a town or village rubbing shoulders must be a source of continual gratification and discovery.

## LOCAL CLASSIFICATION SCHEMES

Having tried to justify, on emotional and practical grounds rather than by any scientific proof, the employment of a classification scheme in the local studies library, it is appropriate that the various schemes currently in use are discussed so that an assessment can be made of what is needed in a local classification scheme.

Local studies libraries in Britain, we have noted, are generally part of a public library authority; and every British public library authority, with one exception, uses the Dewey Decimal Classification - hereafter DC.[18] It is hardly surprising, therefore, that a survey in 1970[19] revealed that two-thirds of local studies libraries in Britain were at that date using DC, more or less modified to local circumstances. The remainder were using either schemes of their own creation, or published general or local classification schemes. It will be helpful to examine and evaluate each category, bearing in mind the tendency of local studies enquiries to be concerned with individual places.

Taking published schemes (other than DC) first, three general classification schemes call for comment. J.D. Brown's Subject Classification (SC), in use in eight libraries in 1970, and still used in two at least - Margate and Canterbury - allocates three figures 000-999 in the vacant class Y to denote places, which are then subdivided using categorical subject tables. The last edition of SC appeared in 1939, and Margate's local adaptation was published in 1934. All general and most local studies libraries seem now to have rejected SC.

The one British public library service not using DC for its general stock is Edinburgh, whose advocacy of the Library of Congress Classification (LC) extends to the Edinburgh Room and Edinburgh's Scottish Library. Vacant LC classes X and Y are used for Scotland and Edinburgh respectively, usually prefixed to other LC subject classes (thus XL = education in Scotland). The history and topography of Edinburgh, however, has its own schedules within the class YDA, using a notation based on a gridded map of the city. Using Cutter numbers as a suffix great specificity can be achieved, coupled with hospitality to include streets and buildings created since the scheme was devised (thus YDA 2376 A13 denotes the A.B.C. Film Centre in Fountainbridge). Cutter numbers are also used to give specificity in other classes (thus YLF 1135 G34 denotes 'the story of St. George's School, Edinburgh'). From this it is apparent that LC can be used to classify with great precision throughout the universe of subjects and topographical areas. The combination of places and subjects would seem to present more problems, and this, coupled with its lack of mnemonic notation and most public librarians' unfamiliarity with LC, makes it unlikely that other authorities will follow Edinburgh's example.

At least two authorities, South Glamorgan (Cardiff) and Dorset (Dorchester), are now classifying local material by the Universal Decimal Classification (UDC), although no user of this scheme was discovered in the 1970 survey referred to above. In both libraries the UDC notation is prefixed by an area code, and in the case of Dorset the parish name is added as well on the catalogue, although disregarded for shelving purposes. Dorset's important collections of local authors are also classified by UDC, the author's surname and first Christian name appearing in the classmark in full. UDC allows works to be classified with great precision, the faceted scheme coping well with complex subjects, and in Cardiff it is used with satisfactory results for cataloguing newspaper and periodical articles in addition to the bookstock. This advantage must be weighed against the cumbersome classmarks which result, however, and the consequent difficulties in filing and retrieval. A work on Corfe Castle sheep show, for instance, receives the classmark D:636.3(.78)+D7 Corfe:06.06, or a poster for *Far from the madding crowd* is DB HARDY, Thomas [823"1906"(084.5)]. Clearly such a scheme could not be extended to provide the shelf arrangement for the entire local studies holdings, lending and reference, of an authority, and so the concept of a union classified catalogue is ruled out.

Many local studies librarians, rather than modify an existing general classification scheme, have preferred to devise one of their own. Most never achieve adoption by any except their own library, but three published schemes are more widely known. James Ormerod's classification, published in 1926-1928,[20] was used by four authorities in 1970 and is still used at

Derby, the collection for which it was devised. The kernel of the scheme is a two-digit subject classification of ten main classes each subdivided into ten. For places an adaptation of Cutter numbers is used. In publishing his scheme Ormerod hoped that it would be adapted for use in other collections, and he offered a number of suggestions as to how this could be done. The best-known adaptation, by J.L. Hobbs for the Shropshire Collection at Shrewsbury, employs a two-letter place code, and a third digit after a decimal point for greater specificity. It was published in both editions of Hobbs's textbook[21] and was employed in five collections in 1970, of which at least three (Bromley, Dundee and Shropshire) still use it. Similar concepts underlie the Guildhall scheme, first published in 1926 (and therefore exactly contemporary with Ormerod), which is used by the City of London (Guildhall), some other London boroughs (e.g. Camden) and by Birmingham. The basic two-digit classification is subdivided by a further two or three digits after a decimal point; unlike Ormerod and Hobbs, however, the Guildhall scheme treats places as part of the basic classification, at 80-89 (topography) and 90-99 (local divisions). Cutter numbers are used to give greater precision, and at certain points in the scheme names, written in full, are suffixed and filed alphabetically.

The inventors of schemes such as these, and their many local derivatives, by classifying local studies material from first principles, produced tailor-made classifications which can work very satisfactorily in practice. It is perhaps not too facile to see the Guildhall scheme and Hobbs's scheme as urban and rural equivalents of the same thinking, and it is in many ways regrettable that no scheme emerged in the 1920s as a universally accepted standard. In practice, local adaptations and tinkering produced a multiplicity of dialects, rather than a single language, and consequently no special local studies scheme has been powerful enough to challenge DC as a standard. The pace of standardisation has accelerated as local government reorganisations have thrown together disparate collections using disparate schemes, and this is in many cases leading to the demise of idiosyncrasy.

In approaching the plethora of DC lookalikes ('mangled Dewey', as one county local studies librarian described her classification scheme) two questions should be asked: How has the scheme adapted DC, if at all? How does the scheme cope with works about an individual place?

Many local studies collections use DC with little or no modification, except for the addition of a place qualifier where appropriate. Examples are Cornwall, Devon (Westcountry Studies), Hampshire (Winchester), Hertfordshire, Leicestershire and Somerset among counties, Leeds,

Liverpool and Richmond-upon-Thames among metropolitan boroughs. The latest (19th) edition is not universal, and instances have been found of both the 14th and 16th editions perpetuated as a conscious decision in order to avoid any reclassification. Unadulterated DC has the advantage that it is intelligible beyond the context of the local studies library, and that for material catalogued by the British Library, the task of classifying need not be carried out locally. Many areas of DC are of little application to local studies, of course; any work on Hebrew grammar or Kenyan history, for instance, will not be in the local collection by virtue of its subject (except in Israel or Kenya, of course), but because of local authorship, printing or some other local association. DC assigns to some subjects well represented in local studies libraries, on the other hand, a cumbersome notation of nine or more digits, often including a redundant (so far as we are concerned) place element. In some subject areas, archaeology for example, DC is notoriously unhelpful. Hence many libraries have abbreviated or otherwise modified DC for local studies purposes.

The simplest method of abbreviating the notation while retaining the Dewey 'flavour' is to move the decimal point to follow the second digit instead of the third. A work on Carmarthenshire railways would be classified in Dyfed at C38.5, where DC's notation would be 385.0942965, the 'C' substituting for DC's lengthy area notation. Simple subjects, such as transport, can be expressed by two digits, 38. Nottingham's scheme, which is virtually identical to that used in Bristol, is of this kind, and has been briefly described by Nichols;[22] despite his claim that it is an original scheme, rather than an adaptation, it mirrors DC very closely.

Many modifications strive to combine economy in notation, especially when classifying subjects seldom encountered in local studies, with greater specificity than normal DC in subject areas likely to be well represented. Norfolk and Essex are examples of authorities whose schemes reflect this philosophy. Dumfries & Galloway takes this a stage further by prescribing around 170 subject classmarks, which are enclosed within curved brackets and follow a place notation. The subject classmarks may be conventional DC, with up to five digits, they may be of one or two digits (9 = history, 79 = sport), or in certain cases, such as biographies and local authors, they may include part of the subject's name. A scheme proposed for Mid-Glamorgan retains the decimal point after the third digit, the first three digits signifying the place, up to six digits (corresponding to DC) following the point. In Wiltshire a three-digit subject classification follows a three-letter place prefix. Within each group of ten classmarks (e.g. 280-289, nonconformity) the first number (280) is used for works about the subject in general, the following eight (281-288) are subdivisions (e.g. Baptists, Methodists, Presbyterians, etc.) which correspond as closely as possible to conventional DC, and the final number (289) is kept for miscellaneous subjects (e.g. Salvation Army) which do not fall into any of the prescribed subdivisions.

Concern for individual places is, of course, the distinguishing mark of the local historian, and this concentration on locality is reflected in many of the home-produced and modified-DC schemes in use. Since classification generally dictates shelf order the construction of classmarks and the notation used for places should be decided in anticipation of the resulting shelf arrangement, particularly in so far as it facilitates browsing. Clearly a scheme in which the place element precedes the subject element will result in collocation of places and dispersal of subjects; and vice versa. Schemes which use a mnemonic prefix to describe places, such as the first three letters of the name, will produce an alphabetical arrangement by place on the shelf; whereas schemes which adopt a hierarchical approach - parish within district within county - or a topographical approach based, for instance, on grid squares, will result in a quite different shelf arrangement, collocating adjacent parishes, perhaps, but difficult to use without recourse to the classification schedules.

A second important decision concerns the units of area to be classified. Most county authorities recognise that the civil parish should be the basic unit, and local government reorganisations have resulted in a quite neat hierarchy, of civil parish, district and county/region, which will probably serve as the basis for schemes to come. Some additions to this tripartite arrangement may be worthwhile. For instance, geographical areas or linear features such as Dartmoor, the River Wye or Salisbury Plain fall between county and district level. Certain landmarks smaller than a parish may usefully be given their own classmark; works on Longleat and Stonehenge will be retrieved more easily under the names by which they are known rather than under the parishes - Horningsham and Amesbury respectively - in which they lie. Room may also need to be found within the scheme for vanished administrative units such as hundreds and rural districts, and in certain instances a distinction drawn between modern and historic counties. It should be recognised too that present-day boundaries are not immutable; any scheme should be flexible enough to accommodate changes. In urban areas the county/district/parish basis does not work, of course, and recourse has to be made to ecclesiastical parishes, wards or even streets as the smallest unit of classification. The place facet may be of less importance, however, in a city, and place may be incorporated into the general subject classification schedules, as in the Guildhall scheme.

A simple and obvious way of denoting place in a classmark is to write it out in full. This is the practice in Kent (Maidstone), West Sussex and in Dorset, where UDC supplies the subject classification. In Nottinghamshire the place name in full is suffixed; thus L90.2 Laxton describes a history of Laxton. The resulting notation may therefore be quite long (e.g. W/Stanton Fitzwarren 726.5 in the former Wiltshire scheme) and so many authorities use abbreviated place names. Derbyshire (Matlock) and Somerset use the first three letters of the name, Oxfordshire uses the first four and Norfolk uses one, two or three letters. Ambiguity will, of course, result in the case of some parishes, especially compound names beginning Great-, North-, etc. In Wiltshire strict alphabetical order is sacrificed to overcome this problem (thus BJA = Berwick St James, BJO = Berwick St John), while Essex adds a number (thus ASH.1 = Asheldon, ASH.2 = Ashen, ASH.3 = Ashingdon) so that a strict alphabetical shelf arrangement can be retained if desired. Cleveland's three-letter place notation achieves collocation by district combined with a mnemonic/alphabetical element. The initial letter signifies the district, the second and third are usually the first two letters of the parish (thus HGR = Greatham in Hartlepool District), or the initial letters of a compound parish name (thus LHG = Hutton Gate in Langbaurgh District).

The convenience of a mnemonic notation may be felt to be less desirable than the ability to group parishes geographically, or to retain an entirely numerical classification scheme. Dumfries & Galloway uses a mixed notation for place, of which only the basic division into district/former county has a mnemonic value, thus Dc21 = Moffat, made up from D = Dumfriesshire, Dc = Annandale (an area within Dumfriesshire), Dc21 = Moffat (a parish in Annandale). Geographical units smaller than a parish may be accommodated by adding a third figure, thus Dc211 = Moffat Burgh (within Moffat parish). Although covering a geographically much smaller area the place notation used by Richmond-upon-Thames is similar, thus RB1, which denotes Mortlake parish, is constructed from R (Richmond and Barnes parliamentary constituency), RB (Barnes borough, within the constituency), RB1 (Mortlake parish, within the borough). Entirely numerical place notations are used by a number of authorities, particularly the Welsh counties. In Dyfed (Carmarthen) a three-figure notation is used, each area having a block of 50 or 100 numbers which are used for communities within that area. Gwent (Newport) is also using a three-figure notation, although this may be subdivided, after the decimal point, for greater specificity. Clwyd's scheme illustrates the problem caused by local government reorganisation. A simple two-figure (for places in Flintshire) and three-figure (for other places in Wales) notation has required expansion to four figures to accommodate Denbighshire places.

## ASSESSMENT

If the writer wished to end this chapter on a note of dejection at the state of local classification in Britain it might be worth quoting the comments of one local studies librarian in reply to the writer's informal questionnaire: 'In practice it is used simply as a filing system for books and pamphlets . . . I do not find it a particularly good scheme, but it is not sufficiently inadequate for us to embark on a new classification scheme, even assuming we had the staff time available for such a major task.' All historians are at the mercy of their sources, of course, and the local studies librarian in Britain may be saddled with an impracticable scheme left over from a different era of library history. There is little in print (in languages familiar to this writer) about local classification schemes in use in countries with less of a legacy of local studies libraries, but what there is suggests that similar problems are encountered abroad. In English-speaking countries, such as the United States and Australia, variations of DC seem to prevail.[23] The outline of a German scheme, the result of a project funded by the Deutschen Bibliotheksinstituts, was published in 1981[24] which, it is intended, will be applied to many collections. The notation is entirely numerical, and is divided into two parts, a three-digit 'core classification' by subject, prefixed by three digits which, in blocks of 100, denote historical land divisions, 'landscape units', administrative units, biographies and family history. In Denmark, however, there has been no standardisation. Local studies libraries form part of local archives, and a decimal library classification is felt to conflict with the arrangement of the national archives.[25]

Clearly there is no classification scheme (nor catalogue, for that matter) which is ideal in every situation, and even if there were it would not be implemented because of the prohibitive amount of retrospective processing that would be necessary. The aim here has not been to advocate a single *modus operandi;* rather the writer has tried to fit specific examples of current practice into a framework of more general considerations. Conclusions may be summarised thus:

1. It should be recognised that cataloguing and classification, whether in traditional or mechanised guise, are not the sole means of retrieving local studies information, and that their usefulness may diminish as technological advances permit indexing and searching by other means. However, for shelf ordering, and therefore for browsing, and for general access to relevant information, some form of cataloguing and classification will continue to be desirable.

2. Ideally a library authority should produce a union catalogue to its entire stock, including therefore all its local studies holdings in lending and reference collections, arranged by one classification scheme. The current cataloguing rules (AACR2) cope satisfactorily with the various media encountered in a local studies library, although some works of interest to the bibliographer rather than the local historian may need separate treatment.

3. It is, alas, probably too late to devise a classification scheme for local studies material which would be adopted nationally. General classification schemes are not wholly satisfactory in local studies libraries, either because they cannot satisfy the very close topographical classification that is demanded, or because, in attempting to do so, the resulting notation is too cumbersome for shelving and retrieval purposes.

4. Since it is envisaged that a local classification scheme should be applied to an authority's entire local studies holdings, it should be reasonably intelligible to both librarians and public. The widespread use of DC in other library departments argues in favour of a modified form of DC for local studies stock.

5. It is essential in rural areas (and of considerable importance in metropolitan districts as well) that stock should be retrievable by place as well as subject, and the catalogue must permit both. In practice the civil parish or equivalent is an appropriate basic unit of place, although there should be flexibility in the classification scheme to describe smaller and larger areas, and to accommodate boundary changes in the future.

6. The notation used for a local classification scheme should be easy to use; in other words it should be capable of being carried in the

head from catalogue to shelf, basic subject notation should be recognisable to anyone versed in DC, and place notation should contain mnemonic elements. The resulting shelf arrangement should assist the browsing historian and the busy librarian.

7. The pace of technological change, coupled with the growth of interest in local studies (and, one hopes, a corresponding growth in resources) may convert the wishful thinking of this chapter into reality sooner than most of us think.

## NOTES

1. Hobbs, J.L. *Local history and the library.* 2nd edition revised by G.A. Carter. London, Deutsch, 1973, p. 247. Lynes, A. *How to organise a local collection.* London, Deutsch, 1974, p. 74.
2. Petty, M.J. The role of the local studies library. *Local historian* 14 (8) November 1981, p. 460.
3. Hobbs, p. 248.
4. Nichols, H. *Local studies librarianship.* London, Bingley, 1979, pp. 72-76.
5. Cave, R. *Rare book librarianship.* 2nd edition. London, Bingley, 1982, p. 67.
6. Nichols, pp. 71-72.
7. Cave, p. 69.
8. Tedd, L. Computers and networks. In: *British librarianship and information work 1976-1980,* edited by L.J. Taylor. London, Library Association, 1983. Vol. 2, p. 217.
9. Nichols, pp. 63, 71.
10. Walker, C. and Jamieson, I. Local studies and the new technology: report on the L.S.G. Weekend School. *Local studies librarian* 2 (1) Summer 1983, 11-13.
11. Wood, A. *et al.* Local history catalogue for West Sussex. *Vine* 30 August 1979, 34-36.
12. Wood, *et al.,* p.35.
13. Hobbs, p. 179.
14. Smith, J.S. Local studies and the new local authorities: local studies collections in Cumbria. In: Library Association. *Study school and national conference proceedings, Brighton 1978.* London, LA, 1978, p. 152.

15. Maxted, I. The ESTC and its importance for the local studies librarian. *Local studies librarian* 3 (1) Summer 1984, 3-5.
16. Evans, M. A national information resource for local studies: the York University local bibliographic project. *Local studies librarian* 3 (1) Summer 1984, 19-21.
17. Reed, M.A. Local history at Loughborough. *Journal of education for librarianship* 16 (2) 1975, p. 101.
18. Bakewell, K.G.B. Cataloguing and classification. In: *British librarianship and information work 1976-1980,* edited by L.J. Taylor. London, Library Association, 1983. Vol. 2, p. 180.
19. Hobbs, p. 266.
20. Ormerod, J. The classification and cataloguing of local collections. *Library world* 29 1926-1927, 147-151, 168-174; 30 1927-1928, 119-123.
21. Hobbs, pp. 284-303.
22. Nichols, pp. 53-57.
23. Hine, J.D. Headings in the right direction: a report of a Sydney workshop. *Cataloguing Australia* 7 (2) April-June 1981, p. 8; Smith, C.E. Building a local history collection *Australian library journal* 21 (10) November 1972, p. 414.
24. Lepiorz, W.-D. Projekt 'Landeskundliche Klassifikation der ASpB': Aufruf zur Mitarbeit *Bibliotheksdienst* 6 June 1981, 483-486.
25. Møller, J. Local historical archives - a theme with variations. *Scandinavian public library quarterly* 12 (3) 1979, p. 109.

# 12

# Indexing

John Chandler

This chapter is intended to complement the preceding chapter on cataloguing and classification, by examining various other methods of information retrieval which are, or which could be, used in local studies libraries. 'Indexing' is here used, therefore, as it tends to be throughout librarianship and life in general, as an omnibus term. Detailed consideration of indexes which might more properly be described as bibliographies, as well as indexes to photographs and oral history recordings, is not given here, since they are described elsewhere in this book. Back-of-book indexes and indexes contained in record society publications are likewise omitted. They cannot be entirely excluded, however, since their existence and use impinge on local studies information retrieval in general.

A certain haziness about what distinguishes an index from a catalogue or a bibliography is understandable and forgivable in the users of local studies libraries. Local history handbooks are themselves unclear: '...most local collections have an index arranged by place, which should locate any published parish histories'.[1] Such a use of 'index' is not strictly speaking inaccurate, according to current usage, since the word 'is sometimes taken as synonymous with "catalogue" or inclusive of both "catalogue" and "bibliography" ';[2] however, most librarians would probably describe such an 'index' as a catalogue. Harrod offers no fewer than six relevant definitions of 'index' as a noun,[3] while Langridge distinguishes a bibliography as 'a record of documents in general', a catalogue as a 'record of the documents in a particular collection' and an index as a 'record of the detailed contents of a particular document'.[4] The latter, with the substitution of 'a particular group of documents', will serve our purposes nicely.

With this definition in mind, therefore, we are better placed to consider the role of indexing, as opposed to cataloguing and classification, in the local studies library. We may divide the library's stock into three categories: items which should be catalogued but need no indexing; items for which, by virtue of medium or presence in a homogeneous group, cataloguing would be pointless or unnecessary, but for which indexing is necessary; items which should be catalogued, but which, for maximum retrieval, also require analytical cataloguing or indexing. Thus a parish church guide may be quite adequately retrieved by using the classified catalogue alone, whereas a collection of newscuttings requires indexing, and a run of a local periodical, while appearing in the catalogue, should also be indexed, or analytical entries should appear in the catalogue for each article. A typical local studies library, therefore, will use for retrieval purposes a catalogue and a number of discrete indexes, which to some extent will overlap the catalogue in the material they describe. Some libraries, as we shall see, have merged some or all of their indexes into their catalogue, thus realising a 'one-step' searching procedure. The feasibility of this depends on whether all indexes have been produced in a compatible format to the same consistent standard, and this in turn frequently depends on who has had responsibility for compiling them.

That local studies libraries have not been in the forefront of indexing advances may come as no surprise; Langridge attributes the slowness of the humanities to adopt modern indexing methods to the more contemplative and leisurely nature of the disciplines involved.[5] Be that as it may, the production of keyword indexes, PRECIS headings and thesauri is expensive and time-consuming, and lack of resources is a more reasonable excuse for local studies librarians' backwardness. In the field of controlled-language vocabularies no published thesaurus of local history or a related discipline was known to Aslib in 1979.[6] A thesaurus of subject headings for local studies collections was published in Australia in 1981, and although some of the terms would have little application in Britain - 'eucalyptus dieback', 'swagmen', for example - the work's thoughtful introduction repays study.[7] In the related field of museology, work carried out in conjunction with the Museum Documentation Association has resulted in a simple manual of thesaurus-building for museum curators,[8] and a very detailed thesaurus of terms for museum objects was published in the United States in 1978.[9] Keyword indexing and controlled vocabulary were discussed in a paper (alas, unpublished) by Ian Maxted to a Local Studies Group seminar in 1983,[10] and standard indexing terms are employed in the York

University local bibliographic project.[11] Nevertheless, the question of consistent subject indexing in local studies has been very little discussed in print, and this is due partly, no doubt, to the very high proportion (80 to 90 per cent, according to J.D. Hine) of proper name entries that occur in local studies indexes.[12] Place and personal names do not, of course, present the indexer with hierarchical problems of relationships between subjects, but the question of orthography is more complicated than many local historians (and librarians) might imagine. The difficulties are set out by Hunnisett in a work intended for record publication editors, but his recommendations could well be considered for use also in local studies indexes.[13]

We shall return to the question of how local studies libraries may benefit from recent advances in indexing techniques at the end of this chapter. Before we consider specific indexes we should briefly discuss responsibility for indexing, since this clearly affects the finished product.

Indexes (excluding back-of-book indexes) in use in a local studies library may be the work of any of four categories of indexer - the library staff, volunteer or government-training-scheme labour working under library supervision, independent workers over which the library has no control and professional indexers outside the library authority providing an indexing service for publication or as a computer database. Here, of course, is one of the simplest distinctions between common use of 'catalogue' and 'index', the catalogue is the preserve of professional librarians, an index may be of more dubious origin.

Previous works on local studies librarianship assume that the library staff themselves will perform most of the indexing tasks. Nichols cites the practice of passing local studies material, 'to be indexed at odd moments by staff in a home-reading library where the flow of work depends more directly on readers' attendance' - a recipe for inconsistency and incompleteness, if ever there was one.[14] Hobbs, while recognising that available staff time limits the production of indexes, describes successful projects in which, for example, library staff have indexed the local parish registers.[15] It is probably true that a much smaller proportion of the indexing carried out for local studies purposes is now the work of library staff than formerly, and this is partly because indexing of a discrete group of material makes a suitable and interesting project for the growing number of volunteer helpers and workers on government-funded employment schemes. Such projects may be at the instigation of the library staff, who may exercise a supervisory role, but where librarians have no direct involvement it is nevertheless important that they try to offer advice based on their professional training and experience, and their knowledge of user needs. Many indexes in local studies libraries, of course, are the legacy of independent researchers, and sometimes represent a lifetime's work, begun without the library in mind and perhaps before it even existed. At the other end of the scale the library will buy in commercially produced current awareness indexes. The *Local studies index,* begun in 1981, offers a useful service by identifying fugitive material in serials unlikely to be held in local studies libraries. Some 800 entries from 90 serials appeared in the first four-monthly issue; a recent issue indexed 123 serials ranging from *Brick bulletin* to *Youth in society, Fire prevention* to *Recusant history.* Other indexing and abstracting services, such as *British archaeological abstracts, British humanities index* and *Writings on British history,* will be familiar to many local studies librarians.

Having considered a few basic principles - the relationship between indexes and catalogues, advances in indexing techniques and types of indexer - we should now consider some categories of index maintained in local studies libraries.

## INDEXING LOCAL NEWSPAPERS

Its file of local newspapers probably represents the least accessible and yet one of the largest information resources in the local studies library. Until the widespread use of microforms to preserve newspapers such inaccessibility was perhaps to be welcomed; had the demands now placed on newspapers existed 50 years ago few of the newspapers would exist today. Interest in local newspapers mirrors the post-war reawakening of interest in local history; indeed it was the evangelist of local history, W.G. Hoskins, who brought them to many people's attention by devoting part of a chapter to them in a famous book, *Local history in England.*[16] Increasing concern for the social and economic aspects of local history (and their corollary, the local aspects of social and economic history), coupled with the greater use of local sources in history teaching, have placed further pressure on them.[17]

Researchers use local newspapers for four main reasons. First they wish to read a contemporary account of a newsworthy event, or more simply they wish to discover the date on which an event occurred. In the latter instance a local newspaper index should provide an answer without the enquirer needing to consult the relevant newspaper. Since the key to reading about events in newspapers is knowing when something occurred an index to one local newspaper will often serve as an approximate index to all the others.[18] Enquirers are to be encouraged to read as many newspaper accounts of the same event as they can, of course, since only by this means will they counteract the inherent bias of the newspaper as a historical source.

Secondly, the historian may be interested not in single events but in the fluctuating week-by-week life of the local community. The state of an agricultural market, timetables, property sales and situations vacant, can all yield important information and may be the best, or only, source available. In eighteenth-century newspapers this is the local historian's main concern, since at this period little local news is reported.[19] In later newspapers the regular reporting of various board meetings, quarter sessions and assizes, ecclesiastical and parochial affairs, all put flesh on the bones to be found in minute books in the local record office. For such matters an index is of less importance, since relevant dates may already be known, or can be discovered by other means. Noteworthy events described in such reports, and named individuals, should nevertheless be indexed.

Thirdly, the local newspaper may operate as a secondary source, carrying articles by antiquaries and local historians which might otherwise have appeared in a periodical. Such pieces may take the form of accounts (sometimes verbatim) of public lectures, or the newspaper may have been regarded by the author as a legitimate alternative to the county archaeological or historical magazine. To use a Wiltshire example, the Devizes historian Edward Kite published 40 historical articles, including a series of 15 on old houses in Devizes, in the *Devizes gazette* between 1917 and 1929. His choice of a newspaper as the organ of publication resulted from a quarrel in 1866 with the Wiltshire Archaeological and Natural History Society (publisher of the county magazine) and the demise in 1916 of an alternative periodical, *Wiltshire notes and queries.*[20] Clearly work of this kind should be regarded in the same light as periodical articles and catalogued, or indexed, in the same fashion.

A fourth use of local newspapers is not historical at all, but is concerned with their input to a more general local information index such as is maintained in some local studies libraries. These are described below.

Such an embarrassment of riches has led to a proliferation of indexes. The idea of indexing newspapers is not a recent one, of course; Palmer's index to The *Times* is well known, and there are other long-running published newspaper indexes, such as the annual index to the *Glasgow herald,* 1906-1968.[21] Local newspapers need to maintain their own indexes to their backfiles, and there is a branch of special librarianship devoted to news libraries, with its own indexing procedures.[22] Any current, as opposed to retrospective, indexing project contemplated by a local studies library should be considered in the light of the quality and scope of the newspaper's own index, since this may one day become available for public use.

A survey in 1981/1982 discovered more than 650 indexes to British local newspapers.[23] Many, presumably, are maintained by news libraries, but others have been created on the initiative of local authorities. Retrospective indexing is a laborious and time-consuming business, as a few statistics will show. Each annual volume of the *Stirling journal* took an indexer ten to twelve working days, and about 18 000 man hours were involved in indexing 151 years, exclusive of filing, checking and typing.[24] An Australian newspaper index took a little over 7000 man hours to create 38 000 records, rather more than five per hour.[25] Since an average local authority employee works about 1700 hours in a year it is obvious that most projects of this kind cannot be funded from the rates. (The *Stirling journal* project, at 1984 local government clerical scales, would probably cost between £50 000 and £100 000 in salaries alone.) Recourse has been made, therefore, either to volunteers, or to government-funded training schemes. In Suffolk, a county noted for its amateur local history involvement, seven volunteers began in 1982 indexing bound volumes of the *Ipswich journal* from 1800. Lincolnshire, Liverpool and Devon are examples of authorities who have used training schemes. In the latter an index to over a century of *Trewman's Exeter flying post* (1763-1885) was produced. Workers employed on schemes of this nature do not necessarily stay for very long. The *Stirling journal* project began with a supervisor and four school leavers; two supervisors had left within the first five months, and at one point earlier underspending enabled the team to grow to nine. Under these circumstances considerable time must be spent in checking and training, in order to achieve consistency.[26]

Compiling an index is one of those activities which has to be right first time. Consequently various rules must be made and decisions taken before the indexing begins. Apart from the medium - which is still usually manually sorted cards or slips - these rules and decisions fall into two categories: the material to be included and excluded, and the form and vocabulary of headings to be used.

236

Preliminary decisions about what is to be indexed concern the period to be covered, the newspaper title(s) to be indexed and the geographical area to be covered. Most indexing projects concern a single title, as in the examples mentioned above. However, in Cheshire the published *Chester newspaper index,* beginning in 1955, indexes three local newspapers and selective references to Chester and Cheshire in others.[27] Lincolnshire's project covers fifteen titles published in six towns in the county. Nottinghamshire's impressive record of indexing involves seven titles each indexed in a different library. In Gloucestershire two indexes to the *Gloucester journal* have been compiled by volunteers, but each is concerned with only one locality. Many indexes begin with the first issue, or the start of the library's file; in the case of small town newspapers this is often shortly after the repeal of the stamp tax in 1855, but many provincial cities had newspapers more than a century before. Liverpool has indexed only the eighteenth-century issues of *Williamson's Liverpool advertiser,* whereas for the *Ipswich journal* and the *Nottingham journal* the indexes only begin in 1800/1801.

Basic decisions such as these should aim to maximise the index's usefulness in the light of the available resources. Bearing in mind that one of the main effects and uses of a newspaper index is to assign dates to notable events, it may be best to concentrate on indexing a long run of one countywide newspaper rather than several contemporary titles published in the same area. As has already been suggested, an index to one newspaper acts to some extent as an index to all newspapers in the area it covers.

The subject-matter indexed may be very restricted, such as Shropshire's index to biographical material in the local press 1892-1932 (which nevertheless includes about 40 000 records), or the indexer may capitalise on a standardised method of presenting local news; thus Cambridge has produced a rapid index to village news reported in the *Cambridgeshire chronicle* 1848-1898 by simply copying the subheadings printed in the newspaper and filing them alphabetically under the village name.[28] More often lists of categories for inclusion and exclusion are prepared to guide the indexer. Lincolnshire and Nottinghamshire have adopted virtually identical lists, and it is a pity that no standard has been adopted more widely. Usually excluded are non-local news items; births, marriages and deaths announcements (although the family historian may argue that these are the most important details in a newspaper); appointments to public office; regular and predictable events; and most advertisements (although this is more controversial). Biographical information, buildings, industries, meetings, services, communications, illustrations, disasters and abnormal occurrences are usually included. Quasi-periodical articles of interest as secondary sources may be included, although it may be better to catalogue them with similar material, as is the practice in Cambridge.[29]

While personal and place name headings in a local newspaper may present few problems, the importance of prescribing a list of subject headings is generally recognised. Hoskins describes the index to the *Hull advertiser and exchange gazette,* and lists its 70 headings to which subheadings could be added.[30] Elliott prefers fewer headings (26), but with a large number of subheadings.[31] Lincolnshire, to simplify the indexing process, prescribes 81 headings, which are not subdivided. Suffolk, by contrast, has compiled a quite detailed and extensive thesaurus of subject headings, using existing indexes as a base. Surprisingly, little work appears to have been done in keyword indexing of headlines, although a free-text index to the opening paragraphs of news items in an American local newspaper was reported as long ago as 1969 and is described by J.J. Hovish.[32]

Alongside the newspapers themselves, and any indexes to them, some local studies libraries maintain cuttings files, which provide another means of access to the rich storehouse of newsprint. Cuttings files tend not to be created retrospectively - few librarians would sanction cutting up an eighteenth-century newspaper - but some have been maintained continuously since the last century, and so offer real meat for the historian as well as providing a ready reference to recent events. From the historian's point of view a good index is to be preferred to a cuttings file, even though the latter may be quicker to use. The bias inherent in a newspaper is only heightened by the cutter's subjective decisions about what is worthy of preservation; even if such decisions do not openly mirror the cutter's penchant, for railways, murder or whatever, he is nonetheless a child of his time, and a century hence views on what is of historical significance will have changed. Such criticisms are not intended to persuade the librarian to abandon the practice of a lifetime (and maybe several lifetimes before him) but merely to recognise how influential the apparent chore may become, and how imperfect the work of previous cutters must now be. 'To an extent, therefore, we are now deciding what future researchers will use when studying our present way of life - an awful responsibility indeed.'[33]

Against their inherent disadvantages must be set a number of factors in favour of cuttings. They may be grouped or filed in a systematic order, based on the classification scheme or some other form of control, from which they may be instantly retrieved, without the intermediary of a microfilm reader or the exertion needed for a bound volume. They may be easily photocopied; indeed a stable photocopy may be better for archival preservation than the original cutting.[34] Where an extensive cuttings file exists it is clearly found useful by researchers: Belfast claims that its series of 88 fully indexed cuttings books from *ca* 1900 is 'possibly the single most used resource in the Irish Studies Collection', and the indexes to the cuttings can also provide access (albeit selective) to the newspapers themselves. Gloucestershire is in the process of cumulating on cards the indexes to its 30 volumes of cuttings which begin in 1859, using headings which conform to those in the main catalogue. Clwyd classifies cuttings according to its local classification scheme and stores them on microfiche, a technique developed to great effect by the BBC News Library.[35] The use of press cuttings as a tool for academic historians and social scientists is becoming more widely recognised following a study by Glasgow University published in 1976.[36] This, however, specifically excluded cuttings maintained in public libraries.

## PERIODICALS

Periodical articles about a locality appear predominantly in periodicals devoted to that locality; as such they will, of course, be taken by the local studies library concerned. But relevant articles may also occur in regional or national special interest periodicals, and these pose problems of bibliographical control. Since the local library and/or record office would in many cases have been used by the authors of periodical articles, complimentary offprints or photocopies often arrive unheralded. But authors' gratitude cannot be relied upon, and does not always apply in any case, and the local studies library must use the commercially produced indexing services described above for bibliographical control. Greater co-operation between local studies librarians in neighbouring authorities might also help in this respect.

Many libraries maintain on cards a separate periodicals index. Essex (Colchester) has an index of over 10 000 records using subject headings and multiple entries. It may be a reflection on the generally healthy and law-abiding interests of Essex people that whereas there are 17 entries under 'Smuggling' and 33 under 'Oysters', there are 42 under 'Cricket' and nearly 100 under 'Railways'. Dorset maintains a separate periodicals card index for Hardy literature, including a subject sequence; while Leeds indexes newspapers and periodicals to produce four sequences - on Leeds, Yorkshire, biography and business history. South Glamorgan (Cardiff) classifies periodical articles and includes details in the library's main dictionary catalogue, which will eventually be computerised. Wiltshire likewise has classified post-1945 articles in the *Wiltshire archaeological and natural history magazine* and other local periodicals, and they appear alongside bookstock in the computerised county catalogue.

Local studies libraries can in their turn act as an indexing agency. Clwyd has produced a title index to the first 30 years, 1952-1982, of the *Denbighshire Historical Society transactions,* and this was published in a subsequent volume. Typescript indexes to two other local periodicals have been produced under a government training scheme. Somerset has published in the *Proceedings of the Somerset Archaeological Society* lists of articles relating to Somerset occurring in non-local periodicals. Gloucestershire sends to all its libraries annually indexes (arranged predominantly by place) to two local periodicals, *Gloucestershire and Avon life* and *Cotswold life.* Most ambitious of all, Nottinghamshire publishes at irregular intervals a periodicals index which is circulated to libraries, schools, museums and other bodies, with an appeal for notification of omissions. This is followed up by a photocopying service of material indexed.

## A MIXED BAG

Indexes to newspapers and periodicals were mentioned far more frequently in the replies to the writer's informal questionnaire than any other kind of index, and so have been accorded special treatment. But at least 30 other categories of local studies material are being, or have been, indexed in various places, and the writer has divided them into groups here so as to offer a brief description. Some of these indexes should more properly, according to our definition, be described as catalogues, and some (genealogical indexes, for example) describe non-bibliothecal material. Nevertheless the diversity of retrieval tools which may be appropriate in a local studies library is both impressive and (to those of us not employing most of them) alarming.

Illustrations form a very considerable and valuable resource in the local studies library, and are frequently indexed or catalogued. Photographs, which form the major part of most illustrations collections, are discussed elsewhere in this book, and it is appropriate that prints and drawings, including portraits, and audio-visual material should be included with photograph indexes wherever possible. Early printed maps may perhaps be considered alongside prints, since the techniques of production are similar. Map catalogues, often relying on the published bibliographical works of Thomas Chubb and others, feature in many local collections, and the production of indexes to features described on maps, such as place names, street names and man-made structures, has been advocated,[37] although seldom, so far as the writer is aware, has the suggestion been acted upon. The need for a library-produced place name index is in any case questionable, as enquiries about the whereabouts of places may usually be answered from published gazetteers, directories, or, for certain English counties, from volumes in the English Place-Name Society series. The Public Record Office is currently (1984) initiating a place index to Victorian census returns.

'Because of the sheer quantity of items you cannot index an ephemera collection', says David Reid.[38] It is questionable, in any case, whether very much organisation of current ephemera should take place, other than the discarding of duplicate items and storage in a non-detrimental environment. Current ephemera is a resource for the future, and it will be for future generations to catalogue and index it according to their own needs. We may be concerned to retrieve ephemera of the past, however, and catalogues and indexes have been produced to playbills, sale catalogues and trade advertisements.

Biographical indexes and prosopographies are at a premium among family historians, who now constitute the largest user group in many local studies libraries. The panoply of genealogical sources which the librarian may command has been described in an excellent manual by Harvey,[39] and indexes of various kinds play a significant role in genealogical searching.[40] In general, family historians may be expected to create their own indexes, and few indexes of any kind can match the massive *International genealogical index* of christenings and marriages in parish and non-parochial registers compiled by the Genealogical Society of Utah (the Mormon index), which is held on microfiche, either for a group of counties, for the United Kingdom or for the world, by many local studies libraries. The results of some local parish register indexing (on the Isle of Wight, for example) have been deposited in libraries, and a number of family history societies have indexed Victorian census enumerators' returns, thus providing a virtually complete directory of inhabitants in a town or county at a given date in the nineteenth century. Some local studies libraries, especially in metropolitan authorities, administer archives collections, and have produced indexes and catalogues to their holdings.

On the principle of, 'when found, make a note of', many local studies librarians keep some kind of index of general information, such as the answers to frequently asked questions, and odd facts which have been particularly hard to trace (in newspapers, for instance), or which have turned up in surprising places. Compiled on the basis of serendipity rather than systematic indexing, such *aides-mémoires* do not fall within our definition of indexes describing the contents of discrete groups of documents, although their usefulness cannot be denied. Akin to such indexes, however, is the ability to retrieve information from the local studies library's correspondence files. Replying to written enquiries occupies a great deal of a local studies librarian's time, and a competent answer often results in a further letter of gratitude which may add more information (or may, to the recipient's annoyance, pose further questions). Much scholarship changes hands in this way, and may profitably be indexed.

Finally in our round-up of indexing diversity, we encounter indexes relating to specific categories of books or to the library's bookstock in general. Special collections of books in libraries may warrant special cataloguing or indexing treatment, and in the previous chapter rare books were cited as a case in point. Some local studies libraries have inherited special private libraries, such as the Colman Collection at Norwich and the Castle Library at Colchester, and these have their own catalogues. Elsewhere quasi-bibliographies, in the form of card or slip indexes, have been inherited, of which the one million cards of the Burnet Morris Index in Devon's Westcountry Studies Library must be one of the most impressive. Libraries which have built up collections of specific types of book (such as the Guildhall Library's directories and pollbooks), or works on very specific subjects (such as Dorset's collection by and about the Powys family) may produce catalogues and indexes. As suggested in the previous chapter, some authorities appear to be rejecting traditional cataloguing and classification for their bookstock, relying instead on an index. Brent maintains a single card index to information, books, pamphlets, newspapers and photographs; Borders is proposing to index its bookstock along archival lines so as to provide a clear link with the region's archives, which are housed alongside.

# CONCLUSIONS

In concluding the previous chapter, a slightly pessimistic note was struck about local cataloguing and classification, largely because of the amount of work involved in making radical changes. Indexing is a much more cheerful business, because the creation of any index, where none existed before, is a step towards better retrieval of information. The prognosis for indexing must be seen against the backcloth of three fundamental changes which have occurred in recent years.

First there have been changes in the uses to which local studies materials are being put. The explosion of interest in census enumerators' returns, to take a single example, reflects the emergence of family historians and social historians as major users of local studies libraries. Reawakened interest in the Victorian antiquaries, and their work buried in the proceedings of county societies and field clubs, accompanied archaeology's spectacular progress in the 1960s and 1970s, and they now appear in the sites and monuments records of the 1980s. Every town suddenly has its book of old photographs, quarried in the main from libraries' photographic collections. All such attempts to extract new wine from old bottles - and long may they continue - need new retrieval tools.

Secondly the basic reorganisation of work, leisure and society, which is still in its early stages, is having the twin effects of pruning all but essential work by salaried staff while opening up new possibilities of interesting unsalaried work as a leisure interest for volunteers, or as stopgap temporary employment funded by central government. Responsibility for creating indexes is therefore passing into other hands.

Thirdly the use of computers to remove all the non-intellectual aspects of indexing - sorting, storing, recalling - has enforced a re-examination of the way in which indexers go about their work, and the result of this, coupled with the emergence of a professional body, the Society of Indexers, has served to improve indexes and enhance the status of indexing. This process has not been confined to local studies, of course; on the contrary, local studies has lagged behind, and can now follow in the wake of pioneering activity in other fields with a reasonable chance of avoiding the pitfalls.

Faced with these three developments, and in the light of the traditions of local history indexing, local studies librarians (as a community, rather than as individuals) should now be making some important decisions. The annotated agenda might run as follows:

1. The index and the catalogue: Should we be attempting to integrate our catalogues and indexes? Although a 'one-step' retrieval system has obvious advantages, these must be weighed against the difficulties of reconciling two basically dissimilar databases. Purpose, method and agent of construction are fundamentally different. It may be preferable to decide, as suggested above, that some categories of stock require indexing, some require cataloguing, and some require both.

2. A thesaurus: Faced with the reality that many hands are currently engaged in many places to index many categories of material, all on the common theme of local studies, and with the likelihood that many similar projects will be initiated in the future, the standardisation of indexing procedure by means of a controlled-language thesaurus must be considered to be the first priority. Its absence jeopardises co-operative indexing and the merging of indexes in the future.

3. The microcomputer: Since it is likely that microcomputers, if not already present, will soon be a feature of all local studies libraries, it is desirable that appropriate software packages be developed for use in indexing local studies, and that developments in local studies computing are discussed and agreed at a national level. Such discussions should involve local studies librarians' colleagues in the related fields of archives, museums and archaeology.

4. One or many? Just as there are advantages in producing a union catalogue so a single index to many categories of materials saves retrieval time and offers a better chance of success. The adoption of a standard indexing language and procedures would enable discrete indexes to be merged into a single file. It would be possible, therefore, not only for an authority to combine its own indexes, but also for it to co-operate with its neighbours to produce indexes of relevance to a wider area. The promotion of local studies to the status of a legitimate academic subject, and their use as an integral part of other branches of historical enquiry, demand the broader view that can be obtained by regional and eventually national co-operation.

5. New indexes: Although any new index, provided it is not actually misleading, is to be encouraged, the local studies librarian has a more active role to play than simply making available the

material to be indexed and begging or buying the resulting index. Librarians are in a position to suggest suitable material for indexing, to advise on indexing techniques and to impose standards, such as a controlled vocabulary and consistent proper-name indexing. Librarians may actually initiate and take part in indexing projects, as well as make available hardware and software. In a more general sense, local studies librarians should be aware of any indexing projects taking place independently of the library, and take steps to benefit from the result, if possible. More generally too, they should encourage a high standard of back-of-book indexing among the writers of local history and in the output of local history societies.

6. Dissemination: Whereas a card index cannot easily be disseminated, except by microfilming or transferring to some other medium, computerised indexes may be easily printed and made widely available. Mention of a network, offering an on-line local studies indexing facility, is perhaps premature, but is is no longer the science fiction that it would have been a decade ago.

## NOTES

1. Riden, P. *Local history : a handbook for beginners.* London, Batsford, 1983, p. 26.
2. Langridge, D.W. *Classification and indexing in the humanities.* London, Butterworths, 1976, p. 119.
3. Harrod, L.M. *The librarian's glossary. . . and reference book.* 4th edition. London, Deutsch, 1977, pp. 412-413.
4. Langridge, p. 119.
5. Langridge, p. 118.
6. Gilbert, V. A list of thesauri and subject headings held in the Aslib Library. *Aslib proceedings* 31 (6) June 1979, 264-274.
7. Flint, J. and Franklin, A. (compilers). *Local studies collections: guidelines and subject headings for organizing and indexing resources.* Sydney, Library Association of Australia, NSW Branch, 1981. (Occasional paper no. 5.)
8. Orna, E. *Build yourself a thesaurus: a step by step guide.* Norwich, Running Angel, 1983.

9. Chenhall, R.G. *Nomenclature for museum cataloguing: a system for classifying man-made objects*. Nashville, American Association for State and Local History, 1978.

10. Winterbotham, D. Access to local studies material. *Local studies librarian* 2 (2) Winter 1983, p. 23.

11. Evans, M. A national information resource for local studies: the York University local bibliographic project. *Local studies librarian* 3 (1) Summer 1984, p. 19.

12. Hine, J.D. Headings in the right direction: report of a Sydney workshop. *Cataloguing Australia* 7 (2) April-June 1981, p. 9.

13. Hunnisett, R.F. *Indexing for editors*. London, British Records Association, 1972.

14. Nichols, H. *Local studies librarianship*. London, Bingley, 1979, p. 88.

15. Hobbs, J.L. *Local history and the library*. 2nd edition revised by G.A. Carter. London, Deutsch, 1973, p. 256.

16. Hoskins, W.G. *Local history in England*. London, Longmans, 1959.

17. Milne, M. The historian and local newspapers. *Local studies librarian* 1 (2) Summer 1982, p. 3.

18. Dewe, M. Indexing local newspapers. *Assistant librarian* 65 (4) April 1972, 58-59.

19. Milne, pp. 4-5.

20. Bradby, E. Edward Kite, antiquary of Devizes (1832-1930). *Wiltshire archaeological and natural history magazine* 78 1984, pp. 85-86.

21. Fisher, J. Local studies in the Mitchell Library: the Glasgow Collection. *Local studies librarian* 2 (1) Summer 1983, p. 14.

22. Knight, G.N. *Indexing, the art of: a guide to the indexing of books and periodicals*. London, Allen and Unwin, 1979, pp. 141-150.

23. Green, S. The newspaper library and the local library. *Local studies librarian* 1 (2) Summer 1982, p. 9.

24. Elliott, B.J. The problems of indexing a local newspaper. *Local historian* 14 (3) 1980, p. 146.

25. Hine, pp. 13-14.

26. Elliott (1980).

27. Nichols, p. 85.

28. Petty, M.J. The role of the local studies library. *Local historian* 14 (8) November 1981, p. 461.

29. Petty, p. 461.

30. Hoskins, pp. 162-163.

31. Elliott, pp. 144-145.
32. Hovish, J.J. The local newspaper in the British public library: problems of storage, bibliographical control, and exploitation, M.Phil. thesis, University of Wales, 1983, pp. 140-141.
33. Petty, p. 464.
34. Lancashire Library. *Standards of provision for local studies: report and policy statement.* Preston, The Lancashire Library, 1981, p. 15.
35. Hovish, pp. 74-78.
36. Mason, C.M. Press cuttings and the social sciences. *Aslib proceedings* 28 (6-7) June-July 1976, 230-242.
37. Lynes, A. *How to organise a local collection.* London, Deutsch, 1974, p. 78. Nichols, p. 80. Nichols, H. *Map librarianship.* 2nd edition. London, Bingley, 1982, pp. 215-216.
38. Reid, D. Ephemera and local studies. *New library world* 80 September 1979, p. 175.
39. Harvey, R. *Genealogy for librarians.* London, Bingley, 1983.
40. Chandler, J.H. Indexes for local and family history: a user's view. *Indexer* 13 (4) October 1983, pp. 225-227.

# 13

# Services to users and extension activities

Bernard Nurse

The increasing interest in local studies has had a considerable impact on the use made of libraries. It has encouraged most public libraries to improve their facilities in this field but has also placed a burden on the staff who have to cope with a rising tide of complex enquiries.

Statistics of use are notoriously unreliable. If the number of readers using the local studies collection is counted, no distinction is made between people who study all day in the library and casual visitors. If the number of enquiries to the staff is counted, those who can find out what they want without seeking the help of the staff are unrepresented. If the number of items consulted is counted, the person who spends all day studying one volume is calculated as using the library less than someone who looks quickly through a pile of press cuttings (which some libraries would count as 100 or more issues). A sample count of readers at a given time can be misleading because the use of libraries can vary enormously from busy peaks (especially October to March) to quiet lulls (especially in the summer).

Although a few libraries have given up counting completely, when arguing for increased resources, it is useful to have some uniform method of counting over a period to demonstrate how much use is increasing (while lending library issues may well be static or declining). Whatever method of counting is used, most local studies libraries have experienced an increase in the number of readers, enquiries or reference issues, often by a factor of three, over the last ten years.

## USERS OF THE LOCAL COLLECTION

A small local collection like that of the London Borough of Southwark, for example, has recorded an increase from 883 visitors and 238 letters in 1974 to 2615 visitors and 335 letters in 1983. This is probably typical of the picture elsewhere. Norma Armstrong asked for comments on recent changes in use for the survey published in 1977 in *Local collections in Scotland*. Most of those who responded remarked on the increase in use by younger readers, and of particular sources such as press cuttings, photographs, maps and newspapers. An increase was, however, often seen to be connected to improvements in the services provided: Caithness, for example, reported a 'wider range of users since opening Caithness Room', and Inverclyde claimed 'more readers since open access'.[1] A large collection such as that at Birmingham now receives 30 000 to 40 000 visitors a year and Newcastle almost as many.

An earlier survey, by George Carter in 1970, for his revision of J.L. Hobbs', *Local history and the library,* asked local studies librarians where their users came from. The results showed that 85 to 95 per cent belonged to the locality; only in the larger cities with regional collections was local use reported to be less than 75 per cent of the total.[2] Fifteen years later, many libraries find that at least half their users come from outside their administrative area. This is certainly the case in inner London boroughs where the population may have dropped by two-thirds during this century. In the Westcountry Studies Library at Exeter, where two-thirds of the users are genealogists, a half of those come from outside the county.

There are two particular fields of interest which have provided the majority of new readers. Visits made for educational purposes (which will be discussed in the next chapter) and visits to trace the history of one's family or house. Local libraries have traditionally possessed sources helpful to genealogists such as directories, electoral registers and local newspapers, but when other sources have been acquired which show the relationship between members of a family, such as census returns, parish registers and the *International genealogical index,* the effect on the number of people using the library has been dramatic. Such sources have become readily available in microfilm or microfiche over the last ten years. Those libraries that cater for this interest may find that a half to two-thirds of their readers are researching their family trees; those libraries that do not (such as the Cambridgeshire Collection) find the proportion to be nearer 20 to 25 per cent.

The experience of the Glasgow Room is shared by many other public libraries who have also acquired copies of basic genealogical sources. The senior librarian reported that:

the build up of such resources has changed our lives in the Glasgow Room and exasperated members of staff, faced with yet another elderly but eager local (Is this whuer we get wir family tree, hen?), have been known to beg that no more such acquisitions be made. But as our Visitors' Book too clearly shows, the service is appreciated; the demand is there.[3]

Other people who may also be unfamiliar with specialist libraries are also being drawn in increasing numbers to the local collection for personal research. The trend to conversion rather than demolition of older properties has encouraged owners to investigate the past history of their houses without appreciating the complex searches required. Large-scale maps and other sources can be used to establish that a particular house was built before 1919 and so qualified for an improvement grant. An entry in the relevant electoral register can prove residence in a council house for long enough to obtain the maximum discount under the 'right to buy' legislation in the 1984 Housing and Building Control Act.

Individuals may have strong personal motives for trying to trace missing relatives or friends, often last seen many years ago; adopted children may wish to find their natural parents. The considerable amount of personal information recorded in electoral registers, local directories and newspapers, rating records and other sources in the local collection, can sometimes provide a starting point which may help. Collectors trying to date objects in their possession, treasure hunters looking for likely sites to search, model makers looking for plans and illustrations, are all familiar readers. The staff cannot always be sure what users want at the time, as demonstrated by the example of the Russian 'spy' who consulted press cuttings on the armed forces and civil defence in the Cambridgeshire Collection.[4]

Professional and commercial reasons attract an important category of users to the local studies library. Lawyers may be attempting to find information on rights of way, land use, boundaries, market rights or residences. Surveyors may be looking for plans of particular sites and structures, or the existence of streams, wells and former buildings. Planners may be concerned with conservation areas and listed buildings or ideas for the names of streets and blocks of flats; archaeologists may be tracing the development of sites being excavated or the potential of those threatened by development.

Commercial use of the collection comes from market researchers investigating areas of possible sales, for example, and from the public

250

relations side looking for information about the history of a particular business, or illustrations for publicity material. Owners of public houses and restaurants may wish to decorate their walls with copies of old photographs. Publishers and television companies find the illustrations collections of great value, partly because much of the material has been previously unpublished, but also because libraries are generally cheaper to use than commercial picture agencies.

An active local collection should become the focal point for all matters of local interest and as such will often be used by the media, as well as by members of the community, as a starting point for enquiries and the natural place to look for information about the locality. The up-to-date details of local organisations that are often maintained by the local studies staff are always much appreciated by newcomers to an area, as well as by long-established residents.

Some of the more regular users of the collection may be members of local history or amenity societies. Their interest in the locality is deep-rooted, and knowledge within their own fields considerable. Their value to the library is more than their numbers might suggest, as these readers will often pass on the fruits of their work to the local collection. The staff in return may inform them of any relevant new acquisitions or information, and may also put researchers in touch with them when they are likely to be able to help. The development of personal friendships with particular readers as a result of common interests over a long period is one of the more rewarding aspects of this branch of librarianship.

These informal and personal arrangements have been developed by some libraries into a more systematic approach. The Cambridgeshire Collection has recently revived its former selective dissemination of information system by which researchers fill in a profile form and coloured cards are added to the subject catalogue at the sections which represent their interests. They are then notified of relevant new books and researchers with the same interests brought together. This sort of scheme is more a feature of American libraries which are trying to build up their contacts in a community. Bristol Public Library in Virginia-Tennessee, for example, has constructed a simply designed and easily maintained 'Genealogy and history referral file'. Each potential participant is sent a questionnaire and asked to list any local families or historical items of which he or she has knowledge. The information from those who respond is entered on index cards divided into four sections - genealogy (by family name), history (by subject), important individuals and the list of participants. A 'Want file' is also maintained in which people can indicate what information they are looking for. According to the librarian, 'the effectiveness of the file as a tool for access to genealogical and historical information has been attested to many times by statements and letters from grateful users'.[5] As far as genealogists in the United Kingdom are concerned, the names of the families being researched can be published in the magazine of the local family history society and members with common interests brought into contact this way.

## ENQUIRIES

Because of the unique nature of each local collection many people will write or telephone to a particular library to find out whether the information required can be found there. Such preliminary contact is advisable anyway before travelling a distance to visit the library, if only to check on the opening hours. No other section of the public library service receives so many enquiry letters. They may be sent direct, but are often forwarded because of their vague addresses from other council departments, local museums and information centres; it is sometimes surprising that they ever reach the library at all. Birmingham Archives and Local Studies Departments receive about 1000 letters a year; in 1983 the various departments of the Guildhall Library received in total over 2700. (Although to put these figures in perspective, it should be noted that the Society of Genealogists receives about 18 000 letters a year.)

Dealing adequately with such a volume of enquiries can occupy a considerable amount of staff time. In order to cope with other demands, libraries have generally had to modify the traditional public reference service whereby every request for information by letter or telephone is met with an attempt to provide a comprehensive answer within the limits of the collection. The trend in most local studies libraries is to move towards the policy of a record office where replies are restricted on the whole to listing particular sources and facilities available.

The chief difficulty arises with genealogists who may ask for a considerable amount of research and live a long way away. The staff of the Glasgow Room will do 'a fair amount of work' on background searches, 'providing pictures and details of great grandfather's place of work, street, house, life-style; a limited amount of genealogical information will be provided for enquiries of a very specific nature; a list of record agents will be sent out to those whose enquiries are of a diffuse nature'.[6] Essex

Local History Department at Colchester Library will carry out a maximum of 20 minutes' searching of census returns for postal enquiries; Essex residents are expected to visit the library. Other libraries have refused to carry out any searches, arguing that people can write to the Census Room of the Public Record Office whence the library copies have been supplied and where limited searches will be done for a fee; or the writer can employ a professional researcher. Genealogy is seen as a hobby for active people who should be expected to carry out their own research; yet it is undoubtedly a cause of ill-feeling that some libraries will provide considerable help to genealogists by correspondence and others will not. A list of researchers can be obtained from the Association of Genealogists and Record Agents and occasionally libraries can refer to local researchers with a particular knowledge of local records who are willing to work for a fee. Libraries must be careful, however, not to recommend any particular person or assume any responsibility for the quality of their work. Although public libraries are unable to charge for work done by staff, some will note in a reply that donations are gratefully received.

In America the situation is similar but libraries are more willing to lend microfilm copies. The library of the State Historical Society in Missouri, for example, receives about 20 000 written or telephone requests a year. The staff will supply information from indexed sources for specific enquiries whenever possible. If extensive research is required, they will suggest ways for the enquirer to do the research personally either by visiting the society's library, other libraries, or borrowing materials through the society's inter-library loan system. Microfilm copies of federal census records and Missouri newspapers can be borrowed by residents of the state through any public or college library. The society will also provide a list of professional researchers.[7]

Difficulties arise in a different connection in the United Kingdom over requests for information from electoral registers. Searches through old issues of the registers can be treated in the same way as requests to search directories; the library staff would use their discretion over how long to spend. More troublesome are the frequent enquiries, usually by telephone, to check the current edition for a particular entry. Many libraries will refuse to undertake this, ostensibly because to check an entry for one means that it would have to be done for all; and pressure of other duties would not permit this. However, behind this attitude is often the suspicion that most of such enquiries originate from debt-collecting or other agencies who are not necessarily working in the interests of the person concerned. The local registration office would require a formal letter before providing the information. As always, the librarian can state that the registers are available in the library for personal inspection only. Birmingham, however, employs a member of staff specifically to answer such enquiries. One part-time librarian has been employed since 1984 in the Local Studies Library for half of each week to answer all such enquiries not just those from statutory authorities. The number of the Local Studies Library is given in the telephone directory as the place to ring for electoral register enquiries, and two entries will be consulted for each enquirer.

Encouraging people to visit the library does not always lessen the work placed on the staff. Some libraries therefore prefer to carry out research themselves for enquirers rather than spend a great deal of time showing readers unfamiliar with complex historical sources how to use them. The effort involved, however, is usually worthwhile, not just because people who would not normally come into the library are brought in, but also because they can appreciate better the richness and variety of the local studies collection. Useful sources previously unknown to the enquirer can be introduced, and appreciation sometimes leads to donations or help with indexing projects. The librarian's first priority is to ensure that users find the material that is in the library and that will help them satisfy their particular needs for information. Personal enquirers are always given precedence over written and telephone enquiries. Letters sent to libraries where the staff are particularly busy may take a month or more before they get answered, although it is more usual to send a reply within two weeks.

Unlike a county record office, which may only be open office hours during the week and perhaps one evening late, a local studies library will try to remain open the maximum number of hours possible to suit the public demand, the only limitation being the number of staff available for duty. If run as a separate department from the reference library, it is preferable to open for only those hours when it is certain that specialist staff will be available, rather than open for long hours and rely upon temporary relief from other sections who may not be familiar with the collections. With a small number of staff, this means closing at lunch times, some evenings and probably one day a week. If there are going to be some occasions when it is not certain that staff can be on duty, it is advisable to make all visits by appointment only, for example on Saturdays or some evenings.

Public libraries are open to any member of the public to use, and the local studies library in particular contains collections with popular appeal and general as well as research interest. Reference libraries may exclude children below a certain age but the local studies collection may be open to any child who can make use of it and behaves responsibly. People prefer library stock to be accessible so that they can browse through material at their own pace and make their own discoveries especially when they are not always sure what specifically to ask for. However, the rarity, value and delicate nature of many of the items necessitates much of the local collection being kept on closed access. Some collections are almost entirely on closed access. More common is for libraries to place duplicate copies of standard works and recent publications on open access. Occasionally long runs of heavily used volumes, such as directories and electoral registers, will also be on the open shelves, although this is becoming more rare as heavy indiscriminate use leads to excessive wear and tear. Duplicates, photocopies or microfilm editions are beginning to replace them.

## LIBRARY REGULATIONS

Some rules are essential to safeguard the stock and respect the rights of other readers and these need to be made clear to users. All readers requesting items on closed access should put their name and address and subject of enquiry in a visitors' book; proof of identity may be required if particularly valuable items and rare books are requested. In general, regulations governing the care of documents follow those of the Public Record Office and the British Library, in that only pencils are allowed for making notes from manuscripts; they must be handled with great care - in particular no mark should be made on them nor should anything be leant on them; tracing is only allowed at the discretion of the librarian and with the protection of a transparent plastic sheet over the original. The rules governing the conduct of readers are often incorporated into library by-laws to aid their enforcement and support the staff in cases of difficulty. They usually forbid such anti-social behaviour as smoking, eating, drinking and loud talking in the library and sometimes prohibit the use of typewriters and tape-recorders except in specially provided rooms.

Some matters can be left to the discretion of the librarian. The number of items a reader may use at any one time should be limited to a reasonable number. Material should not be left on the tables when not in use; readers should be asked to return items to the staff when finished with. The staff should make frequent checks and observe what members of the public are doing to ensure that materials are treated with care and that anything not in use is shelved. Local studies libraries are reference libraries and it is often necessary to insist that unique items cannot be borrowed otherwise the public will not have access to all the material. The demand for local books for home reading should be met where possible by the lending libraries. The local studies library may have several copies of a standard work, a recently published book and copies of books withdrawn from the lending libraries. These can be used for home reading, loans to schools or to other libraries via the inter-library loans system; but their availability is not usually advertised or the stock will soon be depleted and deteriorate. Readers are advised to make their first approach through their local lending library unless the local studies librarian knows there are several copies in stock and the request is particularly urgent.

If lending is restricted to the minimum in this way, it is unlikely to be extensive and rules can be applied with some degree of flexibility. Special tickets should not be needed; a duplicate loan form would suffice, or details can be entered into a ruled book if statistics are required. The number of items issued and the period of loan can be left to the librarian's discretion. Extended loans can be made to known readers, institutions or other departments of the local authority, subject to immediate return if requested. The same principle that unique stock is never lent applies to all material in the library; but there is no reason why duplicate photographs for example should not be loaned.

The local collection will contain much material suitable for exhibition especially illustrations and ephemeral items such as posters and playbills. Every opportunity to co-operate with other bodies in presenting a display should be taken for the sake of publicising the collection to a wider and different public and encouraging interest in the area. Requests to borrow material will come from those experienced in mounting exhibitions such as other libraries, museums and art galleries, but probably more often from local groups, schools, churches or shops with less experience and fewer facilities, who may want to celebrate a festival, an anniversary, their area or a particular occasion. Care must be taken by the library staff that only items appropriate to the event are lent and that no item which cannot be easily replaced is liable to be damaged, lost or taken. However, in exceptional circumstances, unique items can be loaned for special exhibitions arranged by outside bodies when written assurance is given that all loans will be adequately protected in secure premises and sufficiently insured.

## COPYING FACILITIES

Restrictions on the use of materials to the library itself make the provision of good-quality copying equipment essential. A photocopying machine should be available as a basic requirement, preferably a plain paper dry copier capable of taking up to A3 paper. A reducing or enlarging ability is not absolutely necessary, but only a plain paper dry copier can produce permanent copies on archival paper. As much of the copying done will be for the library's own collection, it is advisable to obtain the best possible machine that the library can afford without making copies too expensive for the public. Photocopying machines can also provide a useful source of income.

Nevertheless, librarians are becoming increasingly concerned about the damage which can be caused to irreplaceable material by photocopying. In 1984 Brent libraries carried out a brief survey of local studies libraries in the London area to find out what other libraries permitted to be copied. Many libraries replied that they would not allow the copying of large bound volumes, electoral registers or directories; about half did not allow any maps to be copied, others would not copy manuscript maps or were cautious about copying large maps; early or fragile photographs would not be photocopied, or manuscript volumes; some drew the line at any item dating from before 1800 or even 1900.

Libraries are increasingly arranging for maps and plans to be copied on to microfilm or aperture cards to reduce the handling of the originals. The provision of further copies then becomes relatively straightforward if the library possesses a microfilm reader/printer. Birmingham has put a collection of about 200 000 plans on to aperture cards and the Vestry House Museum Local History Library at Walthamstow is copying many of its older maps on to the same format. Copies can be supplied from these up to A1 in size, larger than those from a normal photocopying machine. Some of the most frequently used materials such as census returns, Ordnance Survey plans, the *International genealogical index* and local newspapers, can be obtained on microfilm or microfiche. Despite the high initial cost and variable quality of the machines currently available, a microfilm reader/printer ranks as the most useful piece of copying equipment after the photocopying machine.

257

Where items are liable to be damaged by photocopying or a better-quality reproduction is required, especially of photographs, the copy has to be made with a camera. Libraries which receive sufficient orders or which have sufficient work of their own can probably justify the expenditure on a camera, lights and copying stand. Copies can then be made fairly quickly and cheaply by the staff, the library retaining control over the quality of the work and keeping the negatives. Sometimes a photographer in another department may be able to carry out copying work; but the library will have a low priority against other demands on his time. The cost will be considerably greater if a commercial photographer is commissioned to visit the library and he/she insists on keeping the negatives for future orders. This should be resisted and outside photographers only employed if they agree to deposit the negatives with the library, because they cannot be relied upon either to keep or to find the negatives after a few years and there is a danger that libraries will lose control over reproduction rights. Not all photographers will charge an additional fee for handing them over. Those libraries that can provide photographic copies at reasonable rates may refuse readers permission to use their own cameras in the library. Otherwise readers should be allowed to film material themselves if it is for their own private use.

## COPYRIGHT

In the United Kingdom copying in libraries is subject to the provisions of the Copyright Act 1956 and the Copyright (Libraries) Regulations 1957 (Statutory Instrument no. 868, 1957). Copyright law, however, is fraught with difficulties and different libraries interpret it in different ways. As far as local studies librarians are concerned, particular problems arise over the copying of maps and illustrations and the question of fees. Most photocopying carried out in a library is for the convenience of the public, in order to save time by not having to take so many notes and to ensure accuracy of quotation. Copying therefore does not usually replace purchase and is rarely a financial threat to the copyright owner. Section 6 of the Copyright Act clearly states that 'no fair dealing with a literary, dramatic or musical work for purpose of research or private study shall constitute an infringement of the copyright in the work'.

Although most copying would come under this category, it is necessary for the librarian to be aware of the restrictions. Anything dating from before

1957 is in copyright for 50 years after the death of the author in the case of a published work, or 50 years after publication in the case of a map, or 50 years after the date a photograph was taken, or for ever (until published) in the case of a manuscript. The Copyright (Libraries) Regulations state that a 'reasonable proportion' of a copyright work can be copied by public libraries but only if the copyright owner cannot be traced. The Society of Authors and the Publishers' Association have defined a reasonable proportion as no more than 10 per cent. These two organisations representing the interests of the copyright holders have declared that they are willing to allow libraries to copy up to this amount without permission even when the copyright owners' identity is known, although some libraries do not appear to be aware of this agreement.[8] Only one copy may be taken. At the time of going to press however, copyright law is under revision.

The Ordnance Survey has also defined fair dealing more precisely as meaning, in so far as their copyright plans are concerned, 'up to four copies of any extract not exceeding 700 square centimetres (about A4 size) may be supplied'.[9] Copies of maps required for submission in court may be freely supplied as may copies for other council departments of the library's own authority. This covers most of the users of the local studies library and any requests for uses other than private study, for more than four copies or larger extracts, can be referred to the Ordnance Survey or their nearest agent. The Ordnance Survey will licence libraries to provide copies of non-current maps published within the 50-year copyright period and authorise them to collect royalties on their behalf, but few libraries have sufficient need to apply for this.

The question of publication arises often over illustrations; and extreme care must be taken that copies are not supplied for this purpose if the copyright owner is known. All enquiries should be passed on, and only if the copyright owner cannot be traced or cannot supply a copy should the library allow a copy to be made. A clear summary of the complex legal situation is given in the Museums Association's Information Sheet no. 7, now unfortunately out of print.[10] Duration of copyright in a photograph taken before 1 June 1957 is 50 years from the end of the calendar year in which the photograph was taken. A new copyright cannot be established in a copy photograph; the date of the original photograph is what is important, not that of any copy negative taken later. However, if the original illustration is in a different medium such as an engraving or watercolour, a photograph of it would have its own copyright. According to the above publication it is not an infringement for anyone to make a single copy of a photograph for their own private study, or to show a slide of an illustration in a lecture. Publishing a copyright photograph or broadcasting it on television requires the permission of the copyright owner.

Copyright belongs initially to whoever commissions the taking of a photograph and pays for it; the owner therefore is not necessarily the person who holds the negative or even the photographer. A library does not necessarily hold the copyright of photographs which it purchases or is given; and photographers are very sensitive on this point. Wiltshire Library Service earned itself a sharp rebuke in the *Amateur photographer* for 18 July 1981 when launching a competition to attract photographs recording the local environment and social activities. Rule 5 claimed that: 'Prints, negatives and copyright become the exclusive property of Wiltshire Library and Museum Service. All entries are non-returnable.' This rule was withdrawn after protests and only the right to retain and display prints claimed.

The issue is of more financial importance with photographs taken by commercial agencies, as fees are their major source of income and libraries may possess photographs which were taken originally by an agency but which no longer has copies of its own. The copyright owner can charge whatever fees he likes for the use of copyright material or just for the use of the collection if the item is out of copyright. In the latter case they are called reproduction fees, and libraries seeking to enlarge their income are increasingly applying fees for the commercial use of any material in their collections which is not somebody else's copyright. Non-profit-making publications, local newspapers and educational users are usually exempt or charged a much reduced fee. Business firms and media organisations are accustomed to paying high fees to commercial picture agencies and expect libraries to make a charge for the use of their facilities, although less than a commercial agency would charge.

Some libraries base their fees on the Museums Association's guidelines, or those of the Radio Times Hulton Picture Library; the Guildhall Library has its own list of charges and receives an income of several thousand pounds a year from this source. It is sometimes difficult to keep a check on whether publishers have used particular illustrations or not, as a picture researcher will often take copies of several for final selection much later. The library has to rely on the honesty of the publisher in declaring which pictures are going to be used and invoice the publisher accordingly.

It is important also for the library to ensure that suitable acknowledgement is made, and not always just to the library. Even if a picture to be used is out of copyright, it may have been donated by a member of the public or copied from an original held by a member of the public. It is a matter of courtesy rather than law for a publisher to inform the donor if any of their material is to be used and to acknowledge them in the credits. People who would otherwise be extremely helpful to a library can become upset and annoyed to find their pictures used without being aware that they were to be published and without acknowledgement.

## LIBRARY GUIDES

Proper reference to the library in a publication that uses its material is essential to inform the reader where the items come from and it is good advertising. Some people may not be aware that the library collects photographs as well as books and may not be conscious of the wealth and range of local studies collections generally. For this reason the library should issue a printed leaflet as a minimum requirement giving the basic details of hours of opening and how to get there, and also outlining the extent of various holdings of books, maps, newspapers, photographs and manuscripts. London local studies libraries have more detailed duplicated 'guides to local history resources' produced in a uniform format initially in response to a questionnaire sponsored by the Association of London Chief Librarians. One copy of each is deposited in every local studies library in the area and some authorities have published guides based on their own replies to the questionnaire for public use. Camden's *Guide to the collections* includes a list of library publications, a select bibliography and a list of local history organisations in the borough. The most lengthy, as befits the library with the largest collections, is that of the Guildhall, which has made copies available for purchase.

Other popular guides concentrate on sources that will assist particular categories of user, especially those tracing the history of a family or building. Such guides answer the most frequently asked questions about holdings of census returns, electoral registers, directories and newspapers, for example; and they can suggest other relevant but less-well-known sources in the library, other record offices and libraries to visit and books on how to go about researching the subject.

Libraries are continually adding to their collections and such guides rapidly become out of date. They are best produced therefore as cheaply as possible; if the library has the use of a word processor, updating is a relative straightforward matter; if not, they may be duplicated and perhaps issued loose-leaf in a folder and given away if not too substantial. The Glasgow Room in the Mitchell Library has about 30 guides available and the range has been widely extended. Among the most popular are: *Glasgow newspapers, 1715-1979: a chronological guide; Index of early Glasgow views, 1693-1850; Acts of Parliament relating to Glasgow, 1488-1973; Glasgow theatres and music halls;* and *Glasgow O.S. maps 25" to 1 mile, County Series.*

Wiltshire Library Service adopted a different approach in compiling a series of eight leaflets to coincide with the 1982 BBC 2 series *History on your doorstep.* The leaflets are aimed at members of the public with particular interests and describe sources for the study of parish, family, transport, building, agricultural and industrial history together with a brief bibliography of the county, a list of useful addresses and advice on how to publish local history. These have been typed onto A4 paper and reduced to A5 by photocopying so that an eight-page leaflet only occupies two sides of A4 paper. Assembled in a wallet under the title *Studying Wiltshire,* over 700 at £1.40 each were sold in the first 18 months.

By presenting the information as a series of leaflets, it is a simple matter to revise and replace one, as has already been done with the family history leaflet. Copies of individual leaflets can also be given away in response to enquiries. The local studies officer for Wiltshire claims another advantage for this sort of guide:

> When one is working in an organisation with fifty or more service points it is very difficult to ensure that a uniform level of service is presented to the public throughout the system. . . By depositing a copy of 'Studying Wiltshire' in every Wiltshire Library, I can try to ensure that most of the basic information necessary to answer commonly asked local studies enquiries is available throughout the system.[11]

Detailed guides such as these can help to inform the public as to the resources they can expect to find in the local studies library and can therefore save the staff much time in not having to explain the collections to visitors. Particular groups, whose members are likely to want to use the library or at least have an interest in what can be found there, often also find it helpful to hold special sessions or arrange special visits when material can be shown to them and its potential value discussed.

The staff need to be free of other interruptions on these occasions, and may arrange for the library to remain open late one evening or set aside time and use suitable premises like a lecture hall if available, to devote to such groups. Visits by school and evening classes will be considered in the next chapter, but other particular interest groups like local family history societies, amenity, literary or transport societies will also find sessions useful. The library staff can use these opportunities not only to interest potential readers in the library but also to draw to their attention parts of the stock that could be better exploited. Some family history societies have arranged with their local library certain regular times when more experienced members will be available to advise other members on how to tackle personal problems of research. The Glasgow and West of Scotland Family History Society, for example, holds worknights in the Glasgow Room and bewildered newcomers to genealogy can be assisted by knowledgeable members instead of the busy staff.

Large public library systems have many visitors during the year, and also a large turnover in staff. The staff of the Edinburgh Room in the Central Library have experimented with a tape/slide programme designed both to instruct visitors and train new staff. They found that the saving in staff time was considerable, especially in dealing with library school students in groups which may number 50 at once, and have to be divided into several parties to be shown around. The students apparently also preferred a tape/slide show to being shown round because they could sit down and concentrate during the performance. However, the criticism was made that there was no need to travel to the library to see the presentation and visitors were deprived of the opportunity to handle original material.[12]

## EXTENSION ACTIVITIES

The level of service provided to users depends ultimately on the resources of the library and the staff time available. At a time when growing demand has not been accompanied by a proportionate increase in staff, local studies librarians have been forced to give first priority to those individuals and groups who visit the library, then to deal with telephone and written enquiries when free to do so and finally to exploit the riches and popular appeal of their collections by 'outreach activities' or what used to be called 'extension work'.

Librarians' annual reports provide evidence of the conflicts that can arise. In his annual report for 1983/84 the chief leisure services officer of the London Borough of Brent expressed the feelings of many local studies librarians under pressure, when discussing the problems faced by the Grange Museum of Local History:

> The increasing popularity of local history has resulted in a greater demand for assistance with local history enquiries and research projects. . . The result is an increasing backlog of work to be done on the documentation of the collections. . . as staff spend so large a proportion of their working time helping members of the public. . . the increasing demand is something which is beyond our control and will eventually put such pressure on the local history library, that users will suffer. . . The increasing demands of the public visiting the museum. . . and the small numbers of staff have made it more difficult to find time for talks outside the museum building.
>
> Nevertheless, the museum keeper and local history librarian did manage to run an evening class over two terms on Willesden history.

Despite the pressure of other work, a lively local studies service will attempt to be active outside the library and within the community because of the publicity value to the library service as a whole, and because it encourages donations, provides useful contacts and enhances local people's understanding of the area in which they live. As with many aspects of local studies librarianship, the level of activity varies throughout the country but it would appear that the greatest emphasis today is placed on local studies publications, (see Chapter 17), exhibitions and supplying material to the local media.

Local newspapers have always seen the local studies collection as a source of good copy, especially in the form of old photographs, and libraries have been able to use the excellent relationship built up over many years to their advantage. The example of Cambridgeshire demonstrates the possibilities of using local newspapers and more recently local radio stations. Cambridge Newspapers Ltd made a permanent loan of back copies of the *Cambridgeshire chronicle* to the Cambridgeshire Collection in the Central Library; the *Cambridge evening news* has naturally featured the indexing of these newspapers which led to a series of booklets on different villages, and also the work of the library. The 'Down your street' series in the *Cambridge weekly news* is mostly researched in the library and has culminated in a paperback compilation. The pictures from the past theme often produces further pictures and useful anecdotes; a variation on this idea in the same newspaper was to publish photographs showing old cars which readers wrote in to identify. Local community newspapers, newsletters of local groups and magazines of local authorities are also willing to publish details about the local studies library, especially if sources relating to their area are discussed and old pictures used. The librarian would have to use discretion as to whether a commitment can be made to provide a regular column.

The Cambridgeshire local studies librarian has contributed a regular weekly spot to Radio Cambridgeshire since the station opened in 1982. Originally indexes to the local newspapers were used to compare events of the current week with similar happenings in the past. More recently a four-minute script has been prepared on a suitable subject and listeners invited to telephone in with their own memories. In the Peterborough district of Cambridgeshire, an early agreement with Hereward Radio for a local history spot rapidly matured into a five-day-a-week all-year-round broadcast with a topical, seasonal, anniversary or special events theme.

A large number of people who would not otherwise consider using library services are made aware of the work of the local studies library by learning about it through such promotions in the media. In contrast, the much heralded BBC 2 series in 1982, *History on your doorstep,* was disappointing, although local studies libraries were extensively featured. The timing of this series and that of Yorkshire TV's *Sense of the past* perhaps made them unlikely to attract a large audience. The BBC series, however, did stimulate libraries to organise their own activities, prepare leaflets, mount exhibitions and stage workshops. Many libraries found that while their own list of sources was popular, the BBC's was not. According to the head of reference services, the response to the three workshops held in Edinburgh was excellent and press coverage at least in Scotland was encouraging.

Regional television, like local radio, may prove to be a more promising way forward. In the Midlands, Central TV's production of the *Country diary of an Edwardian lady* had a linked activity pack which included notes on how to write a nature diary, local walks, and family and local history. Much of this had been supported by groundwork from Birmingham Public Libraries, and the follow-up to the series was undertaken through local libraries.

Exhibitions on a local history theme usually attract considerable publicity if a popular enough subject is chosen. One of the most successful presented by Tower Hamlets Libraries was on 'The Jewish community in East London'; interest in the subject aroused national publicity, including a feature in the *Guardian,* a film presentation on the television, as well as an article in the *Jewish chronicle* when the exhibition was extended by public demand. The exhibition was held in conjunction with an annual local history lecture given each November by a distinguished authority; in 1984 it was Lord Asa Briggs. The mayor usually presides making it an important civic occasion and a capacity audience fills the library hall.

*10. Local history display, Local Studies Department, Colchester Central Library.*

Commemorations often provide the incentive for a major exhibition. The 150th anniversary of the Garnkirk and Glasgow Railway, for example, kept the staff of Strathkelvin District Libraries busy in 1981 with a comprehensive project involving work with local schools, the production of publications and souvenirs, and the preparation of an exhibition; this was seen by over 10 000 people at a British Rail open day and afterwards circulated around libraries in Scotland. The Edinburgh Room used the opportunity of their own fiftieth anniversary in 1982 to invite local authors who regularly used the library, as well as past and present members of staff, to a reception at which the guests were welcomed by the chairman of the Recreation Committee. The Scottish press featured articles on the work of the department and the librarian-in-charge was interviewed on BBC Radio Scotland.

Special events and large exhibitions can only be arranged occasionally as they are time-consuming to prepare. However, small travelling exhibitions are relatively easy to arrange and can circulate around lending libraries, churches, building societies, banks, advice centres, schools and other similar venues where a wide audience will be attracted. If perspex is used to protect original items or only photographic copies are displayed, nothing valuable should be damaged or lost. Sponsorship can sometimes be found, especially from local banks and businesses, to help towards the costs. Wiltshire Library and Museum Service found a bank to sponsor the series of annual history competitions which started in 1984/85. It is hoped that the competitions will encourage original work and provide material for an exhibition which will travel around libraries and other places in the county with a description of local studies facilities in Wiltshire.

What can be achieved on a small scale in an inner city area is shown by the activities of librarians at branch level in Manchester where the local history service is seen as a part of community information. In the east area, libraries always try to display something of local interest, whether photographs, objects or maps, and displays are taken to schools, churches and shopping centres. One successful exhibition at Longright Library was of drawings of houses in the area by a local unemployed school teacher; and local people apparently saw their district in a new light as a result.

More direct contact with individual members of the public can be achieved by giving talks or leading history walks, common features of the programmes of local history societies. Working in a local studies department over a period of time inevitably leads to the librarian becoming a storehouse of information and well aware of the topics that interest people the most. Long experience, and a collection of slides and other visual aids, makes the preparation of such talks easier. Some librarians eventually become regarded as experts on their locality and enjoy sharing their knowledge with others. There are distinct advantages to the library if staff can gain this public image. The librarian-in-charge of the Cambridgeshire Collection for almost 20 years now finds that he gives about 40 talks a year to groups such as Women's Institutes, old peoples' clubs and local societies, and has made many useful contacts and received a number of invaluable donations as a result.

There is an insatiable demand for talks about the locality by all local groups from luncheon clubs for old age pensioners to mother and toddler groups. Such talks are very popular, especially if illustrated, and provide an undoubted service to the community. These are generally social occasions, the audiences are usually very friendly and will do much of the talking themselves, but the librarian will have to decide whether time is available to give talks to these groups and whether the number of people reached, which may be very few, justify the effort involved. The ability to talk convincingly to more critical audiences is a by-product of long experience of local history work. Librarians should not necessarily be thought of as historians, nor should they be expected to devote their own time in the evenings to give talks if they do not want to. Many librarians find that they spend enough time after work attending meetings of local history and other societies, where they may be members of the committee by reason of their official position, so that they are reluctant to take on any extra activities.

Local studies librarians provide a much appreciated service to the general public and the demands have increased enormously over the past decade. Librarians will endeavour to assist the public as much as they can and try to exploit the popular appeal of the collections in their charge. However, the services provided to any one individual or group will always be subject to the staff and resources available, the care needed to conserve material for future generations and the requirements of other users. The chairman of the Local Studies Group in 1979, Dorothy McCulla, questioned whether the failure of the Committee to Review Local History under Lord Blake:

> to recognise the exciting work now being done by local history librarians, which contributes greatly to the betterment of life, [is not] also the failure of the profession to realise in full the value of

the local history collection in every public library? And does this not in turn account for the reticence of many local history librarians to publicise their work because of the impossible work load that would ensue?[13]

It would appear that despite other pressures, local studies librarians are willing to promote their collections, but how they do it varies according to their own abilities and the resources of their particular library.

## NOTES

1.  Armstrong, *Local collections in Scotland*. Glasgow, Scottish Library Association, 1977. See comments under individual libraries in the directory sections.
2.  Hobbs, J.L. *Local history and the library*. 2nd edition revised by G.A. Carter. London, Deutsch, 1973, p. 37.
3.  Escott, A. Cut price genealogy? The Glasgow Room experience. *Locscot* 1 (6) Spring 1984, p. 108.
4.  Spotted spy. *Library Association record* 85 (5) May 1983, p. 165. And, Notes and news, *Local studies librarian* 2 (1) Summer 1983, 25.
5.  Barclay, R.L. Access to information with a genealogy and history referral file. *RQ* 18 (2) Winter 1978, pp. 153-155.
6.  Escott, p. 109.
7.  Goodrich, J. The State Historical Society of Missouri. *Show-me-libraries* 33 (11) August 1982, 5-9.
8.  *Photocopying and the law*. London, Society of Authors, 1968.
9.  Ordnance Survey. *Copyright regulations for libraries*. Southampton, Ordnance Survey, January 1983.
10.  Gibbs-Smith, C.H. *Copyright law concerning works of art, photographs and the written and spoken word*. 3rd edition. London, Museums Association, 1978.
11.  Chandler, J. Local studies and archives. In: *Archives and education: conference proceedings 1982 and 1983*. Society of Archivists, 1984, pp. 14-19.
12.  Armstrong, p. 60.

13. McCulla, D. Report of the Committee to Review Local History (The Blake Report). *Newsletter* (Library Association, Local Studies Group) 2 (2) December 1979, p.1.

## FURTHER READING

Ansell, R. History on your doorstep - a review. *Local studies librarian* 1 (2) Summer 1982, 16-17.

Bunch, A. Local history on air. *Local studies librarian* 3 (2) Winter 1984, 8-11.

Fisher, J. Local studies in the Mitchell Library: the Glasgow Collection. *Local studies librarian* 2 (1) Summer 1983, 14-16.

Harvey, R. *Genealogy for librarians.* London, Bingley, 1983.

Lynes, A. *How to organise a local collection.* London, Deutsch, 1974. Chapters 9 and 10.

McDougall, S. Edinburgh images and reflections: treasures of the Edinburgh Room. *Local studies librarian* 3 (2) Winter 1984, 18-22.

McDougall, S. The golden jubilee of the Edinburgh Room. *Locscot* 1 (3) Autumn 1982, 57-58.

Martin, D. 'Garnkirk and Glasgow 150'. *Locscot* 1 (1) Winter 1981, 12-13.

Nelms, W. Using local history and genealogy to build library support. *Library journal* 104 (6) 15 March, 1979, 686-687.

Petty, M.J. Working with wireless. *Local studies librarian* 2 (2) Winter 1983, 17-19.

Reed, M. International local history - paradox or prospect? *Libri* 26 (3) September 1976, 231-242.

Sharp, M. Local history - making it a community resource in Motherwell District. *Locscot* 1 (5) Autumn 1983, 87-89.

Sussex, G. '. . . and on the right, past the chippy we have Edwin Chadwick's birthplace'. *Local studies librarian* 1 (3) Winter 1982, 12-14.

Sussex, G. Local studies at branch level - vicars, pensioners and Whitwalk photographers. In: Library Association Conference, Cliftonville 1981. *Papers: learning through life.* London, LA, 1982, pp. 39-46.

Taylor, L.J. *Copyright for librarians.* Hastings, Tamarisk Books, 1980.

# 14

# Local studies and education

Andrew Blizzard


Nowhere has the impact of education on library services been so strongly felt than in the field of local studies. Since the early 1950s, and particularly in the last ten to fifteen years, there has been a dramatic increase in the use of local source material at all levels of education - school, college, university and adult classes. This has had a profound effect on the institutions that provide such material, notably libraries, record offices and museums. Significantly, the demand for local resources in education is not limited to the United Kingdom but has been experienced in a number of other countries, such as the United States, Australia, Denmark, France, West Germany and the Union of Soviet Socialist Republics.

This chapter complements the previous one by considering the implications of the use of local studies collections for educational purposes. All uses may, in some way, be regarded as 'educational', but here the concern is principally with children, students, teachers and tutors who are required to use local material. Despite the important position of local studies within libraries, little has been written from the librarian's point of view on its educational value, although an increasing number of articles and papers by archivists have appeared in recent years. The main contributor in this area, however, remains the teacher, college of education tutor and other educationalists, who often acknowledge the help of the local record office and, occasionally, the local collection in the library. The inspiration for this present chapter is drawn largely from the writer's experience as liaison librarian for local studies at Birmingham Reference Library; although perhaps not representing a 'typical' model of a local studies service, the initiative nevertheless provides an excellent example of work with education. There is, however, much good work being undertaken elsewhere, in libraries, record offices, museums and other institutions.

## EDUCATIONAL SIGNIFICANCE OF LOCAL STUDIES

The place of local history (rather than local studies) in education is not a new phenomenon, it was advocated by the Board of Education in 1908: 'It is essential that in each school [secondary school] attention should be paid to the history of the town and district in which it is situated'. Local history was, in its early stages of development, seen fit merely to illustrate national history, rather than as a subject in its own right. Local history/studies was not fully established in the education curriculum until the late 1960s and at examination level some ten years later. Local history teaching and local history project work were, of course, present well before this period, but they were the exception rather than the rule. The Local Studies Department, Birmingham, for example, has an interesting school project, dated 1924, on the Redditch bicycle industry. The most significant developments in local history study and teaching, however, took place after the Second World War. For school teachers, the most significant development was *The school looks around,* by Elizabeth Layton and Justin B. White, which appeared in 1948, written under the auspices of the Association for Education Citizenship and described as 'a book for teachers about local surveys'. This is probably one of the earliest published works aimed at helping teachers of local history, providing information about local survey methods and referring to specific case studies taken from different types of school in both rural and urban areas. The official view of the place of local history was again clearly expressed in 1952, in an HMSO pamphlet, *Teaching history,* which stated that local material 'offers many opportunities for individual initiative and cooperation', but further expressed its illustrative function of general history. More recently there has been a major debate on the place of history in the school curriculum due to falling interest, particularly at examination level. Sir Keith Joseph, the Secretary of State for Education, at a conference of the Historical Association in London in February 1984, argued that 'history is an essential component in the curriculum of all pupils' and that 'it can develop skills in analysis and criticism. . . by encouraging pupils to evaluate primary source material.[1]

## LOCAL STUDIES IN SCHOOLS

It was not until the late 1960s that the study of the local environment and the use of local source material began to find a place in the education curriculum, both in the primary and secondary school. The evidence for this is the number of articles and books published by teachers and other educationalists and the increase in the use of local resources from libraries, record offices and other resource institutions. The local study becomes an increasingly important element in history, geography, social studies, local studies, environmental studies or simply 'project' work; local information could also be successfully utilised in science, mathematics, English and art work. There came a realisation that the study of the local environment could more than illustrate the broader national pattern, that the study of identifiable communities had more relevance and interest for the children, that it introduced a range of skills (e.g. observation, deduction, linguistic expression, mathematical calculation) and attitudes about the past and present (e.g. awareness, enjoyment, curiosity and empathy), and that its interdisciplinary nature was a positive educational asset. What is discernible here is a change of emphasis from content to method, to the process rather than the product. Central to this process is the place of local source material - the 'raw material' of history. Much has been written on the value (and problems) of local history teaching in the school by, for example, Robert Douch and W.B. Stephens,[2] and a number of interesting articles have also appeared in the *Local historian* and in *Teaching history.*[3]

Local history/studies has not been easily accommodated in the secondary (comprehensive) school curriculum (and even less so in the grammar school), because of strict timetabling and the limitations of examination syllabuses. However, in recent years a number of examination boards have introduced project work (personal study) for assessment, and questions about the local area or use of primary source material have been included in the examination paper. Foremost has been the Schools Council History 13-16 Project, 'History around us', a project set up at Leeds University from 1972-1977, to 'suggest suitable objectives for history teachers, and to promote the use of appropriate materials and ideas for their realisation'. The project was aimed at history teaching throughout the secondary school, but has been found particularly useful for CSE and GCE history courses and helped teachers devise their own Mode 3 syllabuses. The Certificate of Extended Education (CEE) West Midlands Examination Board has a history syllabus, 'The methods of a historian', which covers where and how evidence is collected, the types of evidence and its interpretation, together with a course work content of which one option is a local study, for example, 'Industry in the Midlands 1700-1830'. The candidate's

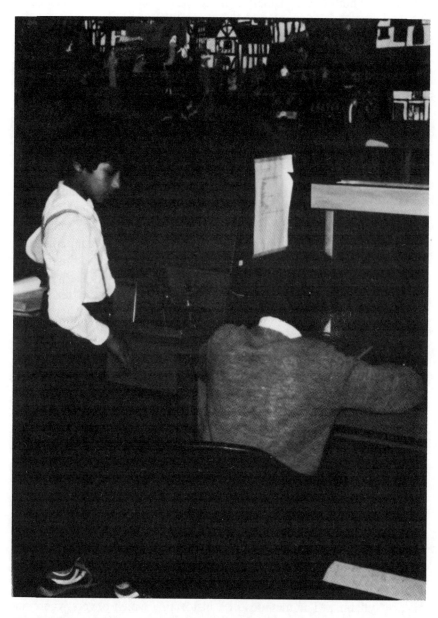

*11. Grove Junior School, Handsworth using census returns on microfilm in the Local Studies Department, Birmingham Central Library, 1982.* [Andrew Blizzard]

fieldwork (visits to historical sites) or course work folder accounts for 30 per cent of the total marks. Many CSE, 16+ and 'O' level syllabuses have a project element and candidates are often encouraged to pursue a local study where there is a good availability of primary source material. At 'A' level, the Associated Examination Board is now offering a history pilot scheme, which includes a personal study, either on national and international history or on local history.

The introduction of new history courses which look, in part, at the ethnic minority presence in Britain can include references to specific local examples. A CSE pilot scheme on 'Aspects of the Afro-Caribbean' has been devised by a West Midlands local authority; and recently, JMB (Joint Matriculation Board) has introduced a similar paper at 'O' level.

A CSE course specifically in local studies has been developed, for example, by a school in the Black Country, which has proved very successful.[4] A local history syllabus at 'O' level is offered by JMB, which includes a project element, accounting for 50 per cent of the marks, and an examination on primary sources. A similar syllabus is also offered at 'A' level. Outside of examinations, many schools have devised or adopted new and interesting courses with a local studies element, either at the lower end or as an alternative to examinations, e.g. 17+: the Certificate of Pre-Vocational Education (CPVE).[5] Family history has played an important part in some secondary schools; a report on three projects is contained in *Family history in schools,* by D.J. Steel and L. Taylor.[6]

History is not the only subject which can utilise local source material, the other major subject area being geography. *Curriculum 11-16: geography,* a working paper by the Geography Committee of HM Inspectorate (July 1978), suggests 'that pupils study the immediate neighbourhood; selected aspects of the home region that have particular significance for the local community. . .' but 'this range of study should be considered at a variety of levels from the local, if possible and appropriate, to the global'. Access to a whole range of source material, for example, maps, aerial photographs and demographic information, is therefore necessary. Candidates' project work for examination assessment will often require local information. Neil Punnett and Peter Webber, in 'Using local resources: town expansion and industrial growth', have highlighted the problem of textbook costs and thus, the need to use local resources, for both their CSE Mode 3 'Local studies' element (60 per cent of which is fieldwork assessment) and 'O' level (University of London Board) 'Industrial location' paper.[7] The project element is also to be found in some 'A' level syllabuses (e.g. JMB). Geography, and indeed history, has also found a place in the government's five-year pilot scheme - Technical and Vocational Education Initiative (TVEI), which is being tested in a number of regions throughout the country. Gill Davidson, in 'TVEI', discusses the retrieval of local information from libraries, resource centres, museums and archive collections.[8]

There has also been an increase in the 'blurring' of subject compartments in recent years, and this is due in no small measure to the growth in local studies which is reflected in, for example, the use of the term 'local studies' in local studies libraries and librarianship. As a term, first used by sociologists and social anthropologists at the turn of the century, 'local studies' has now been widely adopted. It encompasses a broader focus on the local environment, both its past, present and, to some extent, its future. From this, a confusing array of other terms have been used - 'environmental studies', 'environmental science', 'environmental education' or simply 'local project'. These are terms which stress the interdisciplinary nature of the study, focussing on the immediate environment but broadening out to include global issues such as pollution and energy. What is important for local studies librarians, as librarians, is the potential use of their collections for the local component of these courses and as a means to refer teachers and pupils to other sources of information for the broader aspects. Such approaches have been traditionally adopted by the primary school, although increasingly a place in the secondary school curriculum is being found. The West Midlands Examination Board, for example, has introduced a CSE syllabus on environmental science and environmental studies. The successful amalgamation of other areas of the curriculum with environmental studies has been the subject of another Schools Council Project, described in *Art and the built environment: a teacher's approach*, by Eileen Adams and Colin Ward.[9]

The primary school is, however, free from the constraints of examination work and can thus adopt a project approach more easily. Often this will be a study of the immediate environment around the school, or local village, or a particular theme, such as the transport or industry associated with the area. To show the extent of this freedom, a primary school in Birmingham, for example, produced an environmental studies project which was completed over a period of two school terms; for the whole of that time the children worked according to a structured integrated curriculum. The completed project won the Wide-Awake Trail Competition in 1982, organised by the Heritage Education Group of the Civic Trust; a report of the project was published by the Geographical Association entitled *The good, the bad and the ugly*.[10] There are plenty of examples of local studies work undertaken at primary school level in the pages of *Teaching history* and occasionally in *Teaching geography*. What is stressed most often in the teaching of local studies through project work in the primary, middle and lower secondary school, is the child-centred skills aspect: 'Environmental Education is the process of recognising values and clarifying concepts in order to develop the skills and attitudes necessary to understand and appreciate the interrelatedness among man, his culture and his biophysical surroundings. It also entails practice in decision-making and self-formulation of a code of behaviour about issues concerning environmental quality'.[11] Further analysis of the skills aspect in local studies/environmental studies, can be found in 'An approach to environmental studies through historical resources', which also has a useful report on four cases studies from schools in England and Wales.[12]

The most recent and exciting developments in education concern the transfer of data from primary source material to the school microcomputer, and various projects throughout the country have involved the co-operation of librarians and archivists. All schools, both primary and secondary, with the aid of government funding, are required to purchase at least one microcomputer; the majority of schools, at least in the writer's own area, the Birmingham area, use Research Machines Limited (RML) 480 Zs (at primary level) and 380 Zs (at secondary). The first projects, aimed at developing an information retrieval system for use in secondary schools, included Aslib's 'Schools information retrieval project', aided by the British Library, in 1981. Since then, many in-house and commercial computer packages have been developed:

1   Education Computing Section (Chelsea College), Computer Assisted Learning 11-18, e.g. 'Census analysis; average age of death from burial registers'.
2   Micro Education Program (MEP) DES 1981 - which has 14 Regional Information Centres.
3   Longman's (Chelsea College), e.g. 'Canal building' and 'Census'.
4   Heineman Computers in Education, e.g. 'Quarry Bank 1851 census' (which includes room for schools' own census input).[13]

In early November 1984, the BBC announced their plan to create a modern 'Domesday Book' by using information about the local area collated by schools on their microcomputers. A six-part series on BBC television, marking the 900th anniversary, was shown in 1986.

## LOCAL STUDIES IN HIGHER EDUCATION

The present, relatively healthy, position of local studies in schools has been attributed to the training of teachers in the 1950s, 1960s and early 1970s. Many of the influential writers on the subject have been tutors in colleges of education, teacher training colleges or schools of education in polytechnics and universities, and have had experience as teachers in schools. Foremost is John West, the author of *History here and now, Archives for schools, Village records, Town records* and numerous articles. West was senior history lecturer at Shenstone College of Education, Worcester (1955-63), a general advisor in education at Liverpool and a senior inspector at Dudley (from 1967). While at Dudley, he was engaged in a six-year research project, 'Young children's awareness of the past', which also formed the subject of his PhD, thesis at the University of Keele's Institute of Education in 1981.[14] Mention should also be made of Robert Douch, who was lecturer in local history at the University of Southampton Institute of Education, the first post of its kind in the country, created in 1951. A report of the institute's work is contained in 'Local history in school', which includes some information about the local collection in the institute library and stresses the importance of good contacts with librarians, archivists and curators.[15] Details of particular local history projects, undertaken by student teachers, are to be found in *Local history and the teacher,* by R. Douch.[16] Some colleges of education have introduced a dissertation to replace part of the examination and this approach has been described in the *Local historian.*[17]

The problem of students 'invading' record offices for their special study or extended essay is reported in 'College of education students in the archives office', which also includes examples of research projects undertaken at record offices by second-year students.[18] In recent years the faculties of education in polytechnics and universities and the colleges of higher education have tended to introduce the broader 'environmental education' approach, which still, nevertheless, retains an important local aspect. What remains significant about these faculties of education is their

278

contact with local schools and the opportunities for setting up major local studies projects, perhaps with the help of the local studies librarian or archivist. Newman College (Birmingham), for instance, has built up a substantial local collection with the aid of the Manpower Services Commission (MSC) scheme; developed important links with local schools and the library; and has also been involved in the production of local databases for use in schools. For teachers in service, the Historical Association introduced its Advanced Certificate in the Teaching of History in 1982. This course involves 18 months of part-time study and includes a module on library skills and resources, and the techniques of local or family history.

At the university level, local history, as with the schools, had its roots before the war. In 1908 a research fellowship in local history was established at Reading University, but ran for only four years. A reader in the history of London was appointed at University College in 1921 and in 1930 the University of Hull set up a committee to promote research in the history of the region; a staff tutor in local history was established in 1949 and a certificate course the following year. The University of Manchester appointed G.H. Tupling as special lecturer in local history in 1935. Leicester University established the first and only local history department in the country in 1948, although it was and is primarily concerned with postgraduate studies. W.G. Hoskins became the first reader in English local history and H.P.R. Finberg its first professor in 1962. The 'Leicester School' established local history as a useful and serious academic pursuit. A number of universities and polytechnics have followed and are responsible for the publication of serious academic journals like *Social history* (Hull University), *Northern history* (Leeds) and *Midland history* (Birmingham) some of which use a regionalist approach. A number of regional history centres have been established at institutions of higher education, for example at the universities of East Anglia, Lancaster and Keele, North Humberside College of Further Education and Wolverhampton Polytechnic (where a part-time MA course in West Midlands history is offered). Hull University has recently introduced an MA course in historical computation, the first of its kind in the country.

The position of local history in undergraduate courses is not so healthy. In 'Local history in undergraduate history courses', Patricia L. Garside analyses the results of a survey undertaken in 1974/75.[19] Her general findings were that of 28 universities and 9 polytechnics about 50 per cent included local history in their courses; of these, some 60 per cent had a separate local history course, but only 8 history degrees contained a compulsory element of local history. The problem of the increased use of primary source material in record offices by university students has been highlighted by F.G. Emmison, formerly archivist at Essex Record Office. Although not wishing to undervalue the students' use of record offices, he was concerned about the lack of preparation and liaison between the university and record office. Emmison suggested that the archivist's role is not that of student supervisor and the universities ought to be providing more support in the way of finance and staff for the publication of catalogues or guides to archive collections. A number of the universities have their own local collections and departments of manuscripts which contain valuable material covering the local area, for example, at Keele (Wedgewood and Spode archives) and Nottingham (D.H. Lawrence Collection).

Mention must also be made of the education and training of librarians and archivists. As indicated in an earlier chapter, a number of schools of librarianship offer an optional local studies paper in their undergraduate and postgraduate courses, which may require candidates to undertake a small research project into an aspect of local studies librarianship. The training of archivists is at postgraduate level only and includes a number of specialist areas outside the scope of librarianship (e.g. palaeography and Latin); the course leads to the Diploma in Archives Administration (DAA).

## LOCAL STUDIES IN ADULT EDUCATION

The other major development in the study and teaching of local studies has been at the adult education level. The rise in the adult education movement through the Workers' Educational Association (WEA) and extramural studies at the universities, mostly after the war, provided an opportunity to organise classes in local studies and, more recently, in genealogy. One of the earliest publications, aimed principally at tutors and students in adult classes, was *Local studies,* by J.R. Armstrong and P.G.H. Hopkins, published in 1955.[20] Since then many publications on local studies have been written by extra-mural tutors aimed at both the amateur and adult education student, e.g. *Group projects in local history,* edited by Alan Rogers.[21]

In the early years of adult education the audience simply listened to lectures, but through the work of tutors, like Victor Skipp in the late 1950s and 1960s, group research projects were introduced and have now become a common feature of extra-mural programmes. An account of the research projects under the tutorship of Victor Skipp (Extra-mural Department, Birmingham University) is contained in *Local history, objective and pursuit.* [22] In 1957 Skipp started the first of a series of 'Discovering' courses at Birmingham, the results of which have been published, e.g. *Discovering Sheldon* and *Medieval Yardley.* [23] Such courses present a good opportunity for the involvement of the local librarian or archivist at the planning stage; some librarians or archivists may be the initiators of an adult education class and participate as tutors or as course members. Other adult education classes have been developed through correspondence courses, for example, the National Extension College's 'The making of your neighbourhood'. [24] Since 1969, the Open University has had two courses requiring the use of primary source material, 'Great Britain 1750-1950, sources and history' (A401) and 'Historical sources and the social scientist' (D301). There is also a link between the Open University's History Society and the Local Studies Group of the Library Association. The main growth area, however, has been in the study and teaching of local history, particularly genealogy/family history, at adult education centres, which together with local societies for genealogy and local history, have put heavy demands on local collections everywhere.

## OTHER COUNTRIES

The position of local studies and education in other countries is not so far removed from the United Kingdom experience, although overall local studies probably retains a stronger hold in the United Kingdom than elsewhere. At the school level in France, history teaching is controlled by the Ministry of Education, at least at the secondary stage, which is unknown in the United Kingdom. The history syllabus still retains a traditional element of 'facts and figures' but the use of primary evidence has been encouraged through the 'Service éducatif' set up by the Archives Nationales in 1950 and by the archives service for départements providing a valuable support service for history teachers in school since 1952. In the primary school there is a stronger emphasis on local history, particularly where there is a military connection. [25]

In Germany, history at both school and university level has been closely allied to traditionalism and academicism which created a rejection of history teaching in the late 1960s and early 1970s. Since that time history by evidence, teaching by topic units/kits, and more recently the 'source method' and inquiry approach, have been encouraged. But these changes, unlike the position in the United Kingdom, were not accompanied by a 'boom' in the production of archive teaching packs or commercial kits; also there was little interest in family history, urban history or integrated studies.

An article by Lothar Steinbach discusses these developments and stresses the need for history to be linked with social science if it is to survive as a worthwhile discipline.[26] The use of archives with education, on the French model, has been much discussed, and by far the biggest contribution to school history is organised by city archives, for example, at Brunswick (with the help of the municipal library) with its travelling exhibitions. The reform of history teaching in the early 1970s has allowed the introduction of 'group' or 'grade' projects which has resulted in greater use of archives.

In the Union of Soviet Socialist Republics and East Germany, 'it is the duty of the archive services as social educators to cooperate and support the schools'.[27] Many older children (17- and 18-year-olds) are required to undertake research work in archives, with the help of archivists. In Norway, the Norwegian Institute for Local History and Local History Research considers one of its most important functions to be the promotion of local history in schools and in the education of teachers. Similarly, the Home District Federation in Finland is keen to foster an interest in local history and the local environment and sees education as an important aspect of its work. At Helsinki University all graduates are required to study local dialects.[28]

In Denmark, a number of the larger city public libraries have local history collections and there are also regional archive deposits, both of which have been used more extensively recently by educational institutions. The Danish Library School, for example, holds a course in local history work which involves study visits to local collections throughout the country. Since 1980 a number of classes in the primary school have been taught history, which has included three aspects, the development of the local community, national history and projects on local studies. Both teachers and librarians have worked together to supply copies of relevant local material for the school library.[29]

Local history is considered a serious academic discipline in many European countries and a number of the universities publish scholarly journals and monographs on the subject. This aspect is particularly evident in Italian universities where there has been a substantial number of major publications on local history. Post-war trends, as elsewhere, have included the influence of sociology on historical and local historical studies.[30]

The most interesting developments in the field of education, and those nearest to the United Kingdom model, have taken place in Australia and the United States of America. In Australia there has been a growing interest in the use of local source material in education, especially at the lower level. Particularly encouraging has been the close co-operation between the library and the school. The setting-up of a resources project at an education centre in Melbourne, to provide teaching materials about the local community, is reported by Wendy Lowenstein and Muray Loh in 'The Richmond local resources project'.[31] The importance of local history in the school curriculum has been stressed by the History Teachers' Association of Australia since 1976, when a new project, 'Learning through the historical environment', was conceived at their conference. Their particular approach to local history teaching is discussed in a book, published in 1984 by the Association, entitled *Past continuous*.[32] The use of archives by university students, school teachers and others, at the Archives Office of New South Wales, was reported by John Burke in 1977.[33]

The position of local history in American education is also a healthy one. Local history materials have increasingly found a place in history, social studies, family history and other curriculum areas at all levels of education. However, it is at the secondary and university levels that the use of archives and other source materials (together with oral techniques) have had the most effect.[34] Oral history, family history and genealogy also form an important part of the curriculum in American education, particularly at university level. The place of the 'family history project' is discussed by David H. Culbert (Louisiana State University) in 'Family history projects: the scholarly value of the informal sample'.[35]

## IMPLICATIONS FOR RESOURCE PROVIDERS

### Public libraries

It is important for librarians to understand the development of local studies at different levels of education in order to identify the expected demands to be made upon the local collection from this category of user, from child to mature adult student. Having viewed the field of local studies from an educational angle, it is now appropriate to consider it from the standpoint of librarians, and other resource providers.

Local studies resources are provided by a number of different institutions, groups and individuals, including libraries, record offices, museums, resource centres, teachers centres, council departments (e.g. planning offices and information bureaux), community centres, local history societies and individuals; all can offer varying degrees of help to the user in education. It is essential for the local studies librarian to be familiar with and to liaise with as many of these sources as possible, for the benefit of both library and users. In large cities the local studies librarian requires the help of branch librarians, and in the country the help of village and mobile librarians. If a schools library service is in operation, then this can provide a further and very useful means of contact with the community. An educational service for local studies requires additional areas of liaison, e.g. with the local education department, and the local schools, colleges, polytechnics and universities.

Many librarians responsible for the local collection have become increasingly aware of the use of local source material in education, and although opening their doors willingly to the older student or tutor, few have been so welcoming to school children and teachers. There are two possible reasons for this attitude. First, the traditional role of librarian as a custodian, which gives rise to the belief that such material is only suitable for the academic, and that children, if given access to this valuable material, will only damage it. Secondly, that the facilities and expertise to look after school children, especially in large groups, is not available. These problems stem from the fact that many local collections are housed in the reference library and staff have been largely trained in reference enquiry work and have had little contact with children. Experience has shown, however, that children are particularly careful with original material, but that time needs to be spent with them and preferably a separate room provided, away from the main reading area. However, there is need for concern when teachers send or bring their children to the library unannounced and unprepared. This was very much the theme of the Local Studies Group of the Library Association meeting at Stamford in May 1984.[36] It is a problem that can be largely avoided if the librarian has built up good contacts with the local education authority, schools and teacher-training establishments. In Birmingham, the specialist post of liaison librarian, within the Local Studies Department of the Reference Library, has helped to avoid many of the problems experienced elsewhere.

In the late 1960s Birmingham began to realise the tremendous potential of its local collection for educational purposes, particularly at the primary and secondary school level. However, nothing concrete could be done until the opening of the new Central Library in late 1973, which provided a Local Studies Department, together with an Archives Section (and later Conservation Workshop), meeting/classrooms and, most significantly, the creation of a local studies liaison librarian post to promote the use of the department's resources to children, teachers and to others in education.[37] This provides an almost ideal situation, the only disadvantage being the absence of a schools' library service. The provision of such a post is a necessity, rather than a luxury, and has more than proved its worth over the time it has been in existence. It is a pity that other library authorities have not followed Birmingham's initiative, but it is understandable in the light of the recent economic climate.

Many local studies librarians and children's librarians have had to contend with local studies project work along with their other duties; fortunately a substantial number of these staff delight in this aspect of their work. Librarians are often quick to comment on the heavy use of their local collections by children and teachers: 'Many schools visit special subject departments. . . to undertake project work, the local history department being particularly heavily used for this purpose' (R. Malbon, city librarian, Liverpool); 'The departments undertaking the majority of school parties are Local History and History and Topography' (Anne Reilly, young people's services librarian, Glasgow); and perhaps one of the earliest librarians to openly encourage school children, W.H. Shercliff (Local History Library, Manchester) - 'Over the past few years an attempt has been made to interest children at many different levels in appropriate aspects of local history, and, since the library opened in September 1957 a large number of school classes. . . have come to see and use materials in the library'.[38] Other authorities have appointed local studies officers to oversee the work in this area, a substantial part of which includes links with education, for example, Waltham Forest (local studies and museums officer), Bexley, Liverpool (local studies and archives officer), and Wiltshire. In some areas the children's librarian has taken the initiative, often working closely with the local studies librarian/officer, as in Wiltshire.[39] An increasing number of librarians are genuinely interested in local studies work with education, and a number of local and national meetings have been organised on this theme, e.g. Library Association National Conference, Brighton 1978 ('Education and local studies', Local

Studies Group); University of East Anglia, 1975 ('Local Studies, the libraries and the student'); Stamford 1984 ('Local studies and schools') and numerous YLG (Youth Libraries Group) meetings throughout the country, e.g. College of Librarianship, Wales 1984, ('Presenting history to children'). What has been most encouraging about these meetings was the bringing together of interested parties - librarians, archivists, teachers and other educationalists.

## Record offices

It has been particularly enlightening to see the way many archivists and their record offices confront the problems of the educational use of their records. The record office, largely a post-war phenomenon, has played a substantial role in establishing local history in the school and college curriculum. Although there are still archivists who are more concerned with the traditional administrative function of archives, rather than the promotional aspects, a substantial number have appointed full-time education officers, for example, at Essex (education advisor), Wigan, Coventry (teacher for archive services), Northumberland, Suffolk (education advisor), West Sussex (local history advisory officer), Tyne and Wear, Gwynedd Archives Service, Strathclyde Regional Archives and at the National Army Museum, National Maritime Museum, British Library Department of Manuscripts and Public Record Office (assistant keeper, education). A number of proposed appointments have, unfortunately, been suspended due to financial cutbacks, as was the case at Bradford in 1983. Further proof of the archivists' interest in this particular aspect of their work is shown by the number of courses and meetings that have been specifically about its educational role. As early as 1950 Lancashire Record Office organised a weekend course for teachers. Regional meetings on 'Archives and education', organised by the Society of Archivists, were held at Newcastle-upon-Tyne in 1982 and Exeter in 1983. The most important development, however, was the setting up of a Committee on Educational Services by the Society of Archivists in the mid-1970s, which produced the 'Report on the educational use of archives' in 1978.[40] In essence, the report listed four main elements for an effective and balanced educational service:

1   *liaison* - e.g. consultation with teachers centres, workshops and courses for teachers and liaison with education departments, college and university departments of education, museums and libraries;

2 *instruction* - e.g. advice or instruction on the range of documentary sources and their potential for project work;

3 *publication* - e.g. in addition to catalogues, lists and guides, the reproduction of documentary material - facsimile, transcripts and notes where appropriate, and the production of archive teaching 'units' or 'packs', with the aid of teachers;

4 *display* - displays as an introduction to or stimulant of interest in local studies through archives, or the basis for local studies teaching.

The report also stressed the importance of appointing archive education officers (whose training should be in teaching) to provide a service below the further education level. The minimum requirement should be one such officer, supported by an assistant archivist and part-time clerk typist.

In addition, the report also suggested the provision of a separate studies room with teaching facilities, exhibition screens and cases, a collection of basic local history books, access to copying equipment and, finally, extended opening hours. In conclusion, the following problems were raised; methods of finance, the role and training of education officers, and the potential demand which might turn the record office into an education resource centre. The content of this document has important consequences for the development of an education service in record offices and is also relevant to the local studies collection in libraries and museums; some of the main points are discussed later in the chapter.

Earlier, mention was made of the role of archives and education in countries outside the United Kingdom, and it is important to stress here the international interest in this field of work. The International Congress on Archives in 1980, included a number of papers relevant to the theme of the educational use of archives.[41] H.W.L. Payne stressed the general recognition of the true value of archives as an education source in most countries, but stated that this should not 'override the functions of selection, preservation and presentation'. Mrs L. Principe provided some useful statistics on the use of archives in Europe (both East and West), Canada, the United States of America, South America, Africa, Asia and Australia: her general findings were that students accounted for about 30 per cent of the use of archives, and teachers (grouped with office workers) a small but significant percentage; the most popular areas of research were undertaken in local history and genealogy. Mrs C. Berche's survey of archives services in 43 different countries in 1974 showed a high proportion of contact with educational institutions, e.g. lectures on the archive or school premises (e.g. in Bulgaria and France), educational publications (e.g. in the United States, Poland, Union of Soviet Socialist Republics, Canada (use of audio visual aids)), and educational departments (France). France was the first country to establish an archives education service (the 'Service éducatif', set up by the Archives Nationales in 1950), and played host to the first International Congress on Archives in 1954, which was on the theme of 'Archives and schools'. At its inception, the Director-General of the Archives de France and the Director of Secondary Education agreed the attachment of a secondary school teacher, on a part-time basis, to set up an education service to schools. There are now at least four secondary teachers on full-time attachment to the 'Service éducatif', and further teachers are seconded to the départments' archive services on a part-time basis. The services to education include sessions both in the schools and in archives offices themselves, production of teaching aids and document folders, organisation of exhibitions, courses for young historians and film shows. Although these archives are generally of national interest, there is much scope for local research, particularly in conjunction with the local library and local historical association.

In Australia, the Archives Act of 1960 provided a number of government (state) archival institutions in addition to those of the universities. A survey of the provision of one such institution, the Archives Office of New South Wales by John Burke, has already been referred to; this gives some indication of the use of archives for local history research by students and school teachers. W.I. Smith (Dominion Archivist of Canada) has stressed the need for archivists to acknowledge 'the demand for the use of archival material at all levels of education' and that they 'must be sympathetic to a massive interest in archival materials and to the possibility of revitalizing the teaching of history by the use of materials that [they themselves] find exciting'.[42] In the United States, as elsewhere, a variety of institutions provide valuable source material for the study of the local area or region, e.g. libraries, government offices, museums and archive repositories; in fact, similar material to that found in the United Kingdom (although, of course, covering a shorter time-span). Of particular importance are the archive records housed in many of the state universities - the Department of Archives and Manuscripts at Louisiana State University, for example. One very important development in the American model of archives service has been the production of resource packs, e.g. 'World War I - the Home

Front' and 'The Great Depression and the New Deal', published by the Office of Educational Programs, National Archives and Record Service (1979). Canadian archive repositories have been particularly active in reproducing some of their records on microform for student use, and have provided extended opening facilities, some operating for 24 hours.

This brief survey of other countries' initiatives has shown that a positive attitude to the educational use of archives has existed since the early 1950s, at least in France, and in most other countries since the late 1960s. Although concentration has centred in this chapter on the work of archive repositories, this has been largely out of necessity, rather than desire, because of the lack of information about libraries in this field of work. However, the role of libraries as a resource for local studies has been hinted at, and obviously they form a necessary and important point of contact for some types of material. However, it seems certain that the initiatives for co-operation with educational institutions and individuals has come from archivists (as in the United Kingdom), because of the increase in the use of primary source material at all levels of education. Therefore there is a need to plan a systematic and more cohesive approach for the demands created by this new group of users.

## Other resource institutions

There are, in addition to archive repositories and libraries, a number of other resource institutions that have had increasing contact with educational groups, for example, museums, industrial archaeological sites and country houses. A visit to such local places often forms part of a local study and can supplement the documentary evidence found elsewhere. Of course, these places may well have valuable documentary material themselves (some museums have collections of photographs, maps, directories, etc.), but mainly they are concerned with artefacts, which are outside the scope of most record offices and libraries, unless they are attached to form one service (e.g. the Walsall, Leicestershire and Wiltshire Library and Museum Services). Many of these places now have education officers, largely drawn from the teaching profession, who are responsible for educational groups and who organise guided tours of the exhibits, hold activity sessions with children, aid the production of suitable material (e.g. worksheets, information leaflets and postcards), operate a loan service of artefacts and costumes, and arrange courses for teachers.

An additional resource agency for education, which has evolved in the last nine or ten years, is the planning departments of local councils. Schools liaison officers (who are trained planners) have been appointed by a number of local authorities e.g. London Borough of Hammersmith and Fulham in 1978 and Avon in 1977.[43] Their work involves direct contact with teachers and schools, the production of information packs, town trails and exhibitions. The subject of planning has fitted neatly into the local/environmental studies approach and the realisation of its contribution to the school curriculum resulted in the Schools Council 'Art and the built environment' course.

## MATERIALS AND THEIR EXPLOITATION

The largest collections of local material are to be found in reference libraries but immediately librarians and their users are confronted with the problem of 'for reference use only', and also the dilemma of 'original' versus 'copy'. These are problems that exist for all users, but present particular difficulties for those in education, especially school children. However, this very situation has certain distinct and positive educational advantages; first, that children and students are confronted with a new environment, and one that is typically an 'institution'; secondly, the necessity for the teaching of library and information skills and social and communication skills, and thirdly, the particular educative value in using the material itself. Local studies librarians should be aware, as librarians, of the educational thinking behind the local studies approach, as discussed earlier in the chapter, i.e. the importance of the 'process' of finding, selecting and using material rather than the informational content.

The local collection provides the opportunity for the education user to explore a whole range of secondary and primary source material (which is further extended by the archives department, if one exists). Nowhere can such a collection of maps, photographs, directories, newspapers, health and crime reports and theatre and sports programmes, etc., be found, and this is the value of the local studies library. Despite the practice of closed access, which is largely unavoidable because of the nature of such collections, except perhaps for a small collection of secondary sources and duplicates, the learning of the necessary skills to retrieve the material, is an important aspect of education. The notion of original versus copies, forms part of the larger debate that has confronted local studies librarians (and especially, archivists) for many years - conservation versus promotion. There is no doubt that part of the librarian's function is to preserve material for future generations and that some material, due to its condition, will be unavailable for some time, but, everything possible should be done to help any user who needs a particular source for his or her research (whether a school child, student or professional researcher), either by making a photocopy (or other suitable copy) or by allowing use of the item under supervision. The withdrawal of items for repair that are being used for examination projects or any long-term research is not recommended without full consultation with the user. The principle should be that the whole of the collection is open to all that have cause to use it, but that special arrangements should be made for group use, either using a separate room or sectioning off the reading area, and, that overall supervision of the group should be undertaken by the librarian. Copies of some types of material should be used if the original is in a fragile state, e.g. microfilm copies of newspapers, parish registers and census returns, but this requires the use of microfilm readers and therefore limits their accessibility. Most children are, however, fascinated by any form of machinery and will enjoy the chance to use microfilm and microfiche readers. If a group is doing detailed work from newspapers, then the original copies, if their condition allows, will have to be used, although under supervision. Recently, at Birmingham, a class of ten- and eleven-year-olds recorded the headlines for their birthdates, while another school needed to see the papers of 100 years ago for the school's centenary.

It is useful to have a selection of duplicate copies, of documents especially to show to classes of children and students, e.g. original newspapers of different periods, photocopies to illustrate particular types of sources, for example, extracts from school log books, photographs, sections of maps, directories, etc., and to illustrate popular themes, such as health, crime and industry. They can also be useful for introducing sessions with examination project groups. Duplicate copies of popular secondary source material should, if finance allows, be purchased for the use of classes. Some types of material will only be available in their original form, therefore it is necessary to stress the value of such items and to demonstrate the correct way of handling them so as to avoid damage. The conservation staff at Birmingham have laminated some heavily used items and made clear wallets (from archival quality polyester film) to house maps, photographs and other single items, which has helped protect the material from the eager hands of ten-year-olds and the even more eager hands of teachers!

A special problem in the field of local studies has been the lack of suitable material for children, as much of what is produced is teacher orientated. However, this has also been a strength, for the child must discover the facts for him or herself, with the guidance of teachers (and librarians) and books such as the *Finding out about* series (Batsford Academic and Educational Ltd), which has nine titles including *Villages, Victorian schools* and *Victorian towns,* are aimed at ten- to fourteen-year-olds. For individual work or classwork, the *History around you* series (Oliver and Boyd), developed in association with Granada Television in 1976, includes books on family and neighbourhood, the street and transport and are aimed at lower primary school age. *How we used to live 1936-1953,* by Freda Kelsall (Macdonald), was produced to accompany Yorkshire Television's programme of the same title in 1981; and the Macdonald Educational series *Town and around,* e.g. *Life in the past* and the *Past around us.* It is important for the local studies librarian to be aware of what is being commercially produced and used in local schools, together with television programmes of local interest, broadcast especially for schools. Often this will indicate a particular demand for certain types of material; a number of schools in Birmingham, for example, had been watching *How we used to live* but wished to relate the events of the time to Birmingham and, therefore, required a range of source material, especially about the 'home front'. It is well worth purchasing these publications, or at least examples, for the local collection. Although they may not be relevant to the particular locality, the information about the approaches to local studies in schools is most valuable.

What has been highlighted is the shortage of books for children specifically on the local area, giving straightforward factual information in a readable and interesting manner. This is important, because there are going to be some events that are peculiar to specific localities, and guidance, other than the 'academic' secondary source, is needed. Attempts have been made to remedy this situation but these are too few to be of any significance. This shortcoming can to some extent be filled by children's fiction, as an increasing number of stories based on sound local historical research have been written, e.g. *Kipper's turn* and its sequel, *Kipper skips,* by Marjorie Darke (set in the Jewellery Quarter of Birmingham in the 1880s); *A question of courage* by Marjorie Darke (set against the background of the suffragette movement, early this century); *Goodnight Mister Tom* by Michelle Magorian (the evacuation of children from London's East End in 1939) and *The canal children* by Brian Wright (the canals of the Midlands in the 1840s), which was also a successful BBC series for children. Fiction can be used in conjunction with original material to add interest and 'realism' to what might otherwise be considered a 'boring' topic, and provides the opportunity for greater liaison between the local studies librarian and the children's librarian. Similarly, autobiographical accounts (e.g. *Her people* by Kathleen Dayus - recalling her working-class childhood in Edwardian Birmingham) and published diaries (e.g. *Few oranges and no eggs - a diary showing how unimportant people lived in London and Birmingham, during the war years* by Vere Hodgeson), can be usefully coupled with original source material to check facts and experience the problems of interpretation which confront the historian.

## EDUCATION PACKS

In the early 1970s, many libraries, record offices, museums and commercial publishers attempted to resolve the difficulty of finding suitable source material for use in schools, by producing 'resource packs', 'archive teaching units' or 'document folders' containing copies of selected documents with notes for teachers or pupils (the best known are the *Jackdaw* wallets published by Jonathan Cape). The advances in reprographic processes enabled good-quality copies to be made, but often the selection of documents and the accompanying notes were not compatible with the aims and objectives of the education process. Some educationalists have been opposed to the concept of 'resource packs'; Paul Topham, inspector for environmental studies, Birmingham Education Department, has stated:

> We have not gone into the production of local studies kits. These are often too stereotyped, not based on or linked with field evidence, and often stifling initiatives. We do not need to produce archive teaching units or packs for local studies works. We have a first class service where children can be fully involved in research at firsthand; [although such units can have a] place when they are dealing with national, or perhaps regional events. . .[44]

These packs may give an indication of the types of resources available, but they should not be used, or encouraged to be used, as a substitute for the 'real' documents and the associated research skills. The best examples have been those produced by teachers, as Paul Topham said: 'It is actively undesirable that any agency other than practising teachers should select documents for use in the classroom'.[45] The Longman Resources Unit at York has produced a useful set of units, 'Sources for history 1700-1900', devised by Rosemary Rees and Sue Styles (1982). These include units on maps and plans, pictures and photographs, journals, posters and propaganda, official records, people in their communities and records of small groups and companies, with reproductions of documents from Bradford's Local Studies Department and Hertford Record Office. Some books, such as John West's *Village records,* are in fact detailed resource units, containing facsimile illustrations of documents (in this case relating to Dudley) with full commentaries about them. Others stress the range of sources available for any given locality and provide guidance on where to find them and how to use them, e.g. Robert Dunning's *Local sources for the young historian.*[46]

The largest producers of resources packs/archive teaching units have been the record offices, providing much-needed source materials for the 'new' history being taught in schools, i.e. the local study and use of primary evidence, which have also provided a means of publicity for their 'valuable' holdings. Typical units include 'Agriculture in Essex c. 1840-1900' (Essex), 'The Poor Law' (Gloucestershire) and 'Suffolk Turnpikes' (Suffolk). Further examples of archive units are listed in 'Archive units for teaching' by Robert G.E. Wood.[47] The nature of the record office as traditionally research orientated has meant that archive teaching units have played an important role in bringing them into closer contact with schools; this was particularly important in the early stages of their education service. However, better communication and facilities in many record offices has allowed children to gain greater access to the original sources and to learn something of the researcher's skills.

The publication of collections of documents is also undertaken by many archive repositories abroad. In France, for example, folders financed by the Société des Amis des Archives containing documents, translations and written commentaries are produced on a wide range of topics, mostly reflecting national events, e.g. 'Everyday life during the Revolution'; and in America, teaching units often reflect the social studies approach, e.g. 'World War II - the Home Front' (Office of Educational Programs, National Archives) which contains copies of government papers, letters, photographs, newspaper clippings and sound recordings.

The other major producers of resource packs/archive units have been the colleges, or faculties of education, teachers centres and schools. Such packs have been produced in the libraries or, more often, the resource centres, of these institutions. They require the use of reprographic equipment, the time of teaching staff, and the help of librarians, archivists and others that hold resources for the locality. Some colleges of education will have built up a substantial collection of local material, particularly in the boom years of the 1960s when local history studies became a major part of the students' work. Subsequently resource packs have been produced for use by students and teachers in local schools, by, for example, the Archive Teaching Unit, Department of Education, Newcastle University (e.g. 'The Northumberland election 1826'); Sheffield University, Institute of Education (e.g. 'Sheffield Enclosure Act 1791'). At Warwick, the Department of Arts Education has produced a series of guides to local history sources (e.g. 'Books and archives', 'Castles', and 'Canals'), and Newman College (Birmingham) publish extracts from local source material in 'Resources for teaching; Birmingham and the Black Country'.

A number of teachers centres have also been involved in the production of resource packs, e.g. at Bangor ('The Menai Straits'). The most successful examples have been those which form part of a resource centre's collection. The resource centre is an extension of the library, containing material in a variety of formats (maps, charts, plans, slides, illustrations, pamphlets, etc.), and undoubtedly there will be a substantial local studies collection; many will also have reprographic equipment. At Dudley, a resource centre (based on the Schools Council General Studies Project at York University) was developed at the teachers centre, Himley Hall, to serve local authority schools. John West set the project in motion with the help of teachers, the borough library and the local colleges of education and technology. The centre reflects the importance of local studies, with units, for example, on local transport, industry, poor law, pollution, and guides on the study and use of local source materials. Each unit contains a variety of formats, including newscuttings, copies of documents, photographs and three-dimensional models.[48]

Some local education authorities have set up advisory bodies to co-ordinate the production of resource packs. In Staffordshire, for example, the county advisor for history formed the School History Service and with the help of the County Record Office produced a series of local history source books (e.g. *Coal in Staffordshire, Elementary education in Staffordshire*), a total of over 60 titles in all. The books contain about 30 pages of source material with introductory notes and are aimed primarily at children.[49]

A substantial number of schools have now adopted the idea of resource centres as an extension of their library service. Changes in the curriculum, away from textbook towards resource-based learning and 'finding out for yourself', has resulted in the need for easier access to a wide range of resources; local and environmental studies have played a significant part in forwarding this type of approach. The school resource centre, at both the primary and the secondary level, has often built up a large collection of local material with the help of the local studies library and perhaps the record offices and other resource agencies. A detailed survey of resource centres in schools was undertaken by Norman Beswick in the early 1970s and the results published in 1975 as *Organizing resources: six case studies.*[50] One of the major restrictions on the production of resources is the Copyright Act, and under a new agreement between local authorities and publishers through the new Copyright Licensing Agency, further restrictions are to be imposed on the storing of copies, with obvious consequences for resource centres.

A few libraries with large local history collections have gone into the production of resource packs (e.g. Sheffield - 'The Sheffield Canal', and Manchester - 'Peterloo 1819'), but this has tended to be on a small scale because most libraries do not have access to the sort of reprographic equipment available in teachers centres and in general, the library has been more approachable than the record office, as it often has accommodation for class visits and photocopying facilities. Local studies librarians have often helped teachers centres, other institutions and individuals, with finding suitable material for duplication in resource packs. At Birmingham, no resource packs, as such, are produced, but collections of illustrations and slides of local views can be borrowed from the Visual Aids Department, and an art pack on Birmingham artists is available for loan from the Fine Arts Department. Some museums have produced resource packs (e.g. Portsmouth - '1870 Education Act in Portsmouth', and Luton - 'The Turnpike Age') and most have a loan service to schools of artefacts and costumes, which can be a useful supplement to the documentary evidence found in libraries and record offices. The concept of a 'local history resource centre', combining the resources of libraries, museums and record offices, has also been put forward as a 'natural' and necessary development for the provision of a comprehensive service to users. Centres of this type are in operation, e.g. the Local Interest Centre at Oldham and Local Studies Centre, Coventry, but the pattern of separate institutions remains predominant.

296

Norman Beswick's survey mentioned above showed the distribution of resource centres as follows: teachers centre (1), schools (12), colleges of education (7), networks and regional centres (2), public libraries (2) and two research projects at Coventry and Aberystwyth. There have been many developments in the provision of resource packs and resource centres since the date of his survey. One notable contribution has been in the production of packs by independent bodies, although often working in conjunction with libraries, archive repositories, museums and teachers centres, e.g. the Lincolnshire Educational Aids Project (LEAP), which involved unemployed people (including teachers) under the Manpower Services Commission (MSC) scheme, and produced trail booklets and archive packs.[51] A number of teaching resource packs, based on Birmingham Cathedral (e.g. 'Your cathedral' and 'The building of St Philips - an act of worship') have been produced under the MSC scheme, based at the Bordesley Teachers Centre, Birmingham. Local resource projects have also been a feature of educational developments in other countries, particularly in Australia. The Richmond Local Resources Project, for example, was set up at an education centre in Melbourne in 1977. Two teachers, who had resigned from their schools (one was a school librarian), worked on a voluntary basis, gathering local material about the Richmond community for use in primary and secondary schools. The project was funded by a Schools Commission Innovations grant for two years, with the aim of depositing the collection in the local library after this period, but as this was rejected it had to be run on a voluntary basis and financed by the selling of resource packs and other publications.[52]

So far the discussion of local resources has concentrated on the holdings of libraries, record offices, museums and resource centres and has been principally concerned with the needs of children and teachers, but a brief mention should also be made of the holdings of academic libraries. This has already been referred to earlier in the chapter (and discussed more thoroughly in Chapter 4). Suffice it to say that many of the larger city university and polytechnic libraries have important local collections. Mention has already been made of the collections at Wolverhampton Polytechnic, Keele and Nottingham, and the list could be extended to include Birmingham University, the Modern Records Centre at Warwick, Leeds, Leicester, Kent, Newcastle Polytechnic and University College, London. However, their collections, many of which contain record-office-type material, are largely 'limited' access; a criticism levelled at them in the Blake Report, which recommended the opening of university library collections to bona-fide non-university students and the provision of copies in public libraries and record offices. Some university libraries, such as the Manuscript Department at Nottingham, have, in collaboration with local teachers, produced archive teaching units. Many universities with extra-mural departments have small collections of local material for loan to adult classes.

## SERVICES AND PUBLICITY

The fundamental aim of the local studies librarian should be to promote and encourage the use of local source material at all levels of education. This is best achieved by arranging group visits to the collection in order to see at first hand the range of material available. Every effort should also be made to visit individual schools and other education establishments with a selection of resources, including original documents, copies, books and audio-visual aids where appropriate. For example, Essex Record Office (one of the most progressive of archive services) undertook 61 visits to county schools, both primary and secondary, in 1980, with original documents.[53] Teachers or tutors should be encouraged to visit the library personally, before arrangements concerning their groups are finalised, in order to see what material is available, assess its suitability and to discuss the project(s), and numbers, age, abilities and other points, such as special requirements for handicapped persons. Photocopied examples of relevant material, such as map and directory extracts, can be supplied at this initial meeting, enabling some preparatory work to be done before the group visits, and guidance on other possible sources of information can also be given. In fact it has been suggested, and indeed practised by some authorities, that teachers should spend as much time with the local material before the visit as they would with their class!

In the writer's experience the majority of requests for assistance come from primary schools, but there has been a notable increase in secondary school usage, for reasons already discussed. Students from higher education, particularly from the universities, are expected, often misguidedly, to be able to use the collection without formal instruction; therefore group visits should be encouraged. Teacher-training establishments are still keen on promoting the use of local studies material and groups of students will often visit the library or be sent individually for help with their teaching practice. At Birmingham, regular visits are made by the Department of Librarianship, initially for an 'in-depth' tour and then for follow-up sessions to see particular types of material. At the adult education level, several courses have been held at the library, e.g. 'The making of the suburbs' (run jointly by the Archives Section and the Museum, under the Extra-mural Department, Birmingham University) and the Sutton Coldfield History Research Group, based at the Sutton Coldfield Reference Library, which is tutored by the principal librarian there. Open University tutors also arrange frequent group visits to see local source material.

In large reference libraries, such as Birmingham, it is necessary to meet groups at the entrance and introduce them to the official and commonsense procedures. Despite the obvious disadvantages of using escalators to reach the Local Studies Department (Birmingham) on the sixth floor, it does provide the opportunity to see the various departments, and extent of the building generally. The size of a group will depend on individual circumstances, but an average class of children number about 30, which obviously requires good organisation; smaller groups of 10 to 15 are to be preferred. An important point to stress is that the librarian should have overall responsibility for the group on his/her own ground. Once the group is assembled in the department or classroom, a brief introduction about the library and its services should be given, followed by a talk, illustrated with appropriate examples, on the particular project area(s), stressing the uniqueness of the materials and the need for careful handling. Some may be horrified at the prospect of nine- or ten-year-olds (although rarely younger) using original documents, but with careful preparation no harm should come to the material. Children are often very careful once they realise how precious such material is. After this introductory talk the teachers can take over; any worksheets should have been prepared by the teacher, who knows the abilities of the children best. The length of visit will again depend on individual circumstances but on average about 90 minutes is sufficient; some may last a half or full day if the teacher and librarian can sustain the pupils' curiosity; visits to other places of interest may also have been arranged. The primary school project may be limited to a particular local theme, e.g. transport, Victorian times or industry, but the most popular is the study of the pupils' own area, which offers the opportunity for much original research ('detective' work) and integrated study. Such a study might include the following range of material: enclosure and tithe maps (and schedules), census returns, street and trade directories, OS maps, newspapers and illustrations.[54]

Questions have been raised about the value of local studies for ethnic minority children. The majority of groups the author has had contact with are from the inner-city area and they get as much out of it, and in some cases more, than white children. One project, undertaken about ten years ago, on the history of an inner-city suburb, managed successfully to bring together through oral history techniques the cultures of the old residents of the area and those of the young Asian and West Indian children. Projects on religion offer much scope for teaching about the cultures of different countries and can also relate to the local area. Often a local study about the changing face of a suburb, from 100 years ago to the present, can be developed into a broader context (the 'global perspective').

Despite the significance of documentary evidence, schools should also be referred to the local museum, where artefacts and further information about particular local buildings may be found. This also offers the possibility of the library joining forces with the museum to present combined sessions to school groups. Some teachers may wish to take full advantage of the service and arrange regular visits to use the material, giving the children confidence and familiarity with an otherwise strange building, in addition to developing their research skills. An introduction to the catalogues and indexes can be made if the group is small enough, but care must be taken not to confuse the children, particularly if a classification other than Dewey is used. Library skills can perhaps be better taught at other times with the children's librarian and teacher. Sessions with the children should be closed with a question and answer or discussion period, to assess the usefulness of the visit. Photocopies and postcards may also be requested before the group finally leaves the library. Contact with the school should be retained, if at all possible, as the childrens' finished work on the project(s) may be suitable for displaying in the library (at Birmingham a huge frieze depicting the growth of the city is on permanent display), and possibly used in its original or copied form in teachers' or library courses.

Secondary school visits mainly consist of examination groups for history or geography, which often requires individual project work. In a large library, the size of the building can be somewhat overwhelming for the student, who will need to use the library by himself or herself to complete project work; therefore the visit (perhaps their first to the library) needs to be well organised. Other departments may be relevant to their studies, particularly if the course requires a broader national or international context. It was for this reason, that the role of liaison librarian at Birmingham was extended, in 1981, to incorporate a broader brief than local studies. Also significant was the formation of the Young People's Information Services Team (YPIST), comprising of individual departmental members, to co-ordinate services to young people. These developments have contributed to the 'opening up' of the Reference Library for the use of children, as well as academics. Sometimes project titles have been decided on before the visit, but it is quite likely that the purpose of the visit is to see what resources are available and to give students some ideas for their personal study. Popular themes for history include: education, poor law, transport, the 1939-45 War, industry, political movements, health and crime, all of which involve the use of a range of primary source material (e.g. newspapers, broadsides, acts of Parliament). Some sources may be held by the archives department or record office, therefore close liaison is necessary. Although there will be recurring themes, we should be aware of possible future trends in the history syllabus - 'which deals with the radically changing position of women in society; it must explore the multi-cultural nature of Britain and the contribution that ethnic minorities have made; it must show how Britain is part of a globally interdependant World...'.[55]

On the initial visit to the library the students will need to be shown a range of source material, and possible lines of enquiry discussed. Time should obviously be spent in explaining the catalogues and indexes thoroughly, as the students will have to work largely on their own next time. Again, finished projects should, if possible, be borrowed and copies made to add to the local collection. The geography student will often require up-to-date information about population, unemployment, industrial location, urban sprawl, etc., which can be more difficult and time-consuming to locate than history project work.

The school visit to the library has a very important role to play, for both the child and the library. For the child it is often a new experience (it is surprising to learn of children who have never been into the city centre before, let alone the library!) and the impression he or she gets can have a lasting influence. For the library there is the opportunity to build up a lasting relationship with a young and future adult member of the local community. It is for this reason that all children, not just the bright ones but the 'under-achievers' too, can get something out of visiting the library. To take the service out into the community further extends these ties. An important part of the librarian's role is to visit local schools, to show slides (of the library or the local area) and other materials from the local collection and to talk with children and members of staff. Some schools are perhaps too far away to visit the local studies library but may prefer to use the local library, and use local source material there. This enables the local library to become involved, and many will already have good relationships with the schools in the area. Other schools may wish simply to invite the librarian in as an outside speaker. Either way, the children and the librarian will thoroughly enjoy the experience. At Birmingham, regular visits are also made to the Accident Hospital School, to help children with their projects, which hopefully has some therapeutic benefit. Visits to other education establishments should also be made. The liaison librarian at Birmingham, for example, has been lecturing on the history of Birmingham at an adult education centre for some years now, and the present class has over 35 members.

## PROMOTION OF THE LOCAL STUDIES LIBRARY

Central to the successful exploitation of the collection is the need for close liaison and co-operation between the various resource institutions (libraries, museums, record offices, planning departments, etc.) and the education establishments (the education departments, teachers centres, schools and colleges). The local authority education departments can form a very important point of contact, particularly through their inspectorate (e.g. the inspectors for history and geography). In Birmingham, the inspector for environmental studies had a very progressive outlook on promoting the environment and, most importantly, in utilising local source material. Members of the inspectorate and its team in the teachers centres provide information about the service and refer teachers to the department. The most significant form of publicity is by word of mouth. Teachers who have used the service often pass on their enthusiasm to colleagues in the school and in the teaching profession generally and those who once used the service may now be in head or deputy headship posts and thus promote the service to their staff. Members of staff within the libraries, both central and branches, who have contact with teachers may also provide publicity about the service and refer teachers to the local studies library. In Birmingham, the Education Department publishes a fortnightly bulletin, which is received by all local education authority schools, and information about forthcoming courses and exhibitions, organised by the library, can be publicised in it. Any circular or posters about courses, exhibitions, etc., can be distributed throughout the schools by internal post. Library publications, e.g. guides to the collection or leaflets about services to schools, can be handed out to teachers on courses, at schools and when visiting the library; some record offices publish guides and catalogues for students. The local press, school magazines, local radio and television are all potential sources of publicity about the local studies library and its services to schools.

Promotion to groups of teachers can be achieved through the organisation of courses, seminars, day schools and meetings. These may be initiated by the library or education department, teachers centre, colleges of education, individual schools, local museums and local education associations. At Birmingham, a number of very successful courses for teachers have been run by the libraries department, in collaboration with the Inspectorate. Early in 1983 a series of five courses were organised jointly by the Museums' Local History and Education Departments and the Local Studies Department, linked to the annual Environmental Studies Exhibition. The theme was 'Village Birmingham', and some sessions were held in historic buildings. Similarly, a series of Saturday morning courses have been held at Aston Hall, an early-seventeenth-century house owned by the city. Visits to classes in schools often present an opening to talk with a number of teachers, in addition to visits arranged specifically for this purpose. The Urban Base at the Teachers' Centre in Birmingham, which has a resource collection, runs a number of courses for teachers which have involved the liaison librarian. A course on the 'appreciation of libraries' run by the Inspectorate, School of Librarianship and Libraries Department, required a small input by the liaison librarian about services to schools. Training courses for library staff may also provide the opportunity to promote the local studies collection. In some regions teachers and other educationalists have formed committee groups on aspects of the local environment, which the local studies librarian may find useful to join. In Birmingham, there is the Birmingham Environmental Studies Association which organises regular meetings and courses. A Directory of Local Resources was also produced by this association. Another group is the Birmingham Urban Studies Committee, with representatives from the museum, library, education department and university, which has published a number of 'Brum trails' aimed at the teacher, school child and the general visitor to the city.

Exhibitions of local studies material in schools and other education institutions and establishments such as church halls can provide another means of promoting the collection, but adequate publicity is necessary if it is to reach as many people as possible. Exhibitions on services to schools can usefully be organised in schools, teachers centres and libraries. Some libraries set quizzes about the local area for children, particularly in school holiday periods. Birmingham's Local Studies Department was involved in compiling questions for the Super School Quiz broadcast on local radio in 1981 and 1982. Any form of contact with education, whether through visits, or help with particular research, especially for material, such as resource packs or booklets, which acknowledge the help of the librarian, can provide useful publicity. A collaboration between the liaison librarian and a head teacher in 1976 resulted in the publication of *Erdington past and present* (a history of a Birmingham suburb from primary source material), and similar projects are being planned for the future. Mention has already been made of publicising the importance of local studies material in education at professional meetings of librarians and teachers, both local and further afield. (The first liaison librarian at Birmingham was involved in an environmental education course in France in 1979.) Finally, the publication of articles in professional journals, can also provide useful publicity and should be encouraged.

The aim of this chapter has been to show the significance of local studies work in education and the consequences for the providers of local source material, such as public libraries, acadaemic and school libraries, record offices, museums, planning departments and resource centres. Many new and interesting developments within education and libraries are taking place, e.g. oral history, video, computer software - all of which have a place in the area of local studies. Although it is perhaps too much to expect, in the present economic climate, the appointment of education liaison officers, in libraries and resource institutions, this would do much to ensure that the user in education, whether a primary school child or adult education student, will be adequately served.

## NOTES

1. Why teach history in school? *Historian* no. 2 Spring 1984, p. 11.
2. Douch, R. *Local history and the teacher.* London, Routledge, 1967. Stephens, W.B. *Teaching local history.* Manchester, Manchester University Press, 1977.

3. Lowe, R. Local history in the school curriculum. *Local historian* 12 (5) February 1977, 223-228. Daniels, C. and Brown, R. Our future local historians. *Local historian* 13 (3) August 1978, 140-145. Jones, G. Schooling the local historian. *Teaching history* no. 31 October 1981, 7-9.

4. Dunphy, A.W. and Lewis, T.C. Local studies at Ellowes Hall School. *Blackcountry man* 11 (2) Spring 1978, 51-52.

5. Kerwood, B. 17+: the Certificate of Pre-Vocational Education (CPVE) *Teaching history* no. 38 February 1984, 3-7. Waddington-Feather, J. Sixth-form local studies. *Teaching history* 3 (2) May 1974, 217-219.

6. Steel, D.J. and Taylor, L. *Family history in schools.* London, Phillimore, 1973, pp. 165-175.

7. Punnett, N. and Webber, P. Using local resources; town expansion and industrial growth. *Teaching geography* 4 (4) April 1979, 153-157.

8. Davidson, G. T.V.E.I. *Teaching geography* 10 (1) October 1984, 3-4.

9. Adams, E. and Ward, C. *Art and the built environment: a teacher's approach.* Harlow, Longman for Schools Council, 1982.

10. Palmer, J.A. and Wise, M.J. *The good, the bad and the ugly: the study of an urban housing estate by a primary school class.* Sheffield, Geographical Association, 1982.

11. National Association for Environmental Education. *Environmental education: a statement of aims for the formal education service.* NAEE, 1976, p. 1.

12. *Environmental studies 5-13 - the use of historical resources: the report of a working party of the Schools Council Committee for Wales.* London, Evans/Methuen, 1973. (Schools' Council working paper 48.)

13. For further information, see: Computer update. *Teaching history* 40 October 1984, 26-28, and Wood, D.J. Computers and geography: a classroom experience. *Teaching geography* 3 (4) April 1978, 159-160.

14. West, John. Young children's awareness of the past. *Trends in education* no. 1 Spring 1978, 9-14; See also: Testing the use of written records in primary schools, 1979-80. *Teaching history* no. 32 February 1982, 32-35.

15. Douch, R. Local history in school. *Amateur historian* 6 (7) Spring 1965, 218-222.

16. Douch (1967), pp. 139-165.
17. Phelps, P.J. et al. A curricular experiment. *Local historian* 11 (6) May 1976, 331-335.
18. Fines, J. and Steel, D.J. College of education students in the archives office. *Archives* 9 (41) April 1969, 22-28.
19. Garside, P.L. Local history in undergraduate history courses. *Local historian* 13 (2) May 1978, 67-74.
20. Armstrong, J.R. and Hopkins, P.G.H. *Local studies*. London, Workers' Educational Association, 1955.
21. Rogers, A. (ed.). *Group projects in local history*. Folkestone, Dawson/National Institute of Adult Education, 1977.
22. Finberg, H.P.R. and Skipp, V.H.T. *Local history, objective and pursuit*. Newton Abbot, David and Charles, 1967, pp. 87-102.
23. Skipp, V.H.T. *Discovering Sheldon*. Birmingham, Birmingham University, Department of Extra-Mural Studies, 1960. Skipp, V.H.T. *Medieval Yardley*. Chichester, Phillimore, 1970.
24. Ravensdale, J. *The making of your neighbourhood*. Cambridge, National Extension College, 1972.
25. Behr, H.J. Archives and school education - possibilities, problems, limits. *Unesco bulletin for libraries* 28 (3) May-June 1974, 131-138. Duboscq, G. The educational role of archives. *Unesco bulletin for libraries* 24 (4) July-August 1970, 205-10. Ward, L.O. Trends in history teaching in France. *Teaching history* 7 (24) June 1979, 12-13.
26. Steinbach, L. New approaches to the study and teaching of history in West Germany. *Teaching history* 5 (19) October 1977, 15-17.
27. Behr, p. 132.
28. Fladbury, R. The Norwegian Institute for Local History and Local History Research. *Local historian* 11 (4) November 1974, 217-224. Kennerley, E. Local history in Finland. *Local historian* 13 (3/4) November 1976, 149-151.
29. Ott, L. and Eriksen, S.H. Biblioteksskolens kursus i lokalhistorisk arbejde: lokal-historisk opsang. (The library school course in local history work: local historical exhortation.) *Bogens verden* 58 (1) 1976, 11-15. Peterson, C.O. Er der pladstil historie i Skolebiblioteket? (Is there room for history in the school library?) *Børn och bøger* 33 (3) April 1980, 138-140.
30. Bertelli, S. Local history in Italy. *Local historian* 11 (5) February 1975, 251-262.

31. Lowenstein, W. and Loh, M. The Richmond Local Resources Project. *Archives and manuscripts* 8 (1) June 1980, 17-21. Gilbert, L.A. Local history for schools and community. *Australian library journal* 28 (3) March 1979, 41-45.

32. Mackinolty, J. (ed.). *Past continuous: learning through the historical environment.* Rozelle, New South Wales, History Teachers' Association of Australia, 1983.

33. Burke, J. Archives and reader services: a statistical survey. *Archives and manuscripts* 6 (8) February 1977, 325-342.

34. Metcalf, F. and Downey, M.T. Local history in American education. *Local historian* 15 (4) November 1982, 204-211.

35. Culbert, D.H. Family history projects: the scholarly value of the informal sample. *American archives* 38 (4) October 1975, 533-541.

36. Petty, M. Local studies and schools. *Local studies librarian* 3 (1) Summer 1984, 12-13.

37. Baird, P.C. Local studies and education: a librarian's viewpoint. In: Library Association. *Study School and National Conference Proceedings, Brighton 1978.* London, LA, 1979, pp. 143-145.

38. Shercliff, W.H. The school and the local history library. *Manchester review* 9 Summer 1960, 33-38.

39. Fea, V. Education and local studies. In: Library Association. *Study School and National Conference Proceedings, Brighton 1978.* London, LA, 1979, pp. 141-142.

40. Society of Archivists. Committee on Educational Services. Report on the educational use of archives. 1978. (Unpublished report.)

41. Berche, C. The popular use of archives. Payne, H.W.L. 'Education and archives. Principe, L. Everyman and archives. Papers given at the International Congress of Archives, London, 1980.

42. Smith, W.I. Broad horizons: opportunities for archivists. *American archivist* 37 (1) January 1974, p. 9.

43. Armstrong, A. and Russell, G. Schools liaison officers in planning departments: innovations in Hammersmith and Avon. *Teaching geography* 6 (3) January 1981, 119-121.

44. Topham, P. Education and local studies. In: Library Association. *Study School and National Conference proceedings, Brighton 1978.* London, LA, 1979, p. 150.

45. Ibid.

46. Dunning, R. *Local sources for the young historian.* London, Muller, 1973.

47.  Wood, R.G.E. Archive units for teaching. *Teaching history* 11 (6) November 1971, 158-165.

48.  West, John. Resources centre. *Teaching history* 11 (7) May 1972, 228-235.

49.  Lewis, R.A. A local history service for Staffordshire schools. *Local historian* 13 (5) February 1979, 291-296.

50.  Beswick, N. *Organising resources: six case studies.* London, Heinemann, 1975.

51.  Acton, R. and Hall, T. L.E.A.P. - a successful launch into historical aids. *Teaching history* no. 38 February 1984, 8-11.

52.  Lowenstein and Loh. (1980).

53.  Mason, I. The "Records Road Show" or documents in Essex classrooms. *Teaching history* no. 31 October 1981, 4-6.

54.  Wheeler, S. Young children, documents and the locality. *Teaching history* 1 (2) May 1969, 181-187.

55.  Editorial. *Teaching history* no. 40 October 1984, p. 2.

# 15

# Oral history recordings

Rheinallt Llwyd and Geraint Evans

## I

Local history has a remarkably wide scope and the range of evidences at the disposal of the local historian and researcher is often considerable. W.G. Hoskins, the doyen of English local history, once maintained that:

> To the true local historian no human record, whatever its form - a hedge-bank, a wall, a street, a headstone, a farmhouse, an old man's gossip, wills and tax assessments and the thousands of other written things, a memorial tablet on a church wall - a multitude of evidences in every shape or form - no human record fails to tell him something about the past. All these evidences, whatever form they take, are interrelated.[1]

In this chapter, the writers are concerned with oral evidence, what Hoskins referred to as 'an old man's gossip'. At times it may indeed be nothing more than gossip and may have little historical significance. More often than not, however, oral testimony obtained from the minds and memories of older men and women within the community, and from those who are not so old, will provide information that is unique and invaluable.

The term 'oral history' is a fairly recent one and has been defined as: 'A record of information gathered in oral form, usually on tape, as a result of a planned interview.'[2] There is, however, a tendency to use the term in a collective sense to encompass a wide range of oral information gathered on tape, and many oral history collections consist not only of individual interviews and reminiscences but also of recordings of local events, folksongs and folklore and a range of other materials.

Although the term 'oral history' is a modern one, the use of oral sources in history is a very old practice. Paul Thompson, in his book *The voice of the past,* gives a comprehensive account of the uses made throughout the centuries of oral evidences. Thompson maintains that: 'In fact, oral history is as old as history itself. It was the first kind of history. And it is only quite recently that skill in handling oral evidence has ceased to be one of the marks of the great historian.'[3] Even to this day in certain parts of the world where pre-literate societies are found, the only history available for those societies is the oral traditions which have been handed down from generation to generation and in less literate times, in Europe and elsewhere, the main method of transmitting information was orally. Herodotus (484-424 BC) based much of his accounts of the Persian Wars on evidence he obtained by interviewing former soldiers, and Bede during the early part of the eighth century states clearly in his preface to *A history of the English church and people* that he had used evidence of 'countless faithful witnesses who either know or remember the facts, apart from what I know myself'.[4] There are numerous other examples of historians and authors using evidence obtained by listening to oral accounts of past events related to them by people who had been directly involved.

## 'TO OBTAIN FROM THE LIPS ... A FULLER RECORD'

The term 'oral history', nonetheless, is associated with the work initiated by Professor Allan Nevins of Columbia University. He is regarded as the founder of the subject. In 1938 Nevins maintained in the preface to *The gateway to history* that there was an urgent need for an organisation that would make 'a systematic attempt to obtain from the lips of living Americans who have led significant lives, a fuller record of their participation in the political, economic and cultural life of the last sixty years.'[5] It was ten years later before Nevins actually began recording the memoirs of his 'significant' Americans and he concentrated almost entirely on the reminiscences of the famous and influential, those who had changed in some way or other the course of American history. This was the beginning of élite oral history and in America elaborate projects were soon set up to study in as complete a detail as possible the careers of leading politicians, diplomats, industrialists, etc. Oral history became almost an industry in itself, with a wide range of projects being initiated, large funds being attracted and elaborate teams of researchers engaged. Nevins argued that it was necessary to develop this new, modern technique for historical documentation because 'oral history is an essential defence against oblivion in history, against the absolute loss of historical fact that would otherwise occur.'[6]

One of the main reasons why this technique had to be developed was the rapidly changing nature of modern communications systems, and the fact that these systems were replacing long-established traditional methods. Letter writing was being replaced by telephone calls, recording devices were replacing reports. 'All the while the hurry and complexity of modern politics, modern financial and business affairs, and even modern literary and artistic life slice away the time that men need for methodical, reflective writing.'[7] To a professional political historian such as Nevins, who was aware that a great deal of invaluable material was constantly being lost as important personalities, often eye witnesses to major national events were dying out, something had to be done. He was seeing 'in the daily obituary columns proof that knowledge valuable to the historian, novelist, sociologist and economist was daily perishing without yielding any part of their riches'.[8] Something drastic had to be done. 'Oral history', Nevins maintains, 'was born of modern invention and technology'.[9]

It was the history of the 'significant' and the eminent that Nevins was concerned with, the 'great men' of America, and for almost two decades oral history in the United States concentrated mainly on this area. Since 1967 and the establishment of the American Oral History Association, the frontiers of oral history have expanded dramatically, outwards and downwards. It has extended into the spheres of minority interests such as Indian history, aspects of American women's history and the history of black communities. The emphasis also moved from individuals to themes and specific subjects, and from significant men to insignificant persons, those who had had really little choice in the way their country or their own lives had been run.

The origin and development of oral history in Britain differed from the American scene. Some of the earliest examples of using sound recording equipment to collect oral evidence are found in Britain, not among the works of political historians, but in institutions specialising in the study of folklife and linguistics. In Scandinavian countries, particularly Sweden, the value of collecting oral evidence had been an established practice, since the 1830s. The emphasis had been mainly on collecting linguistic phenomena, provincial words and expressions and the terminology associated with various crafts and customs that were rapidly disappearing.

In Ireland, the realisation that a wealth of evidence was vanishing forever as older members of communities were dying was the main reason for setting up the Irish Folklore Commission in Dublin in 1935. The old way of life that had existed for centuries, particularly in rural Ireland, was gradually changing with the advent of new communications systems and the advancement of technology.

During the 1940s and 1950s other centres were established in Britain, which were primarily concerned with collecting materials for folklife scholars and linguistic specialists, notably: The Institute of Folk Life Studies at the University of Leeds, the School of Folklife Studies at Edinburgh and the Welsh Folk Museum at St Fagan's, Cardiff. At the Welsh Folk Museum, for example, the Department of Oral Traditions and Dialects was established to investigate and accurately record oral evidence relating to three major areas of study, namely:

1. *The pattern of livelihood and everyday life* in both rural and urban Wales;
2. *The lore of everyday life,* which included subjects such as seasonal customs and customs relating to birth, marriage and death, children's games and pastimes, and a whole range of evidences available in folk songs and traditions;
3. *The language of everyday life,* which dealt with the recording of dialects, investigation into phonological and grammatical features, and the collecting of the vocabularies of agriculture and industry, of domestic life and cultural activities.

Although the amount of evidence of interest and value to local historians amassed at establishments such as the Welsh Folk Museum is enormous, some of the really pioneering work in oral history in Britain was undertaken by individuals.

## 'TOMORROW MAY BE TOO LATE'

Notable among such individuals is George Ewart Evans, a Welshman, who spent much of his working life as a teacher and writer in East Anglia. Shortly after the end of the Second World War, Evans had moved to the small village of Blaxhall in East Suffolk and soon realised that he had moved to an area which still had evidences of a prior culture. During the 1950s

Evans began tape-recording the reminiscences of some of the older inhabitants of Blaxhall and in 1956 he published *Ask the fellows who cut the hay,* a book based on those recordings. George Ewart Evans was painfully aware that he was witnessing the final break-up of the old community - its customs, beliefs, vocabulary and above all its way of life:

> The book has taken this particular shape from the writer's conviction that the oral tradition is at this time of the greatest historical importance... At present, old people in this countryside are survivors from another era. They belong essentially to a culture that has extended in unbroken line since at least the early Middle Ages. They are in some respects the last repositories of this culture; and for this reason should have some of the respect given to any source of valuable historical information. Their knowledge of dialect, folk tales and songs, old customs and usages, and craft vocabularies, and their ability to identify and describe the use of farm implements that are now going into limbo after being used for centuries, are sufficient reasons why they should have the local historian's greatest attention. [10]

This meant meticulously recording their reminiscences, an exacting task, but one of prime importance. Unexcavated sites can wait to be dug up, even the collecting of printed local material can be postponed for another day, but not the recording of oral evidence: 'While the sort of knowledge that is waiting to be taken down from old people is always on the brink of extinction. Tomorrow may be too late; and once this knowledge is under the soil no amount of digging will ever again recover it.' [11] Since the appearance of his remarkable book, Geoge Ewart Evans has produced a series of other notable volumes based on oral evidence. Most of these, such as *The pattern under the plough* and *The farm and the village,* are concerned with aspects of folk life in East Anglia. He also ventured in *From mouths of men* into urban history, and a section of that book relates to community life in the south Wales mining valley where he was brought up. In all his writings, George Ewart Evans emphasises again and again the importance of oral evidence: 'It seems to me now that the value of oral history ... is not so much in the new material it can reveal, although this is manifestly of great importance, as in the bringing home to the student or researcher a new consciousness of history which is entirely different from the knowledge or enlightenment he can obtain through the conventional methods.' [12]

The real impetus for oral history in Britain, however, came during the mid- and late 1960s, when a group of academics, mainly social historians and sociologists, began making extensive use of oral evidences and forcibly arguing its case. Paul Thompson and Thea Vigne at the University of Essex's Department of Sociology, Bill Williams at the Manchester Studies Unit and Raphael Samuel at Oxford, instigated a number of impressive projects. At Essex they undertook a major survey of family life, work and community before 1918, and the Manchester Studies Unit was involved in subjects such as Jewish studies, the cotton industry and pawnbroking. One result of the activities of these academics was the establishment in 1973 of the Oral History Society 'to further the practice of oral history in all appropriate fields'. The journal *Oral history* began to appear regularly and became a forum for monitoring developments in oral history studies. Also, during the early 1970s the Social Service Research Council began funding a number of oral history projects; the South Wales Coalfield project is an interesting example. Although the coalfield's history goes back to the beginning of the nineteenth century, there was, a century and a half later, surprisingly little documentary sources available to record its growth and subsequent decline. Before nationalisation was finally achieved in 1947, most of the coal-owners had systematically destroyed colliery records. What remained was soon sold off to second-hand book dealers. It was obvious, however, that a wealth of information relating to various aspects of the coalfield's history was available in the reminiscences of former miners and lodge officials, and indeed a great many other inhabitants who had experienced life in the south Wales industrial communities. This project was essentially a salvage operation, 'an essential defence against oblivion' as Nevins would maintain.

A number of other oral history projects were salvage operations, obtaining invaluable oral evidence before the tomorrow that would be too late. But whereas Nevins was concerned with élite oral history, the projects of most of the British social historians investigated the conditions of the working classes in rural and urban areas. The non-élites of this world often possessing invaluable information about the societies they had lived in. Oral history therefore became a process of redressing the balance. History was no longer the sole territory of royalty and the ruling classes, whose every movement had been so well and amply recorded throughout the centuries. At last there was an opportunity to record, literally, the voices of ordinary men and women. History would be given back to the people.

# THE SIGNIFICANCE OF ORAL HISTORY

Despite the increased recognition of the value of oral history during the last 15 years, it is still viewed with suspicion by a number of the more orthodox traditionalist historians, who are mainly used to, and who would rather rely on, documentary sources of historical evidence. They would claim that histories based entirely on non-documentary sources tend to be less satisfactory than those drawn from documents. The main argument concerns the objective validity of oral history. The human memory, it will be argued, is notoriously unreliable and an informant can quite unintentionally provide evidence that is entirely false. It is also maintained that oral testimony is often no more than superfluous gossip, and not only unreliable but also unfair, over-simplified and distorted. The personal nature of a recorded interview makes the evidence far less reliable and far less objective than evidence in documentary sources. A.J.P. Taylor was dismissive when talking about the value of oral evidence: 'In this matter I am an almost total sceptic ... Old men drooling on about their youth -No'.[13]

Another major criticism, and sometimes a valid one, concerns the role of the interviewer. The type of questions asked and the manner of their asking can be crucial. Biased questioning can produce the sort of answers the interviewer wishes to hear:

> One serious danger does exist for the oral historian. When he is himself conducting the interview ... he may be tempted into moulding the evidence he receives; the barriers against doing this are less formidable with oral than with documentary material. By asking leading questions ... or by approaching only those informants who will give him the answers he wants, he may halfconsciously use the interview to distort the truth.[14]

The third major area of criticism concerns the actual process of interviewing. Certain informants may dislike the prospect of speaking into a tape recorder and will therefore refuse or fail to be frank and forthright. Others may feel inhibited and nervous when faced with the interview situation and may not always provide the real evidence they possess: 'This is the drawback of interviews ... the final product is a wholly accurate record of what has been on the speaker's tongue but rarely in his mind or heart'.[15]

The above criticisms must be carefully considered by oral historians. No oral history project should be instigated and no interview undertaken unless clear objectives are laid down and detailed guidelines observed. The basic question that must be returned to, however, is whether oral testimony is less objective and less reliable than evidence obtained from various documentary sources. But are the documentary sources always objective and entirely reliable? The words of the late Richard Crossman on this subject are interesting:

> I've discovered, having read all the Cabinet papers about the meetings I attended, that the documents often bear virtually no relation to what actually happened. I know now that the Cabinet Minutes are written by Burke Trend (secretary to the Cabinet), not to say what did happen in the Cabinet, but what the Civil Service wishes it to be believed happened, so that a clear directive can be given.[16]

George Ewart Evans holds a similar view. Having been a parish councillor for many years he was intrigued with what he found in the offical minutes: 'Not that there was any blatant inaccuracy ... but since the time of the meeting so recorded, a selective intelligence had been at work, omitting almost everything that did not contribute to fortifying the main decisions reached.'[17]

Throughout the centuries has there not been 'a selective intelligence' at work ensuring that the official establishment view of events is recorded, whether it be on a national or local level? Some of the major criticisms of oral history are equally applicable to some of the more respectable traditional sources. Had George Ewart Evans taken the view of A.J.P. Taylor and rejected the evidences of 'old men drooling on' we would not have his remarkable volumes on folklife in East Anglia. Evans, however, makes no apology for his reliance on oral testimony:

> Can oral tradition be relied upon? From my own experience in one particular field - the recording of old skills and craft of the old prior society in East Anglia - I can say unequivocally that in this field I would much prefer to trust the craftsmen, the farmer, or the farm-worker who had done the job probably for his lifetime, rather than any printed sources dealing with the details and nature of his work ... To a man who had spent his life at a certain work or craft it is a point of honour to describe its details fully and without distortion.[18]

Oral testimony, like all other historical evidences, must be used with the greatest of care and subjected to the rigorous standards of scholarship. Having applied these standards, it will be found that the advantages of oral history in areas of study where other documentary evidence already exists can provide useful supplementary material to reinforce or possibly correct that evidence. It enhances the task of historical interpretation. In areas of study where documentary evidence is non-existent or under-documented, the use of oral history can be unique and unsurpassable. And in local history there are often subjects which are often totally undocumented. Raphael Samuel, another notable practitioner of the use of oral evidence, advocated the case forcefully:

> Oral evidence makes it possible to escape from some of the deficiencies of the documentary record, at least so far as recent times are concerned ... There are matters of fact which are recorded in the memories of older people and nowhere else, events of the past which they alone can elucidate for us, vanished sights which they alone can recall. Documents can't answer back, nor, beyond a point, can they be asked to explain in greater detail what they mean, to give more examples, to account for negative instances, or to explain apparent discrepancies in the record which survives. Yet there are certain kinds of inquiry which can only be undertaken with the aid of living testimony, and whole areas of life in which its credentials are beyond question.[19]

The old people in whose memories so much is hidden are, to use the analogy of George Ewart Evans, 'people who are themselves living bridges to the past'.[20] Paul Thompson would go further and claim that oral history, because of its unique position as a historical source, has radical implications for the future:

> The discovery of 'oral history' by historians which is now underway is then unlikely to be obscured. And it is not only a discovery but a recovery. It gives history a future no longer tied to the cultural significance of the paper document. It also gives back to historians the oldest skill of their own craft.[21]

## ORAL HISTORY AND LOCAL STUDIES

As the validity of oral history gained recognition among historians, the implications for libraries, particularly for those (both public and academic) which had established comprehensive local studies collections, became apparent. American librarians had realised long before their British counterparts that no local studies collection would be complete without the inclusion of oral evidence: 'Local history may benefit most from oral history. Local history tapes are an excellent way to record the changing lifestyles, speech patterns, and customs that are rapidly disappearing, and to assess how larger issues affect local areas'.[22]

Librarians have always realised that they have an important role to play in preserving the records (in whatever format) that embody the unique heritage of their communities. As cultural and educational resource centres, no library can therefore afford to ignore the challenges of oral history:

> Why should a library collect tape recordings? The basic principle is quite simple: a library - and I am thinking particularly of a local history library - must comprehensively collect information about its locality, and if it neglects an information source, or any type of material, it cannot claim to be catholic in scope. Tape recordings … are just one more type of non-book material which add another dimension to the range of sources available.[23]

Accepting that local studies collections should be as comprehensive as possible, it is imperative, however, that libraries who intend to become involved in the acquisition of oral history materials are fully aware of the implications. For the collection of oral history materials is expensive and time-consuming. Furthermore, it invariably involves the production of new and unique historical material and librarians may not always be competent to undertake such a task. In deciding whether or not to establish an oral history collection each library must do so in the light of its overall objectives and only after having carefully considered its own priorities. 'The library must consider the needs of its users, its budget, staff, and space, the resources and services of other historical agencies in determining its optimal contribution to the preservation of the historical record.'[24] To instigate such a collection and to develop it systematically and comprehensively will demand considerable resources in terms of finance, staffing, equipment and accommodation.

## Finance

At whatever level of commitment the library is involved in collecting oral history, some expense will be involved. Even where the library is only concerned with collecting materials created by persons outside the library, staff will be required to process materials, storage facilities must be provided and expertise available at hand to document and exploit the collection. If the library becomes directly involved in collecting oral history then the financial implications will be greater and any oral history project will need to be carefully budgeted for. Allowances must be made for adequate equipment to undertake the work, for proper storage facilities to retain the finished products and for the transcription of tapes and their detailed cataloguing and indexing. The cost of fulfilling all these duties can be high.

## Staffing

By far the most expensive element in the development of any oral history collection will be the staff time involved. That oral history is a very time-consuming activity cannot be over emphasised. Unless adequate time is provided the task cannot be done well, and unless it is done well it may indeed be better left undone. It is therefore important to ensure that adequate time will be allowed for:

preparation in advance of an interview, i.e. checking background information and drawing up of questionnaires;
adequate time to undertake the interview itself and to obtain a record of the highest quality possible;
sufficient time to document the taped 'interview' and maximising its availability to potential users by indexing, transcription, etc.

The use of volunteers and others for oral history recording work has been discussed in Chapter 7.

## Accommodation

Adequate accommodation facilities must be provided by libraries who seriously wish to develop oral history collections. Few libraries will be in a position to provide purpose-built premises catering for the use and storage of magnetic tapes and cassettes. All libraries, however, must attempt to store their materials under the best possible conditions given the range and quality of accommodation available. Not only must there be appropriate working accommodation for technical staff involved in editing work, etc, but there must also be adequate storage space to house all tapes (master and working copies), and there should be listening facilities for users.

## LEVEL OF COMMITMENT

Having decided that it will be involved in the collection of oral history materials, the library also has to decide on its level of involvement or commitment. Basically there are three possible approaches:

First, it can act as a *passive depository* for oral history materials produced entirely by outside sources. The library assumes therefore archival functions for the storage and exploitation of materials, although it has not been involved in their production. It can accept materials from individuals or institutions and be responsible for their safekeeping. On this level, however, the library must be absolutely clear as to what type of material it is prepared to accept. It should not accept material which will be of little use to its clientele or which would be better deposited elsewhere. Materials accepted should ideally be those which supplement or complement other historical sources available in its own local studies collection.

On a second level of commitment the library acts as *an active depository*. Again most of the material will probably be produced by outsiders - by individuals working on specific subjects or by local history or other interested groups. But on this level the library can become much more directly involved. It can act in a co-ordinating role and provide useful preliminary information for interviewers, even equipment for recording, and once the interviews are completed, be mainly responsible for ensuring that they are competently catalogued, indexed and transcribed if necessary. The library's unique position in the community, and the access its staff has to all sections of that community, means it can establish links with institutions and individuals concerned with oral history. On this level of commitment the library will obviously need to invest time and money in projects which may originate elsewhere but the return for the local studies collection can be very substantial.

On the third level of commitment the library becomes directly involved in the creation of an oral history collection. In a sense it becomes *a creative depository*. During the late 1960s and early 1970s a substantial number of

320

public libraries and a few academic libraries in the United Kingdom saw the value of setting up such collections. A number of these were the products of short-term projects which secured additional funding for the libraries concerned. Short-term projects often produce excellent results but the collection of oral history should if possible be an ongoing activity. Before a library undertakes that activity, however, it must assess the implications realistically:

> A full commitment to establishing an oral history program in the library is not undertaken lightly. Oral history projects are often more expensive and time-consuming than anticipated and the creation of an oral history program may jeopardize the quality of the library's other established programs by draining funds or staff from them. Can the library make its greatest contribution to preservation of the historical record by establishing an oral history program? Or can it make a greater contribution to the collective memory of the community or its parent institution by comprehensively collecting and preserving its published documents?[25]

Once it has decided to establish an oral history collection a library will need to carefully plan its development.

## PLANNING THE COLLECTION

The precise nature of the collection will need to be defined so that all involved know exactly what the end result should be. Whether a library embarks on an oral history project entirely on its own or in conjunction with other interested groups, a clearly laid out policy statement listing the main objectives should be produced. What areas of local studies need to be covered and what gaps in existing documentary evidence need to be filled? More important still what level of commitment should be adopted? These are some of the vitally important questions that need to be answered before any project can commence in earnest.

### Guidelines for research/interviews

It is important from the start that those involved in the process of collecting oral history should be given detailed guidelines relating to the amount of preliminary research required of them and advice on the preparation of questionnaires and on the technique of interviewing. At all times it should be remembered that it is the quality of the interviews within a collection that counts as opposed to the quantity.

## The storage and documentation of the collection

It is equally important at the outset to lay down a policy for storage and documentation. Often in the past, the oral history collections developed in libraries have been inadequately preserved, and poorly documented. As with all historical records, ensuring their availability and accessibility is of paramount importance.

## STORAGE AND PRESERVATION

Having successfully conducted an interview and produced a new and unique historical record, it is imperative that the librarian and his/her staff should ensure that it is adequately stored and preserved for future use. Creating a historical resource on the one hand and allowing it to be destroyed through neglect on the other would be nonsensical. Therefore, those involved in developing oral history collections should pay careful and constant attention to the best means and methods of preserving magnetic tape recordings. Even though few libraries will have the facilities or the resources to store their tapes under ideal conditions, all libraries can take basic precautions. As to the storage of tapes it is generally maintained that:

> The recommended storage temperature for magnetic tape is 45 °F to 35 °F (7 °C to 13 °C), and the recommended relative humidity is 40 to 60 per cent. Stability of temperature and humidity is particularly important; it has been suggested as a general guide that, in the absence of an air-conditioned storage room, tapes be kept in dry areas with comfortable working temperatures not subject to variations of more than 10 °F (6 °C).[26]

Tapes must always be protected from the effects of dust, sunlight and dampness and from the influences of magnetic fields. In order to avoid deterioration a number of other precautions should be observed such as the correct manner of shelving tapes, the importance of routine rewinding

322

to reduce print-through effects and periodic testing for magnetic degradation. Before contemplating the creation of an oral history archive expert advice on the storage and preservation of magnetic tapes should be sought. Most librarians, whether academic or public, will have access to media specialists within their institutions or authorities, and further advice could be obtained from tape manufacturers or indeed from some of the major national archives specialising in the development of oral history collections (for example, the Imperial War Museum and the Welsh Folk Museum are able to give advice).

## DOCUMENTATION

In order to maximise the use made of an oral history collection, it is necessary to ensure that each recorded interview is fully documented and made as accessible as possible to potential users. The degree of accessibility will depend on a number of factors, particularly the extent to which a library is able, within its resources, to process, catalogue and index its tapes as soon as they have been recorded. Libraries may often be faced with the dilemma of whether to conduct more interviews or to actually document those already produced. It can often be an exceedingly difficult decision. Unless undertaken immediately, 'tomorrow may be too late' to record the views and reminiscences of a unique informant; on the other hand there is nothing more infuriating for the serious researcher than a badly organised and under-documented collection of interviews. Ideally, therefore, each recorded interview should be accessioned, catalogued and possibly transcribed and indexed as soon as it is completed. This does not mean that the procedures adopted should be cumbersome or overtly complicated, indeed they should avoid over-sophistication at all costs. The essence of a good documentation system for oral history is that it should provide quick and effective information retrieval for its users. In order to ensure this a number of fairly elementary steps are recommended:

### Identification of tapes

As soon as they have been recorded individual tapes should be clearly identified in two ways:-

1.  A verbal label at the beginning of a tape in which the interviewer

announces the name of the informant and the date of the interview.

2.  By written labels attached to the tape itself, its spool and container on which will be inscribed the accession number of the interview, the names of the interviewer and informant, and the date of the interview.

Without these two basic precautions, tapes can be accidentally wound on incorrect spools or replaced in wrong boxes, with all the ensuing complications!

## Accessions list/register

Each taped interview must be identifiable and the easiest method of ensuring this is by the production of an accessions list/register. Each new recorded interview is treated as a unit and given a unique number from a consecutive series. Such an accessions list/register need only contain basic information giving the name of the informant, the date of the interview and a very brief description of its subject-matter. Where more than one tape was used during an interview, this can easily be indicated as part of the accession number e.g. 107/4. This accession number should henceforth be used in all references to this particular interview.

## Cataloguing

To adequately provide a retrieval system to a collection of tapes, it is essential that information should be provided relating to:

the circumstances of the interview ➡ *interview card*
the informant and his background ➡ *informant's card*
the subject-matter of the interview ➡ *summary/contents card*

The degree of detail which any particular library will record will depend very much on the amount of staff time it is able to afford.

### Interview card

This will provide two categories of information, namely

1.  *information relating to the informant (interviewee)* - i.e. full name and title, date of birth, qualifications, occupation, nationality, topic of interview,
2.  *information relating to the interview* - i.e. accession number, location, date, duration, name of interviewer, language, speed, tape width, transcription, access and copyright, associated materials.

## Informant's card

Many libraries and archives have felt that as much information as possible relating to the informant should be collected, thus creating a 'personal file' providing invaluable background material. In addition to information about the informant's date of birth, education, career outline, marriage, etc. information about parents and grandparents and their respective careers should also be collected. Thus an informant's card would not only provide basic data, but also place the informant within a wider social, economic and political context.

The library may also wish to attach to an informant's card other relevant materials such as correspondence, photographs, copyright agreements, pre-interview notes compiled by the interviewer, etc. The aim of any informant's card would be to provide as comprehensive a picture as possible.

It is also fair to note in this context that a number of oral historians, particularly those involved in political and social history, would claim that it is equally important to collect background information relating to interviewers, so that their education and upbringing and beliefs are known.

## Summary/contents card

This would provide a synopsis of the main topics discussed during each interview, to assist potential users in deciding whether they would wish to listen to the original tape or consult a full transcript if that were available. Any synopsis would concentrate on the most important topics discussed, personalities and places referred to, etc. The importance of intelligently and well produced summary/contents cards cannot be over-emphasised. Their value for staff and users alike is obvious - they will provide the most useful guide to the subject-matter of each taped interview. One expert suggests that; 'A synopsis of fifty to seventy five words per thirty minutes of recording is appropriate ... When preparing the interview synopsis, it must be borne in mind that the information given rather than the questions asked is to be catalogued'.[27]

Where possible, each summary card should also indicate the precise location of items on the tape so that users wishing to hear the original evidence can do so with the minimum of bother.

## Transcription

It would be argued by most oral historians that it is highly desirable for recorded interviews to be transcribed, thus increasing considerably their accessibility. Not all such historians would place the same emphasis on the transcript. Some would argue that what really matters is the content of a tape, the quality and value of the information provided. Others, such as David Lance, who developed the Department of Sound Records at the Imperial War Museum, would argue that the real value of any recorded interview lies in the verbal record itself: 'The only form in which the full content and quality of oral information can be reproduced is that in which it is recorded. It is in the spoken word, not the written, that the oral history interview is encapsulated.'[28]

'The sound recording', as Lance maintains, is therefore 'the primary oral history document'. What a transcription does is merely provide a useful finding aid for the tape itself and serve as a printed copy of the verbal document, thus making the task of cataloguing and indexing tapes easier. Historians representing both the above points of view, however, insist that a transcript must at all times be an accurate printed facsimile of the oral document. The task of ensuring this is a highly skilled and specialised one and finding a competent, intelligent and interested transcriber may not always be easy: 'The task of the typist is to produce an accurate typescript of the interview and - by the appropriate use of sentences, paragraphs and punctuation - to make it as literate a document as possible without altering the words or sense of the speakers. Thus the informant's choice of words should always be retained ...'[29]

The decision whether to produce transcripts of tapes or not will depend on factors such as the resources available to undertake the work, the quality of the contents of individual tapes and the desirability of transcribing them. Transcribing is an exceptionally demanding and time-consuming task, and it is generally recommended that between six and nine hours is required to transcribe a tape of one hour's duration. Providing full transcripts, however, increases considerably the value of any oral history collection for potential users.

## Indexing

For certain small-scale oral history collections the production of well-produced summary/contents cards may be sufficient. For large collections in academic and public libraries alike, an in-depth subject indexing of collections will be desirable to further facilitate their accessibility. This again is an expensive and time-consuming activity, but if undertaken should be done as soon as possible after the recording of the interview and the production of the summary/contents card. If both tasks could be undertaken by the same person it would further ensure consistency and accuracy.

The depth and detail of indexing will depend on the resources available, the nature of the collection and the type of user likely to consult it. The range of subjects to be indexed and the detail of indexing will remain a major decision. One important factor which has made that decision-making process easier has been the development during the last few years of computer-based cataloguing and indexing systems. Nowadays it is perfectly feasible for even large and moderately sized oral history collections to be indexed by computerised methods, thus increasing considerably their accessibility.

## THE EXPLOITATION OF ORAL HISTORY

It is not only accessibility to oral history collections that is important, it is also imperative that such collections should be further exploited wherever possible. The unique voices of the past should not be left in silence on the library shelf or in the archival vault. The one obvious method of ensuring that material collected orally reaches a wide audience is by reproducing it in printed form and this can be done in a variety of ways ranging from substantial biographies to small local booklets or information packs. Oral history reproduced in both audio and printed form provides invaluable educational materials not only for schools and colleges, but also for a wide range of adult education classes. In the reproduction of oral evidence the library can often benefit from the experience of individuals involved with local history societies or educational projects. Where material is reproduced on tape or audio cassettes, the quality will obviously depend on the standard of the original recording and that standard must always be of the highest order possible.

II

## INTERVIEWING FOR ORAL HISTORY

It would be invidious to suggest that one path exists which, if followed with diligence, will create a perfect oral history interview. The changing circumstances of each interview, and more especially the role of interviewer and respondent, should bring a new dimension to each interviewing experience. However, against this essential chemistry it is important to consider the practice and methodology which should be adopted if the interview is to approach success. Such consideration is crucial if the interview is to be of any lasting value to future researchers; it will ensure that the effort of interviewer and respondent is not wasted and that the end product does not descend to the standard described by one commentator: 'Too often oral history recordings are of appalling technical quality, the interviewee being virtually unintelligible. A little more thought in advance and the interview and the recording could be improved considerably'.[30] Thus while successful interviewing is to some extent an art, certain guidelines can be offered; these are the accumulation of experience and observation of many interviews and interviewers. They will yield success and ensure that certain fundamental pitfalls are avoided.

### Preparation

Thorough preparation is required if any interview is to be fully exploited. This will include a search of print and non-print sources, and preliminary discussions with respondents. It is only by undertaking such research that the interviewer will familiarise himself/herself with the subject area, leading of course to the asking of meaningful questions. This research can also be incorporated into a formal questionnaire, resulting in a structured approach for one or more interviews. Care should be taken, however, when presenting the fruits of the research to respondents at initial meetings or prior to the recording of an interview. Citing articles and the views of academics in the subject area will immediately place the respondent at a disadvantage. The interviewer will be speaking to 'amateurs' - people who have worked as blacksmiths or chambermaids, as opposed to others who have written about these occupations. Oral history evidence has the advantage of bringing first-hand experience, but this can quickly dissipate into worthless recollections if ranged against the views and writings of authorities in the field.

A related question is, when should an interview be carried out? Is it necessary to complete all research prior to interviewing or can early interviews or initial discussions form part of this research, leading to a final session in which the interviewer is by now thoroughly familiar with the territory and can thus react quickly and easily to points raised during the interview? There is no ideal answer and again the circumstances of each interview will call for individual assessment. A great deal will depend on the respondent: on the one hand it may be necessary to seek several meetings to become clear on the pattern of the interview; one disadvantage of this approach is the loss of spontaneity or of memory and recollection. On the other hand, there is one factor that may be crucial in deciding on the timing of the interview. Without descending to the morbid and macabre, it is important to consider the age and state of health of potential respondents. The historian, Lord Briggs, is succinctly clear on this point: 'In my experience, you have to watch age above all: I've lost some notable people through not seeing them in time'.[31]

The next step is to discover the location of the interview. There is need, of course, to be clear on the geographical location but far more important is whether the location chosen is likely to have any bearing on the success of the interview. Recording in the open air, or at an industrial location may bring advantages of providing memory triggers and actuality, but such locations will inevitably call for special equipment. Clearly open-air recording will require the use of battery-driven rather than mains tape recorders, and it is essential to take along an ample supply of batteries. Even the smallest reel to reel machines have a voracious appetite for batteries and it is important that each set used is at peak power. If this power is not maintained the tape spools will turn at a lower speed than that chosen, and thus when that tape is transferred to a mains machine the interviewer will find that there is a distorted recording. Recording at open locations or in areas where there is a good deal of background noise also means that the interviewer must use a windshield over the microphone. This simple cover of foam rubber is exactly what it says: a shield which will effectively absorb any wind or background noise. What may seem to be a gentle breeze or the idyllic splash of a mill wheel turning, can be transformed into a howling gale or earth-shattering rumble when transferred on to tape. The objective is to obtain a balance where both parties are clearly audible with the background noise not distracting in any way from the quality of the recording. Remember also to have a sufficient supply of tape and adaptors. It is no good if the interviewer discovers half way through a fascinating interview that he/she has run out of tape, the reserve stock being 30 miles away at headquarters! Always use the highest-quality tape that can be afforded, and when choosing cassettes stick to well-known brands such as TDK or Maxell, restricting your choice to C60 or C90, rather than C120 which are too fragile and far more likely to tangle or break. A golden rule is the thicker the tape base, the better the overall prospect of preservation. In particular, thicker tape bases, such as standard play, will minimise print-through - the condition where a signal present on a tape is transferred or printed through to the next layer of tape and so on. No one brand is ideal in this respect, but modern advances in tape technology have lessened the likelihood of print-through.

Using the correct equipment is extremely important, and potential oral historians are likely to require some advice on this area. There is now a wide range of audio recorders on the market, but when one seeks high technical quality the choice is narrowed to a few machines designed to broadcast standards and thus carrying a professional price tag. Examples are reel to reel recorders manufactured by Nagra and Uher. Those made by Nagra are expensive, but have a high reputation and are extensively used by professional sound recordists the world over. The Uher tape recorders are a familiar sight at any BBC or commercial radio station and are excellent machines offering very good value for money. Later models have a variety of tape speeds, are unobtrusive and relatively light-weight (around 8 lb), virtually silent in operation and almost idiot-proof once a few basic controls are mastered. Uhers are also well made and will consistently give good results, recording to broadcast standards. They do, however, have one disadvantage which can be of significance to oral historians. The size of the recorders mean that they will only accommodate a maximum spool of 5 inches diameter, which with standard play thickness of tape recording at 7½ inches per second (the only real choice if the tape is to be copied) allows a recording of 16 minutes per side. An oral history interview of one hour would thus require four changes of tape on a standard Uher, with all the resultant interruptions, and likely loss of flow. The commercial market is awash with a wide range of cassette recorders, but unless one is prepared to pay a very high price, such machines cannot be seriously considered as suitable for oral history recording. One distinct, but commonplace, disadvantage is that many of these cassette recorders have an in-built microphone. This facility will usually ensure that there is a fair reproduction of the cassette recorder motor which then invariably affects any material on the tape. A further problem is that cassettes are designed to run at a far slower speed than reel to reel, resulting in loss of quality, again made apparent if and when the tape is copied. A final reason for choosing reel to reel instead of cassettes is that the former make it considerably easier to edit the tape if this is necessary for any reason.

The results obtained from any tape recorder will ultimately depend on another piece of equipment - the microphone. Here the key word is compatability. There is no point in attempting to improve the performance of a cheap machine by coupling it to an expensive microphone; it is also false economy to spend a large sum on a tape recorder and then curb its effectiveness by using a cheap microphone. Low-cost microphones tend to have an uneven frequency response, giving rather flat dull recordings on which the full speech range is not represented. Another weakness is that they pick up and emphasise the hard consonants and sibilants used in speech, such as p's and b's and s's, resulting in distorted recordings, peppered with pops and hisses. A further fault in many cheap microphones is that they are over-susceptible to handling noise - the noise caused by the friction of the hand against the microphone case or cable. A partial solution to this problem is the microphone stand: the microphone is placed in position at the beginning of the interview and left in that position until recording is ended. Remember, however, that a microphone so placed must have the capacity to provide a balanced recording from at least two participants - the interviewer and respondent. Choice is therefore between uni-directional microphones, which have the disadvantage of providing a degree of protection against unwanted noise, and omni-directional microphones which pick up sounds (including background noises) equally well from all directions. A further solution is to use small clip or lapel microphones of the type frequently worn by television interviewers and presenters. The latest examples give high technical quality at a relatively low price. Such microphones are also unobtrusive and overcome the difficulty of variations in recording levels which can occur as respondents change their position relative to a stand or mounted or other fixed microphones. Nagra and Uher manufacture a range of microphones specially designed for use with their machines; other reputable names in this field are AKG, Sony and Eagle.

12. *Oral history interview : retired station master providing information for an MSC sponsored project undertaken by Dyfed Cultural Services on the development of railways in West Wales.* [*Harold Richards*]

332

A final word on preparation. Be familiar with all the equipment before leaving base. Fiddling with pause buttons and fumbling with spools of tape will do little to win the confidence of the respondent and will draw attention to the technical side of the interview, which ideally should be as unobtrusive as possible.

## Preliminaries

Before commencing interviewing the first task is to check the location once again, viewing it with a practised eye, and more especially listening to the location with a finely tuned ear. This is the only opportunity to listen out for extraneous noises which could mar the recording. As indicated already, some background noises can contribute to the success of a tape giving it actuality and 'feel'. There are, however, many other noises which will contribute nothing, indeed will have the opposite effect of causing annoyance and irritation to any future listener. First there are internal noises, or noises from within the room or chosen location. Examples here are doorbells, crackling fires, ticking clocks, pets, telephones and creaking armchairs. Noises can also emanate from outside the room: traffic, trains, hooters and industrial plant are perfect examples. It is the task of the interviewer to be aware and awake to these noises, curbing their effect if at all possible. Whereas it may seem tranquil and conducive to record an oral history interview in front of a roaring fire, with a grandfather clock gently ticking in the background, it should be remembered that a listener turning to the tape in five years will find the crackling coals totally mystifying, and the grandfather clock will assume maddening proportions. Avoid recording against 'hard' surfaces, such as large windows, as these will give the recording a harsh resonant tone. Of course, in attempting to solve these and other related difficulties, the interviewer must try to seek a balance. To move half the furniture around the room and silence the budgerigar may achieve a congenial recording atmosphere, but it is also likely to create domestic chaos, ensuring discomfort and ill-feeling. Thus the whole exercise defeats its own object. There are, however, quite simple things that the interviewer can request and indeed set up in a quiet and unobtrusive manner. A move to the rear of the house can lessen the problem of traffic noise, whereas a room well draped with soft furnishings will always improve the overall quality of the recording. One set of guidelines takes this search for an effective recording atmosphere to a logical, if surprising, conclusion: 'Technically, the bedroom is probably the best recording area'.[32] Bearing in mind that one other common piece of advice to enhance sound quality is to draw the curtains, it is easy to imagine that such a progression could well cause alarm for respondent and perhaps also interviewer!

Interruptions can also emanate from other individuals in the room, presenting serious obstacles. While it may be incorrect to suggest that problems are doubled every time another member joins the interviewing 'party', it is true to say that it becomes increasingly difficult to handle groups of respondents. Again while certain respondents can draw comments one from another and get the conversation going, it remains the task of the interviewer to control that situation if necessary and this task can become well nigh impossible if faced with a welter of enthusiastic, but contradictory, statements. Furthermore unless all respondents wear individual clip microphones there is the danger of having one or two members of the party within microphone range and the remainder sounding as if they were some thirty feet distant. A related issue centres around interviewing husbands with wives present or vice versa. Such respondents may wish to refer to early periods in their lives prior to marriage, and while the interviewer is unlikely to be the recipient of intimate disclosures, it is obviously easier to talk about some topics without the presence of another party. Even if third parties say nothing, their presence will distract the respondent, make him/her feel uncomfortable and conscious of being interviewed, whereas the objective is to achieve the exact opposite. Thus unless the interviewer is an expert at handling group interviews, the best and simplest solution is to record interviews on a one to one basis. If it is discovered that a second or third member of the household has something relevant to contribute, then the interviewer can move on to other interviews, but again on an individual basis.

Now the stage has been reached which can make or break any oral history interview, the crucial requirement to talk freely and fully before starting to record. This will ensure that both parties do not go 'cold' into any interview; to pursue the analogy the ice will be broken by having a general conversation with the respondent, which will get him/her talking and place him/her at ease. Thus when the interviewer is ready to start, he/she can move gently from this opening conversation to the actual interview with the respondent hardly noticing the change. This talk beforehand will also provide an invaluable opportunity to go over the ground to be covered during the interview. It is an unswerving human characteristic that points will be mentioned before and after an interview which would not be revealed at all during its course. This may arise because of lapse of memory or an awareness of the artificiality of the interview situation, but whatever the reason it is the responsibility of the interviewer to carefully note these points and weave them into the interview. Here it becomes apparent that, while it was suggested above that the overall plan of the interview may have been structured into a questionnaire, it is essential not to adhere rigidly to it. It should not be felt that because background research and other interviews suggest that there are fundamental points to be covered, that those points must be covered whatever happens. The interviewer has to be prepared to adapt and change this overall plan, especially as a result of information conveyed prior to the interview. To return to this exploratory conversation, a constant problem is whether the respondent should be told the questions he is going to be asked. It is impossible to offer blanket advice, as the course of action will have to depend ultimately on the attitude of the respondent. Some individuals may demand to see a list of points beforehand (and if such a request is made then it should be respected); others will be prepared to follow an easier, open approach, which offers a greater prospect for successful interviews. The ideal is to chart a middle path: cover the ground before hand, changing and adapting as necessary, but avoid a list of typed questions, unless these are demanded. The great difficulty with such a list is that it becomes the final blueprint for the interview, the respondent being unwilling and indeed surprised when an attempt is made to move beyond the ten questions listed. A list of questions can also result in the ultimate disaster: the respondent carefully prepares 'answers' and reads them to the microphone, all of which negates the whole purpose of oral history interviewing.

## The interview

Before starting to record a voice test must be undertaken to ensure that the microphone is placed in the optimum position and that the controls on the tape recorder are adjusted to attain good recording levels. Switch off or turn down the speaker on the machine or there will be 'feedback'. A table-standing microphone should be placed no further than 18 inches away from the interviewer or respondent, and at such an angle that both parties are speaking across the microphone rather than directly into it. To achieve a balanced recording it may be necessary to compensate for the member of the interviewing party with the weaker voice by having him or her move closer to the microphone. Using clip microphones will overcome this problem if these are attached to a stable part of the clothing (such as the lapel), so that they do not swing or rub in response to movements of the body.

Practically all tape recorders will have recording level indicators; some, such as later Uher models, also have automatic level control devices. These bring the advantage of coping with respondents whose voice levels rise and fall dramatically, or those who shift their position during the interview. Such devices can, however, make certain words sound clipped, but more relevantly they can bring a sort of ebb and flow effect to any interview - this becoming particularly apparent after any halt or pause. What happens is that the automatic level control takes a few seconds to readjust itself, and the first few words after a pause may be lost or picked up at a significantly lower level. There are, therefore, firm arguments for setting recording levels manually, with the meters showing that a strong, undistorted signal is being recorded. To echo a piece of advice given by bank managers to their clients, the interviewer should be careful not 'to go into the red' as levels are taken prior to recording. Although this process may sound involved and complicated it can in fact be achieved quite easily by incorporating the task into the preliminary conversations, flicking the pause button on the machine while exchanging social pleasantries. This brief section of tape can be replayed to check on the quality of the recording, but this must be done quickly and unobtrusively, as many respondents find the sound of their own voice on tape somewhat off-putting. Despite this the interviewer must listen to this section, as it is of no use to discover at the end of the interview that the recording is distorted or, worse still, totally void of any material! This taking of levels will also provide an opportunity to verbally 'tag' the interview, which should be kept simple and avoid at all costs the jargon-laden words 'this is John Smith, recording William Brown - take one' or other similar phrases which can cause alarm and discomfort to the respondent. The tape recorder itself should be out of sight if possible and, once the controls are adjusted, left well alone during the interview. If the interviewer appears to concentrate intensively on the turning spools, so also quite naturally will the respondent, making both conscious of the one item in the room which both should try to forget. The last task before the interview is to pose the question, 'Are you sitting comfortably?' The respondent may have to sit in that position for an hour with little or no movement; the time for settling into that favourite armchair, with attendant shifting of furniture, is before rather than after the start of the interview.

To capitalise effectively on the preparation undertaken, certain pitfalls have to be avoided during the interview. The first suggestion is to move gently into the interview, opening with two or three general questions which can easily be edited out of the final tape. This approach can be especially relevant when dealing with nervous respondents: by the time these first few questions have been gone through, the respondent is more likely to have forgotten about the microphone and tape recorder, leaving the interviewer to shift imperceptibly to the actual start. Ideally the interview will from now on develop into a natural unfolding of relevant reminiscences, but all experienced oral historians would acknowledge that such development needs to be carefully nurtured. The greatest threat to this progression arises from interviewing sins which can cause havoc in any oral history interview. They can be summarised as follows:

1   The posing of long, rambling questions.
2   The posing of questions which can be answered by 'yes' or 'no'. For example, instead of 'Was it cold when you worked on narrow boats?' the interviewer should ask, 'Did the weather cause you problems in your work as a narrow boat man?'
3   The stringing together of questions. Three combined questions are likely to receive answers to one or perhaps two.
4   Cutting in with a secondary question before the respondent has finished answering the first.
5   Failing to follow up a question which has not been fully or satisfactorily answered.
6   Allowing the respondent to stray into irrelevancies or unsubstantiated statements. The interviewer should try to regain control by interposing with something like - 'Before you go on, I'd like to hear more about . . .'.
7   Allowing the respondent to overflaunt opinions and prejudices.
8   Failing to follow a logical pattern, (which may be chronological) and confusing the respondent by jumping, mountain goat fashion, from one subject to another or one time period to another.
9   Finally, and perhaps most importantly, the posing of leading questions.[33]

Beyond these essential requirements, an overriding consideration is that the interviewer must listen astutely throughout the whole interview. As an interviewing skill, this is one of the most difficult to master, yet it is crucial if the interview is to follow any discernible pattern. It is only by listening that the interviewer can come in with the relevant point, basing the next question on what the respondent has just said. This will give the interview a natural 'feel' and although this practice is constantly adopted in everyday conversation it can be extraordinarily difficult to instill this element into an oral history interview. Interviewers can be tempted to think only of the next question to be posed, and to relentlessly present that, regardless of what the respondent has said. This blinkered attitude can be mystifying and perplexing to the respondent - particularly if he has just covered the points raised in the question. As the interviewer listens he/she should also be careful not to constantly agree with the respondent with 'uhms' and 'ahs' and 'reallys'. Although this is a common feature of conversation, it becomes increasingly infuriating when transferred on to tape. An interview full of ponderous 'yeses' will be remembered (and probably discarded) for that very reason, no matter how fascinating the recollections of the respondent. Interviewers must thus get out of the habit of offering continuous verbal agreement; if encouragement is necessary it should be offered in a non-verbal way by nodding or smiling or through an expression of pleasure. However, when some form of response is natural and called for, it should be given. A respondent's amusing story greeted with stony silence will appear most odd - at the time to the respondent, who will surely begin to have niggling doubts as to the course of the interview, and in the future to listeners of that tape, who will surely dub the interviewer as a dullard and devoid of any sense of humour!

Any audio interview can only convey a partial impression, and the interviewer should seek and grasp any opportunity to amplify or extend that impression. Visible aids to memory, such as artefacts, tools, newspaper cuttings or photographs, can all prove useful in this respect. As well as jogging the memory, they can make abstract descriptions much easier for the respondent. George Ewart Evans, testifies to the value of this approach: 'In the countryside I often take along an old serrated sickle. With that there is no need of any abstract explanation of what you are going about. He sees the object and if you choose well he won't need any prodding to open up. We are both into our subject from the beginning'.[34]

Nevertheless these devices must be clearly incorporated into the interview. This is especially true of photographs or press cuttings, present and visible to both parties at the time of the interview, but bewilderingly absent to any future listener. So if such material is being used this should be made clear through constant references - this is essential as an attempt is made to assimilate a visual image into an audio interview. There are also other natural ways of amplifying the interview and in certain instances it would be strange if the interviewer did not heed them. Folk singing is a perfect example: in addition to the interview on the origin and history of the songs, it is natural to include examples; indeed it is in this way that oral testimony becomes particularly valuable as aspects of a culture are collected on tape which are neglected in print-based sources.

Through these and careful questioning it should be possible to create a valuable and valid interview. To this end the interviewer should try to obtain and record verification and substantiation for the facts offered. This will mean asking about the dates and sequence of events (help may be required with calculations) and checking on the person's involvement in those events. Did they, for example, take part in the march to Westminster, were they bystanders, or did they hear about the whole thing from someone they knew?

One relevant and all-pervading point remains and that is that the interviewer should not under any circumstances use the interview as an ego-trip. The objective is to get the respondent to speak, and so the interviewer should keep himself/herself in the background as much as possible, avoiding any temptation to air knowledge. Gentle guidance and prodding may be necessary, but essentially the interviewer's task is to build an easy and relaxed relationship between himself/herself and the respondent. Within this relationship the interviewer's role, although critical, is subsidiary.

## After the interview

The respondent will quite rightly feel offended if the interviewer leaves as soon as the recording is finished. This is most likely to be the time when the tea-cups are brought out, giving another opportunity for a relaxed chat about the course of the interview. The interviewer should also replay at least a brief extract of the tape to check on quality, and a longer section, or the whole of the tape, if this is requested by the respondent. Individuals normally divide fairly evenly into two camps: a group, as already suggested, who find their voice on tape strange, and consider their job done once recording is over, while a second group may be fascinated to hear what they sound like and indeed will wish to check on what they have said. This, of course, is where a thorny question can present itself. The respondent, on listening to the tape, asks whether certain answers can be amended or extended. It is very difficult to offer concrete advice as changes to each interview will have to be accepted or rejected on the merit of their contribution to that interview alone. Despite this, it should be recognised that some changes are easier to incorporate than others. If a respondent feels that he has forgotten something important, then the interviewer can simply record this at the end of the interview and 'cut' this section into the relevant point of the conversation. The erasing or alteration of whole answers is a different matter. On the one hand the respondent may feel that he has been incautious or indelicate in his comments; the interviewer may feel that the material on tape is exactly what he/she wants and will only suffer as a result of changes. This should be explained fully to the respondent, but ultimately if the respondent sticks to his/her ground, his/her wishes must be respected. Another alternative is to plan a second interview, but this again must be a matter of judgement. The interviewer has to decide whether further recollections justify a second visit, or will it be a question of simply covering the same ground once again? A decision may turn on a question of time: in a perfect world the interviewer would return to a second and perhaps third interview, but there may be seven other respondents to contact and record, and their recollections now take priority.

A sound piece of advice on the interviewer's and respondent's reaction to the tape is, leave well enough alone. If both parties are satisfied with the first attempt, it could be disastrous to try and improve sections by re-interviewing. In this respect all interviews are susceptible to a law of diminishing returns. The second attempt will never be quite as good as the first, the third try significantly worse than the second and so on. They will lose out on the keynote element of the tape-spontaneity. The interviewer will try to remember the way the question was posed, the respondent the supposed faults in the answer that was first offered, and the whole effort will disappear into a confusing tangle of contradiction and repetition.

There is one other area which will call for the interviewer's attention before he/she takes leave of the respondent - the question of copyright and access. It may seem strange to have to talk of these requirements in the warm afterglow of a successful interview, yet if such arrangements are left to chance they can create horrendous problems in the future. Whereas the interviewer may feel happy to depend on the verbal agreement of the respondent as to what use may be made of the tape in the future, such an agreement may be found worthless when angry listeners beat a path to the interviewer's door. A large proportion of respondents may be aged, and other members of the family (especially if mentioned on tape) may be not quite so amenable after the respondent's death. They will ask

340

(quite justifiably) who gave the interviewer permission to use the tape and to give members of the public access to that interview, and at that point the verbal agreement so cosily reached will offer little or no defence. Thus to avoid these and other obstacles it is best to get the respondent to sign a clear written statement at the end of the interview. It may be slightly Machiavellian to leave such a request until this point, but it could be argued that the presentation of such a document, no matter how simple, at the start of the interview could be a disincentive to convey worthwhile information. The statement will clarify the terms under which the tape can be made available, and will give the interviewer copyright to the material. This is also essential, as the copyright in the information in an oral history recording - the respondent's actual words - is the respondent's own. The interviewer may own the tape, and copyright of the recording as a whole may be the property of the interviewer or institution that he/she represents, but this in no way changes the equal right of the respondent to copyright. This means that the interviewer may not make available extracts or the whole interview without the respondent's permission. A willingness to be interviewed can in no way be construed as a legal entitlement of access to that interview and it is the responsibility of the interviewer to obtain access.

Here as an example is the copyright statement used at the Department of Sound Records at the Imperial War Museum; agreement is requested on the recordings and any subsequent transcripts and this obviously saves having to recontact the respondent if and when a transcript is made:

1. May the recordings and any transcripts of them be used for educational, research and study purposes within the Museum?
2. May the recordings and transcripts be made available for sale to bona fide educational establishments at a charge sufficient to recover the Museum's overheads? This service is provided only on the prior written undertaking by a responsible member of the establishment's staff that no further copies whatsoever of the material will be made and also that it will only be used on the premises of such establishments strictly for teaching purposes.
3. May the recordings and transcripts be made available for sale to private individuals for strictly personal use under comparable conditions to those specified under 2 above?
4. Would you be prepared to assign your copyright in the information in the recordings to the Trustees of the Imperial War Museum?

This would enable us to deal with such matters as publication and broadcasting, should they arise, without having to make prior reference to you. If you agree to this assignment it does not, of course, preclude any use you might want to make of the information in the recordings yourself.

## Conclusion

Interviewing for oral history can be a rewarding experience for interviewer and respondent. The interviewer will feel that he/she has been given an opportunity to eavesdrop on long-forgotten conversations of a bygone age and respondents will usually feel pleasantly surprised that someone has taken time and trouble to 'listen to their story'. The task of interviewing will be approached with enthusiasm by all oral historians; this chapter has, however, shown that enthusiasm alone is not enough.

## NOTES

1.  Hoskins, W.G. *English local history the past and the future.* Leicester, University Press, 1966, p. 20.
2.  Quoted in: Seldon, A. and Pappworth, J. *By word of mouth.* London, Methuen, 1983, p. 234.
3.  Thompson, P. *The voice of the past.* London, Oxford University Press, 1978, p. 19.
4.  Bede. *A history of the English church and people,* translated by L. Shirley-Price. Harmondsworth, Penguin Books, 1955, p. 34.
5.  Nevins, A. *The gateway to history.* New York, Appleton-Century, 1938, p. iv.
6.  Nevins, A. *Proceedings of the First National Colloquium on Oral History.* California, 1966, p. 31.
7.  Nevins, A. Oral history: how and why it was born. *Wilson library bulletin* 40 (7) 1966, p. 600.
8.  Nevins, p. 600.
9.  Nevins, p. 600.
10.  Evans, G. *Ask the fellows who cut the hay.* London, Faber, 1956, pp. 13-14.
11.  Evans, p.14.
12.  Evans, G. *From mouths of men.* London, Faber, 1976, p. 17.

13. Quoted in: *Oral history* 1 (3) 1972, p. 46.
14. Harrison, B. Oral history and recent political history. *Oral history* 1 (3) 1972, p. 36.
15. King, F. *Sunday telegraph* 3 January 1982, p. 12.
16. Crossman, R. *Listener* 1 February 1973, p. 148.
17. Evans (1976), pp. 174-175.
18. Evans, G.E. Aspects of oral tradition. *Folk life* 7 1969, p. 9.
19. Samuel, R. Local history and oral history. *History workshop* no. 1 Spring 1976, p. 199.
20. Evans (1976), p. 18.
21. Thompson, p. 64.
22. Pfaff, E. Oral history: a new challenge for public libraries. *Wilson library bulletin,* 54 (9) 1980, p. 569.
23. Reid, D. Full of noises. *New library world* 81 (962) 1980, p. 155.
24. Pugh, M.J. Oral history in the library: levels of commitment. *Drexel library quarterly* 15 (4) 1979, pp. 23-24.
25. Ibid., p. 23.
26. Brooks, M. Methodology for oral archives. In: Seldon, A. and Pappworth, J., p. 101.
27. Brooks, p. 110.
28. Lance, D. *An archive approach to oral history.* London, Imperial War Museum, 1978, p. 20.
29. Lance, p. 22.
30. Howarth, K. Tape recording oral history. *Museums journal* 82 (2) September 1982, p. 105.
31. Quoted in: Seldon, A. and Pappworth, J., p. 57.
32. Lance, p. 17.
33. For a useful list of model questions see, Thompson, pp. 243-252.
34. Evans, G.E. Approaches to interviewing. *Oral history* 1 (4) 1973, p. 56.

**FURTHER READING**

Bird, J. *Oral history collections.* London, Polytechnic of North London, 1983. (Occasional publication no. 5).
Humphries, S. *The handbook of oral history: recording life stories.* London, Inter-Action Imprint, 1984.

Storm-Clark, C. Some technical means for higher quality: recording in oral history. *Oral history* 6 (1) Spring 1978, 114-119.

Winstanley, M. Some practical hints on oral history recording and interviewing. *Oral history* 5 (1) Spring 1977, 122-133.

# 16

# Visual materials

Chris Baggs

To collect photographs is to collect the world. *(Susan Sontag)*

## THE NATURE OF THE INFORMATION RECORD

Should clichés truly be an indication, if no more, of common knowledge or general opinion, then it would appear that the value and function of visual images, be they still or moving, are clearly understood by the average person. After all not only does every picture tell a story, but a picture is also worth a thousand words. And yet, and yet. Is it really as simple as such phrases suggest? Is it not more the case that *a* picture, on its own and out of context, tells no story or tells many stories? Furthermore, although a visual image can capture an historical instant, or a mood or atmosphere frozen forever at a particular moment in time and can at times relay information faster and more economically, one picture is seldom worth a thousand words. Many words may indeed sometimes prove necessary to describe one specific image but by contrast many photographs might be needed to depict what can be said or written in a thousand words.

Invariably what a picture or photograph needs for the visual image to be understood or to make its true impact is a context within which that frozen instant in time can be viewed. A problem with older material is often that the further away the viewer is from the moment when the photograph was taken, the more difficult it is to know why certain things were picked out for photographing. What is or was their significance? Lifting single images out of their context and using only those appropriate for conveying a predetermined idea is a dangerous game, more akin to propaganda than rediscovering historical reality. But does not such thinking conflict with yet another time-honoured adage, namely that 'the camera never lies'? Of course it conflicts; and for the very simple reason that, as with many maxims, an element of general truth cloaks a potential can of worms. A visual image taken by an inanimate object - the camera - may be thought to be a neutral information tool, but pictures can just as easily and convincingly be used to deceive, to provide misinformation as well as real information. This deception can be carried out inadvertently as well as deliberately, the fault, if fault it be, lying with the subjective mind behind the apparatus. Whether it has been done with malice aforethought or not, any photographer must clearly be selective in *what* he/she chooses to photograph and also in *how* the photograph is taken.

Once taken the visual image is virtually defenceless against eccentric and individualistic interpretations of its significance. If, to quote Susan Sontag again, the camera can be used as a gun, providing alternative views of the world, then the individual has far more power to abuse and misuse the images created. Michael Lesy's work appears to be a prime example, arousing bitter controversy over the way he has utilised historical photographs as documentary evidence. In *Wisconsin death trip,* [1] for instance, Lesy seems to have decided beforehand on his 'line' regarding the psychic and social crises faced by small town middle America around the turn of the century and then selected from the work of one local photographer only those visual images which reinforced his thesis. For one historian Lesy has developed 'a radical, innovatory technique...exciting enough to send social historians scampering to local photographic archives'.[2] To others, 'Lesy is doing a disservice to historians and to serious users of photographs'.[3] In any event it is an interesting but not isolated case of image manipulation.

There are further problems with visual images even when they have gained the sanctuary of an institutional collection. To begin with some control and judgement will very probably have to be exercised in deciding from the wealth of material available what to keep and what not to keep. In addition to the human dimension vis à vis this selection, there is also the self-selection of time, fashion and custom which will affect the nature of the collection. Certain areas of life may, for whatever reason, be under-represented visually or simply not be represented at all. Thus, although high spots in local life such as civic occasions, royal visits, the opening of major new buildings, etc., are generally well recorded, are they in the right proportion to the more mundane happenings of ordinary, everyday life? At the more humble social level it is the annual family outings and

346

get-togethers, major events such as births, marriages and war, which normally called for the photographer's art. The 'reality' of the vast array of early studio portraits, with their carefully positioned symbolic props, evocative backdrops and best Sunday clothes, must be seen for what it is. The record is neither perfect nor complete. Yet at the same time photography has recorded aspects of society often ignored or glossed over. Photographs are highly complex structures and are among the most intriguing of archival materials.

All this may seem at some remove from the practical day-to-day activities of a local studies librarian. Yet such considerations about the nature and value of the visual record, merely hinted at here, are fundamental to the working of local studies visual collections. Thousands of photographs are not assembled just for the sake of it, nor simply because they are there. There must be a purpose to this activity - namely to act as a particular type of information resource about a community for a community. Local studies librarians therefore owe it to themselves as information workers and more vitally to their users to be aware of the limitations and difficulties associated with the specific source they are handling - the intellectual as well as the storage and retrieval difficulties.[4]

## USERS AND USAGE

It seems to be generally recognised that ours is increasingly a pictorial society, that television especially has conditioned the general public into demanding and expecting a visual window on the world. If seeing has not yet quite become believing, some commentators at least feel that images now challenge words as the dominant means of communication. Whether or not this development is based on the supposition that photographs, etc. are per se accurate and infallible carriers of information, there is an apparently insatiable demand for images, and for many people a clear preference for visual images over the printed word. Within the library and information world, this is likely to mean an increasing demand for pictorial images, for use in a variety of ways. As the future will contain more and not fewer pictures, information services as a whole should develop a more positive attitude to their collection, preservation and effective use. Local studies collections may well be in the vanguard in this respect, as photographs have long featured in them as a valuable resource.

Primarily the visual image collection is valued as an historical record, a remembrance of the past.[5] Over many years publishers, including library authorities themselves, have cashed in on the popularity of these links with former times, producing numerous volumes of local photographs with titles such as 'Old X in pictures' or 'Victorian life in Y', simply as profitable commercial ventures. Specific prints may also be wanted for individual publication, or for use by advertisers, or perhaps by a local newspaper for a column such as the 'Flashback' column in the *Aberdeen evening express*. They may even be used for local radio and television series. So the local studies library can expect all manner of picture researchers, young and old, professional and amateur. In education, studying a local community is commonplace at all levels, and with adult education classes on local history and local history societies themselves growing in numbers and popularity, they can be expected and should be encouraged to make full use of local photographic material. Among professional historians at least there has recently been a change in attitude towards the use of the pictorial record. Whereas previously the photograph may have been seen chiefly as 'wallpaper', as giving a feel or impression while acting as an adjunct to the hard information of printed sources, it is now being studied more closely as primary material and documentary evidence in its own right. Photographs have moved from being illustrations of a point to being the point themselves. For such purposes the images have to be examined in some detail, and the skills of reading and interpreting the historical signs contained visually in this constantly expanding information source need to be better developed.

But it would be wrong merely to see photographs as simply commercial fodder, a professional research resource or educational materials. Many users of such collections are casual enquirers, who derive basic pleasure from reconstructing a byegone age in a familiar environment and can while away happy hours comparing, contrasting, possibly even reliving. Other users, such as illustrators, designers or art students, may require specific examples of such items as clothing, household furniture, long-lost buildings, early modes of transport, etc., or a general portfolio to try and capture the mood of an era or place. Photographs are also being used by social workers in charge of elderly patients and in geriatric wards of local psychiatric hospitals. Prints can be displayed in these wards or used in 'reminiscence' therapy sessions to stimulate, to encourage participation and discussion, and to help patients maintain viable contact with the outside world. Libraries themselves use their own materials to mount exhibitions

348

at schools, community centres, old people's homes and elsewhere. These are just some of the uses to which visual images can be and are put, but such diversity is an important factor in considering both how the collection should be organised and made accessible and also indeed what the collection should include.[6]

## THE MATERIALS

So far the term 'visual record' has been used to cover a multitude of types of image-bearing materials, although normally it has been taken to mean some form of still photographic medium. This is probably as it should be, as the photograph in its many shapes, sizes and forms constitutes the bulk of local studies picture collections. However, even in the stills world there are other formats which may just as reasonably be and are included in certain collections - art originals (prints or reproductions for instance), postcards and posters, and newspaper clippings, for example, all of which can carry relevant visual information. Motion picture film is essentially the same medium as certain kinds of still photography, but with video, at the moment basically a magnetic tape medium, there is a different range of storage, handling and retrieval problems to be faced. To cope in detail with this wide spectrum of potentially appropriate materials is beyond the bounds of this chapter. The writer will concentrate, therefore, on photographic materials - mainly because of their pre-eminent position and overwhelming value in any collection of visual images - and video - primarily because this is a major growth area for recording moving pictures and as such should be given active consideration by local studies librarians anxious to preserve an appropriate contemporary record.

The whole range of types of photographs is unlikely to find its way into many local studies libraries but the librarian should nevertheless be prepared. Their history, development and individual characteristics, both chemical and aesthetic, have been chronicled fully elsewhere,[7] and the very diversity of the materials and processes used can cause quite considerable management problems. Indeed if this has not already been undertaken, a thorough survey of a collection's photographs is a valuable exercise in terms of pinpointing precisely whether the collection does include delicate daguerrotypes, easily breakable lantern slides or potentially dangerous nitrate stock; all of which require specific but different storage conditions. In crude terms the pre-1900 period provides the greater variety of processes and formats, with daguerrotypes, ambrotypes and albumen prints as three examples among many. Albumen prints, for instance, were the dominant printing medium in the final quarter of the nineteenth century and were still being used until the late 1920s. This was the format invariably used for *cartes-de-visite* and cabinets, which were evidently popular enough for many examples still to be in existence today. The librarian may well find himself/herself confronted by negatives as well as prints, and although paper and plastic are now, and have been for some time, the commonest base substance for photographic images, other materials have been successfully used. The inert nature of glass made it a popular material, both for negatives and slides, until well into the 1930s. Both Coventry and Manchester Public Libraries for instance have sizeable collections of lantern slides.

Even before the librarian adds any new material, a particular collection can be an amalgam of photographic formats, reflecting different processes, utilising different materials and subject to different problems. Nor is the position static; new technology could well add to these processes, materials and problems! Even now it is not always a simple job to determine what kind of a photograph is being dealt with.

Generally photographs will be black and white, as colour photography is essentially an unstable process with the colour dyes used steadily but surely deteriorating, unless relatively extreme counter measures are taken. The question of colour reveals an interesting dilemma. Although deemed an unstable medium for long-term archival storage, to deny a place in collections for colour materials is going against one objective of those collections, namely to provide accurate and appropriate information. Part of the value of an image may lie precisely in the fact that it is the *colour* of the object or scene depicted that confirms its importance as a visual record. This means that collection development policies will have to weigh up this importance against the difficulties of preserving the integrity of the image. This problem will only get worse. Whereas users may be prepared now to accept black and white material - partly because they have little option with pre-1935 photographs and partly because black and white somehow confirms their venerable status and matches users' expectations - the ubiquity of colour in television, commercial video and home still photography must increasingly force a general reassessment with time. The record of the current era is a colour record, and future generations have a right to expect such a record from local studies photographic collections. Perhaps technological advance will come to the rescue.

Another medium which could and should form a growing proportion of the visual record, and which shares with colour photography well-founded reservations about its archival qualities, is video. Although moving images have been available on cine film for over 70 years and some local studies libraries have built up useful but normally numerically small collections,[8] certain factors have always militated against cine film becoming as popular and as widespread a format as still photography and, at an increasing rate, video. This does not mean that local studies libraries should simply shun donations of home movies. Their value as a sometimes unique historical record has been amply shown by the inclusion of amateur film in various BBC and ITV documentary programmes.[9] Once again it must not be overlooked that the dimension of motion may be *the* dimension specifically required by the user, and it is incumbent on some side of the library/archive world to preserve that record, be it professional or amateur in origin. Whether or not a more appropriate depository for such material is a regional, dedicated archive, such as the North West or East Anglian Film Archives, is a matter for further debate.

Looking to the future, a similar situation may well develop with video materials, given that the tapes' message physically survives that long. The difference would seem to lie in the greater amount of material potentially available for deposit. Should video, in whatever format (and therein lies a further problem), become generally acceptable for local studies collections, there are good reasons for believing that its inclusion could have a more discernible effect on those collections than cine film ever had. What is beyond question is that an increasing amount of visual information is being originated and retained in video formats and that much of this material, be it from professional television production companies or from amateur groups and individuals, would be of immense value to a local studies library. It may never replace still photographs, but it represents a vital supplementary and complementary resource that should be tapped.


## ACQUISITION

On the surface there would appear to be few problems concerning general acquisitions policies. Admittedly acquiring particular formats as outlined above will force the library into certain practical decisions regarding storage, handling, user access, etc. But fundamentally the only real restriction on acquiring materials would appear to be space and their suitability to the collection. In the case of photographs - described by John Szarkowski as being 'as plentiful as bricks' - this should be relatively easy given the large numbers of them. But is it as straightforward as that? Perhaps in the early days when a collection is developing the answer may be an unreserved yes. But a collection cannot simply go on continually adding images regardless. Proper consideration must be given to the questions of numbers and quality.[10] Just because users are becoming more aware of the value of photographs does not take away from the librarian the responsibility for making choices. Clearly every photograph is an illustration of something, and it is always hard, if not impossible, to determine what contemporary material is potentially of value to future users of local studies collections. However, the question of selection will have to be broached. Perhaps this is not yet a burning issue, primarily because material currently being acquired is largely historical, and time is a great ally in unselective weeding. But what of the contemporary record? Once photography became a democratic pastime the number of individual items of possible relevance soared. Consider the following and compare it with the output of books: in 1979 in the United States over 10 billion exposures were made by 45 million cameras, with over 19 million photographs being taken on average daily by amateur photographers. Some of this prodigious output is the visual record - in just one medium - of the contemporary local environment. Time will once again come to the rescue with material being lost, thrown away or otherwise destroyed. Many images will thereby be consigned to the oblivion they doubtless merit; others however deserve better. Collectively there will be more than enough, and the local studies librarian's job will be to isolate the best, the most representative, those most likely to meet the users' requirements, etc. Whereas with older materials a poor quality, fading or blurred print may have proved acceptable because of its uniqueness, this is far less likely to be the case with post-1950 material. Richard Noble, an archivist with the National Historical Publications and Records Commission, Washington, DC, has devoted some time and thought to the whole question of evaluation in a recent article.[11] He would apply four basic tests concerning the value of photographic contents, namely potential uses, uniqueness, availability and importance. The article as a whole raises other interesting points about the nature of the record, the origination of the material and so forth. Although it is probable that the bulk of new material for the collection will come from donations, loans, in-house or co-operative production programmes, outright purchase must not be ignored even in these days of economic constraint. Purchase should

352

be actively considered where particular collections or individual prints are *unique* in terms of their local value or where they are the product of a local photographer or studio. Local studies librarians should therefore keep a sharp eye open for relevant items becoming available on the market. In general, however, purchase should be avoided wherever possible, partly so that a 'market' is not created, but mainly because other options are available for acquiring the information of a particular photograph without buying it. Serviceable copies could be made, for instance, or material acquired on permanent loan.

Indeed it is through copying, loans and donations that the local studies library is most likely to increase its stock of photographs. Hampshire County Library Service has even organised a sponsored photographic competition with cash prizes to help improve its local collection - all entries being donated to the local studies library. Donations can come in all shapes, sizes and numbers, ranging from the unwanted prints in the attic to the files of a local newspaper which has no further use for its vast collection of photographs. Prints may also turn up as part of a personal bequest of books, manuscripts and papers, where they are just one format among several.

Assuming that donations are an outright gift, problems over copyright should technically not exist, although it may be advisable to explain to donors precisely what the position is. There have been enough instances of local donors being upset or made angry by the tactless reproduction and publication of personal material. Although legally the library may be acting within its rights, donations obviously rely on the goodwill of the public, so some care should be taken to avoid creating offence. The right to re-use photographs can become even trickier where the library has borrowed items or made copy negatives or prints from an original which has been retained by the owner. In the latter case the letter of the copyright law must be tempered by commonsense. The problem here is that copyright, not normally an area widely understood, can seem even more bizarre than usual as regards photographs, particularly in respect of the early material which invariably forms the bulk of the collection. Copyright in any photograph taken before 1 June 1957 is 50 years from the end of the calendar year in which the photograph was taken, *whether or not the photograph has been published in the meantime.* Technically therefore any photograph taken before the end of 1937 (at the time of publication) is within the public domain and can be published freely by anyone - assuming, of course, that they can get hold of it, which is precisely what a programme of acquiring prints, etc. and making copies is designed to achieve! Other difficulties can arise with pre-1957 material still in copyright where the owner of a print or negative did not *take* the photograph or was actually commissioned by another body to do the work. Post-June 1957 material is less problematic in that copyright remains perpetual until the photograph is first published from which time the 50-year rule applies. Few people enjoy copyright wranglings, so proper appreciation of the law is vital, together with an ability to explain adequately to members of the public the consequences of their action in relation to donations, loans or allowing copies to be made. Collections can still benefit enormously from material available for reference use only, even if those same items may not be used for publication or exhibition purposes. The information is intrinsic to the photograph, not to its use.

Donations or copy programmes as major methods of acquisitions are excellent ways to begin or build up a collection but they are not without potential problems. There is the possibility at some stage of being overwhelmed by sheer weight of numbers. What begins as a good idea for winkling out those elusive and long-lost unique images, turns into a flood of mundane duplicates, which tax the system's capacity to copy and/or organise them for use, without really adding anything to the informational content of the collection. The librarian is thus squarely faced by the awkward problem of having to make choices, of turning away or throwing out material actively solicited. Clearly any move towards encouraging ordinary people to think of their family albums as valuable sources of information is almost bound to run into this difficulty. (It is an interesting fact that families often retain old photographs though they have destroyed other useful historical records.[12]) So a wealth of material is there to be tapped, and its acquisition, if it is to be done deliberately, must involve an effective appeal campaign. This can be incorporated into regular public relations visits and talks to WI meetings, old people's clubs, etc. Tameside Local Studies Library even produced a handout for the public entitled 'Wanted', in which they appealed directly for, among other things, photographs relating to life in Tameside before 1950. Material can either be donated, placed on permanent loan, or copies made and the originals returned. Overall the handout tries very succinctly to explain the value of this material and assuage any reasonable fears about its storage and use. One further minor consideration which might cause an organisational headache is whether to index such material by donor, as it has been known for donors or their relatives to wish to see 'those photos we let you have a few years back'!

Part and parcel of any scheme to encourage donations is, as has already been mentioned a number of times, the ability to make and retain copies rather than receive the original. A number of local studies libraries, including Tameside, are actively engaged in this area which has met with promising results. Admittedly such a policy requires an outlay of capital for cameras, copy stands, enlargers and other equipment, but wise purchasing can keep this figure down to a few hundred pounds. Dark room facilities would be a boon if finance and staffing will allow for them; otherwise developing and printing will have to be done commercially, preferably by someone near at hand. In any event all members of the local studies unit should be trained in basic copy photography techniques, so that where necessary a copy can be made virtually on the spot. Tameside's 'while you wait service' provides customers, at a price, with a copy of a photograph they have brought in, while the library endeavours to retain a copy negative and contact print for its own collection. The additional dark room facilities would mean that the library can then easily produce further copies as required - contact prints for aiding access to the collection, regular prints for exhibitions, for retail or to replace deteriorating prints - let alone the ability to make original prints from in-house produced photographic work. The Manchester Studies Unit, for instance, makes five sets of contact prints from each film for a variety of purposes including three sets for subject index work.

Until recently still photographs were the only visual material where copies could be made cheaply, easily and efficiently in house. The advent of video, especially in the cassette format, has changed that; this is a development which could have repercussions for local studies collections. Previously as far as moving images were concerned appropriate materials on cine film were available for purchase commercially, but in limited quantities and at relatively high prices. Local amateur film-makers could still be encouraged to donate unwanted films of whatever gauge, but lack of the necessary playback facilities among other things might well discourage libraries from pursuing this line too far. The possibilities opened up by video in most cases go far beyond those offered by film. Outright purchase of appropriate programmes is less expensive and making copies - with permission - is a relatively easy and cheap process, assuming the basic hardware has already been acquired. Moreover the ease with which programmes can be copied might encourage local studies libraries to broaden their loans' policy and thereby help spread the material's use throughout a community which is increasingly regarding the video cassette player as a standard item of home hardware. At least it would offer users an interesting alternative to a diet of feature films! The earlier reference to obtaining the necessary permission is, however, going to act as a powerful brake on this development. Although there are a growing number of independent or amateur video-makers and groups producing material relevant to local studies collections and from whom programmes can be bought and copies made, the overwhelming bulk of appropriate information is being produced by the major television companies. Unfortunately, purchasing this material can be expensive if not impossible, while making off-air copies without prior permission is recognised to be illegal with a few clear exceptions. This means that copies of local documentary or news broadcasts are sitting, scarcely used, on the shelves of assorted television company video libraries. Eventually when past their useful lives, and assuming they are neither junked nor recorded over, they may be handed on to regional film and TV archives (as has been the case in some areas with outdated film material). It is nevertheless a great pity that such a wealth of potentially valuable material is not readily available now and is consequently so sadly underused. One can only hope that a way can be found quickly to allow institutions like local studies libraries the freedom to record, store and utilise these contemporary source documents. The implications of any possible legislation arising from the government's recent white paper (*Intellectual property and innovation.* 1986. Cmnd 9712) cannot yet be worked out, although an optimistic reading of the document would suggest a rosy future.

Making copies is only one form of in-house production; genuine origination is another - clearly more creative, probably more interesting and rewarding, and certainly actively engaged in by various local studies libraries. Lancashire County Libraries, for instance, regard 'record photography' as an important method for acquiring material and will send out a member of the library staff for emergency record work, i.e. where buildings are to be demolished imminently. They also do a limited amount of non-urgent record work. Such active involvement obviously implies the necessary equipment, adequately trained staff who know what to photograph and, if the volume of in-house production warrants it, internal developing and printing facilities. Similarly modern portable video equipment could be obtained, staff quickly and easily trained in its use, and a dynamic programme of library-shot material initiated. Llanelli Public Library is perhaps a unique example of a public library authority which began in the 1950s with 16 millimetre cine film for making local history programmes and has since progressed, with some reservations about picture quality, to using video.[13]

Even if the local studies library cannot be actively engaged in in-house production, it can lend its support, involvement, interest and expertise to other groups, both official and independent, who are concerned with making a visual record of a particular locality. In fact in certain instances a large percentage of a local studies library's collection has stemmed from just such surveys.[14] It is also worth remembering that the products of these surveys, including aerial photographs, may well be stashed away in another department of the authority, such as the Engineers Department or the Planning and Public Works Department. Although the local studies library might not want a copy of every photograph taken by the Engineers Department, building by building, street by street, an awareness of such alternative collections and inter-departmental co-operation when necessary might help to open up these resources to other people who could put them to valuable use.

There is quite a lengthy history of such co-operative approaches to creating a visual record. Perhaps the most famous example is the Chester Photographic Survey begun in 1963 with the aim of producing 'a house by house photographic survey of the City of Chester'.[15] Although its scope has widened since then, with special projects on old crafts, manufacturing processes and trade signs, for example, it is essentially a social and architectural record of the changing face of Chester. Run under the joint auspices of the Chester Civic Trust, the Chester Photographic Society and Chester County Library, the ten thousand or more slides taken by volunteers from the Photographic Society are kept for consultation in the library. All in all it is a fine example of what can be achieved over a period of time through practical co-operation of interested parties. Similar methods could be adopted using local enthusiasts and history groups for joint ventures in video formats.[16] Although clearly the size of output would be limited, structured and well-organised video histories would make a valuable addition to the collection.

## ACCESS, ORGANISATION AND EXPLOITATION

It has been said that cataloguing and classifying photographic materials involve unique difficulties. In a specific collection this may not be true simply because existing working practices already predetermine precisely how this or that activity will be carried out. Thus discussions over the efficacy of AACR2 or Dewey, or whether photographs should be handled entirely separately from the rest of the collection, are not strictly necessary. Nevertheless such theoretical deliberations are intrinsically and professionally interesting, and could prove of practical value in cases of reorganisation, rapid expansion and so on.

The basic difficulty to be overcome with organising photographic collections for use is that, no matter how competent and complete the cataloguing, classifying and indexing processes are, there is no substitute for actually *seeing* the prints, etc. themselves. It is a question of a visual medium, and any surrogate between those images and the user is a handicap. Users like and want to look at photographs rather than catalogue cards, and for obvious reasons. Skimming through an album of prints is a very effective and rapid way of separating the wheat from the chaff, while using catalogues, subject indexes, etc. simply cannot provide, via written details, the instant recognition of the appropriate visual information. The catalogue card may state that the collection has eight general views of King Street in 1910, but perhaps only one is just right for the particular purpose, provides the right nuance or reveals a specific or extra feature not mentioned on the card, and only examination of the image itself highlights that. This is not denying indexes and similar tools a valuable, indeed crucial, role where user access is limited or non-existent. Visual material is often not self-explanatory and therefore more effort may be required on the librarian's part in providing written, even interpretative, access, although clearly general policy decisions and attitudes regarding physical access will largely determine the overall organisation. Thus a local studies library which is more archival in its approach and which contains a fair number of unique and valuable photographs may baulk at the idea of too much handling by the users. On the other hand, browsing is vital and collections can be so organised as to meet heavy use, allowing ready access to the stock via contact print files, or copy prints. Indeed one advantage of the copying approach to acquisitions is that negatives are available from which some form of print can be made and access facilitated. Should the time, staff, facilities and finance all be available, the best solution of all would be some form of dual collection, with initial access to copies - either normal or contact print sized - for every photograph in stock. Such an approach clearly offers great advantages for both the exploitation of the materials and the proper storage of the originals. For most institutions this must, however, seem like a pipe-dream, and working compromises will be the order of the day, with the librarian having to weigh up a number of factors including types of user and usage, amount of use, types of indexes and catalogues, financial implications of the various strategies, etc., before deciding on an acceptable access policy. In Leeds Central Library, for instance, experience and observation has allowed the staff to produce a sample selection of the most frequently requested items which users can browse. Other requests are channelled from the catalogues, etc. to the staff who retrieve the appropriate photographs from store. In a brief survey carried out by the writer of a selection of major local studies libraries and other institutions with large picture collections, it was interesting to note the relatively high number which did not allow the users physical access to the materials nor used copies or files of contact prints as an alternative to the originals. Without any direct access to the materials, the pressure on the efficiency and reliability of retrieval devices offered instead is greatly increased, and libraries must look very carefully at how they can provide the most effective surrogates to the images themselves. These surrogates may include catalogues, subject indexes, classified lists, information sheets and other documentation - or most probably combinations thereof. Manchester Central Library, for instance, maintains three indexes - alphabetical subject, Dewey classified and alphabetic topographical.

Despite the appearance of the second edition of the Anglo-American Cataloguing Rules in 1978, many custodians of photographic collections would agree with Nancy Malan that when it comes to cataloguing or describing photographs, 'the picture professional will find no rule book of universally accepted standards... There is no agreement on the information that should appear on a catalog card, its order or format, or the level of description'.[17] Although much has been written on the care and use of picture collections, relatively little has been produced on cataloguing.[18] General problems, however, include the likely waste of effort in detailed descriptive cataloguing: as photographs are normally unique items it is unlikely that anyone has catalogued a particular item before, so co-operative networks are of little use. Photographs are also often quite anonymous and without a recognised title, so that a more conventional author/title approach is inappropriate if not irrelevant. The fact that they come in a variety of shapes, sizes and chemical compositions does not make the physical form description easy for the individual cataloguer either.

One important and immediate decision to be made is whether to go for item-by-item cataloguing which will be very time-consuming, costly and wasteful when dealing with large numbers of photographs which individually have little aesthetic or informational value to distinguish them from each other. The main alternative is group cataloguing, linking numbers of related photographs under one broadly appropriate description. Such an approach cuts down on the bulk of any catalogue and the time taken to produce it - important considerations perhaps for a growing collection. However, as a system it is obviously unable to reflect the differences between the photographs listed on a particular card, although dividing the entries further by period is relatively easy and clearly helpful. If ready access to the photographs themselves is allowed then the amount of descriptive cataloguing needed is marginal, although there will be instances where the size of image, process of printing is worth noting. Fuller cataloguing is more crucial where such access is denied.

The catalogue card itself can be turned into a more effective tool if a reduced visual image is added to it, thereby meeting the user's requirement to be able to see the image. Such systems are described in two American instances,[19] and Tameside Public Library in the United Kingdom also employs this basic method. Unlike the 'norm' which literally consists of a copy of the item described on the catalogue card being affixed to that card, Tameside not only attaches a contact print to a 5 inches by 3 inches envelope acting as a catalogue card but also stores the appropriate negative inside the envelope. This general approach has the clear advantage of instant visual access to the item, but it also raises problems and implies a certain overall policy towards the nature of the collection. For instance, unless the collection is relatively small it could prove fairly expensive, especially if it were further decided to adopt this method retrospectively. However, for a newly started service relying mainly on copying for increasing its stock, and assuming that acid-free envelopes are used, it is an option well worth considering.

It is far more important, given the nature of the type of requests generally encountered in local studies work, that adequate subject access to the materials is provided. Enquirers are invariably after a specific named place or feature. Subject analysis of images is, however, often more complex than for other materials: as individual units they can work on different levels and may be used for purposes far removed from the original intention. In such cases retrieval must be by characteristics not immediately obvious and a variety of approaches to organising picture collections have been used in an attempt to aid this process. General classification schemes, perhaps slightly amended, can be used - Manchester and the London

Borough of Hammersmith and Fulham use Dewey, for instance - and it may at least have the advantage of providing some continuity with the way the stock is arranged in the rest of the library. There are specialised schemes for use solely in local studies collections and many libraries (Birmingham, Norwich and Nottingham Public Libraries, to name but three) have devised their own local systems to reflect local peculiarities. Yet other libraries (Newcastle Central Library, for instance) avoid classification schemes altogether and rely on an alphabetical subject approach which is generally deemed more appropriate for photographs,[20] especially where they can be dealt with separately from the other materials in the collection.

This method is greatly helped by the idea that photographs are said to be self-indexing, with the subject descriptors simply being taken from the image itself, i.e. X canal in 1897, a view of Y Street or Mrs Z opening the new library in 1924. Subjects divide neatly into three broad groups - people, places and things - and so, it would be possible to file the material in three simple alphabetical sequences reflecting those three divisions. Users might then enjoy easy access to a collection arranged in an eminently understandable fashion. Superficially another simple solution, but like all subject approaches to information, it is not that straightforward! Quite apart from the usual problems of compound headings, phrase headings, the order of adjectival phrases, synonyms, etc., etc., it is very often the case with visuals that either a photograph's subject cannot be accurately delineated by one subject term - unless so broad as to be virtually meaningless - or else there are numerous items of subsidiary interest on a picture all of which are worthy of some note. It is the 'things' category that is the most troublesome. Michael Petty's article provides a good example;[21] an early print of Petty Cury, Cambridge, is indexed under the headings of: street scenes, post office, buses, cyclists, police, news-vendors and lamp-posts. All of these are quite valid and cover topics likely to be asked for, although it can be argued that other topics are also visible and are not indexed. As the individual photograph can only be filed in one place (unless numerous copies are made), the main subject is chosen - not always a simple matter - with appropriate 'see' and 'see also' references and added entries in the subject index from which the relevant image can be located. One alternative might be to keep all the photographs in accession number order, give each image as many subject descriptors as thought necessary and rely on co-ordinate indexing techniques to pull items together. This presumes that the users are not being allowed physical access to the collection but have to rely on the staff using the catalogues to find the right pictures.

With all subject indexing there is always a question mark over how far one should go, to what depth, etc., and even indexing by personal name can become a daunting task once taken beyond well-known personalities. Creating a bulky catalogue with many additional subject entries per individual item may produce an unwieldy and ultimately ineffective retrieval system. Over-indulgence becomes counter-productive. It may be that only good or unique examples of specific extra items are really worth indexing or cataloguing; yet another milk cart in a street scene could be quietly overlooked. Even so an authority file of terms used must be constructed to avoid confusion both for new staff and for the clientele. A general published scheme, such as the Library of Congress or Sears, or even one specifically for picture collections could be used,[22] although an in-house scheme reflecting the particular requirements of a specific local studies collection is most appealing, largely because of the undoubted specificity that can be obtained.

In time it is highly probable that microcomputers can be used to good effect, allowing as they do for subject terms and accession numbers to be placed on file and thus provide faster, easier and better access to the subject information of individual images. Such systems are already being increasingly employed in large fine arts and other institutional libraries in the United States, and it seems to be a development being planned for in the United Kingdom.[23] Newcastle Local Studies Department have indicated an interest in this direction as computerised indexing clearly provides for that greater degree of flexibility which is needed with photographic collections and which the present variety of indexes, catalogues, etc. is designed to achieve, but with varying success and at not inconsiderable costs of time, effort and thought.

A further valuable aid to the effective utilisation of the collection is the production of information sheets describing individual photographs in more detail probably even than item-by-item cataloguing. The Manchester Studies Unit made extensive use of such sheets and a similar one is used by Sheffield City Libraries. In any library, especially where the local population is being encouraged to deposit originals or allow copies to be made, it is essential that the librarian tries to elicit as much information about a print, etc. from any donor and then fully documents it. Even though on occasions such information may be suspect, any clues to the who/what/when/where/why of the image are indispensable both for elucidating the picture's subject content and for enabling the library staff to incorporate the material correctly into the collection. Otherwise identification, dating and so on is a far more troublesome and time-consuming business.

Access to cine film or video information is generally far easier to achieve. First of all item-by-item cataloguing should not create the problems associated with photographs - certainly not as far as volume is concerned. Secondly either classifying or using alphabetical subject terms should also prove easier in that as so often with handling books, one class mark or subject heading can generally be found to describe the subject content of a programme. Should it prove desirable, more detailed indexing techniques can be used, such as sequence or shot listing for dealing with small, discrete units within the programme.[24] It is, however, a lengthy process. Unlike photographs, neither video nor cine films are 'browseable', so that users have no choice but to rely not just on surrogates like catalogues, etc. to obtain the correct programme but of course on replay facilities to view them.

## STORAGE AND CONSERVATION

Numerous manuals, handbooks and so on have been published recently which look in some detail at the practical sides of how to conserve, preserve and even restore materials likely to be found in libraries and archives.[25] Conservation and storage are inextricably entwined. Once it is clear what factors are causing deterioration in specific materials then measures, including appropriate storage, can be taken to retard, prevent or even reverse those processes. Leaving finance aside for a moment, and the cost of proper storage per item is usually higher for photographic than other materials, one crucial decision the local studies library will have to take relates to the type of service it sees itself offering. Although not simply an archive collection, there is no questioning the important archival functions of local studies libraries. At the same time for a department of a public library system the collections are there to be used by the public at large, and with increasing interest being shown in local history, that use is growing in magnitude. Materials may be in for a hard time! Local studies libraries will have to show a degree of flexibility and make fine judgements over the rights of access to the collection versus the need to preserve the stock.

With visual materials two specific problems come to the fore. Photographs as opposed to many print items are unique - that particular negative or print will be the only one available and if destroyed, the information is lost forever. All due care should therefore be taken to preserve such items. On the other hand, it is in the nature of the medium that duplicates or copies can be made relatively cheaply and easily. This frees the original for archival storage, while the duplicate or copy is available for hard work and storage appropriate to its function. Two levels of storage and conservation may therefore be necessary, although instances have already been given in this chapter where collections are essentially based on duplicates or copies - archival worries are then far less pressing.

The second feature worth stressing is a point made by K. Hendriks,[26] namely that photographic materials based on the light sensitivity of silver halides (as most photographs are) are more sensitive to environmental conditions than many other materials in libraries. This may mean that a disproportionate amount of time, effort and money is spent on preserving visual images in the collection than other items.

Some of the manuals referred to earlier contain detailed sections or chapters dealing with photographs, motion picture films and video, so there is no need here to do more than scratch the surface of the problem. Invariably these manuals carry too much information for the needs of the average local studies librarian. They are written by professional conservationists specifically for the archive and conservation markets and involve processes, etc. which are clearly beyond the reach of many institutions. Nevertheless they provide a good basic grounding in the area and it is possible to supplement this understanding and keep up to date with the theory and practice of, as well as developments in, conservation by reading appropriate technical and professional literature.[27] One word of warning: as technology progresses, processes or storage systems originally deemed to be beneficial or at least not harmful are later shown to be quite the reverse. If possible therefore only consult recent literature in the field. Changing practices can be expensive, especially for a large undertaking, and even if future reassessments clearly cannot be allowed for, there is no excuse for introducing methods and materials already regarded as suspect or worse.

When dealing with visual items it is worthwhile having at least some broad understanding of the materials being used. Photographs, either negatives or positive prints, stills or moving picture film, consist of a base or support and an image-forming substance, together with a binding agent to link the two elements. Videotape, on the other hand, consists of a base on to which are fixed magnetic particles capable of being realigned electronically to record the information. Looking in more detail at photographs, the support materials may be paper (including resin-coated paper), glass, plastic, even metal or other miscellaneous substances, while the image-forming materials are generally some kind of silver (for black and white images) or organic dyes (for colour). What the librarian needs to understand is that each element in an image's make-up can react differently towards the same environmental conditions, and that optimum conditions to suit all the materials involved do not exist. Where possible therefore, different types of material should be stored separately, although compromises will generally have to be made.

In relation to the support materials and the image-forming substances, the former are normally the most stable element of photographs. One need only think of glass (widely used for lantern slides) photographic paper (often of outstanding quality) or plastic (now some kind of polyester and remarkably resilient and stable) to confirm this. Luckily in a way, or perhaps merely reflecting the quality of those particular substances, the bulk of photographs in local studies collections will be negatives on plastic film or black and white prints on paper. However as the detailed studies show there are problems with all materials; some problems such as the fading of the dyes used in colour photography or the oft-stated basic instability of nitrate plastic film are very serious and call for relatively specialised measures to overcome them. One spin-off from any detailed survey and examination of the collection mentioned earlier is that the librarian can make more informed decisions on the nature of the conservation measures and storage systems needed, given that he/she knows precisely what physical materials are being dealt with. Unfortunately it is not always possible to identify the processes and materials used quickly and accurately, while the quality of the original processing, which can greatly effect the survival chances of the image, will only very rarely be known without sophisticated testing techniques.

The main enemies acting against the permanence of the record as with other materials are essentially five - the human factor; relative humidity; temperature; light; and chemical matters. Short of denying totally any access by users to materials, there is little that can be done practically to prevent damage caused by handling. Given that such damage is accidental and is occasioned by carelessness and lack of knowledge about the harmful qualities of greasy fingers, some effort could be spent on educating users in the correct ways of handling prints, negatives, etc. Only where contact prints in binders or copy prints in albums are being viewed, or where originals are individually stored in transparent plastic sleeves, can the staff be comparatively sure that the human factor is being controlled. And even staff have been known to drop glass negatives!

K. Hendriks is quite certain that the main enemy facing visual materials is relative humidity, and effective control of this within acceptable parameters is the key to their long-term stability. This is not simply because of the effects too high, too low or wildly fluctuating relative humidity itself has physically on the constituent materials of photographs, but also because moisture, associated with high relative humidity, is a catalyst for other chemical reactions, such as fungal growth. However, there is no one level of relative humidity which is just right for all materials, although somewhere between 35 and 40 per cent seems to be the value best suited to a range of different materials. In no event should it exceed 60 per cent. Whatever value is fixed on, it should be constant, day and night, winter and summer.

Similarly with temperatures. Once an appropriate storage temperature has been decided on, cycling of more than 4 °C should be avoided. Temperature is slightly more problematic than relative humidity. Although for prints, plates and short-term storage of photographic film a value around a comfortable working temperature for staff, i.e. about 20 °C is acceptable, low temperatures are recommended for long-term or archival storage and especially so for colour film, where such conditions greatly retard the fading of the dyes. Here a temperature of 2 °C is far more suitable, although it also means that the relative humidity will have to be adjusted accordingly. At the moment when most photographic materials in local studies collections are black and white, this may hardly cause an eyebrow to flicker. Yet the point has been made earlier that the record of our period is a colour record - up to 85 per cent of all photographs are taken today on colour film. A small 'fridge in the corner for such 'troublesome' material may soon no longer be an adequate solution. This assumes, of course, that the collection has both a short-term and a long-term archival function requiring appropriate storage and conservation policies.

Although it is true that light can have deleterious effects on visual materials, particularly once again on colour materials, such effects can be overstated. Well-processed contemporary black and white photographs are essentially stable to light, and if older materials are generally stored in sleeves, boxes, albums, etc. and are therefore protected from the light, there is little problem. Clearly continued over-exposure, especially to ultra-violet light and direct sunlight, will be harmful, so originals should not be used for displays or exhibitions unless absolutely unavoidable. They should also be reshelved as quickly as possible after any normal reference use. One basic problem with using opaque storage devices is that users are then forced to handle the prints in order to view them properly. Once more the logic of the materials and the service implies copies and duplicates for viewing, while effective storage conditions can be lavished on important, unique and valuable originals. Thus a collection consisting overwhelmingly of copies and so on can afford to treat storage and conservation aspects with a lighter touch.

The final factor is chemistry. In one sense virtually all the factors affecting the permanence of the record are chemical, but some, such as the role of temperature and relative humidity, can be isolated, measured and dealt with comparatively easily. Others such as inherent instabilities of the materials used - such as nitrate film stock - are beyond simple, if any, control. Likewise there is little that can be done now about inadequate processing of original material, even supposing that such inadequacies can be readily detected. It is the environment in which the materials now exist, the air that circulates around them, that is a constant problem and about which something can be done. Many particles, chemically dangerous to photographs, float around in the atmosphere, particularly in urban, industrialised areas. Invariably they react with the image-forming silver substances, oxidising them and causing discolouration of the image. For example, industrial gases, ozone and exhaust fumes contain aggressive oxidising chemicals (sulphur is often the culprit), so photographic materials should be stored in dust- and pollution-free areas, with incoming air filtered and purified. However, the enemy can be much closer at hand. Fumes from certain paints, contact with newsprint or unsuitable storage containers can also be chemically harmful. The problem with many of the chemical factors affecting permanence, as opposed to temperature and relative humidity, is essentially that there is no data on threshold values, no agreed working parameters. There are no simple instruments for measuring either the causes or the effects - what is the maximum permissible level of air pollution beyond which visual images suffer?

This section has tried to delineate the major factors causing the deterioration in the visual record, and although there may be disagreements over details, commentators do at least seem fairly united on the importance of proper and stable temperature and relative humidity control and the respective values required. These would seem to be factors more within the power of the average local studies library to control than some of the others.

Given basic financial support, appropriate storage containers, such as boxes, sleeves, envelopes, etc., should also be within the grasp of most institutions, although their range and the extent of their use will depend on the materials stocked and the type of service offered. Ideally every item should be put into an acid-free enclosure, but this may be a trifle excessive for a collection consisting mainly of copies and duplicates, as well as expensive even for the more critical prints and originals. However, there are now a few generally recognised dos and don'ts with regard to storage.

If using paper-based envelopes, boxes, etc., only acid-free papers should be bought, and Kraft paper and most glassine paper envelopes therefore avoided. Some experts would generally favour inert plastics, such as Mylar or cellulose triacetate, partly because their transparent nature allows for easy visual access to the materials. However, writing information on plastic sleeves is not easy as compared with paper materials, and there is some dispute over just how effective some plastics are, as they do not allow the photographs to 'breathe' properly and static electricity can build up. Hendriks goes so far as to suggest placing prints and negatives in plastic sleeves and then placing these in paper envelopes on which appropriate information can be written. Prints and negatives should, of course, be stored apart. Relevant-sized sleeves and envelopes for negatives, prints (including contact prints) can be obtained from certain manufacturers - see the appendix to this chapter. Once in sleeves, etc. (and the positioning of their seams is another factor to watch out for), the material can then be kept in boxes on shelves or in cabinets - again ensuring that there are no constituent elements present likely to affect the photographs adversely. First-class storage systems are clearly available at a price; other factors will determine to what extent such systems can and should be utilised.

A few minor points are worth paying attention to no matter how sophisticated or not the storage system is. All of these involve materials which are harmful to photographs. If mounting is necessary, avoid pressure-sensitive tape (like Sellotape), rubber cements or water-absorbing glues and pastes. Dry mounting techniques can be used but make sure the mounting board is chemically acceptable. Dry mounting is itself not now universally accepted as good practice, so only non-critical materials or copies should be mounted. Do not use rubber bands or paper clips to keep photographs together, and avoid using wooden boxes, cabinets or shelving for storage. If it is necessary to write on the back of photographs, and sometimes it is, use a soft pencil and not pen ink, felt tip or ball point pens. There are other simple dos and don'ts suggested in the literature, but the ones given above seem among the most basic and easy to comply with, as are obvious precautions like insisting on no smoking, eating or drinking in the vicinity of the collection.

Video as a medium has been in existence for far less time than photography and therefore the effects of particular types and levels of storage are less easy to quantify or predict. It is normally thought that video tape is not made to archival standards, although manufacturers are continually striving to produce longer-lasting tape. It is partly this fear that video materials will not last - each play of a tape for instance causes some loss of quality and drop-out can occur - that convinces some librarians and others that video should not be considered as an appropriate medium for archival collections. However, as with photography, material can be copied quite easily and the future use of digital techniques may help allay worries over the drop in quality generally associated with repeated analogue copying. Video is a medium in which appropriate information is being generated, and its storage is a problem that must be faced.

There are guidelines in the literature on proper storage conditions for video[28] but they are far less elaborate than those needed for photographic images. Although storing in a cool environment is considered beneficial by some, especially for longer-term storage, normal room temperatures with a controlled relative humidity of 40 to 60 per cent are quite acceptable. The boxes and cassette cases within which the tape is housed have no effect on the material and also allow for easy shelving. Although it is recommended that tapes be kept well away from strong external magnetic fields (lift motors and loudspeakers, for example), tests indicate that a distance of a metre is more than adequate. Otherwise the guidelines are basic and commonsense in relation to handling, dust, cleaning, etc. The extra problems associated with video (and motion picture film) concern the playback equipment required to make effective use of the medium. Looking after this hardware could be the straw that breaks the local studies librarian's back!

Proper storage and conservation procedures are easier in the abstract than in the practice. Not even the Library of Congress Prints and Photographs Divison has the time, staff or money to store items in the way they would like to ideally. There are often very good reasons why a particular approach cannot be adopted and advancing piecemeal may be the only practical solution, i.e. systematically replacing negatives, for example, in acid-free envelopes as and when the negatives are used. Nor do appropriate storage conditions stop 'mysterious' damage from occurring occasionally, while less than ideal conditions do not inevitably mean the disintegration of the collection. The niceties of storage and conservation can be followed in the literature, where more specific instructions can be found. What is noticeable is that the experts invariably disagree over the finer points. After all concern over the preservation of visual materials is a comparatively recent phenomenon, experience and knowledge relatively limited and some of the research currently being carried out may well lead to changes in practice. In two areas there is basic agreement: firstly, whatever the conditions, make sure they are constant, and secondly, it is generally a combination of factors, rather than one single cause, that leads to serious damage. Even then restoration can sometimes save the day, but that, as they say, is a whole new ball game, best left to trained restorators.

## THE FUTURE

This is not really the place for crystal-ball gazing, although it is clear that technology is likely to have further profound effects on the development of local studies libraries' visual collections. New advances in materials, formats and so on, may significantly alter the nature and type of images stocked, while the ways in which collections are organised, accessed and stored could also change quite considerably. Extending computerised systems is just one example. Reading the literature also reveals a number of other interesting ideas - for example, microfilm or video copies of the images have been suggested as alternative methods for encouraging increased visual access to a collection.[29] Introducing video disc technology has also been put forward. However, on closer inspection it is hard to see how some of these suggestions could, in the short term, be applicable to a general and often impoverished service like the local studies collection of a public library. Some of the more down-to-earth practices outlined in this chapter may be more feasible, and other more limited goals such as converting certain formats to a more stable or more accessible alternative might be worth considering. Lantern slides could, for instance, be turned into 35 millimetre copies which should then be lent to the public more easily.

One fact is quite clear: this is, that millions of visual images have been collected which contain information of value to local studies work, and not all of them are housed in local studies libraries. Museums, including national examples like the Welsh Folk Museum and the Museum of English Rural Life, or local institutions like the Dorset County Museum in Dorchester; record offices, such as the Strathclyde Regional Archives;

specialised organisations like the Royal Commissions on Ancient and Historical Monuments in England, Wales and Scotland; all of these and numerous other institutions will have photographic material of quite considerable relevance. What is extremely difficult, of course, is tracking down particular appropriate images when often only general descriptions of a collection are publicly available.

In an attempt to increase information about and access to the wealth of items in these various storehouses, many short-term Manpower Services Commission schemes are being set up to collect, store, index and even generate the relevant visual record. At the time of writing, Strathkelvin District Council are running a Strathkelvin Local Studies Project which involves photographing sites and collecting material from the local population; Canterbury City Council needed someone to index visual materials on local people and buildings; Ilfracombe Community Archive is trying to bring together the large quantity of local material available, including photographs. So even if funds are not available for the library to take giant steps forward in technology, resources are there for more limited, but essential, foundation work.

Eventually some effort will have to be made on a national scale to collate all this disparate information and try to provide a working guide to these numerous collections.[30] At the local level, despite clear lessons that can be learned from observing other collections' solutions or reading the professional literature, it should never be forgotten that each collection is unique, reflecting the character of the community it serves. Specific approaches to organisation and access may work well in one instance, but they should only be adopted where they are in harmony with the content and state of the collection and above all where they meet the users' needs.

## NOTES

1. Lesy, M. *Wisconsin death trip.* London, Allen Lane, 1973.
2. Smith D. The camera as historian. *Welsh history review* 7 (2) December 1974, p. 238.
3. Daniel, P. and Smock, R.W. Michael Lesy's sideshow. *Picturescope* 29 (2) Summer 1981, p. 52.
4. See, for instance: Weinstein, R. Why collect photographs? *Picturescope* 29 (4) Winter 1981, 120-124.

5. McCord, N. Photographs as historical evidence. *Local historian* 13 (1) February 1978, 23-36. Miller, S.T. The value of photographs as historical evidence. *Local historian* 15 (8) November 1983, 468-473. These are just two among numerous examples of articles, etc. which assess the value of photographs.

6. An interesting view from the angle of the user and potential uses is: Cox, L. Picturescope: getting the picture in focus. *Picturescope* 29 (1) Spring 1981, 12-13.

7. The classic work which deals with all aspects of the photograph in local history collections is: Weinstein, R. and Booth. L. *Collection, use, and care of historical photographs.* Nashville, Tennessee American Association for State and Local History, 1977. In certain areas it is, not surprisingly, showing its age, but it is nevertheless *the* basic guide to the subject.

8. One or two like Llanelli Public Library or Sheffield City Libraries and certain record offices, in Bristol or Suffolk for instance, are mentioned in: Oliver, E. (ed.). *Researchers guide to British film and television collections.* 2nd edition. London, British Universities Film and Video Council, 1985.

9. The value of cine film in local studies collections was dealt with some years ago by: Hardman, A.R. Films in the local history collection. *Library world* 69 (812) February 1968, 190-193.

10. Horvath, D.G. Archival appraisal of photographic materials. *Picturescope* 29 (2) Summer 1981, 44-47.

11. Noble, R. Considerations for evaluating local history photographs. *Picturescope* 31 (1) Spring 1983, 17-20.

12. The role of the photograph for family historians has recently been covered by: Steel, D. and Taylor, L. (eds). *Family history in focus.* Farnham, Lutterworth Press, 1984.

13. Prescott, H. Movie films as local archive material. *Audiovisual librarian* 11 (1) Winter 1985, 26-29.

14. The idea of such surveys has a long pedigree; see for instance: Gower H.D., Jast, L. and Topley, W. *The camera as historian.* London, Sampson Low, 1916.

15. Fennell, Y. Chester photographic survey. *Library Association record* 72 (5) May 1970, 197-199. Radmore, D.F. Suggestions for a photographic survey. *Local historian,* 9 (5) February 1971, 222-225.

16. For a more detailed look at the whole area of the use of video in local studies work, see: Baggs, C.M. Video and local studies librarianship. *Audiovisual librarian*, 10 (3) Summer 1984, 128-138.
17. Malan, N.E. Organizing photo collections: an introspective approach. *Picturescope* 29 (1) Spring 1981, 4-6.
18. Maounis, J. Cataloguing historical photographs: a select bibliography. *Picturescope* 28 (4) Winter 1980, 21.
19. Clawson, C. and Rankowski, C. Classification and cataloguing of slides using color photocopying. *Special libraries* 69 (8) August 1978, 281-285. Evans, G. and Stein, L. Image-bearing catalog cards for photolibraries. *Special libraries,* 70 (11) November 1979, 462-470.
20. For an overall discussion of the problems of the subject approach, see: Jirgensens, M. Thinking visually about subject headings for picture files. *Picturescope* 26 (4) Fall 1978, 100-125. Shaw, R. Picture organization: practices and procedures. *Special libraries,* 63 (10) October 1972, 448-456; 63 (11) November 1972, 502-506.
21. Petty, M.J. The role of the local studies library. *Local historian* 14 (8) November 1981, 460-467.
22. Dane, W.J. *The picture collection.* 6th edition. Hamden, Connecticut, Shoe String Press, 1968. Hill, D. *The picture file.* 2nd edition. Hamden, Connecticut, Linnet Books, 1978.
23. Examples from the United States include the University of Louisville, Photographic Archives; Yale Center for British Art; Smithsonian Institution/National Museum of American Art. In the United Kingdom, the Design Council Picture Library and the Property Services Agency Photographic Library see this as a significant development.
24. Harrison, H. *Film library techniques.* London, Focal Press, 1973.
25. In many recent published general works on conservation there is a section or chapter on photography, motion picture films and video. Among the more valuable and lengthy treatments are: Swann, A. Conservation of photographic print collections. *Library trends* 30 (2) Fall 1981, 267-296. Swartzburg, S. (ed.). *Conservation in the library.* London, Aldwych Press, 1983. (Chapter 4 by Gary Albright is on photographs; Chapter 5 by Nancy Schrock and Christine Sundt is on slides; Chapter 7 by Eileen Bowser is on motion picture films; and Chapter 8 by Swartzburg and Deidre Boyle is on videotape.) The area has also been covered in a recent British thesis:

Eaglestone, S. Storage of photographs in libraries, MLS thesis. University of Loughborough. There is also a useful bibliography: Walsh, T. The conservation of photographic records; a select bibliography. *Archives and manuscripts* 9 (1) September 1981, 72-82.

26. Hendriks, K. *The preservation and restoration of photographic materials in archives and libraries.* Paris, UNESCO, 1984.

27. The most consistently valuable periodical in the general field of photographs in library collections is *Picturescope,* the quarterly bulletin of the picture division of the Special Libraries Association in the United States. Although American in emphasis, there are numerous general and relatively specific articles to make it a more useful journal than some of the dedicated, highly specialised periodicals in the field of conservation. Library journals may well carry the occasional relevant article, especially those in the art library field.

28. Apart from the chapter in Swartzburg (see Note 25 above) a basic set of guidelines can be found in: Weston, M. Videotape storage and handling; guidelines. *BUFC newsletter* no. 43 May 1981, 15-16. Weston, M. The storage and handling of videocassettes in libraries. *Audiovisual librarian* 8 (1) Winter 1982, 31-33.

29. Leary, W. Microfilming photographs. *Picturescope* 28 (4) Winter 1980, 10-11, 13-14. Lewis, E. Video scan picture searching. *Visual resources* 1 (1) Spring 1980, 40-51.

30. Two guides to photographic collections are: Wall, J. *Directory of British photographic collections.* London, Heinemann, 1977. Although still a very valuable guide, a new edition is needed by now and of course it is not restricted to local studies materials. More specific, but not comprehensive, information can be found in: West, J. *Town records.* Chichester, Phillimore, 1983. This includes a gazetteer of two collections of photographs, p. 339-348.


## APPENDIX

Here is a select list of manufacturers/distributors of appropriate storage materials:

Ademco Ltd, Coronation Road, High Wycombe, Bucks HP12 3TA.
Conservation Resources International, 33-35 Markham St., Chelsea Green, London SW3 3NR.

Cundell Coutts Ltd, Violet Road, London E3 3QL.
G. Ryder, Denbigh Road, Bletchley, Milton Keynes, MK1 1DG.

# 17

# Publications and products

Roy Field

One of the great success stories in British public librarianship has been the richness and strength of local studies collections. Even the smallest urban libraries, and later even county library branches, acquired materials related to their areas and these provided a breadth and depth of local knowledge unsurpassed by any other agency. Donations both of single items and whole private libraries, allied with judicious purchasing, has resulted in collections which are sometimes the only true specialist departments in a particular library authority. In spite of these strengths, these collections have never been well known to the general public, although scholars have always known of their existence for their researches. In common with other sorts of libraries, the role now of local studies collections has changed from the concept of conservation and acquisition of materials to their exploitation. Although exhibitions of material had taken place and there had been a certain amount of publication such as bibliographies of collections, it was not until the 1960s, and more particularly the 1970s, that the full range of materials available were drawn to the attention of the public. Exhibitions and talks in branch libraries not normally associated with local studies certainly encouraged the trend, but a significant development has been the making available directly to the public, by publication, of material not otherwise available.

## DEVELOPMENT OF PUBLICATIONS PROGRAMMES

Publications programmes in libraries often began by being allied to some sort of event or celebration. It could have been a town pageant, charter day celebration, foundation ceremony or even the anniversary of the

376

establishment of a library service. There usually was a reason for the early library publications rather than just the whim or bright idea of a local librarian. Yet even when allied to some sort of local celebration, the reasons for publication often became a definitive statement for the establishment and maintenance of a proper publications programme. A good example of this is in the minutes of the Derby Borough Libraries Committee of 1970 which refer to celebrations for the centenary of the Derby Library Service to be held in 1971. The committee approved the publication of a book of old photographs of Derby on the basis of 'making available at a modest cost to the residents of the town and surrounding area, material in the local history collection that would otherwise not be available'. This minute clearly establishes the social reasons for the publication and any subsequent continuation. It is to 'make available at a modest cost' - implying that profit on publications was not the main reason. Also the material 'would not otherwise be available'. which is acknowledging the reality that local studies material was often locked away and known only to scholars and researchers. It is the beginning of a legitimate exploitation of local studies stock. At a later stage in the development of publications programmes, particularly in the late 1970s, the concept of exploitation for profit unfortunately began to come to the fore, while the earlier justification, as evidenced in the Derby and other minutes, became less important. Within the terms of the Derby minute it is clearly acceptable and indeed desirable that a public library authority become a publisher to make known more widely material within its care.

Libraries do not stand in isolation from social trends and developments and it is not surprising that this rise in the exploitation of local studies materials coincided with the increase in visits to ancient monuments and stately homes and a general interest in local history. Any visit these days to a National Trust or English Heritage property may result in being enticed into a gift shop to buy guide books, reproductions, postcards and other mementoes connected either directly or vaguely with the building in question. This is not to decry these gift shops or the quality of the merchandise that they sell, but it is a fact that 20 years ago such gift shops were almost unheard of. Guides to properties, be they in national or private care, were poorly produced and badly written, contrasting markedly with the high quality and usual value for money of the books and merchandise on sale now. This quality is also mirrored in the increased professionalism of library authorities involved in publications and other products compared with the frankly amateur approach of library publicity and printing in years past.

It is not the intention of this chapter to survey the broad range of commercial publications available in any locality. This is unnecessary as local printed material is a basic source for local studies collections and its location and acquisition is well known by local studies librarians. Suffice it to say that commercial publications range from major volumes such as the Victoria County History at one end of the spectrum to the small, privately produced, pamphlets relating, say, to someone's reminiscences of their time 'below stairs' or in the trenches at the other end. This chapter will look at publications and other materials produced by a library authority, demonstrating the problems and benefits of the production of such material. Although selected examples will be given, it is not intended to list the full variety of publications from all local authorities. For those who wish to get a reasonable impression of the broad range of material produced during a five-year span, a survey in *British librarianship and information work 1976-1980* gives a clear indication of that activity.[1] Inevitably the author's comments will be from the viewpoint of a senior manager in a library authority with overall responsibility for a publications programme and who deals with problems in a particular manner. Other authorities' approaches to library publications may be equally valid.

## REPRINTS

Although, as indicated earlier, many library authorities began publications programmes on the basis of some event or celebration, which very often resulted in commemorative books of photographs or maps or print reproductions, a starting point for many others was the production of reprints of important books in a local studies collection. Reprints correctly handled can be the easiest and indeed the most profitable of local studies publications to deal with. All local studies librarians know of significant books in their collections that are either very heavily used and in their original editions begin to show signs of wear, or other volumes where very few copies still exist but for which there is still a demand. In both cases the cry from the heart from librarians is 'Why on earth is this book not reprinted?' Very often, through local commercial printers with an entrepreneurial spirit, or indeed under the aegis of a local historical society, reprints were undertaken but the cry from the heart could equally well be solved by the library itself undertaking publication of the reprint. For ease of reproduction, and to avoid complications, it is obviously better to choose a book for reprint publication that is out of copyright. Copyright problems can be overcome by negotiation with the copyright holder but as a general rule the older the book the less chance of copyright problems. These days good quality lithographic printing can ensure a very high-quality facsimile reproduction of an original work, but as a facsimile copy the end product will either look old-fashioned or contemporary according to the typeface and quality of the original.

At this point it has to be decided how to market the final end product. Do you simply market it as an exact facsimile copy of an old book, that fact being its marketing strength, or use a revised title page, and perhaps a new introduction together with new artwork on the cover, and pretend the book is more up to date than it actually is? There is no hard and fast rule here and individual titles and circumstances may vary the decision. An example which comes to the writer's mind is of a facsimile reproduction of a series of small, local topographical guides produced at the turn of the century, which were frankly boring at the time of first production, and which were equally or more boring in the 1970s when they were reprinted! In their reprinted form they were not bestsellers but they were not designed to be so. They were, however, available at a modest cost for those who wanted them. On the other hand, the decision can be made to clearly enhance the publication. *The bridges of Shrewsbury,* originally produced in 1931, and now published by Shropshire Libraries, is a good example of this. The text and illustrations are the same as in 1931, but the title page and new jacket are such as to attract sales through local book shops. If necessary this concept can be taken even further by alterations to the positioning of the text itself while still retaining the concept of a reprint - *Shropshire canals* (also published by Shropshire Libraries) is an example of this. The printed matter originally appeared in the 1950s and 1960s as a series of articles in the local *Shropshire magazine.* As with most magazine publication, the articles were set in columns and inevitably interspersed with advertisements for local services and products. Although these advertisements by the time of consideration for reprint publication in the 1970s had a certain period charm, it was felt more desirable to remove them. Therefore the columns of print relating to canals as they appeared in the magazine were cut out and repasted into a logical sequence. This repasted text was then lithographically produced and thus constituted a reprint, albeit looking very different from the original. This approach is by no means the easiest method of reprint production and involves either skill on the part of the library service in preparing the reprint or skill and expense by the printer dealing with this particular publication. It has to be decided whether the end result justifies the expenditure of money or time.

In general the printing costs for reprints are considerably less than for new materials because there are no setting-up costs and artwork, which are the expensive elements of new printing. It is likely, therefore, that reprints can retail at a lower cost than their size would indicate. This can be beneficial to the consumer, and falls well within the Derby remit of 'modest costing', unless the authority expects a suitable mark-up to keep the publication in line with other publications of a similar size. If saleability is a factor in reprint publications, rather than the strict criteria of simply making a worthy book available once more, then as well as new covers to attract, the subject-matter of the reprint itself should be seriously considered. Topographical guides of small communities, however worthy, might not be economically worth reprinting, but some topics can achieve sales over a much larger area, for instance, across a county rather than just sales within a specific town. *Shropshire canals* referred to above, is a case in point, in that it sells throughout the whole of the county and not just in a specific town. A town guide to, say, Ludlow, would only really have a sales potential in and around Ludlow.

*Shropshire canals* also exemplifies how sales can reach beyond a county to the whole country, in that the topic, i.e. inland waterways, has a strong national appeal. Industrial archaeology and transportation are also big sellers nationally, even if a book's title seems to refer only to a specific locality. The subject-matter rather than the local connection is the prime sales generator with these books. Careful advertising in national journals connected with industrial archaeology and transportation history for books such as these can result in considerable national sales to individuals as well as libraries.

## ORIGINAL TEXTS

There is inevitably a limit on the number of titles suitable for reprinting and the logical development of a library's publications programme is to move from reprints into original work. These can take two forms. The first is the creation by library staff of an original work on the basis of material held within a local studies collection. The most common forms are the photographic and illustrative guides to an area. These are usually based on the photographic and/or print collections housed in local studies departments and if attractively packaged can be both socially interesting and financially rewarding. Even more than books, the usually extensive files of visual material housed in local studies collections are rarely seen by members of the public unless put on exhibition or occasionally used in local newspapers to illustrate articles. A compilation of interesting photographs of a town or area is therefore popular. Many local authorities over the last few years have been involved in such productions, e.g. Derbyshire, Shropshire, Wigan, Lambeth, East Sussex and Hampshire. A popular theme for these is 'before and after' by utilising new photographs taken from the same position as old photographs or prints in the collections.

As well as 'before and after'-style books, collections of old photographs and illustrations are popular. Sometimes they can be allied to a specific theme or period, e.g. Edwardian photographs, architectural views or rural life. Sometimes the theme can be a subject which in itself moves the book into a different category. For instance, books of photographs of old railway scenes link strongly again to industrial archaeology and transport, with the consequent benefits of country-wide sales, as described previously. Different books of photographs can be produced for some time but eventually there is a limit to the standard of quality and variety of illustrations available for reproduction. It is, however, always worth bearing in mind that new generations come along and a best seller of old photographs kept judiciously out of print for a number of years and then revised can be an equally good seller.

Although the prime source of material for old photographs in any locality is often the local studies library, there are, of course, many photographs in private hands which if made available can be advantageously used in a publication. It must be remembered that commercial publishers also regard this field as a potential gold mine, especially for publication towards the Christmas period, and have produced similar sorts of books commercially. Such firms include Batsford and Barracuda but there are also many more localised publications, often issued by local newspapers or local civic societies, which cover a similar field. It is ironical that initially some of the commercially produced books of old photographs relied heavily on the goodwill of local librarians to provide the source of material often before library publications programmes were established. The quality and the verification of the brief descriptions and notes which usually accompany the photographs can more easily be controlled if the publication is an in-house one from a local library; indeed some of the statements and dates in some commercial publications leave something to be desired.

Nevertheless if the local library does not have a publications programme it can be equally well argued that it is for the public good to have these books produced by commercial publishers or local societies.

Narrative local histories produced entirely in house are less common. Certainly local studies librarians do often act as local authors but the fact that the publisher is the local authority rather than a private company is more coincidental than anything else. There is the time factor involved in library staff sitting down to write a text of a book to be published, as usually a librarian's role in serving the public is a full-time commitment. Nevertheless, a number of local studies librarians have produced texts of books for publication by their own local authority in their own time using the source materials at hand. In this case they act more as an independent author than an employee of the authority and indeed should be treated as such in terms of correct financial arrangements.

Far more common are the approaches made by local authors to have their own manuscript or text printed. It is a fact that if the local authority begins to establish itself as a publisher of local historical material then the manuscripts do come flooding in. This situation raises a number of important points which need analysis.

Any library that decides to become in effect a publisher should deal with it in the most professional way possible. The end product must be of such a quality that it will stand up to scrutiny within a local bookshop or newsagent against highly glossy, commercial publications. Equally the library publisher should deal with a client author in a very professional manner and negotiate correctly all along the way.

By establishing these standards, manuscripts or texts can be received by a library publisher and dealt with impartially on their merits alone. There is no doubt that a lot of badly written or inaccurate material is submitted to local libraries for possible publication which, without undue amendation or correction, could not be dealt with realistically. It is very desirable for a library publisher to have a first refusal for a local publication but the keyword is indeed *refusal* if the manuscript or text does not come up to a desired standard.

Many books on the shelves in local studies collections have been collected over the years from material on a locality produced locally often by private means. There is a long and indeed worthy tradition of amateurism within the field of local studies. It is for the local studies librarian and indeed scholars to interpret the value of material in care, but by acting as a publisher itself, the library has to consider a reasonable return on the investment on behalf of the local authority or indeed consider whether the text is of such great social and historical value that it really must be produced. Having said this, one is aware sometimes that interesting social documents are slipping through the net. There are differences of opinion between local studies librarians about the value of such material. For instance, take the small village history which is in effect reminiscences of an elderly lady or gentleman telling stories of times past. Some of these stories may be strictly inaccurate in true historical terms but they nevertheless give a clear picture of social conditions in communities. An example of this, from Bradford in 1979, was the *Reminiscences of a Bradford mill girl* by Maggie Newberry, which, it was clearly stated, in the preface, would not have been printed commercially or in learned journals. In these terms the social/historical content was of paramount importance. Scholarship should not be taken to extremes when considering manuscripts and texts for eventual publication. Remember that anything connected with a locality has some value within a collection, even though it is known that some of the information may have to be regarded with caution. Professional judgements as to the value of a publication have to be made, however, within the limited budgets usually available for a publications programme: refusal is an inevitability of serious consideration of manuscripts and is not something that should be shirked.

Local authors, either individual or corporate, are usually delighted to have material published, as very often this will be the only time that they have their names in print. They are sometimes so embarrassingly grateful that there is almost an impression given of them wishing to pay for publication rather than the other way round. It is important, therefore, to deal with such authors on a professional but realistic basis and not try to press them too hard in order to get the best deal for the authority. They should be entitled to royalties or their equivalent on the publication.

Authors of the relatively short booklet of 60 or 70 pages are quite happy to receive a lump sum in lieu of royalties, thus avoiding the complications of receiving periodically only very small amounts of money. This approach is perfectly legitimate, but should be clearly stated in a formal contract which is important for all parties to consider and sign.

Reference books, such as the *Writers' and artists' yearbook,* give an indication of the standard form of publisher's contract and this can be used as a basis for a local contract in consultation with the council's legal department. It need not be a complex document, as it is unlikely that the subject-matter of books and pamphlets within this field would, for instance, form the basis of television or feature film material, with the necessary protection of rights of performance. The contract between the publisher and the author should thus be simple and concise and should state the responsibilities of each party. Topics that need to be covered in the document include copyright ownership, assignments of the right to print and publish, responsibility to determine the print run and selling price, competitive works for other publishers, royalties or other payments, format and artwork, reprint rights and disposal of copies. Never forget that without the author of the book there would be nothing to publish and treat him or her with respect.

Corporate bodies very often approach a library involved in publishing to collaborate in specific publications. Sometimes the approach is simply from the corporate body themselves acting as an author, but often it might be a genuine collaboration with both parties being involved in the funding of the project. Such collaboration could be in-house within the local authority. For instance, books on roads or bridges might be produced in collaboration with a highways and surveyor's department; books on country walks and nature trails might be produced in collaboration with a planning department; while guides to local monuments and places of interest might be produced in collaboration with a museums department. An interesting collaboration which has taken place in a number of shire counties is with the Victoria County History, particularly when an editor is on the county's establishment. Essex, Staffordshire, Somerset, Shropshire and other authorities have collaborated with the Victoria County History in issuing reprints from sections of the major published volumes. This has the advantage of making better known to the public the major volumes, but also offers the possibility of extracts applicable to specific villages or communities at a modest price. Reprinted sections have the virtue of being reasonably cheap to produce in that they consist of facsimile reproductions of existing pages of the main volumes with the addition usually of a distinct new cover. Local Victoria County History editors can also collaborate by writing abbreviated histories of different aspects of an area, especially when related to published volumes. For example, a pamphlet on *Monastic Shropshire,* which was written by the editor of the Shropshire Victoria County History in 1982, proved most popular and acted as a good piece of public relations for the work of the editor and his staff. It also publicised the existence of the previously published volume used as the source material for the text.

Collaboration need not, however, be just within the local authority. Successful collaborations can take place, particularly with local newspapers, on the production of the 'before and after'- type photographic surveys. Regular coverage within the newspaper of photographs to be produced in the book can result in mammoth sales for this type of production. Collaboration in this way also has the virtue of the library, with its expert local studies staff, being involved in the verification of the facts connected with the photographs.

## PRODUCTS

Although most library publications programmes are concerned with books and pamphlets, many also reproduce illustrative material in a variety of formats. These can include individual maps and prints, portfolios of maps and prints, postcards, greetings cards, slide sets and a variety of souvenir material. Maps, prints, postcards and greetings cards can all add considerably to the total image of a library's publication programme. They can look very eyecatching on a display stand of library publications organised either within the library or at an outside venue. They usually cost less than the books or booklets on display and very often come within the pocket money or Christmas gift finances of visitors. It is unlikely that such illustrative material makes vast profits unless one is fortunate to be able to provide something which is of great interest to the broad commercial market. This often depends on the nature of the area in which the library is located and its tourist potential. A tourist area, for instance, will have many commercial postcards available already through a range of outlets in the area and to add to that range would not be particularly profitable. On the other hand, a more urban area with few regularly published views of the locality might well find that postcards and prints are an attractive proposition. Greetings cards using old prints, in particular those in colour, are a far better commerical proposition but it is sensible *not* to put a greeting inside the card or at the very minimum 'Best wishes'. This then makes the card appropriate for a heavy sales campaign during the Christmas period and yet also suitable for the rest of the year.

With other products it is often wise to watch the commercial market and see if any gaps can be identified. For instance, if small mats or coasters are on display in an area with illustrative material on them not connected with the area, it might well be worth a library's while to produce such items itself, utilising small illustrations and vignettes from material in local studies collections. This undoubtedly involves the library in contracts with commercial producers so the library must be very sure of the market before it goes into this area. The writer was once involved in the sale and exploitation of notepaper with small vignettes of local interest scenes as a commercial venture. Attempting to put together the packages of vignetted notepaper and envelopes in appropriate attractive packaging was a horrendous experience although in sales terms the eventual product was popular. The staff time involvement is, however, too great to justify dealing with such products if the library tries to do it all itself. The market has to be clearly defined for these sorts of additions to a library's stock of publications and products, as one must remember that most visitors to libraries come in without the intention of spending money and they are conditioned mainly to purchasing in other types of institution. Collaboration with local beauty spots, stately homes, museums, etc., would probably be necessary to deal with non-book products and it is up to individual libraries to determine whether the public relations benefits of such products is really worth while.

## PUBLICITY/ADVERTISING

Financial arrangements for the establishment of a publications programme will vary very much from local authority to local authority, so the precise financial details of a publications programme are not included here. In general the local authority will have to determine whether its publication programme is designed for profit or a simple recovery of costs. When these facts are known then a costing formula can be applied to determine mark-up, bearing in mind that a discount of a third will have to be offered to the book trade. The formula used for the unit costing will include such factors as printing costs, publicity costs, gratis copies, specialised artwork and, if necessary, elements of salary and administration costs.

The discount of a third to traders is vital if it is wished to sell the products outside the confines of the library service points. Only knocking pennies off the selling price of a book is not acceptable to the trade, nor is it professional, in that it implies a lack of care in determining correct unit costing and applying a strict formula.

Some libraries which act as publishers have a policy which restricts the sale of their publications to libraries and other premises belonging to the local authority. This policy might be acceptable if there are a number of suitable outlets but great potential for sales and effective publicity for the library service is being missed by not using commercial outlets. If the product is good then up to 70 per cent of effective sales of the product can be achieved outside the public sector. There are a number of factors, however, which need to be taken into account to achieve these sort of sales figures. The first is the necessity of offering a proper trade discount as referred to previously. The second is making the product so attractive that it stands up to comparison with commercially produced books and pamphlets. This in turn relies on good design and artwork for the covers of the books or effective commercial packaging for other products. A reproduction of an historic map, for instance, is better sold rolled up in a cardboard or plastic tube rather than attempting to sell it flat with the hazards of transportation home by so doing. These extra touches add to the cost of the product but are very essential for effective sales and should be built into the basic unit costing formula. Posters advertising new and forthcoming books are quite cheap to produce and are effective. Advance publicity for a new publication (possibly including a small reproduction of the book's cover) can go to commercial outlets with a tear-off return order slip; at the time of publication, effective use of press releases and review copies is essential. Usually the local press will respond to press releases about a book relating to their locality but to reinforce this the library service would be well advised to organise some sort of book launch or event. Certainly it is courteous to the outside authors to have a modest book launch ceremony. These events can easily take place in most libraries and at the very minimum they should consist of light refreshments and an opportunity for library staff and other invited guests, e.g. councillors, trade representatives and press, to talk to the author and his or her family. Brief speeches and responses are in order and this makes the launch of a new book something more of an event which can be picked up by the press, perhaps with appropriate photographs. Taking this idea much further one can utilise the theme of the book for major displays or events. Books on a locality during wartime might result in a book launch using wartime recipes for the refreshments; a book on local railways could involve the launch in a waiting room or bar at a local station with the co-operation of the local station manager; while a book on canals or water transportation could even involve a launch afloat! Anything that is out of the normal run of things is usually welcomed by the press and is certainly worthy of consideration.

Some three or four years ago income generation in libraries was very much the 'in' subject and indeed a number of libraries did involve themselves in income generation by such methods as the use of bookmarks with advertisements. Advertising has also been considered as an additional method of financing local publications. Opinion is split, however, as to whether advertisements in books so diminish the quality of the finished product that whatever income they achieve they are counter-productive. On the other hand, books are increasingly expensive to produce and if the aim is to keep the price reasonably low to the public and advertising can assist in this, then it is worth consideration. The problem is obtaining the advertising. For a one-off publication of modest size it is probably not worth while involving a commercial advertising agency in trying to obtain sufficient local advertising. If, however, staff are left on their own to obtain the advertising, then one must consider very carefully the time involved, and hence the cost, in getting this additional source of revenue. The writer's experience has shown that the time involved can be prohibitive, and having had a single book with advertising produced as an experiment, it is not an experience the writer would repeat. It must also be recognised that although local government might have financial problems at the time of writing, so indeed have local commercial enterprises, and advertising is very often a part of their budget that is severely under pressure. It is far better to get the unit costing absolutely right and the book sold at the correct price rather than be involved in the difficult problems of obtaining additional finance through advertising.

Many of the comments made in this chapter are based on the writer's experience over many years in library publishing, and so to widen the scope of this chapter reference will be made to some reports produced through the British Library about publishing in one specific shire, Devon,[2], and a survey undertaken there by Capital Planning Information Limited. Devon was a county that had not been very much involved in library publishing but recognised that many publications were being produced from other departments under the imprint of the County Council. The reports indicate a move toward the establishment of a corporate publishing policy for the County Council, and this corporate approach might indeed be a more politically acceptable way forward for many local authorities. The reports also identifiy and comment on the possibility of creating closer relationships with all elements of a 'publishing chain' - author, publisher, bookseller and library. These reports are worthy of consideration even if a library is already involved in publishing in that the consideration of the inter-departmental approach to publishing can always be reappraised and also its connection with the local book trade in all forms. It should not be forgotten that local authority publishing is inevitably subsided in some way or another. Staff, be they in a library's department or other department, work in an office environment which is heated and lit and has other appropriate services. A commercial publisher would have to provide such premises and services himself. Although library publications might be carefully costed and a perfectly acceptable return on investment made, it must be said that if they were produced purely commercially, then the cover price would no doubt have to be somewhat higher. This recognition of subsidy is important to consider, as publications programmes begin to move away from their original conception of making available material housed in collections, to acting as an agency for outside manuscripts and texts. If local publishing houses exist within a locality, they may have some cause for objection if books are being produced under subsidy by a local authority that they could well publish themselves. This is a topic which must be seriously considered by all libraries which act in effect as publishers.

Even commercial publishers cannot, however, accept every local manuscript or text. There is still the very small publication which would be of great value in a small locality but not valued much further afield. The writer refers to those village histories and the like which are most useful social documents but whose cost of production would be so great that they rarely see the light of day. This is where the local authority might be able to legitimately involve itself in publication if only by the use of the new technologies that are beginning now to come into most libraries. Word processors, for instance, can be used to reproduce text of such small histories in-house very easily and with appropriate litho reproduction can make even small-scale pamphlets economic.

Experience has shown that once a library establishes itself as a publisher, manuscripts and texts begin to flow in. There is always something new that people are finding out about a locality which in decades to come will be of great value for historians and others. If libraries can assist in their publication, often in alliance with the commercial sector, then public libraries, and in particular local studies departments, will be succeeding in maintaining their long tradition of assisting scholarship and providing information about a local community.

## NOTES

1.  Field, R. Library publications. In: *British Librarianship and information work 1976-1980*. London, Library Association, 1982. Vol. 2, pp. 165-172. A survey of library publications for 1981-1985 is due for publication in 1987 in the next volume in this series.
2.  Capital Planning Information Ltd. *Devon County Council publishing programme*. Exeter, Devon County Council, 1984. (British Library research and development reports, no. 5803.) Capital Planning Information Ltd. *Local government publications: their packaging and marketing*. Exeter, Devon Library Service, 1982. (British Library research and development reports, no. 5745.) Capital Planning Information Ltd. *Publishing and local government: a report of a seminar on the packaging and marketing of local government publications*. Exeter, Devon County Council, 1983. (British Library research and development reports, no. 5748.)

## FURTHER READING

Betty, P.K. Publishing and local studies. In: Library Association. *Study school and national conference proceedings, Brighton 1978*. London, Library Association, 1979, pp. 135-138.

Dean. J.R. Local authorities publishing of local history. In: Library Association. *Study school and national conference proceedings, Brighton, 1978*. London, Library Association, 1979, pp. 132-134.

Field, R. The library as publisher. *Library Association record* 81 (8) August 1979, 383-385.

Kennington, D. and Shute, A. Devon's new departure in local government publishing. *County councils gazette* 77 (8) November 1984, 229.

Nurse, B. London boroughs look at their past. *London journal* 1 (6) Summer 1980, 70-76.

Orton, I. The library as publisher. *Assistant librarian* 73 (5) May 1980, 70-73.

Reid, D. Publishing for profit. *New library world* 81 (964) October 1980, 199-201.

Shute, A. Low cost innovation in the Devon Library Service. *Local government policy making* 9 (3) 1983, 71-77.

# Index

398

Geography
  use of local material, 275-276,
    300, 301
Geographical Association, 277
Geography Committee (H.M.
  Inspectorate), 275
German Democratic Republic
  use of archives in, 282
Germany, Federal Republic of,
  local classification schemes, 227
  local history in schools, 282-282
  local studies resources in
    education, 271
  regional bibliography, 176
Glasgow and West of Scotland
  Family History Society, 263
Glasgow District Libraries, 36, 47,
  127-128, *158*
  *see also* Mitchell Library
*Glasgow herald,* 236
Glasgow University, 239
  Library, 57, 58, 67
*Gloucester journal,* 237
Gloucester Public Library, 35, 40,
  128
*Gloucestershire and Avon life,* 240
Gloucestershire County Library,
  237, 239, 240
  *see also* Gloucester Public Library
*Good, the bad and the ugly* (Palmer
  and Wise), 277
*Goodnight Mister Tom* (Magorian),
  292
Granada Television, 292
Grange Museum of Local History
  (Brent Library Service), 130
Greater London Council, 2, 49
*Group projects in local history,*
  (Rogers), 280
Group rooms, 135, 139, 152, 156
Guidelines for local studies libraries,
  4, 114, 132
*Guidelines for reference and*

*information service to public
  libraries* (Library Association), 98
Guildford Library (Surrey County
  Library), 128, *129*
Guildhall Classification Scheme, 61,
  223, 226
Guildhall Library, London, 27-28,
  35, 44
  accommodation, 130, 138, 139
  directories and poll books, 242
  guide to the collections, 261
  number of letters received, 252
  reproduction fees, 260
Gwent College of Higher Education
  Library, 66
Gwent County Library, *see* Newport
  Regional Library
Gwynedd Archives Service, 286
Gwynedd Library Service, *see*
  Caernarfon Library

HMSO, *see* Her Majesty's
  Stationery Office
Hackney Library Services, *see*
  Shoreditch District Library
Hallworth, Frederick, 48
Halon gas, 149
Hammersmith and Fulham, London
  Borough of, 290, 360-361
Hampshire County Library Service,
  353, 381
  *see also* Portsmouth Central
    Library; Waterlooville Library;
    Winchester Library
*Handbook to county bibliography*
  (Humphrey), 171
Hanworth, *Lord* (1861-1936), 40
Haringey Libraries, *see* Bruce Castle
  Museum
Hendon Publishing Company, 197
Hendriks, K., 364, 366
Her Majesty's Stationery Office, 119
*Her people* (Dayus), 293

401

130, 296

Local studies collections (Academic libraries), 3, 52-69, 297-298
finance, 58
historical development, 53
oral history, 318, 321
relationship to main collections, 56-58
role, 65
scope, 54-55
staffing, 58-59
survey questionnaire, 52-53, 64, 67-69
use, 55-56

Local studies collections (Public libraries), 1-5, 21-22, 376
abroad, 2, 4-5
as local studies and information departments, 101
centralisation and decentralisation, 42-47, 112
formerly local history collections, 1
historical developments, 27-42
objectives, 97-99, 102, 104, 130
opening hours, 254
policies, 98, 99-105
present structure of provision, 42-49, 211
subject departments, 128, 130
*see also* Local studies centres

Local Studies Group of the Library Association, 4, 118, 232, 268, 284
'Education and local studies' National Conference 1978, 285
Open University History Society link, 281
proposed standards, 4, 114, 116
*Local studies index,* 234
*Local studies librarian,* 4
Local studies librarians, 20, 48, 97, 103, 108-112, 114

as authors, 382
as local experts, 268
contacts with schools, 283-286
continuing education, 117-118
in-service training, 118-119
professional education, 39, 40, 108, 114, 116-118, 281, 283, 299-300
role, 20-22, 42, 115
*see also* Liaison librarians

*Local studies librarianship* (Nichols), 182

Local studies packs, 103

'Local studies, the libraries and the student' (meeting), 286

*Locscot,* 4

London
boroughs, 42, 44, 46, 108, 110, 249
archive services, 2, 49, 70
guide to local history resources, 261
structure of public library local studies provision, 43-44, 45, 46, 49, 110
local studies centres, 19, 48, 130

London and Home Counties Branch of the Library Association, 173

London County Council, 38

London Government Act 1962, 70

London Museum, 16

London Society Library, 65

London University, 52
'O' Level Board, 275
University College Library, 61, 66, 67, 297
University College reader in the history of London, 279
University College School of Librarianship, 40

Longman Resources Unit (York), 294

Longright Library, Manchester, 267

Nevins, Alan, 310, 314
New South Wales Archives Office, 283, 288
Newark Public Library, 128
Newcastle City Libraries, 35, 55, 362
  number of visitors, 249
  photographs collection arrangement, 361
  refused official repository status, 40
Newcastle Polytechnic Library, 55, 61, 66, 67, 297
  School of Librarianship, 55, 61
Newcastle University
  Archive Teaching Unit, Department of Education, 295
  Library, 60, 66, 67
Newman College, 295
  Library, 67, 279
Newport Regional Library (Gwent County Library), 227
Newsagents, 202
Newscuttings, 232, 238-239, 249
Newspapers
  *see* Local newspapers
*Niedersächsen-bibliographie 1908-1970*, 176
*Niedersächsische bibliographie*, 176
Noble, Richard, 352
Non-book materials, 149
Non-metropolitan counties, 42, 70, 110, 211, 212
  structure of public library local studies provision, 45-46, 47
*Nordrhein-Westfälische bibliographie*, 176
*Norfolk bibliography* (Darrock and Taylor), 172, 178
Norfolk Library Service, 213, 224, 226
  *see also* Norwich Central Library
Norfolk Record Office, 48, 129,

159-160, 162, 163
North Cheshire College Library, 66, 67
North-East London Polytechnic Library, 66, 67
North-East Wales Institute of Higher Education Library, 66
North Eastern Library Board, 175
North Humberside College of Further Education, 279
North London Polytechnic Library, 66
North Staffordshire Polytechnic Library, 57, 66
North West Film Archive, 351
North West Regional Library System, 171
North Western Museum of Science and Industry, 193
North Yorkshire County Library
  *see* York Central Library
Northampton Central Library, 106, 128
*Northern bibliography*, 173-175
*Northern history*, 279
Northern Ireland, 42, 44, 71, 111, 173
*Northern Ireland local studies*, 44, 173, 175
Northern Regional Library System, 173
Northumberland Record Office, 286
*Norton on archives* (Norton), 73
Norwegian Institute for Local History and Local History Research, 282
Norwich Central Library (Norfolk Library Service), 35, 36, 40, 48, *159*
  building, 128, 130, 134
  classification for photographs, 361
Nottingham County Library (Nottinghamshire County Libraries)

Record agents, 252-253

Record offices, 2, 10, 22, 47, 52,
65, 98, 119, 174, 219, 278, 280
educational role, 14-15
relationship with library service,
109, 113, 114
resource provision for education,
286-289, 294
*see also* Archives; County record
offices; Local records

Record societies, 172

Records Commission, 1830, 27

Records management, 19, 76, 90-92,
94, 158

Records Management Society of
Great Britain, 94

*Recusant history*, 234

Reference libraries, 31, 47, 284
as location of local studies
collection, 30, 108, 130, 131,
133
proximity to local studies
collection, 133, 134
staffing, 110, 111, 113-114

Regional film archives, 351

Regional history centres, 279

Regions (Scotland), 42, 46, 71

Religious denominations archives,
78-79

*Reminiscences of a Bradford mill
girl* (Newberry), 383

Renfrew District Libraries, see
Paisley Central Library

'Report on the educational use of
archives' (Society of Archivists),
286

Reprography, 114, 293, 295
*see also* Photocopying;
Photography

'Rescue' work in archaeology, 20

Resource centres, 297

Resource packs, *see* Education packs

Rhyl Library (Clwyd Library

Service), 111

'Richmond local resource project'
(Lowenstein and Loh), 283

Richmond Local Resources Project,
Melbourne, 297

Richmond-upon-Thames Library
Services, 224, 226

Rochdale Libraries, 35, 45, 71

Rodents, 81

Royal Commissions on Ancient and
Historical Monuments in England,
Wales and Scotland, 371

Rumney College Library, 66, 67

Runcorn District Library (Cheshire
Libraries and Museums), 133

Ruthin Library (Clwyd Library
Service), 111

St. Andrew's College, Glasgow, 66, 67

St. Andrews University Library, 54,
66, 67

Salford City Libraries, 28, 45, 130
*see also* Swinton Central Area
Library

Salisbury Library, Cardiff, 58

Samuel, Ralph, 12, 314, 317

Sandwell Libraries, 45

Savage, E. (1878-1966), 128

*School looks around* (Layton and
White), 272

School of Folklife Studies,
Edinburgh, 312

Schools, 114, 271-278
and local studies collections,
283-286, 290-293, 298-302
and oral history, 327
and promotion of local studies
collections, 302-304
local studies in, 272-278
resource centres, 296, 297

Schools Council, 14, 273, 276, 290,
295

Scotland

413

417

Weald and Downland Open Air
Museum, 17
Wedgewood and Spode archives,
(Keele University), 280
H.G. Wells Collection, (Bromley
Library Service), 184
Welsh Folk Museum, 323, 370
Department of Oral Traditions and
Dialects, 312
West, John, 278, 295
West Devon Record Office, 127
West Glamorgan County Library
see Swansea Central Library
West Midlands County Council, 70
West Midlands Examination Board,
273-275, 276
West Sussex County Library, 3, 46,
130, 216, 226
see also Crawley Library:
Worthing Library
West Sussex Record Office, 286
West Yorkshire Archive Service, 71
West Yorkshire Metropolitan
Council, 71
Western Education and Library
Board, 44
Westminster City Libraries see
Marylebone Library
*Wheelwright's shop* (Sturt), 12
Wide-Awake Trail Competition, 276
Wigan Libraries and Archives, 111,
286, 381
see also Leigh Library
*Williamson's Liverpool advertiser,*
237
Willow Press, 197
*Wiltshire archaeological and natural
history magazine,* 240
Wiltshire Archaeological and Natural
History Society, 235
Wiltshire Buildings Record, 104
Wiltshire Folk Life Society, 104
Wiltshire Library and Museum

Service,
acquisition policy, 183-184
annual history competition, 267
classification and cataloguing of
periodical articles, 240
computer cataloguing, 216
local classification scheme,
224-225, 226
local studies leaflets, 262
local studies officer, 109, 285
local studies policy statement,
104-105
photographic competition, 260
structure and provision of local
studies, 46, 289
*Wiltshire notes and queries,* 235
Winchester Library (Hampshire
County Library Service), 223
Wirral Libraries and Arts, *see*
Birkenhead Central Library
*Wisconsin death trip* (Lesy), 346
Wolverhampton Polytechnic, 279
Library, 57, 58, 60, 66, 297
Women's Institute, 267, 354
Wood Collection (Huddersfield
Polytechnic Library), 54-55, 58,
60
Worcester Divisional Library
(Hereford and Worcester County
Library), 128
Workers' Educational Association,
7, 90, 280
Workrooms, 138, 155, 156
Worthing Library (West Sussex
County Library), 128, 130
Wrexham Area Library (Clwyd
Library Service), 111
Wright, William Henry Kearley
(1844-1915), 33, *34,* 34-35, 37,
127
*Writers' and artists' yearbook,* 383
*Writings on British history,* 234